D1439098

The Changing English Village
1066–1914

The Changing
English Village

A history of Bledington, Gloucestershire
in its setting 1066-1914

M. K. Ashby

with a foreword by
Dr Joan Thirsk
reader in Economic History University of Oxford

Kineton: The Roundwood Press: 1974

By the same author:

THE COUNTRY SCHOOL: ITS PRACTICE AND PROBLEMS
Oxford University Press, 1929
JOSEPH ASHBY OF TYSOE *Cambridge University Press, 1961*

First published 1974 by The Roundwood Press (Publishers) Limited
Kineton, Warwick, England

lc

*Set in 'Monotype' Times series 327 and printed by Gordon Norwood
at The Roundwood Press, Kineton, in the County of Warwick*

Made and printed in Great Britain

To

Margaret Phillips

and to

the village that has given us a true home

contents

vii

illustrations

The maps were drawn by R. G. Sharp of Leamington Spa.

ix

Abbreviations

B.G.A.S.	Bristol and Gloucestershire Archaeological Association
G.R.O.	Gloucestershire Records Office
G.D.R.	Gloucester Diocesan Records (in Gloucester City Library)
Hockaday	Abstracts of Gloucester diocesan records by F. S. Hockaday (in Gloucester City Library)
J.O.J.	Jackson's Oxford Journal
Landboc	Landboc sive Registrum Monastrii de Winchelcumba (Land Register of Winchcombe Abbey) ed. David Royce
V.C.H.	Victoria County History

preface

WE CANNOT AFFORD altogether to despise the literature that dwells on
the charms of village life—on the successful family of high, orthodox
culture, the beauty of Cotswold building, the clever craftsmen, the
benevolent squire, or the rare genius. Illusion we must often have and
we need not draw it from fantasy; we have only to select and ignore.
On the other hand it would today be possible to concern oneself too
exclusively with those who seem most to have needed sympathy—the
poor, or the children. The need of today is an all-round image.

Bledington has its points of high interest—a small church of great
beauty of stone and lingering richness in glass; wherever the art of
dance, especially folk-dance, is valued and practised Bledington's
name is heard: our village had associations for seven hundred years
with Winchcombe Abbey and for roughly four hundred with Christ-
Church, Oxford, Cathedral and College. But with these two famous
institutions our link was by no means romantic; Bledington supplied
them with part of their provender or income. Neither took much
interest in the well-being of the village or the parish of Bledington
till in the early nineteenth century the Chapter of Christ Church shared
in the developing social sensitivity of that time.

Some of the qualities of our village are due to what could be regarded as lacks. We have strictly speaking no manor-house, though
the ancient Steward's House is of interest. We have never had a resident Lord of the Manor nor a long-dominant family. It is a parable
that an able and learned predecessor in my enquiries was entranced
by a chance association and spent precious months tracing a family
history of no significance for the village. I, in similar danger, saw myself writing pleasant chapters on church, comely farmhouses and families stable over the centuries. Especially I hoped to explore the nomenclature of the village. Time was when every group of trees, every little
stream had its name; one saw the patronymic 'North Leach' turn into

xi

Nolledge. But nine years have not been long enough for me to attend to names. As I read the documents, looked at our buildings, and took excursions to nearby villages other and unexpected questions came to occupy my mind.

What is the reality of a village? Most basic no doubt is the day-to-day dependence of neighbour on neighbour, that strictly local and ever-present condition. There are also its relations with neighbouring villages and market towns and those within the sphere of local government—with the ancient county town and the modern Rural District's headquarters, and with the diocesan courts in the cathedral city. Acts of Parliament shape its affairs to their centre: it has its relations with theologies originating in far-off centres of learning; villagers' friends and relatives are to be found in distant countries.

In such connections every village is different. It is necessary to know and so far as in one lies to understand the economic forces, the national events and the attitudes and atmospheres by which one's village has been affected and in what ways they have changed it. A newcomer to Bledington today is struck by the degree of communal life surviving and the services freely rendered to the village. Its history to the eighteenth century shows us a village criss-crossed by internal connections, without rigid divisions, a genuine community. Between then and 1914 there was a long period in which community was at risk, though it never failed as completely as in some nearby villages. Why this change, and why this difference? Those are very important questions for an age to which time has given the tasks of creating a world community and of achieving in older, small communities a new degree of social amenity and justice. Between the Restoration and about 1850 economic evils in this as in other English villages reached a point at which exaggeration is hardly possible and community survives as by a miracle. No careful village historian can fail to see that 'the production and distribution' of goods is basic, but more than one cornerstone of communication, of unity, are necessary. We see at times very strange proportions between material condition and grace, precious personal qualities and even art surviving great and protracted poverty.

Such facts and appearances have interested me and I think that a village history should provide some suggestion as to their causes, but who is qualified to write it? That is, to go back to beginnings, to understand agriculture, crafts, local government, orthodoxy and dissent in religion and many another thing. But one must not despair: the life-long historian would have one qualification and the life-long villager another; the latter I could with some truth claim. It is also true that there is in one's village no farmer, housewife, craftsman, teacher or minister of religion interested in the past but can supply clues. I have been greatly helped and sustained by my neighbour-friends. They have shown me their homes, lent me documents and albums, taken photographs for me, walked the fields to find how they were used before their enclosure. My farmer, farm-worker and crafts-men friends have shown in our discussions a total lack of distortion and fantasy that those of us who live much by books must admire and envy. Other local friends with much to give represent institutions— Friendly Societies, Parish and Rural District Councils, the inn, the brass band and of course the school, the chapel and the church.

Some of these services are acknowledged in footnotes; others have been more general in nature. At first I made no record of services, not knowing how much time would pass, and I may well have forgotten some. In too many cases friends are no longer with us to be thanked. Neighbours in Bledington, or living in nearby villages, who have helped in the ways I have mentioned include Mr Cecil Acock, Mr A. T. Alvis, my nephews James and Bill Ashby, Mr and Mrs George Beacham and Mr Rodney Beacham, Mr Roland Bolter, Mrs Ethel Cook, Mr Aubrey Cook, Mrs Reeve, Mr and Mrs Charles Holdom, Miss Mary Hall, Mr and Mrs Angus Hood, Mrs Arthur Hunt, Mr and Mrs Roy Hunt, of Shipton under Wychwood, Mr E. W. Hunt, of Oddington, the late Harry Jefferies, Mrs Harold Prentice, Canon G. H. Parks, Mr and Mrs Norman Pearson, Mr Will Stayt, the late Frank and Mrs Stow, Mr and Mrs John Stow, the late Harry Slatter and Mrs Slatter, the late Fred Tremaine, the Misses Gillian and Sheila Truslove and the late Mrs Viner; and Mr E. A. Smith of the Ciren-cester Benefit Society.

I have had much friendly secretarial help from Mrs Peter Rivière, Mrs A. D. Stacey, Mrs Michael Joiner, Mrs Frances Chapman and Mrs Robin Peck.

Friends who read the book or chapters of it and made suggestions include Miss Eva Hutchinson, Miss Helen Clinkard, Mrs Eulalie Heron, Mrs Phyllis Plummer and the Rev. David Dendy. Through Mrs Liberty and the late Major Cyril Jackson I received useful papers collected or written by the Rev. Stephen Liberty. Mr Roy Dommett, of the English Folk Dance Society, Mrs Giles Heron and in especial Mr Rolf Gardiner helped my understanding of the nature and history of our ancient dances.

Miss Margaret Jones and Miss Edith Lyle spent much time checking my literary and other references.

Help on some difficult points was given to me by the late Professors Helen Cam and T. S. Ashton and by Professor W. G. Hoskins. I learned much from fellow local historians, in especial Mr Ernest Lainchbury of Kingham, and Mrs Lilian Rose of Churchill, the late John Purser of Ilmington and the Hon. Elsie Corbett of Spelsbury.

To institutions and their representatives I owe much: in 1962 the Trustees of the Leverhulme Research Awards made me a grant for the first two years of my studies. Many years ago the old students of Hillcroft College made possible my life-membership of the London Library: to them and to the Library's staff, with their superhuman care and promptitude, I owe more than can be expressed. I am also indebted to the Record Officers of Gloucestershire, Mr Irvine Grey and Mr Brian S. Smith, the staff of the Worcestershire Record Office, the librarian of Christ Church, Mr J. F. A. Mason and his assistant, and to the following libraries:—the Gloucester City, Gloucester County, Oxford County, the Bodleian, and that of the Department of Education and Science; and to the Public Record Office.

Miss Margaret Phillips has given me constant support with her inexhaustible resouce and generosity. If only I could start afresh I might do justice to the help I have received but time does not permit.

My remaining debt is to Dr Joan Thirsk, reader in Economic History, the University of Oxford for reading this amateur work and for her foreword.

foreword

The lives of all of us are shaped by the family and the village or neighbourhood in which we grow up. What more important subjects for the historian to explore? And yet how few have been brave enough to attempt it. The task is fraught with immense difficulty, for the historian is never allowed to invent; he must always find evidence for his statements. And since the history of the family or village is rarely as well documented as the history of a political figure or a whole nation, it is this grander kind of national history that has been well served to the neglect of the local and familiar. Family and village history has been left to the novelists, some of whom have produced masterpieces. How could the historian compete?

Yet for many of us the most satisfying history is that which comes closest to home. Few of us have taken part in momentous events. The people we know best are ordinary people. So the history that springs most readily to life is that which is set within a local framework. It makes no impossible calls on our imagination, but instead confers instantly on the most homely things of our experience a wider meaning. Finally, it enriches life by giving us some sense of our place in a long chain of human endeavour.

So Miss Ashby's history of her village cannot fail to cast brilliant shafts of illuminating understanding through the reflections and memories of every villager who reads her book. The problems of every village community are the same though the solutions vary. Every reader seeing the similarities or the contrasts with his own experience will learn a little more about the way man in the past has attempted to balance the demands of the individual against the needs of the community in a small village society. One way sometimes works out better than another, but frequently in ways that were not anticipated. Our planners would be more wary if they read more history. Who would have predicted, for example, that the dissolution of the monasteries, and the destruction of Winchcombe Abbey, would have released such a new spirit of enterprise and change in Bledington? Yet it did so simply because the manorial demesne of the abbey's estate here was carved up and a new group of freeholders introduced into the village. Who could have predicted that the growth of larger farms in the eighteenth century, while creating a welcome demand for more labour, would in the end drag the labourer down into a kind of slavery? It is sobering to see change in the village in a long perspective, and not in the foreshortened view of one lifetime.

"What," asks Miss Ashby in the early pages of her book, "is the reality of the village?" What indeed. Miss Ashby clearly owes her sharpened vision of this matter to her family and the village of Tysoe in which she was brought up. She described her mother, her village, and most of all her father, in her memorable book, *Joseph Ashby of Tysoe*. Now she answers her question fully in the history of another village, and one that is significantly not unlike Tysoe in its essential lineaments. It was a lordless community, master of itself. Born a villager, and trained by her family in sensitive observation to be a lifelong historian, Miss Ashby can use a tiny fragment of information from the past to illumine a greater canvas. Through her insights, we perceive in the architecture of the church and its ambitious improvements in the fifteenth century not just a building project, but the powerful personality of the parson and the responsive, proud spirit of the village community that carried it through to completion. We see alongside the beneficial agricultural changes that accompanied enclosure all the other tendencies that flowed from it, causing unforeseen, mostly damaging, social change. Not a word is wasted in this compelling story; not a single, superficial judgment passes. Bledington was a village of husbandmen in 1086, without a resident lord. In the thirteenth century there were two freeholders. Its independent spirit was being forged at those early dates and it still survives. But when the new freeholders arrived in the sixteenth century, while reinforcing the spirit of independence and self-help, they pressed it further into into their service. Property and wealth began to accumulate in their hands. Enclosure was deemed necessary, and this "meant a form of anarchy, every family for itself." By the early nineteenth century Bledington was a village with a few prosperous farmers while all the rest were labourers. The story is sparely told, but it is deeply moving. Yet is does not end in pessimistic mood.

While Miss Ashby writes about the past, she writes unwittingly about herself and her vision of the future. In her village, through her eyes, every individual had a homely place, was known to all his fellows, and respected for his best qualities. There is clearly no reason why the sense of community that pervaded life until the end of the seventeenth century, and the individualism that swept all before it in the eighteenth and nineteenth, should not be blended again into a new harmony in the twentieth or twenty-first century.

JOAN THIRSK

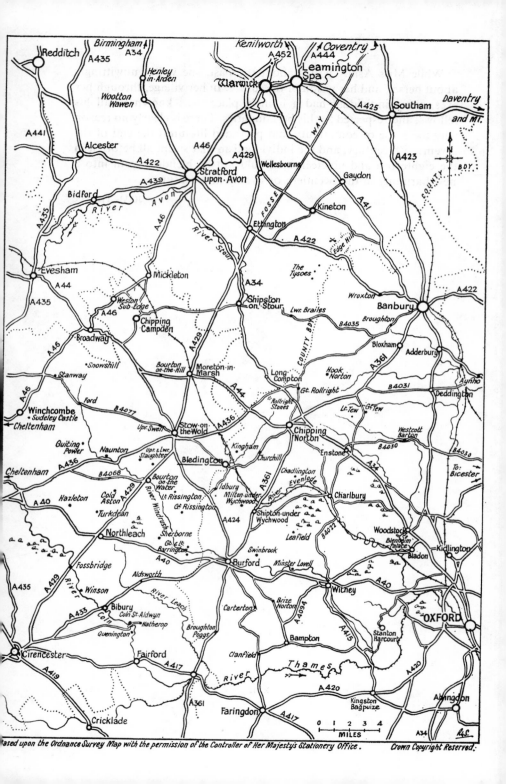

The site of Bledington

BLEDINGTON LIES UNDER the slope of Cotswold, four miles to the south east of Stow on the Wold. The Cotswold ridge, stretching from the north east corner of Somerset to the south west edge of Warwickshire is fifty miles long, with a cliff edge to the west and a long slope to the east and south east. The ridge is of oolitic rock, the egg-stone, of small rounded grains of calcium carbonate, related to chalk and lime, packed—the geologists say—like the roe of a fish. It is good building stone, put to good use as the world knows in its famous small towns—for example, Painswick, Campden, Burford, Stow.

But between Stow, at 750 feet, and Bledington on a level some 350 feet lower there is a change; the soil no longer overlies the limestone; we are in the vale of Evenlode, on the clay plain of a tributary of the Thames, in technical terms on the lower lias. The parish slopes down from Pebbley Hill at 425 feet to under 380 at the bridge across the Evenlode between Bledington and its Oxonian neighbours, Churchill and Kingham. Ours is a small parish of 1539 acres, only sufficient to form say, four large modern farms, but in the middle ages it afforded its folk (entirely agricultural for many centuries, and basically so until 1914 and beyond) some thirty holdings averaging, in modern terms, fifty acres and, later, eight or nine farms with from eighty to two hundred acres, together with a varying number of small holdings. Our border with Oxford county on the south east is the river Evenlode; only a brook and hedges divide us on the west from Idbury and Westcote, also in Oxfordshire, and from Stow and Oddington, to the north west, in Gloucestershire.

Bledington's situation on the edge of its county is an awkward one, thirty miles from the main seat of local government, the county town of Gloucester, and from the cathedral of our diocese (whether Worcester, or later Gloucester) with its Consistory Court; on the edge also of Salmonsbury or Slaughter Hundred whose court was also of great importance to us for some centuries; and again for seven hundred years fifteen miles from the headquarters of our lord of the manor, the Abbot of Winchcombe. Distance from our county town might have its occasional advantage such as freedom from some means of compulsion, e.g. the press gang when soldiers were wanted, and in general from excessive attention. It is said that no bishop ever set foot in our church till 1951, and this reminds us that we were also remote from some of the subtler influences of civilisation.

Our village is surrounded by others of much the same dimensions and style though usually in larger parishes, for many miles around, with also three small market towns. Stow, the nearest to us, with its famous sheep and horse fairs and ancient roads going north, east and west, was the only one much used by Bledingtonians till fairly late; then, as roads improved and horses and ponies were more numerous, Chipping Norton, six miles to the north east, not greatly visited till the late eighteenth century, became more popular than Stow; Burford a little further away to the south, was never of economic or administrative importance to us, but it was somehow a distinguished little town, attracting to itself notable persons and events, figuring in the national story, and from about 1750, with the founding of local newspapers and the annual pleasure fair in Wychwood Forest, became a genuine neighbour of ours. Of large towns Oxford was somewhat less distant from us than Gloucester but until 1546 Bledington folk had little reason to look in that direction. From that year, our clergy and some of our farmers had associations with the University city. From 1753 news of the wide world came to us weekly via the Oxford Journal.

To visitors coming down from Stow, the village looks comely: an elegant, small, towered church looks over fine stone roofs and seems gently to dominate and organise the village. The first houses approached are roomy stone farmhouses set round a spacious green through which flows a slow-moving brook. Along this stream in both directions are other old houses, forming the 'yate' as it was anciently called, or street, which contains now (1972) the Methodist chapel, the old Steward's House of the manor, the shop and the inn. Other houses rise in two lanes from the brook and these are joined together by another lane, thus forming a rough square with its base a section of the street. The interior of the square is occupied by the gardens and orchards of the old houses. Until well within this century these were the yards and home-closes of the farms, with stables, cow-houses and barns. Time was when these were the only enclosed grounds in the village. Here the animals were wintered at need, the young were born, and the small stock—barndoor fowl, geese, and later, pigs—spent their lives.

Until the eighteenth century there were no outlying houses except the mill on the river; one was built about 1780 and three others in the early nineteenth century.

In the greater part of the parish the impermeable clay lies near the surface. Quite near to the brook gardens can only be made by removing clay or making soil above it. On the north side, the clay reaches to the confines of the parish. Ploughs drawn by powerful tractors on our largest farm, Bledington Grounds, still turn up lumps of clay half as large as a wheelbarrow. Along the Icomb Road are the old pits left by digging clay for brick-making.

The brook's slow rate of fall has combined with the high water-table to make the village very liable to floods. In past times they were extensive and deep: once, not so very long ago, a man and his horse were almost drowned, and the water used often to invade the lower houses.

There is of course clay on the south east side of the brook, as on the north west, but as the ground rises the water-table is much farther from the surface. Just above the houses there is, in a state of nature, next to no soil, but a layer of pebbles, laid down here ages ago by ice-bergs, which also left behind some huge smoothish, reddish boulders. The lower farmyards had all one or two of these impedimenta, but by now most of them have been broken up and removed. Above the pebbles come a slope of brash of stones and stone-fragments. At last, still a few feet higher, one comes to level ground with a fair layer of soil, this plateau extending on the modern map from the school to the church and south to the parish boundary, the Westcote brook. This 'riverine' soil, deposited at some period by the Evenlode, drains easily, can be dug with relative ease and made fertile. Where the ground begins to drop again towards the river comes another variation, a bed of gravel a few feet thick, on both sides of the Burford road.

The area on each side of this road, the riverine plateau with the gravel beds, had an ancient name, still occasionally used—the Oars, Upper and Lower. When there was no road between, though perhaps a rough path, they were 'the Oar.' 'Oar' is a celtic word meaning 'earth' possibly allied to 'wyrth'. The Oars are called the 'wyrths' in one pre-enclosure document. This word is an older form of 'worth,' signifying soil or farms.

The Oar, or the Upper and Lower Oars, remained always in a sense separate from the rest of the open fields; they gave their name to the men chosen from early times till enclosure, to oversee the working of the common lands, the 'Oarsmen'; no tithes were ever paid from produce of the Oars; and when the parish was enclosed and private farms organised, the Oars were not thrown into the general pool of lands for division; those who shared them in their open condition were allotted plots within them for private ownership. It seems an essential inference that the Oars were the first cultivated ground within what became in time the parish of Bledington.

Although Bledington is not on the oolite rock it has been a very stony village. The houses, no doubt originally huts of wood and thatch, have long been of stone, and all but a few cottages have had stone roofs as well as walls. Until comparatively recently all the old home-closes of the farmhouses were fenced with great slabs of a very hard local stone, four inches through, sunk as far below as visible above the surface.[1] Remnants of these can still be seen here in their original lines, as in Kingham and Foscote also. There still remain a few gate-posts of single stones six feet high and others may be identified as parts of rockeries in gardens or used to form steps. Our building stones and the hard fence-stones all came from Stow parish or from Westcote, from quarries conveniently above Bledington, the slope facilitating transport. The stone tiles for roofs are also oolitic. These were quarried and exposed to frost for splitting at Stonesfield near Oxford, but also possibly at quarries nearer to us. It is true that within the houses and farm buildings there are massive oak beams, but our own trees are not large nor have we many oaks. The beams must have come from outlying woods or from Wychwood whose boundaries were once nearer our own than now. The bare, stony look of the village was partly lost when the new small fields were enclosed by hedges, in which trees often grew up, but even so to come over to Bledington from the western cliff of Cotswold with its high graceful beeches, or from the deep grass and rich, thick hedges of South Warwickshire is still to pass from richness to a somewhat meagre quality. Our landscape has its beauties but these arise from its distances, so inviting to eye and foot and mind, not from any suggestions of comfort or wealth.

Bledington was never easily fertile nor extensive enough for the great flocks of sheep that enriched some villages. Whatever prosperity its folk came by they had to labour for. It may be doubted whether till 1914 any parishioners made a comfortable living, without both hard work and anxiety: very few inhabitants brought wealth from elsewhere.

[1] This material and technique of fencing was used by the late Stone Age people on Cotswold to edge and support their long barrows.

chapter one

BEFORE THE NORMAN CONQUEST

I   Early times: The Late Stone, Bronze and Iron Ages
II   Roman Bledington
III   From the Romans to the Normans: the Anglo-Saxons

HOW LONG THERE has been a community on the area that is now the parish of Bledington even an archaeologist working over the ground might not be able to say. Still less can we know what is the earliest time from which our village inherits present traits, physical or cultural. The long continuities we find in later times encourage us to trace our story from as far back as may be.

On the high ground we see all round us there is some evidence of very early habitation. Ancient weapons have been collected in great numbers[1] between Stow on the Wold and Upper and Nether Swell; in Lyneham parish on the hill-top road to Chipping Norton is a long barrow; six or seven miles away, for bird or human, are Rollright Stones, a religious meeting place and monument; running through Stow on the Wold are ancient roadways, one from Northamptonshire, along the Edge Hills, the other the Fosse Way, crossing England, known as a Roman road, but more ancient. All these were used by late Stone Age people (2500–1750 B.C.),[2] who fashioned stone into arrowheads and axeheads for hunting or fighting and for cutting down trees. Their tools were made with infinite labour and easily lost. The removal of trees and brushwood must have been extremely slow work. They could do little more than clear and scratch a little ground to grow food, though it seems that they planted barley and later other grains. Hard as their life was, it was human: they 'wasted' time burying their dead in great, elaborate multiple tombs or barrows. They show feeling for decoration and for comfort, occasionally wearing beads and making pottery spoons to stir their hollowed-stone or rough pottery cups. It was they, if not earlier people, who set up the Rollright Stones which show their need to formulate feelings and thoughts about man's wider situation.

Bledington as a community cannot claim to go back even to the Later Stone Age folk who followed the builders of the long barrows. It was not possible with their tools to clear the woods in the valleys or to dig the stiffer soil.

The birds and beasts and fish of the Evenlode river and valley remained undisturbed through the time of the Later Stone Age folk who buried their dead in round barrows, although they came near to our parish; there are a number of their barrows at Wyck Rissington and Longborough. These were better potters and made more effective tools and also weapons; the latter had helped them to displace or mix as masters with the long-barrow builders. But they did not advance the pattern of life in a very fundamental way.

The stone-tool users were at length—about 1750 to 450 B.C.— succeeded by newcomers who knew the use of metal. From using copper, easily melted and moulded, but all too easily bent, they had learned to produce a harder metal by adding tin to it to make bronze, so that they had lighter, stronger, sharper tools for cutting and digging. They had hoes to break the soil with and could grow more corn. A further invasion of Bronze Age folk took place and these brought with them knowledge of a kind of plough and used sickles to cut the ears of ripened corn. They were qualified to settle in such an area as ours, but we have no sign of them.

The last attack and conquest suffered by the inhabitants of our midlands before the Romans came was that of the Iron Age folk, a Celtic people, tall and fair, where their predecessors had been shorter and darker. It seems certain that a group of these were the first settlers on the Bledington site. There are no signs of Stone Age folk or bronze-users but there was certainly a settlement before the Romans came.

They were a more energetic and aggressive people, but their way of life was hardly superior. Their pottery was poor, indicating a low valuation of domestic life; they built no memorial barrows. Iron is a commoner metal than copper or tin and they had more and sharper tools, not at first all of iron, for bronze was harder till they learned to temper iron by repeated quick cooling. Perhaps improved and more numerous tools, affording more food, accounted for their energy.

The iron-users brought with them a religion more highly organised

2

than their predecessors' and yet barbaric. This 'Druidic' system involved a priesthood, who among other duties carried out human sacrifices, more numerous than with earlier peoples. The gods of this people included a thunder-god, a war-god, and a mother-god concerned with the harvest. The priests knew something of numbers and of the movements of the heavenly bodies and taught what they knew to the sons of tribal leaders.

The Celts were, comparatively speaking, an organised people. Their 'tribes' fought each other for territory and for domination. In consequence they needed fortresses for defence and refuge. There are small hill-forts along the ancient ways in this area, and in the parish of Bourton on the Water there are the remains of a defended area, Salmonsbury Camp. Its site is uncommon in its nature, being 'overlooked by hills on all sides,' but its double ramparts and ditches are of the usual kind. It stands near the Foss Way and is thought to have been of the nature of a trading settlement. It continued through changes and vicissitudes for centuries to come to be a place of great importance to Bledington and her Gloucestershire neighbours.

Early tools had made settled communities possible; iron tools had made it practicable to cultivate at least the lighter valley soils. It is probable that the foundations of all the villages in our area had been laid by about 400 B.C. Tools, then, are of fundamental importance. They would continue to improve though very slowly until the present, going from strength to greater strength, greater variety and complexity making possible more prosperous and larger communities, till the present when it may be that the complexity of our machines has passed the point of maximum true profit.

When the Romans decided that Britain must be added to their empire they met a people organised in tribes and alliances of tribes, with effective weapons and high and practised courage. But their own weapons and organisation were stronger still. Celts who continued to resist them were driven far westward. Those who remained were disarmed and later abandoned their Druid religion—a subordinated folk. They continued to farm in their accustomed way.

II Roman Bledington

We all learn something, in school days, of the Romans, a great Mediterranean people. These—being in touch by sea—had learned much from a more civilised people, the Greeks, who in their turn had

3

learned from the ancient cultures of the Near East. Their predecessors in Britain had come from northern Europe and northern France where they had been only most indirectly touched by influences from the centres of old civilisations. Thus the Romans brought a quite new degree of culture to this island.

The Romans had learned the arts of literature, of building, and of statuary. They became, in the service of their empire, great civil engineers, building roads and viaducts to aid and maintain their military conquests and led water to their towns in great aqueducts. Britain was the most far-flung of their territories; even here they built, planned and ornamented towns (the second greatest being Ciren-cester) and their high officials lived in beautiful villas, such as that at Chedworth, with warmed rooms, and pictured, tessellated floors and elaborate baths. They brought trees and numerous garden plants from their homelands and planted orchards.

On the borders of conquered Britain, as in other countries, they maintained their military efficiency and the necessary ruthlessness to keep more primitive peoples at bay, but they gave peace to the areas behind their defensive lines, dreamed of a peaceful world and even of 'one world-wide family, all akin to Rome.'

Like the Stone Age folk at least two thousand years before them and the Normans arriving a thousand years after their own arrival the Romans seem to have been at home in the Cotswold area. From their urban centres and their camps they spread into the countryside. In many a Cotswold village and in some of the lower Evenlode valley, Roman relics have been found.

About 1950 Sidney Morgan, a Bledingtonian of Banks Farm, whose house is on the green a hundred yards on the north west side of the brook, saw tiny unusual specks of colour among the sods he was ploughing. Discs of metal, they proved to be: Roman coins. Collected on two or three occasions, there were eleven of them. He found also from time to time shards of pottery, unlike anything in his wife's kitchen but for some basic likeness to some old-fashioned 'panshons,' used for storage. These proved to be lips and bases of Roman jars of which every Roman housewife had a number, in which she kept grain and other things. Curiously, the pottery was thought by experts to be older than the coins.

Mr Morgan was not the first to find strange objects about Banks Farm. When he required to use an old bread oven in an outside kitchen he found in it a 'double stone,' the lower part circular, with a rim, the upper fitting within it, and having a hole through it—a Roman quern. There was another hollowed stone also, trough-like; can it have been a child's coffin? We shall never know, for it has vanished.

There was a final discovery. One very dry summer we saw, at a short distance from the sites of the coins and the pottery, a rectangle outlined in strips of grass, still green, though the field was withered. Two green strips crossed the rectangle dividing it into three sections. It seems likely that the lines indicated the foundations of a small Roman house—whether inhabited by a Roman or a Roman-British family. And these are the only Roman remains found here.

All the coins but one date from the fourth century A.D.[3]—from Constantine the Great (307–337), Constantine II (337–340), Valens (364–378), Gratian or Valens (364–383). Four coins, though thought to be of the fourth century, are illegible. One stray coin is of the third century, minted perhaps forty years before the earliest of the others, but it seems probable that the Roman or Romanised family were here during much of the fourth century, possibly not before. The engraving of the coins illustrates Roman history and culture: the legendary founding of Rome by Romulus and Remus, the savagery of conquest, the idealisation of the Republic, the success of usurping Emperors. They indicate something of the extent of the empire of which the Bledington settlement found itself a minute part: they had been minted in the Roman towns of Germany and France that became Trier, Lyons and Arles.

In some other villages the signs of such a Roman house have been accompanied by green circles indicating the sites of primitive native huts, but none have at any time been remarked here. Our oldest house-sites, except Banks Farm, are nearer to the brook and chiefly on the other side. It seems possible that the native huts of our Celtic predecessors were covered by later abodes.

There were evidently similar Roman settlements, usually more prosperous, on the sites of many villages within a short radius of us. In Kingham parish[4] there seem to have been two, using coins dating from as early as 41 A.D., and relating also to the third and fourth centuries. In Chipping Norton coins have been collected on a number of sites and in considerable numbers;[5] at Stonesfield and Northleigh, in or just above the Evenlode valley; at Naunton, not far from the Fosse Way, Roman coins of the second, third and fourth centuries

5

have occurred 'in some abundance,'6 including coins of Marcus Aurelius, the great stoic moralist; at Lower Slaughter, a mile from the Foss Way, a larger Romano-British village was found with sites of Roman houses and circular native huts.7 Among these were several wells which have yielded treasures, including sculptures of a military deity, so that we see that Roman religions—of which there were a number—reached our countryside. There is no reason to think that Christianity did so, though there were Christian groups in Roman towns.

Some larger settlements may have been seen by Bledingtonians— the one on the already-ancient site of Salmonsbury, the great town of Cirencester about twenty miles away, and the fine villa at Chedworth, less far, with its work-rooms for crafts (weaving and dyeing) and its well-worked fields.

For approaching four centuries Roman soldiers and some civilians came and went between Rome and Britain. When early in the fifth century A.D. Rome with the whole Empire was in danger from barbarians the army hurried home and with it almost all civilians. Romans had been tolerant masters but never, in Britain, colonisers. They had not trained or educated or in any way permeated the native people. Britain had little hold on the distinguished civilisation that had been shown to them, and the native Celts were left with no organisation for self-defence, and no leaders.

Before we pass to the next phase we must momentarily go back to Banks Farm. Near to the site of Roman finds, and near to the present house is another ancient site. On its little aged pear-orchard are the Town Banks, the meeting place of an early community. Which was the first folk to meet there? If the Celts, can that be why the Roman house was built near? Certainly for the next arrivals a village meeting-place was essential, and it was here.

III   From the Romans to the Normans: the Anglo-Saxons

Between the early fifth century when the Romans left and the arrival of the Normans in 1066 is a long stretch of time. The speedy Roman and Norman conquests make dramatic stories but the Anglo-Saxon and Danish invasions extend over several centuries, affecting the country district by district, When once settled in this country the various invading tribes or nations struggled among themselves for predominance, each always trying to extend the area governed and peaceful. They were meanwhile doing a far greater work than that of Romans or Normans—a work of that detailed, day by day and yet extensive type that the conquest of earth involves. In these six centuries —as long a time as from the Conqueror to Charles II or the Black Prince to Hitler—three great processes went on: the greater part of England was brought under cultivation: the heathen people who did this changed their outlook and religion—a revolution indeed; and they worked out in detail a system of government designed to cover every acre and every man. They did the fundamental work of a civilisation.

It is from these invaders that our village of to-day is descended: our laws are not Roman; our language is neither Celtic nor Roman—they are English, taking this name from one group of the new folk, the Angles. The farming methods of Anglo-Saxons could be inferred in Bledington as late as 1770 and the religion of their early days left traces here till our present century. Nevertheless, to understand how Bledington fared during this time is not easy. There are very few documents that mention our settlement, and no buildings or monuments remain. We have to make every reasonable inference from our own fields and roads, from remains in neighbouring and similar villages and from the network of government in which our village was firmly held by 1066.

While the Romans were gradually withdrawing, tribes from the Dutch, Belgian and North-east French coast (to use modern names) had already begun to invade by the east coast. After they had gone the invading forces made use of the entire eastern coast line where harbours were suitable, and some entered by the Kent coast, the Isle of Wight and the Hampshire harbours. On the whole the newcomers, though they came from widespread areas and bore different names, had all the same basic language, similar tools and modes of agriculture, and the same general aims in their conquest. An exception of some degree was the Kent area: here groups settled whose family and other customs differed from others in a way that would at times affect our history.

Naturally the first invaders were bold sailors and fighters who had to overcome the resistance of the native, settled people who had lost under the Romans some of their aptitude for struggle. The fighters were accompanied and followed by those who would occupy the land, farm it and set up communities. The whole process involved pushing the native British west and north, to the mountains where it was hardly worthwhile to follow them. Such British families as chose to remain had to work for their conquerors, to learn their speech and to accept a position resembling slavery.

It was the West Saxons, who began to arrive on the south coast about 500 A.D., who colonised the south and west of the country, covering the ground between the coast and our own area very slowly. About sixty years passed, it is believed, before they reached Old Sarum above the sodden area where Salisbury arose later. Afterwards some of them came up the Thames which naturally gave the British a line they would try to hold: Saxon sword-blades have been fished out of the river at several points below Oxford. It is from the Anglo-Saxon Chronicles that scholars learn the approximate dates of the later main battles. Under one Cuthwulf the West Saxons captured Eynsham, well beyond the river and only ten miles from the little British group here by the Bladon River. It was not till forty years later that the local British made their last stand at Bampton and were 'very bloodily defeated.'

Meanwhile other West Saxons had been approaching our area from the West, via Gloucester and the site of the Roman city, Cirencester. A large tribe of those who maintained some independence came very near to us on the West. They came as far as the forest the remnant of which still bears their name—Huicca úúdú—in a modified form, Wychwood, the forest or wood of the Huicci. Whether in the end it was Huiccans from the west, arriving via the sites of Idbury, Westcote or Stow who took the Bledington site or other West Saxons coming up the Evenlode river we cannot know. In any case, we seem always to have been on the borders. There would later be struggles between larger, more powerful organisations. Various Kingdoms were formed and pressed upon each other. The West Saxons met the Mercians and later the Mercians were overcome by the Northumbrians, but the few square miles of our area were never central to these struggles.

What is certain is that the British were pushed out. Over the Cotswold area few British words remained, chiefly names of rivers. Here, even the name of our river was changed from Even to Bladon: our settlement became Bladenton, Blaydintun—several spellings, the farm on the river, on the Bladon. Presently the British name of the river was used again, though with a Saxon ending, Evenlode. One settlement Icomb, Iccancumbe, never lost its British name. Perhaps a little group of British families were left there for a time, on sufferance, but presently it was taken over: it figures early in Saxon charters.

Here the Saxons must have found the small British fields on the seventy-five acres or so of the Oars and perhaps on smaller gravelly areas beyond them. For the rest, along the river were many areas covered by rushes, and on higher ground were sparse woods and thick undergrowth. All this was not without its richness—flowering rushes in the river and kingcups nearby with whitethorn trees and blackthorn thickets, many birds and small wild animals. Nor must we lightly decide that spring beauty meant little to these ancestors of ours.

Certainly, they had a great task before them—to cut down woods and root out undergrowth. They would never attempt to cultivate the whole area; the woods provided their only fuel and the wild ground, later to be 'heaths,' their only pasturage, though there was probably a little meadow-ground between the Oars[8] and the river. There are in the parish some 1539 acres: of these in the course of 350 years or so, from 700 A.D. to 1050 some 700 acres were brought into cultivation. The greatness of the task depended on the number of the labourers and the nature of their tools. The cultivated area was, it seems, divided into family holdings (though these were not in separate blocks) known as 'yardlands' or 'hides' or in Bede's Latin translation 'familia.' In later times the hide was calculated to be usually about 120 acres; its extent varied. When the Normans came there were seven hides in Bledington, which may well mean that at an early date seven Saxon families formed the community, together probably with a few dependent British folk. The number of families grew, but very slowly here as elsewhere.

From the small group of British farmers the Saxons took over cultivated acres of the Oars, and with them the organisation—the meetings and the officers, the Oarsmen, this practice being not unlike that with which they were familiar. But neither the small, irregular-shaped Celtic or British fields on the Oars nor the Roman farm beyond the brook suited their ways. They expected to cultivate larger areas, using partly the family unit, and partly the group of families. The area for ploughing was divided into strips, and these were given in turn to the families. Sites vary in height, in wetness and dryness, and in fertility: the turn by turn allotment ensured justice. All the ploughed land was alternately sown and left fallow. There was not much opportunity for family enterprise to be experimental. A whole field of strips was sown to wheat or barley; when it had been reaped, the cattle of all the community wandered over the stubble to eat the luscious weeds that sprang up. Every year the fertile but unflooded ground near the river was divided by lot among the families so that justice held in the meadow grass for the families' animals—a few oxen and maybe horses. Swine and oxen were turned on to the heath ground to feed themselves, and in time it would be necessary to regulate the numbers turned out by each commoner. Thus there were always decisions to be taken in common and to be observed.

But there was room for everyone's strength and prowess and enterprise in the clearing of the hundreds of acres of the woods and wastes. The only tools they had for this great task were picks and billhooks, together with, for cultivation of the freed soil, wooden spades. Rough scythes have also been found but they may not have been made till the ninth century; there seem to have been no sickles. Ploughs were early used, though perhaps not from the beginning. Iron spades came too, but until it was possible to put a steel edge on these, they were more heavy than sharp. Thus, all the work, not only the clearing, was slow and laborious.

For the crops on the arable evidence is slight, but archaeologists tell us that Saxon potsherds from near Oxford bear numerous prints of barley, some of oats, and a very few of flax. Dorothy Whitelock, deriving evidence from writings, says that 'wheat and barley were the principal crops, the latter being necessary not only for bread but also to provide malt for brewing; rye, beans and peas are mentioned sometimes and flax was cultivated also.'⁹ But the pots belong to an earlier date probably than the literary references.

For their diet the early Bledington Saxons may have had, in addition to grains, fish from the river and crayfish from the brooks (the latter hawked round by small boys to housewives as late as 1950.) Birds may have been netted on the heaths and hedgehogs caught, and roasted in clay on the hearths. A few wild herbs may have been brought home and planted near the houses; an apple tree or two would be a matter of great good fortune. Each season yielded few of these products and these uncertain. Hunting implements were as poor as the tools.

What of the homes in which the farmers rested and ate and brought up children and from which they set out in the morning to their long primitive work? The oldest farmhouses and cottages stand today along the brook, or at a very short distance from it, and that in spite of its one-time marsh and its inevitable winter flooding. No one would choose today to build on just these sites, even with our techniques; we must suppose that the brook was the attraction; there were no tools for sinking wells—though it seems likely that the Roman-British household had had one. A little study of the farmhouses shows how each one has been modified time and time again, century after century. One must think that changes now invisible took place in still earlier times and that our fine farmhouses stand where once there were primitive Saxon homes.

Somewhere about 1850 three cottages in a row standing on the close below the homestead of Banks Farm were pulled down. They are sometimes recalled now with the phrase 'the thatch came nearly to the ground.' Reference will be made again to these; they were the changed remains of an old yeoman's house sold at last for the value of the site, because the timbers had decayed and the constrictions of tentlike dwellings had become intolerable. They were the last houses of an ancient pattern, vanished for many miles around, lingering only in this exceptionally poor village. Excavations of Saxon sites in Bourton-on-the-Water, seven miles away, and at Cassington, this side of Oxford and Sutton Courtenay beyond, all show that the oldest Anglo-Saxon houses differed from this old Bledington type with its yard high walls chiefly in having no walls at all. The archaeological diggers in the villages mentioned found trenches $1\frac{1}{2}$ to 2 feet deep and remains of beams along the ground with indications of holes where slanting poles had been inserted. The poles had been 'secured to a ridge pole' at Bourton-on-the-Water. The roofs came down to the edge of the excavation, leaving no head room at the sides. They consisted of well-packed brushwood, with thatch on top, like the cover over the Home Farm's great implement shed, taken down in 1952. These thick roof-sides must have made for warmth; but also how combustible they were. When Penda King of Mercia attacked 'the royal city' (651 A.D.) he pulled down several villages such as this, to pile a vast quantity of beams, rafters, partitions, brushwood and thatch against the city wall and set fire to the heap.[10] In Bede's History and in the poems of the Anglo-Saxons written a century or two after their settlement in this area we find that the churches were built of wood and that the palaces were huge single-storey, tentlike halls. (Why did not the Saxons learn from the Roman houses to build with stone? Today any young Cotswold villager who wants a wall will build it, after a little study of the walls roundabout. Timber was handier, we must suppose, even than stone, and the thoughts in their minds were not of comfort and the extension of houses).

In Sutton Courtenay, a fertile valley settlement, the wooden houses were from 10 to 21 feet in length. We shall not go far wrong to conclude that here the dwellings were small and miserable, with 'never a richer house.' In these the villagers slept, ate and presumably cooked as well as brewed. They cured skins here also and spun wool, and kept their tools. But such buildings were not difficult to erect; a family might have more than one. Meanwhile there were settlements on all the sites around where there are now villages. All of these were increasing their acreage of tilled ground and making more use of their wastes and woods. Questions must arise as to their boundaries. Between Bledington on one side of the Bladon and Kingham and Churchill on the other, the river—not yet bridged—was almost too great a barrier. Idbury and Westcote were on the other side of the deep Westcote brook, a natural, firm limit though easily spanned by a tree trunk. But in respect of Icomb, Oddington and Stow there must have been a more gradual definition, not without dispute; the boundary could never be marked by anything more permanent than hedge or fence. Bledington's most frequent offence against her neighbours for centuries to come was the neglect of fences between our parish and Oddington.

Communal agriculture must have meant meetings of the commoners. There must have been also occasional breaches of the peace to be brought to an end. And then what of ceremonies such as funerals? What of religious observances? Banks Farm has been mentioned. On old maps and in seventeenth century records we see the name Town Banks. These are on the outskirts of the settlement which we may now begin to call the village, in the little pear orchard of Banks Farm, close to the field which yields Roman coins. Here is a mound, now shallow, once rather higher, which may possibly have been a barrow for burials, beside other, longer and higher ridges. We learn from records of the Hundred Court centuries later that here also were the butts where archery was practised during the middle ages and until the seventeenth century. Clearly this small area was sacred to the community. It is reasonable to think of it as the village meeting-place. (On old maps of Kingham and in its lists of field names we meet the name Town Hill for an area in a similar relation to the village).[11]

This was, then, for the village what Salmonsbury near Bourton was for an area comprising many villages. Excavation and archaeological research have established that Salmonsbury (and later the nearby Lower Slaughter) was used as a centre for many centuries. It is possible that skilled excavation would show the use of the Town Banks. For us, so sheltered in our houses, cars and water-proof coats and with our church, chapel, school and village hall for meetings it is difficult to imagine how rain and wind were circumvented. Perhaps sometimes the congregations, like men of the Old Testament, built rough shelters of boughs. Small local meetings would be easily called and postponed when men met in the fields and women had all to sally forth to fetch water. Alongside agriculture and the necessary maintenance of order and of defence there was always the life of ideas and values and imagination—from time to time pleasure or fear or rejoicing to express. We can gather something of the Anglo-Saxon outlook from remnants of paganism lingering late in village life—in Bledington's, and, in that of villages around. Also, there is Anglo-Saxon poetry, dealing with the lives of fighting men and of tribal leaders who were becoming Kings, rather than with the life of farming. The literature suggests an overwhelming sense of immediate and complete dependence on the moods of nature, the sense of threat from thunderbolts and floods and the failure of seasons. The virtues it extols are courage and endurance. Village relics suggest a happier outlook; dance and play and festive meals, games and competitions in skill and prowess were retained generation after generation because of the pleasure they both expressed and gave, while the darker vision was unwanted. All over our small neighbourhood—in Icomb, Shipton, Leafield, Longborough, Heyford, Islip and in Bledington itself the Mummers' Play was still acted till 1860 or 1880. In this the turn of the year is celebrated. It originates in magical ceremonies by which the passing of winter was hastened and the power that caused the sun's heat to wax and the days to be prolonged, was felt to be reinforced. Eostre the goddess of earth and spring is recalled in the name, Easter, of the Christian festival of resurrection. Perhaps it was originally in her honour and to gain her favour that the Churchill folk, like those of many villages, had their Whitsun games and dances. These went on as late as 1721 and probably decades later, together with a rich and costly feast for man, woman and child.

On Bledington's green there stands a Maypole, round which on May

Day the school-children sometimes dance. It succeeds a series of poles, surely going back to Saxon times, before our village had a Christian church or priest. The early May festival survived in many villages in a form but little modified till late in the reign of Queen Elizabeth I. A Puritan divine described it in 1583:[12] '... Against Maie, Whitsondaie, or some other tyme of the year, every parishe, towne, and village, assemble themselves together, both the men, women and children, olde and young, even all indifferently, and either goyng all together or dividyng themselves into companies, they goe some to the woodes and groves, some to the hilles and mountaines, some to one place, some to another, where they spend all night in pleasant pastymes, and in the mornyng they returne, bringing with them birch, bowes and branches of trees, to deck their assemblies withall. ... But their chiefest jewell they bring from thence is their Maie poole, which they bring home with great veneration, as thus: they have twentie or fortie yoke of oxen, every ox havyng a sweet nosegay of flowers tyed on the tip of his hornes, and these oxen drawe home this Maie poole ..., which is covered all over with flowers and hearbes, bounde round with stringes, from the top to the bottome, and sometime painted with variable colours, with ... men, women and children followyng it with great devotion. And thus beyng reared up, with handkerchiefs and flagges streaming on the toppe, they straw the ground aboute it, sett up sommer haules (halls), bowers and arbours hard by it; and then they fall to banquet and feast, to leape and dance aboute it, as the heathern people did at the dedication of their idolles, whereof this is a perfecte patterne ....'

Stubbes was surely right in thinking that pagan gods were being worshipped in these May festivities, but not perhaps in thinking that 'Satan, prince of hell' inspired them. It was rather the goddess of spring who went by a number of names including EOSTRE, Easter.

But nature has other moods than that of joyful renewal. Tysoe's name, a village twenty miles away, shows its devotion to the god Tiw, a dark vengeful god. His sign, the horse, cut in the red soil of Edgehill, showed for miles over the countryside. Customs originating in his worship lingered on till the late eighteenth century. Games and sports took place in early summer, beside the newly-scoured horse, the worship of Tiw having become linked with that of the gods of springtime and growth. There was also Woden, the war-god, and Thor, the god of thunder, and Freja whose emblems were carried round to the fields

14

and to the animals' stalls and stables—the goddess of increase, of harvest.

In their religion our Anglo-Saxon ancestors in the village had not travelled far from their basic need of nature's fruits and animal increase, from the influence of winter's cold and the warmth of spring, and from fear of the thunderbolt. Their governors and leaders, the kings and soldiers, were a little removed from these and their outlook less simple. The Anglo-Saxon epic poem, Beowulf, shows the fighting men's high estimate of the virtue of courage. It shows the heroes loyal to the death to their leaders and to their fellow fighters, and shows also that there were rewards for heroism—rank, effective and decorated weapons (so different from the farmers' poor tools), feasts—with princesses to wait gracefully upon them—and honour at death and afterwards. Golden treasure was given to them in their barrows or ship-tombs (we find it today), and their courage was immortalised in poems. In Beowulf we also find the enemies of mankind personified in dragons and 'the fearful worm.' In this and in references to God as 'the Almighty' it seems that the author (writing about 750 A.D.) knew something of the Old Testament, but he shows no consciousness either of the hopeful outlook or the ethics of the New.[13]

Christianity had reached England early from more than one direction. There had been some Christians in Roman towns, and after the Romans left missionaries had come from the highly developed and enthusiastic Irish church. They came via Iona to the Picts and Scots of the north and to the British people further south, building at Worcester the first Cathedral of our own diocese. They went also, it seems, into Wales. There were many groups of Christians west of the Severn when the West Saxons invaded our area and it is likely that there were some east of the river, nearer to the Bladon valley. The gentle priest and historian, Bede, whose history was finished in 734, chid the British that they had not converted the Saxons but it is not easy for the beaten to preach to their supplanters.

The powerful, highly organised Catholic Church of Rome was more effective with the Anglo-Saxons. In 597 Pope Gregory sent Augustine with forty monks to the Kentish kingdom. Now that the conversion of Britain was one of the great plans and ambitions of a Pope the courage and persistence of a mission could be maintained and if it should fail, renewed. An unsuccessful effort could be followed up. And indeed Christianity did not at first gain steadily in strength;

rulers were converted but sons succeeding to their office were rene-gades worshipping old gods and returning to old ways, for Christian standards of conduct were new. But setbacks were never defeat. Some of the teaching spread easily, almost of itself. Reading Bede and translations of their poems one gathers that Anglo-Saxons responded easily to the idea of one great universal god, who had the powers of all their old gods and, soaring beyond them all, 'wrought glory, the spacious heavens.'

But there were aspects of Christian teaching more difficult than this of the Creator—aspects stranger, only acceptable by contagion of enthusiasm, only proved by the martyrdom of devoted, undismayable men, and the evidence of miracles e.g. the humility of Christ, the the religion of love and forgiveness.

The complex message of Christian teachers drew towards the Church all kinds and ranks of people. For kings there was much to be learned through the Church of the organisation of European states, so much more advanced than their own government; for those attracted to Christian priesthood, among them some pagan priests, there was the hope of learning and influence; and for all there was the hope of heaven and the love of God and of the Saviour himself. Even slaves found that missionaries regarded them as souls of the same value as others, and that sometimes they purchased slaves and set them free.

No wonder that the old, country, traditional pagan religion gradu-ally receded. The church went forward from kingdom to kingdom—from Ethelbert's Kent to Alfred's Wessex, Mercia and the Saint-King Oswald's Northumbria. When kings and their court officials were converted, Bishops were appointed to care for religion over an area, a 'diocese,' but it was a difficult task to reach the people in the small settlements. The best means found was to establish small groups of missionary priests in central villages, in 'minster' churches, who should teach and preach in the area around. One such minster was established at Daylesford, very near the borders of Kingham and Bledington, but we do not know what success it had.

The Christian church has many forms, many moods. It seems that the church in England in early days was often gentle and tolerant. The priests were content to win the people peacefully, accepting whatever they could of the old paganism. The old festivals at the turn of the year, of springtime, and of early summer, were adapted as Christmas, Easter and Whitsuntide. The fields were blessed and the harvest time celebrated, nor were the plays and dances too seriously frowned upon; only the worship of the old gods must and did give way.

Besides the minsters, monasteries where devoted groups of men or women, priests or nuns lived together were also early. In such monasteries as Bede's at Jarrow, the books of the Bible were studied and learned, the rites and ceremonies of the church were practised, classical languages and literature were studied, education was offered to those who cared for it. Whole companies—small at first—learned the pleasure of study and art. Some made very beautiful copies of the books of the Bible, developing the great art of illumination; a few wrote books of their own. They studied architecture and science and poetry. For such men the old ways, the old religion were darkness itself; return to them was inconceivable.

From the late seven-hundreds there was a religious house near us, at Eynsham. Towards the end of the tenth century Aelfric became its head—a man devoted to books, who felt that Christians, even rural ones, even farmers, should be literate. He translated part of the Scriptures into English so that laymen could read them in their own tongue, and used the Bible stories to guide the English people to do their daily duty. He 'set forth Judith in English' for example to his neighbours that they might 'guard their country against their foes.' He even wrote instructions in theology for two local Thanes—that is, farmers of fairly broad acres and some status, Wolfgeat of Ilmington and Siegeforth of Asthall. Bede had insisted on the duty of reading and learning the Bible; King Alfred in the ninth century provided a school for his courtiers' boys and translated books into English for them. Now Aelfric in the tenth was ready to teach all.

At Bledington there is no sign of any church built before about 1150, the date of the pillars and arches of the nave. Nor is there any sign of pre-Conquest churches very near—not at Kingham or Churchill or Chipping Norton. But Christianity was approaching us. At Notgrove a tenth century crucifix may still be seen and nearby at Aston Blank there are also Saxon fragments. At Lemington, by Moreton-in-Marsh a fine if minute Saxon church was built. Oxford was growing quite large; it had several churches before the Conquest. St. Michael's in the Cornmarket has still a tower which is a lesson in how the Saxons built—with rubble walls and short and long stones to make the angles or quoins firm, and with small windows, divided by pillars, making decorative patterns in the walls.

17

But building in stone had been no part of Saxon culture when they first came and many settlements may have had churches of wood or of dry stone walls roughly thatched which would pull apart easily and leave no distinguishable stone when the time was ripe for a better building. Yet, the idea that every township small and large should have its own centre for the new Christian teaching could hardly occur as yet. The new dioceses were immense. Worcester included all Gloucestershire as well as Worcestershire and part of Warwickshire. The diocese of Lincoln covered a great part of England, including Oxford. An occasional travelling teacher or a central church attended by Christians of the area around were the most that could be hoped for; it is possible that the Saxon church at Stow, of which legend though no stone tells, served such a purpose.

Though it had no centre of its own Bledington was still related from 811 A.D. with a well-known Christian institution. In that year the monastery of Winchcombe was dedicated with great ceremony in the presence of three Kings with eleven Ealdormen in their train, the Archbishop of Canterbury and twelve Bishops.[14] King Cenwulf of Mercia took a leading part in the foundation of the monastery and in providing it with an income. He gave to it (the date of the document was November 11th, 811) 'seven hides in Bladenton"—the full measure of our cultivated land. At the same time, he made a similar gift of Sherborne; because of this, the two villages would have certain connections for hundreds of years—as long as our connection with the Abbey lasted.

The connection with the Monastery or convent (for long the latter was the usual word) was not in truth a religious event; at no time did it bear a very religious character. The work of convents was not that of providing for the religious life of the villeins, cottagers and serfs on their lands. This work by the ninth century was coming to be regarded as that of the bishops. Convents cared for the religious life of their members; they served God in their ceremonies and devotions. Some of them provided training and work and dignified functions for sons and daughters of the nobles, and all the larger ones came to be used to provide pensions and refuge for old age for royal officials and servants. Bledington and Sherborne (with later, Hidcote and Snowshill and other properties) served to support these monks at Winchcombe; the tie was economic. Strictly however, it was not ownership. Its precise nature is of great importance, as we shall see.

All this while, there were struggles between kings and armies to control and govern larger and larger areas—the struggle towards unity, a single control of the whole country. The military organisation of each kingdom required rewards for the soldiers—the most natural form for which was land or rights over land. Thus originated most probably the 'manorial' organisation by which every settlement, every 'parish' had its own Lord, with the commoners paying dues to him of produce or service or money, or all three, together with some small military obligation. Some scholars believe that the germ of manorial organisations was very early: it is certain that two centuries before the Conquest saw its wide development. It seems that an assumption was made that the king was the lord of each manor until he and his government (the deed was signed by a number of 'wise men' as well as the king) allocated it to some person or some institution.

As we have seen, the Christian church grew partly through its association with the kings. Thus many manors were assigned to bishoprics and monasteries as well as to royal officials and captains: so Bledington was put under the lordship of Winchcombe Abbey. Manorial organisation was of great importance to villages for some nine hundred years, only dying away into insignificance during the seventeenth century. Beside its private importance to Landlords and commoners it was part of the government of the country. Peace and order on the manor were of great importance both to lord and tenants and these were promoted by the manor court. Just how the dues of tenant to lord were established is not known but it is certain that they had always a large element of custom—the lord could not vary them by his mere wish, nor settle them according to the demand for his land: he was land*lord*, but not a land*owner*, though later he would try to become one, and sometimes succeed. The lord's rights and the relations of tenants to each other were administered by a manor court, usually held once a year. All the tenants attended and the 'chair'—the only one—was taken by the lord or his agent or steward. Every one knew and remembered the customary dues of his own and others' holdings: disputes between tenants were reviewed and miscreants were fined there. An important function of the court was to witness to the customs relating to and changes in tenancy. When a tenant died his widow had certain rights, and it was usual for a son to be allowed to succeed, on payment of a customary entrance fee: there was a right to succession, sometimes for one life, sometimes for two. But still in

Bledington the old meeting of commoners with no officers but its 'Oarsmen' continued to take its co-operative decisions as to plantings and to discuss the numbers of cattle to be turned on to the heaths, and other farming regulations. It seems that if disputes were avoided the manor court did not become involved in these.

It may be that, here, the Abbey had at first no resident agent but where lords did not live on the manor it was usual for them to have a steward who was allotted a holding known as the demesne which he farmed for the lord. Certain rights claimed by lords, e.g. the control of fishing in the river and of hunting called for local control, as did also the delivery of dues in the form of produce. Here, the lord was at no time resident, but the steward lived in the old gabled house now known as the Old Manor. On behalf of the Abbey he farmed two yardlands, in scattered strips in the open field. Another manorial officer was one of the tenants, the reeve, who both acted as spokesman for his fellows and was held responsible for the accuracy of their various claims as to custom.

On many large manors the court could take action in what we may call civic matters: it was not only a 'court manor,' but also a 'court leet.' Offences such as assault and larceny could be dealt with. This right depended on royal approval, only given where there was a sufficient number of freehold tenants, who paid only small special dues, were free to leave the manor if they so wished (as others were not) and to bequeath their property and their holdings to their chosen heirs. These men with their partial independence served as a jury. But here there were for centuries only two freeholders, too few for this purpose. All offences against the peace in Bledington, all dishonest actions except minor ones had to go to a larger court, the 'hundred' or district court. And indeed, from all manors, serious offences had to be referred to it.

There was provision for local responsibility in the matter of crime: men were organised in groups of ten, or 'tithings', who acted as surety for each other and also would bring members to answer charges in the hundred court. Bledington men were too few to form two tithings: their one 'tithing man' must attend all meetings of the hundred court, which met for long on the old site at Salemansburie, in the open air, and later at nearby Lower Slaughter, where a building had become available. This court, already ancient in some form by the Conquest, would continue to have functions far into the eighteenth century.[15]

By the end of the Anglo-Saxon period there was an organisation larger than the Hundred. A larger section of the Kingdom—the county, Gloucestershire—had been organised by 1016. Every county consisted of several hundreds: the Shire-reeve, the sheriff represented the King and was responsible for justice within the county. From the creation of the latter it was the sheriff or his officers who presided over the hundred courts.

Meanwhile the organisation of the Church had also become extended and more detailed.

The idea gained ground that every community should be an ecclesiastical unit, with its own church building and its own priest. The physical site, the 'parish,' usually coincided with the land defined as the community's agricultural, manorial and civic base. But the great work of providing churches went forward very slowly. It was the Normans who completed the great work of providing all midland and southern England with permanent, nearly always stone, churches.

Wulfstan, Bishop of Worcester, who held his office both before and after the Norman Conquest, urged all lords of manors in his diocese to see that their parishes had churches. It may well be that Winchcombe Abbey obeyed this bidding on its manors, although the earliest part of our present church dates from some eighty years after the Conquest. In this way, though not more than many lay lords, the convent assumed some spiritual responsibility.

The problem of providing for the maintenance of the church and its services was solved by laying on parishioners the duty of paying tithes, or tenths, of agricultural produce. At first they were paid on varying products and at various times of year; nor was their destination and purpose always the same. Two objects, however, were always served— the service of the church and help for the poor. In the course of time the custom of their use was settled as the support of the parish priest together with charity for the poor. They became legally payable to those who appointed the parson, whose duty it was to pass them to him. Their payment became compulsory in respect of all land.[16] Sometimes it seemed that a tenth of the parish products was more than the parson and the poor needed and the patron, perhaps with permission, retained a part of them: they gradually became a form of property, of rent, subject to the payment of the parish priest's salary; often he was given the minor tithes, and those only. The claim of the poor on the tithes was forgotten and the duty was ascribed to the parishioners of making special further provision.

The support of the church building was divided, as time went on, between the patron, who should maintain the chancel, used by the priest, and the parishioners responsible for the nave in which they sat.

Life seems to have been quiet in Bledington, in the century after the Abbey became Lord of the manor—the ninth, but the country as a whole bore then another invasion, which eventually almost reached our parish. When King Cenwulf opened the new monastery in 811 Danes had been for twenty years raiding coastal districts. They came from the country north of the home lands of the Angles and Saxons and resembled them in race and language. Their pagan religion and so far as we know the motives of their invasion were also basically the same as their predecessors'. They meant to settle in this more fertile and extensive home.

To-day Danish names bear witness to their succeess in conquering and settling Northumbria and East Anglia. They pushed on south-wards into Wessex where they met a brave and persistent leader in the King, the famous Alfred. With him they fought battle after battle, defeating him many times. But he gathered his forces a last time and the enemy was overcome at Ethandune in Wiltshire in 878. King Alfred is one of the timeless figures, having virtues relevant to all periods. He could fight but loved peace; he cared for songs and poems, understanding the importance of great literature. He was a man ready to make reasonable compromise, and in all this he was devoted to the Christian, the Christ-like life.

But the Danes were still able to press on north of Alfred's Wessex. In 877 they had captured Gloucester and two years later a company of them settled for a time at Cirencester, plundering and living in the country and leaving small settlements. There are still a few Danish names of villages near the two towns—'thorpes': Brookthorpe, Hatherop, Southrop. On the Oxford side of Bledington also, they left two place-names—Heythrop and Dunthrop. The nearest they came to us was Hook Norton. In 906 "An army from Northampton and Leicester made a great slaughter of the English at Hookneretun and plundered far and wide over the county of Oxford.' But they later receded from the area that became Gloucestershire and Oxfordshire. This was perhaps not a deliverance for some families in Bledington and neighbouring villages—for the serfs. Unfree men were few among the Danes, while the Normans when they came found more serfs in Gloucestershire than anywhere else in the country.

The end of the Danes in England was not yet. Sweyn, King of Denmark and Norway, 'swept over England' and after him there were three Danish Kings. One of these was Canute, who was a statesman and a monarch devoted to the unity of the country he ruled. Under him Danes and English were treated alike and grew together. He gave the nation a single law, drawn largely from English sources. Unfortunately his two successors, his sons Harald and Harthacanut, antagonised the country and the English kings came back. Edward, later known as the Confessor, had been brought up in Normandy and is said to have given its Duke a promise of succession to the throne or of the right to present himself to the national assembly, the Witan, for election. Edward was not himself a man of vigour: when he returned to England he employed the famous Godwin of Wessex to strengthen his government. Godwin and his sons became great powers in the land. One of them, Harold, had already largely governed the country for twelve years when the King died. The Witan, the nobles and bishops proceeded to elect Harold to the throne. Now comes the story every Englishman learns: Harold was attacked in the north by his brother and the Danish King and in the south by the Duke of Normandy, who was to be England's conqueror.

[1] Chiefly by the Rev. David Royce of Swell, whose collection is now chiefly in the Bristol Museum
[2] These dates are now thought to be too late
[3] Coins the property of Mrs Rosina Morgan, identified by the Ashmolean Museum
[4] E. J. Lainchbury *Kingham: the Beloved Place*, Alden Press, Oxford, 1957. p. 327
[5] E. Meades *The History of Chipping Norton*, Alden Press, Oxford, 1949. P. 11
[6] E. F. Eales *History of Naunton*, Alden Press, Oxford, 1928
[7] H. E. O'Neil & J. M. C. Toynbee *Scultpures from a Romano-British Well in Gloucestershire*, Journal of Roman Studies, 1958
[8] See page xvi
[9] D. Whitelock *The Beginnings of English Society*, London 1952, Ch. V p. 103
[10] Bede *A History of the English Church and People*. Tr. L. Sherley-Price. London 1964. Bk. III Ch. 17 p. 163
[11] E. J. Lainchbury. op. cit. p. 317

[12] Philip Stubbes *The Anatomie of Abuses* (1583) quoted by James Reeve *The Idiom of the People* London 1958. p. 27

[13] Beowulf, prose translation by E. V. Rieu. London 1963

[14] (i) ed. D. Royce. Landboc sive Registrum Monastrii de Winchelcumba (Land Register of Winchcombe Abbey), Vol. I, pt. V, Vol. II Introduction p. xiii
(ii) G. Haigh. The History of Winchcombe Abbey. London 1950. pp. 17, 18

[15] It was in abeyance for a time, but revived in the early eighteenth century

[16] There was an exception here: tithes were never laid on the ancient Oars

chapter two

MONASTERY, MANOR AND PARISH

IN THE TWO centuries and a half between 811 and 1066 the life of the monks within Winchcombe Abbey went through a number of phases, but change in the relations between the Abbey and its manors appears to have been slow. The manorial system continued to evolve: customs were modified and became more uniform; demesne farms worked by a steward on behalf of the monks, began to be established; more acres or hides were brought under the plough. The social and military system known later as feudalism, was developing; the social ladder led down from king to lord, and from lord to freeman villein, bordar and serf, and each lord had the duty to call out freemen to follow him to battle when the king required.

Whether any Bledington man fought with the English king Harold against the invading Normans in 1066 we shall never know. C. S. Taylor, one of the County's historians, believed[1] that a Gloucestershire man from a village ten miles from here fought at Senlac, on October 14 of that year. Toni de Barrington was a housecarl of Harold's and, faithful like an old Saxon follower, 'was one of the heroes whose bodies lay near their king when night closed in.' The Abbot of Winchcombe also, in his fashion, resisted the Conqueror. He may have called up freemen from his manors, but if so they did not as a body reach the field of battle: in any case, there were as yet no freeholders here. He himself was imprisoned and deposed from his abbey, and after three years or so a Norman was appointed to his place. Wars and invasions had sometimes left remote villages untouched for a while but it was soon evident that none would escape the changes the Normans brought about.

William the Conqueror claimed to be the rightful king of England, not by conquest but by law. He was a most powerful organiser and administrator, but at the same time judicious. He modified law, custom and religious institutions when necessary for his major purposes but where possible he used them. The unification of the country and the concentration of government in the hands of the sovereign were his prime intentions. When any region opposed him, as western counties did early and the Yorkshire area later, he mercilessly devastated them. To achieve centralisation he rewarded his followers with lordships of manors. By 1086 not a single major landlord was an Englishman. Sometimes one of his soldiers received a great number of manors, never a great compact estate but scattered manors so that no man could easily sway a neighbourhood. In the feudal system as William developed it, oaths of fealty set loyalty to the king before that to a man's or a tenant's immediate lord.

Customs in the manors, however, were not greatly disturbed. The manor, hundred and county courts continued to function. So far all this could be regarded as a development rather than an overturning of English law.

The Church in England was a part of William's own, the Roman Catholic Church; he especially respected religious institutions. In spite of the Abbot's recalcitrance there was no plunder of the Winchcombe estates. The Abbot of Evesham was placed for a time in charge of the Abbey and its affairs and he 'treated it with much justice.' The folk of the manor of Bledington must have heard rumours of the stream of starving sickly people who struggled out of William's path as he harried nearby counties, Shropshire and Staffordshire. They died in the streets of Evesham before Wulfstan, our Bishop—the Bishop of Worcester—could get them fed. But Bledington was able to lie doggo in a quiet neighbourhood, much of which was in the lordship of monasteries.

One of the ways in which the Conquest affected everyone was through taxation. The main measurement of land was everywhere the hide, partly a matter of area, partly of value, and only roughly equal from one area to another (from eighty to a hundred and twenty acreas) but serving for nation-wide taxation. The old tax, Danegeld, had been charged on hides; the last English king, Edward the Confessor, had greatly reduced it; on one occasion it was levied at a mere seven-pence a hide, and for a time it was remitted altogether. But William levied geld at six shillings the hide—a sum calculated to have been equal to five shillings (25p) in the pound. After two world wars this rate sounds almost tolerable but it takes no account of taxes in kind, or in labour, of tithes for the church or of military service. It is certain that taxation levied by the Sheriff for the king and by the parson and the convent's reeve for the various purposes of the church partly accounts for the 'utter misery in our shire'[2] from 1066 to 1086.

In the collection of taxes the Normans seemed to reveal themselves in their true colours. Violence and greed seemed greater than the wish to take over peacefully. Says the Old English Chronicle for 1087:—

'The King and the headmen loved much, and overmuch, covetousness in gold and silver . . . The King . . . recked not how very sinfully the stewards got it of wretched men nor how many unlawful deeds they did; but the more men spoke about right law, the more unlawfully they acted.'[3]

Twenty years after the Conquest William had the idea that seems to prove his administrative genius. He would discover the value of all his lands, and thus know how to tax it and what taxes it would yield. His officers should record the lordship of every manor, the extent of its cultivated land, what the value of income from it had been shortly before the Conquest, in the time of Edward the Confessor, and the value at the time of record, in 1086.

The earliest description of Bledington is the one in Domesday Book.[4] It is brief but basic; seven hides—that is, somewhere between 700 and 860 acres—were now in cultivation. (These doubtless included all the more easily worked soil—the two Oars, the land stretching from the Upper Oar to the small heights above the brook; and also some clay land near the houses on both sides of it. There were also twenty acres of meadow land near the river. Seven or eight hundred acres remained in a comparatively wild state—what in the eighteenth century were called the Home Heath and the Far Heath and the land beyond the Home Heath to the borders of Oddington and Icomb.) There were in the parish eight villeins and four bordars. All these held shares in the land but none of them were freemen—none could leave the manor without the permission of their lord the Abbot. Villeins were the superior tenants, with usually more ridges in the open arable fields, more cattle and sheep on the Heath. Villeins and bordars alike helped to till the land—the demesne—which the Abbey retained to farm directly. They worked at it at customary times. Bordars on other manors worked four, three or two days each week through the year; how many were worked here we do not know. Villiens might owe as little labour-rent as a few weeks at hay or corn-harvest. Their work was supervised by the reeve, often one of the villiens who was also farming his own land, which he held 'freely'—i.e. with neither money nor labour-rent, but involving the onerous task of knowing every man's due service and seeing that he gave it, while at the same time bearing witness to the rights of tenants.

The demesne land was farmed by the Abbey's Steward who lived in the house provided for him, that is, in a house on the site of what is now known as the Old Manor House. Beside the customary tenant labour the Steward had other and full-time labour—eight serfs and two 'ancillae,' i.e. women of servile status. We must not think of the serfs as slaves for it would have been a breach of custom to sell them and a shock because a threat to the tenants for they were not men of another colour or even of another race: British and Saxons had long merged into English.

On the demesne there were two plough-teams, while the eight villeins and four bordars had five: this seems to give tenants small holdings but it is possible that these varied: some bordars may have had no draught animals, no share in a plough.

There was one other head of a household—the miller. He owed the money rent of five shillings but may also have yielded to the Abbey some part of the corn deducted as payment for milling. On other manors nearby the presence of a priest is indicated, but not here. Thus we may suppose that if there was a small building for religious purposes it was not regularly served.

The remaining fact given about the manor itself, is that under Edward the Confessor it was worth £4 annually and now is worth £3. This final statement is, for William's government, what the rest led up to. It gives the taxable value and indicates that in times of peace it can be expected to be at least one third higher. The Domesday entry gives us further something of the setting of the 'vill' of Bledington. It occurs—the second item—in an account of the Gloucestershire manors of Winchcombe Abbey, the first manor described being Sherborne, a much larger and more valuable manor near Burford. These two manors and parishes are linked together in many documents, they were visited on the same journeys by Abbey officers. Facts about the larger manor, worth so much more attention and paper-work, throw light from time to time on our own. Both manors we learn are members of the Hundred of Salemansberie.

A hundred years after the Conquest the English still hated their Norman masters, and when they could, avenged themselves for the losses, the taxes and the humiliations they suffered. It was still rash for a Norman to ride among them alone, even in our quiet area. In 1169 a Bledington man named Segrim found the corpse of a murdered Norman somewhere within the Manor. If this were known the whole village would be severely fined, and perhaps the Hundred. Segrim removed the body across the parish boundary, which was also the limit of the Salemanesberie Hundred. But the matter came to light and was reported to the Hundred Court, then to the County Court, and thence to the King's Court. Bledington men do not seem to have been suspected of the murder, but only of concealment. The end of the matter was a fine of £2, levied on the Hundred, and a fine of half a mark for Segrim.[5]

Justice in those days had two aspects—the maintenance of order and the provision of funds for government: fines were valuable. Hence came complications; fines might be paid direct to the king's officers or he might award them to some feudal subordinate, a lay lord. There were also 'the religious' to be placated, or to be paid for religious and other services: fines were given in some areas to monasteries or cathedrals. Thus for a time from 1227 onward Winchcombe Abbey was allowed to withdraw the tenants of its manors from hundred and county courts, and arrange for justice in courts under its own control. But presently Winchcombe rented the fines of the Slaughter court and also of two other Gloucestershire hundred courts, for a fixed annual rent and the Bledington cases reverted to Slaughter.

The relations of our village to the monastery continued to be mainly economic. No question of religious service to the village arose at first nor did the monastery lay any claim to tithes given for the parish church and the poor.

During the greater part of all this period of relation to Winchcombe it is likely that Bledington tenants felt themselves fortunate. Monasteries were usually, though not always, mild and steady-going administrators of their landed estates. Their rents were usually rather lower than those paid to laymen, not that the monks did not want money, or were free of the temptation to exploit, but certainly lay families were more subject to these contingencies; thus rents on manors of 'the religious' remained more constant.

The chief source of our knowledge of Bledington life for this time is the *Landboc*[6] of Winchcombe Abbey. As its name indicates, this is largely a record concerning the Abbey's landed estates. It contains copies of charters and decrees and licenses. All the entries have an aspect related to property, but many have other significances also. From it we learn that in 1282 Abbot Walter de Wickware provided for the raising of some rents—probably not those of living tenants, or even of customary successors to a holding. Few such changes are recorded. Between the monastery and rich personal lords there was a social difference; Winchcombe Abbey was to a considerable extent a local institution, (though also in its connections a European one) recruiting a number of its monks from nearby villages or from its own manors—e.g. from Child's Wickham, Idbury, Bledington and Honeybourne. In 1307 a *de Bladinton* was a monk in the Abbey, 'valet' to the Abbot, his personal attendant, perhaps his writer or clerk; a monk who was a native of Idbury was one of the last Abbots.

At first the rule was that recruits must be sons of freemen, but these multiplied, and their status implied little as to the size of their farms. Soon villeins were received and at length, the entrance of the son of a serf was allowed. Thus in the monks' Chapter, manorial tenants' interests must have had their protectors.[7] Later when there was exploitation of the manor, recruitment was not usually from among the sons of tenants.

Meanwhile Bledington was a parish as well as a manor: it was a unit for religious purposes. The Bishop's and his diocese's work of providing for the religious needs of parishes had gone forward slowly. The organisation at the centre had to be developed before all parishes could be served and the clergy supervised. The diocese of Worcester was divided into archdeaconries, and then again later into rural deaneries. Bledington was one of the parishes of the Stow deanery, as it is again today. The rural dean had some oversight of his group of parishes, and his superior the Archdeacon of Gloucester visited Stow periodically as he still does, to receive reports from the village churches.

By the late eleventh century the Church intended and expected to have a church in every village. If a parish had only a poor wooden church, or a small, poorly-built stone one, it was thought the duty of its lord to erect a good stone building of permanence and dignity.

Thus, a number of churches of Norman pattern are still seen in the Cotswolds—with semi-circular arches between nave and chancel, and when there is an aisle, round pillars joined by semi-circular arches between it and the nave.

Bledington, it seems, never had a church of this pure Norman fashion. Very many village churches were built in the mixed style of cylindrical pillars and pointed 'Early English' arches and those, such as Idbury's, in the relatively pure English style were the result of later building or re-building. Bledington church was built in the mixed style; there is no sign that its pointed arches were preceded by round ones. The monastery, one infers, had built the church for its manor about 1150 or, more probably 1170, just as the lay lords were doing. On 14th July 1175 Pope Alexander III issued a Bill confirming Winchcombe in its possession of its home buildings and also of churches on its manors—Sherborne, Bledington,[8] Twining, Enstone, Stanton and Alne. That does not quite prove that our church was completed by that day and year, but it seems likely, for by that year the governing body of the Monastery, its Chapter of monks, was already claiming the right to nominate secular priests to the livings on its manors as was done also by lay lords. At this date the Pope signified his approval of the claim, and henceforth it seems that when a vacancy occurs, the Abbey nominates and the Bishop confirms its choice. In the monastery's direct relation to the Pope—whereas the Bishop's Diocese is part of a national organisation—we see the ground of later trouble.

The church had been dedicated to Saint Leonard, a French nobleman of the Sixth Century, who had turned hermit. He had lived in a cell—such was the story told to Bledington folk—practising holiness alone for a time, and then had founded a monastery. He had become a popular saint in England somewhat before our church was built, as the patron of 'prisoners, sick folk and peasants.' The dedication seems suitable for a village.

Provision was made, or more probably had been for some time made, for the support of the village priest and for his duty of caring for the poor, and for the chancel of the church, by means of tithes—tenths of the produce of farms and gardens. It would seem that the provision was ample: it naturally grew with every improvement in field, herd and garden—grew, it appears, so considerably as to come to seem more than enough for men on so low a rung of the ecclesiastical ladder.

As one walks, today, down the Stow road to Bledington one sees, glimpse by glimpse, a small ideal picture of a beautiful church rising on a height among and above a cluster of houses, all of the creamy or golden-grey Cotswold stone. It is a parable in stone for a community life dominated by a refined, humane religion, expressed in a church which comprehends everyone. Today this is not so, even though all villagers may be touched by Christian influence but in the Middle Ages there may have been moments when it represented the truth. In the 12th and 13th centuries the church had no tower but it was already higher and finer than the houses which were still built of timber and thatched. The church had no religious rival. Ancient, originally religious, customs and festivities remained, for example the mumming play, and spring-time games and old songs and dances; pagan ideas had passed from full consciousness and expression, but were still the base of much popular life and art.

The church, then, was already as superior in architecture to the homes around as it would always be up to the present. Though towerless and barnlike, it was amply large for its community and its walls were massive. Within, its architecture was distinctive and it had great dignity.

From 1170, perhaps before, there was a resident parson in the village. At first he was a rector, i.e. he received the full tithes—the great tithes of corn and cattle and the lesser tithes of poultry, honey and other relatively small products. Beside the prestige given him, if not by full priesthood at any rate by the fact that he represented the Church, and some superiority through his access to writings and rituals, he would be economically better off than the farming tenants. Of these there had been only 13 at the Conquest, but their numbers grew. As the extent of ploughland grew and cultivation slowly improved the Rector's income from tithes increased. Besides, the Rector had glebe land, though here only a little. Probably his one equal in income and prestige was the Abbey's Steward.

We have, I think, to imagine efficient service to the church: the Bishop of that time indicated his standard for his clergy when he arranged that at Honeybourne there should be services not only on Sunday, but also on Wednesdays and Fridays and on numerous holy days.[9] Working farmers, even more their wives, with their unending and exacting tasks, would surely think the services more than sufficient.

The church now called people to itself by its fine appearance as well as by the ringing of its one small bell, hanging in the bell-cote still to be seen topping the nave wall at its eastern end. Now, with its tiny Norman arch, and the sharp angle of its small coping it has the look of a miniature, small and delicate, but that is because it is dwarfed by the tower. In the 12th century it stood out clear and important. Coming into this dignified place of assembly from their houses of one or two rooms, crowded with people and with cooking, meals and multifarious small jobs, peace and leisure must have fallen on worshippers. The text in Latin and the ritual of the Mass gave the church an air of mystery, and freed minds from common pressures.

In a late decade of the 13th century the church was somewhat enlarged. Experts say that the walls of the chancel date in part from that time and deduce that it was extended. More light as well as space was desired and tiny Norman windows gave way to Early English lancets. The eastern chancel window is an Early English triplet of which the centre lancet rises in height above the others. To the casual and uninformed eye this large window appears simple enough but careful looking in a good light shows much elaboration of great interest to masons.

The technical description may serve to illustrate the great architectural interest of this small church and its fellows in villages around and is not difficult to follow step by step on the spot. ' . . . each light has a trefoil head, and the lights are divided by a bold mullion, rebated and chamfered to an arris inside and out, the thickness of the heads of the window on the inside being less than that of the mullion, the extra thickness of the mullion runs halfway up from the springing to the containing arch, and then stops short. On the exterior the lights form a triplet with a dripstone to each light, but on the interior the triplet is contained under one arch with a label, the mouldings of which finish on a conical stop, carried on a moulded cap, enriched with the nailhead ornament; . . .'[10]

Meanwhile Winchcombe Abbey was growing in wealth—by money legacies, usually on condition of prayers for the soul of donors; or by the 'granting', in fact by the sale, of the right to houseroom and diet and other comforts in the Abbey for life; and also by developing its skills of estate management, by keeping increasing flocks of sheep on upland demesne lands and commons and by careful exchange of properties. A further source of income was the fees and fines paid into manorial courts and into others when the Abbey could gain control of them. This was exemplified in 1223, with regard to Sherborne and Bledington, the two manors being often associated in the Abbey's manorial business. The tenants of both were then 'released from suit' at the Hundred and County Courts. (We have no evidence as to where cases were taken until 1320 when they seem to have returned to Salmonsbury).[11] All successful monasteries were increasing their wealth in such ways while at the same time struggling to be freed from some of the taxes and services laymen were subject to. But while they felt privilege to be their due from the national government, they hoped not to be fully subject to its authority in economic matters. The Abbot of Winchcombe refers all the main business of his house, economic as well as spiritual, to the Pope. Some monasteries retained the right to be, in the spiritual realm, independent of the Bishop, that is of the Church's organisation within the country. Winchcombe never did quite this but was under the Pope's 'protection' and could often by appeal to the Pope resist the bishops within whose dioceses its manors lay. Monasteries were the cause and the centre in and from these years of struggle for control. Hence in the short run, the slow pace of much of the monastery's business and in the long run, one strong motive, on the sovereign's part for the Reformation.

One sample of these processes, and their relation to the manors is seen in the appropriation of a large proportion of the tithes of some parishes. This would happen, but at a rather later period, in Bledington. More typically Sherborne and Enstone suffered (the word seems not unjust) much earlier.

Sherborne was a larger and richer manor and living than Bledington: the monastery drew a larger income from it and took certain supplements from the tithes in earlier decades than from our parish. In 1194 the Abbey had obtained—beside its manorial dues—an annual draft of £5 upon the tithes, the incumbent's income being, of course, reduced by this sum. Twenty years later (1214), the Abbot obtained permission from Pope, Bishop and King to take £1 annually from Bledington tithes, towards the support of the daily Mass to the Blessed Virgin which had recently been instituted at the Abbey. Returning to the attack upon Sherborne's tithes, the Abbey started in 1220 the process of appropriating the whole rectory, obtaining the right to pay a Vicar to do the work of the Parish for one third of the tithes, keeping two thirds for itself. The process was completed in six years. On this occasion, the Archbishop of Canterbury was added to the number of dignitaries whose permission must be obtained, and he had asserted that the poor must not suffer. That could only be prevented by the parson doing as much for them as hitherto on one third of his former income. The poor, the chancel fabric and the parson all suffered by the reduction. Naturally villagers resented this despoliation, as it seemed to them: the reduction of money to be spent in the village affected the whole. Their resentment was poured out upon one of the Vicars sent to them: he was besieged in his house and otherwise roughly treated.[12]

A similar and still clearer story can be gathered at Enstone, a large and fertile manor some seven miles from Bledington, over the border in Oxford county, then in the diocese of Lincoln. The living was a rich one, valued at 40 marks but, it appeared, worth much more. Two thirds of it in perpetuity were well worth a long process and much expense. At long last, in 1307, the Pope gave his permission for the Abbey to appropriate the Rectory, and the Bishop of Lincoln, after much objection, gave way. Thus the Abbot became Rector and was allowed to appoint a Vicar to act in his stead, for a third of the stipend. Again the move was unpopular. This time the rector of the parish resisted and for himself his protest succeeded, at least on an economic plane: the monastery undertook to pay him till he died a pension of twice the alleged value of his benefice.[13]

It seems that the interests of parishioners in tithes, and in the status and, we must suppose, the qualifications of their parson went undefended: their sole legal concern with tithes was to pay them.

When the Abbot was inducted into the rectory of Enstone it was ceremonially done, in Enstone church, but he did not himself attend: he sent two proctors, instead, and one of them was the Rector of Bledington—the Abbot's nephew. It was perhaps to be expected that the same process would not be applied to Bledington until the Abbot's nephew resigned the living.

The reasons given for these appropriations was not that the village clergy's incomes were excessive, but the inadequacy of the monastery's income to the duties it was expected to assume. So many, the monks said, of the 'poor and faithful' clamoured at its gates for the necessities of life; the King's and Pope's demands for money were, it was said, 'ceaseless.' Bishops required much hospitality for visiting officers, and the King sent pensioners to be cared for as long as they lived. It was certainly not for direct provision for monks (by 1307 there were but twenty of them) that higher income was necessary but

35

they had many officers and servants and vast and fine buildings erected to the glory of God, but whose support must be a drain on an economy which could barely feed the population. To take from the clergy and the poor of the villages to make provision for ageing royal servants or for wandering beggars, hardly seems statesmanlike, but village clergy and poor folk had no power to resist. Even the law, which might well have been their defence, decided for the powers that were, as Winchcombe town discovered[14] when it tried to resist appropriation. Bishops, it is true, never gave their warm approval—they had reason to sympathise with the parish clergy—but their objections were overruled by the Pope.

The village clergy were a different set of men from the monks: they entered the profession by a different route. On the whole, it was the Bishop's right and function to certify men fit to serve parishes. A boy wishing to be ordained applied first to be an acolyte or a sub-deacon. To achieve this he must get some teaching in Latin, and learn to recite prayers and psalms. He would in due time be called to some centre to show his progress to the Bishop or much more often to some officer appointed by him. Safely through the first test the candidate went forward to another, and with effort and good fortune became a deacon. Finally, if he pursued matters, but not all did, he was ordained priest.

Quite a number of boys from Bledington started on this road, but some, half-way through turned aside to other goals. To a boy who could not inherit his father's tenancy, to become a cleric must have seemed one of the few ways open to him, and it was the sole way of obtaining some—usually not much—literary education. The situation was parallel to that of the nineteenth and early twentieth centuries when for many the only way to education was pupil-teachership, or 'winning a scholarship,' with a view to teaching.

In the forty one years from 1282 to 1322 inclusive, fifteen Bledington boys were received by the Bishop or his representative into diaconate and priesthood. Of priests there were eight; one other did not go beyond sub-deacon's rank, and one in the year when the available registers cease, was admitted an 'acolyte' and may have gone further. The rest became deacons, and possibly a few of these proceeded to priesthood in later years.[15]

It was evidently feared that there might be an excess of men for the parish ministry: the Bishop must be satisfied that if posts were not available, ordained men would not lack livelihood. The fathers of the

Bledington youths all promised the necessary support.

Who taught the candidates? One boy was put forward as 'approved' by the Dean of Stow: in other cases the approver is not named. No school was available: it seems likely that clerics or lawyers in Stow were the usual coaches for the boys. One boy was approved by Bruerne Abbey and presumably was taught in that small Cistercian house— only four miles away.

One can infer a little as to the family background of the ordinands. None of the Bledington holdings were large and most were small. The only family that could be regarded as prosperous was that of the steward of the demesne. For a longish period a de Bladinton (possibly a short succession of men of that name) was steward and no fewer than eleven ordinands bore that name: one concludes that some of these were sons or nephews of this house. The family had other connections with the monastery: in 1300 a John de Bladinton had given to the Abbot a house in Fleet Street, London, and in 1307 he (or another of the same name) was 'valet' to the Abbot —his attendant, perhaps his secretary. Families called *atte Yate de Bladinton* and de la Broke (later, *atte Brooke*) and Brown sent candidates, and these families in the 14th century, and probably in the 13th also, had holdings above the average size.[16]

Of the eleven *de Bladintons* it is possible that some were not relatives of the Steward, but belonged to families who had not yet come by a very distinctive surname. When one was needed it was sufficient to say 'of such and such a place.' Now we see the process of bestowing more particular names.

The *atte Yates* lived in one of the houses scattered in two vague lines on each side of the brook from the present University Farm to the King's Head Inn, which formed what was called The Yate or Street and the *de la Brokes*' or *atte Brookes*' home was close beside the brook where houses stand now almost opposite the Methodist chapel. To digress a little, there were men in the village called by the surprising names of Dame Ysabel and Dame Emme, perhaps after some person they had served or some notable mater familias of their own. We come across many families named after villages around from which they had hailed—Stow, Northleach, Icomb, Honeybourne, Broadwell. Some names dropped out, others were changed beyond recognition. There is no one named Bledington in the whole county now, so far as I can find; Honeybournes are Honeybones, Broadwell is lost in Bradwell,

Northleach in Nolidge or even Knowledge: Kentys became Kench. How many who see charm in antiques would like to have the surname 'Dame Ysabel,' but no one has.

One exception among candidates for the diaconate was John de Wykewar, not a native of Bledington. He was here in 1299, as 'clerk,' yet it was not till 1306 that he was received as a deacon, the entry in the register describing him as Rector of Bladinton. Something more of this man's story must be told:[17] meanwhile we note that his formal qualification was very low.

It was perhaps more in theory than in practice that sub-deacons and deacons expected to become parish priests. Many earned their livings as paid writers or lawyers' clerks or went round the manors in the employ of the lords, writing down the accounts so far kept in the minds of reeve or steward unable to write, or when that became customary, keeping records of the manor courts. Thus they helped themselves and their families to that familiarity with the use of professional men's services and to a legal way of doing business which is so striking in village documents in these times and long afterwards, while there was still little village education. Those who remained unable to read or write learned to summon those who could do so, just as they did skilled smiths or weavers. A ray of light falls on two of the Bledington rectors in the late 13th century. In 1275 Bishop Giffard of Worcester took up with the monastery the case of Richard de Stodley (or Studley) rector of Bledington and also of Twining, a village near Tewkesbury, and 'of the church of the Blessed Mary in Winchcombe.' He was, that is, in some sense a member of the monastery itself. This old pluralist is deep in debt. Upon what he has spent the income of his rectories we do not learn, but he appears to be accustomed to the ministrations of servants, and to expect to keep a small stable : we may imagine he lived more than comfortably. The Bishop directs that the Abbey shall take the rents of his rectories, pay his debts, and cause his churches to be served. Studley himself is to have lodgings in the Abbey, a servant-cleric with whom he can read the daily services, and also a groom and a boy; these three servants are all to be 'well lodged.' For himself he is to have food and wine, raiment and bed-clothes. Why so prosperous a person running into debt should have so much of the attention of the Bishop and so fine a provision there is no indication.[18] Bishop Gifford was himself a man of Norman descent and had been high in the King's diplomatic service; it may well be that Studley had high connections. A little sympathy for the Abbey is stirred by this case. With Kings and Bishops both ordaining 'corrodies'—life-long entertainment for their nominees—there was reason for gaining support from the Pope, and gave some excuse for annexing a large part of the tithes in some of its manors and parishes.

It seems likely that while Studley lived the Church here was served by a Clerk in minor orders under the direction of the Abbey. At the turn of the century, perhaps at Studley's death, the Abbot of the time, Walter de Wickwar, nominated his nephew John de Wickwar to our rectory. When nephew John was fourteen years of age his uncle had presented him to the living of Hawling,[19] a parish nine miles away over the hills and in no relation to Bledington. In justice it should possibly be said that the church there was not left to the ministrations of a child: his preparation to become a sub-deacon and the services of his church were both to be supervised by a neighbour, the Rector of the parish of Stanton. When John became Rector of Bledington he was thirty years old, and still a sub-deacon, becoming a deacon later as we have shown. As to whether his work here justified the hereditary principle or was a regrettable example of nepotism we have no further evidence. I do not know whether he held both rectories Hawling and Bledington at the same time. But taking together the stories of de Studley and de Wickwar it seems likely that Bledington had glimpses of the ease of life and self-concern of the clergy and monks which contributed to the great discontent and ferment of the next century.

The village parsons produced by the education of sub-deacons and deacons are described by William Langland in his Piers Plowman written in the next century:—

> 'I've been parson and priest past thirty long years,
> Yet I sing not, *nor solfa*, nor saints' lives read;
> I can find in a field or a furlong a hare
> Better than in beatus-vir or beata omnes
> Construe a clause or full clearly expound it.
> I can hold well lovedays or hear a reeve's reckoning
> But in canon law and decretals can read not a line.'[20]

But no doubt if they forgot almost all they had learned of the psalms or canon law and even of Latin there was still in their minds something of literary training and the wider mind.

After gathering information, such as we can, about the monastery's and the bishop's relation to the village, the church fabric, and the available facts about our clergy one notes our almost total lack of knowledge of the mental contents of both shepherd and flock. In particular the intimate religious life of villagers remains hidden. How was the teaching of the gospels presented to them? Did anyone read them translations of the psalms? Did they grasp that Christianity is the religion of a book? We must no doubt suppose that the teaching of Rectors de Studley and de Wickwar was somewhat formal, but there were other rectors before and after.

The Church's message at all times takes some colour from the temperament and experience of every speaker of it: where there is only one speaker that may be an important fact. In the thirteenth century emphasis was laid upon varying parts and aspects of the teaching of the Church. Associated with the massive dark Norman churches had been a large element of threat and fear. In Oddington Old Church, two miles from us along Heath Lane there was a wall painting of the Last Judgement[21] and at the hamlet of Shorthampton, near Charlbury, remains an ancient church with nave and tiny chancel and Norman window. On its walls are pale, fading pictures. These were found, some forty years since, under the plaster. I saw them, with astonishment, thirty years ago when they were clear and lively. The largest and brightest of them was a representation of the day of judgment. Men and women were stepping out of their graves and turning some towards a group of trees in flower and others to a downward path. At the end of a short journey these latter were shown as the damned in hell—in cauldrons of boiling pitch, with Satan's servant-imps stoking the fires. Seeming odd and childish in the twentieth century, these pictures carried a terrifying suggestion when they were painted, perhaps in the late 14th century. This strain of threat and fear continued to be emphasised from time to time. We may see in Chaucer's *confession*, also late in the fourteenth century, how the gayest most cultivated sceptic in England thought it well before he died to allow for the possibility of a judgment day not entirely unlike that of the Shorthampton pictures—'so that,' he wrote, 'I may be of hem at the day of doom that shulle be saved.'[22] The Landboc of Winchcombe shows us a considerable number of men, sometimes with their wives, bargaining—in the way already mentioned—for their own support at the monastery, making over their property to it, on condition of prayer for their souls. Sometimes they arranged to be allowed to wear clothes like those of the monks, feeling—it is said—that this would increase their chance of salvation. We may be sure that fear of judgment day was part of the official religion taught here: but it is certain that great popular movements stressing the loving quality of the Christian life touched our forebears—maybe through our own rectors, but if not, by other means.

For example, in the early and middle twelfth century a great religious and cultural enthusiasm for the Virgin Mary swept over Europe. Between 1160 and 1260 the all but miraculous Cathedral of Chartres was built and sublimely decorated in her honour. Into this cult of the Blessed Virgin all the idealism, the poetry and the artists' passion was poured. Royal persons, the 'ranks of chivalry,' the merchant guilds, all adored the Divine Mother. She warmed hearts, raised the conception of the feminine life, inspired the young and humanised a frequently brutal time—but all we positively know of her effect on Bledington is that in 1214 the Bishop of Worcester granted a yearly pension of 20 shillings from the Bledington tithes to help pay for candles used at the daily mass for the Virgin, in the Abbey[23].

During many decades the Crusades excited and satisfied cravings for novelty and adventure, but we do not know of any Bledington man who visited the Holy Land—only that in 1257 a tax of one twentieth of income was demanded, by way of the Abbey, by King Henry III, for the support of a crusade.

In the late years of the twelfth and the early years of the thirteenth century, St. Francis of Assisi, a sunny and gentle spirit, the product of the warmth of the southern slopes of Italian hills, of beautiful Italian cities, and of Italy's prosperous trade, all combined with the inspiration of the gospels, was preaching the brotherhood of living things, God's love for the simplest of men, and that poverty was no bar to the spirit's wealth. This teaching and his own devoted spirit inspired a great movement in Italy and France and by 1224 some of his followers had arrived in Canterbury. Soon Franciscan friars were travelling through English villages, begging their way, and preaching on the greens. But the only Franciscan we know of in relation to Bledington is the Bishop of Worcester who was in office from 1302, William de Geynesborough. By that time a friar could be something of a grandee as he was—not only a Bishop but also a Reader in the University of Oxford and an official of his now important order with some responsibilities for all the Franciscans of 'the province of England.'

In the constant struggle for authority between King and Pope Geynesborough was a 'stout upholder of Papal claims.'

This scholar and administrator brought St. Francis but little nearer to our village, but still the spirit of the Saint may have reached hither, together with the cult of the Virgin, in the early carols for Christmas in which babe and beast and bird were brought together in affectionate and romantic contemplation.

In 1271 Hayles Abbey, the rival of Winchcombe, some fifteen miles from here, received relics of 'the precious blood' of Christ, and became the object of innumerable pilgrimages. But it is only a supposition, however reasonable, that young Bledington folk joined companies on the road, riding or walking to the shrine on long summer days between haytime and harvest. But such matters as these were part of the common mental furniture of the time, and the question is not of whether Bledington knew of them, but whether it was deeply stirred by all or some of these movements.

Of the ordinary day to day home and working life no full picture can be drawn. But during this time the inhabitants first included freemen. The two families of this status, le Kentys and de Bladinton, were both founded here by men who had been officers or servants of the monastery. It had been among their duties to witness the Abbot's transactions in property; they were most probably clerks. It is likely that both—certainly one—on their first entry to our township acted as stewards of the demesne and manor. The two men were literate and their sons also tended to learn Latin and writing. These two families. free and literate, raised a little the efficiency and the status of the manor

Their help was needed. Life could be rough here and violent crimes occurred though the records show few. Serious offences had to be reported to the Sheriff's court of three judges and might be passed to the Justices in Eyre, representing the King's central government who visted the county from time to time. Their court was awesome: twelve judges sat together. Archbishops, bishops, abbots, priors, barons, knights, and from villages all freeholders, were called to witness its procedures. Violence was frequent it seems, sometimes in the quarrels of young men.

In 1221 Richard the Hayward (or mower or reaper) of Bledington struck John of Sherborne with a hatchet so that he died. Richard fled. Possibly he went no farther than Wychwood Forest for a company of outlaws and outlaws' descendants lived there—ancestors of the Field

Town (now Leafield) people who preferred a rough style of life for long after. No one else could be suspected of the deed; he had no cattle that could be forfeited: he was outlawed.

On this crime followed another probably connected with it. Richard Hayward's house had been taken over by John son of the miller. Burglars entered the house and broke into John's chest. The unknown malefactors went off with its contents. Since the township of Bledington had not been able to present them it was 'in mercy,' that is, liable to a fine. But the records do not tell us how large was this corporate punishment.[24]

If only we could know what the chest contained we might be able to infer much more.

[1] C. S. Taylor, *Norman Settlement of Gloucestershire*, Journal of B.G.A.S. XL 1927

[2] C. S. Taylor Op cit.

[3] J. Ingram, translator *The Old English Chronicle* Everyman edition London 1923 p. 164

[4] Facsimile of the Great Survey of England, the part relating to Gloucestershire. Edition, Sir Henry James 1862. Terra eccle de Wincelcube . . . Ipsa eccla ten[s] Bladintun Ibi vii hide. In duio sunt ii carr and viii villi and iiii bord cu. v car[s] and viii servi and ii ancile. Ibi molin de v sol and xxx ac p a valuit iiii lib modo iii lib

[5] F. B. Welch *Gloucestershire in the Pipe Rolls* B.G.A.S. LXVII 1935 p. 83

[6] Landboc. Vols. I and II EXETER 1892

[7] Clemency was sometimes shown to tenants who were closely related to monks. Landboc I, pp. 204, 5. Haigh p. 49

[8] Landboc. Vol. I p. 24

[9] Haigh, op. cit. p. 42; Lanboc I pp. 216–7

[10] Anon: St. Leonard's Church, Bledington. The Church Builder. October 1876

[11] C.P.R. 1216–1225 p. 415; Haigh p. 61

[12] Haigh, op. cit. pp. 52, 59–60, 90–91; Landboc Vol. II pp. 275–6, 279–81

[13] Haigh, op. cit. pp. 79, 89–92, Landboc. Vol. I p. 313 EXETER 1892

[14] Haigh, op. cit. p. 144

[15] Worcester Record Office. Transcripts of Bishops' Registers 1268–1322

[16] Sir Thomas Phillips. Glos., Subsidy Roll. I Ed. III 1327 Privately printed Winchcombe Abbey Rental 1355 G.R.O.

[17] See p. 63

[18] V.C.H. Vol. VI p. 31; Haigh, op. cit. pp. 69, 70

[19] G. Haigh. op. cit. p. 91

[20] William Langland, *The Vision of Piers Plowman*, edited by Rev. Prof. Skeat. London 1910 p. 84

[21] W. Hobart Bird *Mural Paintings in Gloucestershire Churches* pp. 24 & 25

[22] Chaucer *The Parson's Tale* Last section, Leave taking

[23] Landboc I pp. 108–9, 109–10, 173. Haigh. op. cit. p. 56

[24] ed. F. W. Maitland. Pleas of the Crown for Gloucestershire 1221 London 1884 p. 14 sections 61 and 62

chapter three

FOURTEENTH AND FIFTEENTH CENTURIES

I   Revolt and Religion
II   Enterprise and Unity

THE TWELFTH AND thirteenth centuries had seen the flowering of mediaeval thought, feeling and institutions. There was relative peace in ecclesiastical matters, and beautiful churches were being built or rebuilt; crusades and pilgrimages gave movement and romance to the era; Universities were founded and scholars became more numerous. Manors retained established customs but though there was much peace, it may well be that some of the disturbing changes of the following century could be traced back into the thirteenth.

The fourteenth century in England is one of frequent conflict in the political and military fields and also in the daily life of villages. Great change is, as we shall see, justifiably traced to the great plague of 1348 and 1349—the Black Death; but it is true that this was a point of acceleration, rather than of change of direction.

Some gradual and general changes that formed the background of local specific developments were, for example, the growing trade between England and Flanders, and the war between England and France. Both required sea-travel and knowledge of foreign countries by larger numbers of men than hitherto, and these activities involved stimulus to minds, and to adventure, and will in individuals. There was also the growth of towns and with them of the fortunes of craftsmen and—on a larger scale—of merchants. In the towns, too, were new demands for freedom from manorial restrictions and the need for more labour in the workshops, which attracted men from the countryside.

A most pervasive change in England was the crossing and partial closing of the gap between on the one hand the descendants of conquerors together with those who had contrived to join this high class of lords of lands, and on the other the majority, descendants of the conquered. English had been the spoken language of underlings but by the end of the thirteenth century almost every Englishman spoke English though lords and ladies still spoke French as well. Early in the fourteenth century English began to be used in literary writings as well as for business dealings and all the purposes of daily life. After 1362 it was spoken and written even in those homes of ancient custom, the law courts. The common language encouraged intercourse between classes and some social intermingling, though the gap to be bridged even between landlord and merchant remained wide at any rate till 1400.

Another change was the development of Parliament and other institutions of government The knights of the shire were elected to the House of Commons largely by the freeholders from the manors, whose number was slowly growing. These had also the duty to attend the new courts held in the county by the King's Justices, as well as having functions in hundred and manor courts. In the King's Courts the Justices were aided by twelve local men and in this provision is found the origin of juries. Late in the thirteenth century (1285) certain knights had been given duties as 'conservators of the peace': in 1361 their functions were enlarged and they were known as Justices of the Peace, holding an office of great power over country folk for centuries, and of importance still.

There were also some changes, based on ancient customs, in the military duties of every able-bodied villager and especially of freeholders. Since the time of Alfred it had been the duty of able-bodied men to have arms and skill in their use for local defence only. In 1285 this old national army, the Fyrd, had been fully organised and brought up to date thoughout the country: every freeman, i.e. every man of non-servile status, between 16 and 60 must under the Statute of Winchester have weapons—a bow and arrows if he were poor, but if well to do he might have to provide himself with a horse as well as sword, knife and helmet. Twice a year Constables of the Hundred were to view these arms. Every township, a term which includes villages, had now for the first time its constable whose duties were at first connected with the Fyrd. Some of the weapons were kept in the church where they could easily be checked. The Bledington butts on the Town

Banks[1] must have existed from this time and probably far earlier.

The Fyrd (or militia) had no duty abroad; for that the feudal army existed. It had been the duty of freeholders i.e. of every man who had sworn fealty to his lord and to the King, to follow the lord of his manor for forty days' military service. He might be called upon to fight anywhere in the country or to go abroad. But the period was too short for foreign service in anything but raids, and the character of warfare had changed: on the continent there were large, long-service armies. In 1285 a tax—the shield tax or scutage—had been substituted for the old forty-days duty. With the proceeds the king could hire men who stayed longer in his army and could be more fully trained. The freeholders benefited: they could stay at home on their farms, while there was an opportunity for their younger sons and those of prosperous villeins to enlist.

The amount of scutage depended on the extent of the freeholder's farm. We know that the two Bledington men paid the tax but not how much. Enquiry was made as to their correct assessment in the first year, 1285.[2]

The long war with France, the 'Hundred Years' war began in 1337. France was powerful on the continent: her soveriegns claimed feudal lordship over English kings for their French lands, and later there were English royal claims to the throne of France. Had the French been victorious in the early days of the struggle England might have lost her growing wool trade with Flanders and her control of part of south-west France together with her wine trade with Bordeaux. In the early years English kings had good success but French national feeling grew in the fifteenth century: the sense that the English were foreigners became intense and after the struggle in which Joan of Arc played her famous part they were thrown out (1453) except for a foothold in Calais and a small area around that port.

In the fourteenth century village recruits can have had little knowledge of the country they were to fight in but as with travelled farm workers in 1918, some of them must have returned to their homes enlightened. It has often been noted that in 1346 at the battle of Creçy they saw French knights—mounted on fine horses and in heavy armour—fall before the arrows from their long-bows, weapons of mere foot-soldiers. They would compare the towns and fields and peasants with those of home, returning with a new sense of their own value and of their own situation.

If the archers of Creçy were away from home for a matter of years they might on their return note changes on the home manor. In Bledington before the plague came in 1349 labour rents had been greatly reduced. 'Bederips,' that is labour on the demesne in time of harvest, were still owed by all tenants but apparently few other labour dues remained. Money rents were paid. Serfdom remained and would long do so to some extent, but men were trying to escape from it. Those dependent on money wages had ways of showing discontent and even of demanding more pay. When their number was reduced by the plague and they pressed harder or left the manors stealthily the government took action. The plague had entered the country in 1347 and as early as 1349 a royal ordinance provided that wages should be no higher than they were two years before the plague began. This was followed after the epidemic had died away by the famous Statute of Labourers (1351) which forbade men to leave their parish on pain of imprisonment. We shall see that this risk was taken by Bledington men but we do not know whether any of them were 'branded with a hot iron on the forehead,' the punishment which was prescribed when others failed. It so happened that the price of corn rose very steeply after the Black Death, so that the wages paid before would not maintain a man; he had great reason to try to escape. Yet it often suited the stewards or lords of manors whose own serfs had died or flitted, to employ serfs from other manors, asking no questions; and still more often craftsmen and others in towns were short of workers.

Twenty-two years before the plague reached Bledington, in 1327, some tenants of the manor were assessed as liable to subscribe to the subsidy the King was demanding for his military needs. Seventeen men and one woman were to pay sums from thirty pence to twelve pence, the total amounting to a little over twenty-five shillings. It is interesting to study the list of names. Only eight of the eighteen will recur in the document of 1355 to which we come shortly, which seems to indicate considerable change in the tenancies. But caution is necessary: change in surnames of families seems still to be going on. Such names as 'atte Stretende," 'Dame Ysabele,' 'Dame Emme' are coming to be outside the convention and to be dropped in favour of others, but which we do not know. It is worth while to note that the cost of war was coming home even to husbandmen.[3]

The Black Death entered the country through south-west ports and spread into the counties north of them; Gloucester, Oxford and Worcester towns all suffered; but so, we come to infer, did all the villages. Wherever there are writings of the time, chiefly wills and rentals, there is evidence of a high death rate.

Those persons who have memories of the influenza epidemic that followed the First World War knew a state of affairs in our village in which members of every household were ill, and in some, the entire family. Some sufferers went unnursed, were barely fed, or offered grotesquely unsuitable food. And the death rate appalled us. It gave us some insight into this greater plague. In the Black Death, patients were greatly disfigured; more of them died than recovered. So fast did death follow death that it was impossible to dig graves for each. Pits for corpses were dug deep; there was little knowledge of hygiene, but at least it was known that the bodies of the plague-stricken must be covered with three or four feet of soil.

Winchcombe town and the monastery itself suffered severely. The number of monks fell by about half. Stewards and reeves of manors died, so that manors were disorganised. Rents went unpaid and customary services could not be rendered. Some holdings and cottages were untenanted. The Abbey's income is said to have fallen by half.[4]

The effect of the plague upon the Bledington manor can be inferred from a list of the tenants, with the dues they should pay, drawn up in 1355.[5] (The document we shall refer to as the Rental for 1355). In that year the Abbey's estate officers drew up such lists for all its manors. There was risk that the tenants might forget the customs, make new claims, and discipline break down. Hence it was necessary to restate the Abbey's resources and fix in writing what was annually owing to it. But there was no intention to give information to outsiders or to the future: careful study is required to find the facts.

First we gather that the general framework of the manor is much as it had been during the three hundred years since the Conquest. There are still the open arable and meadowland, and the Abbey still cultivates its generous share of these—its demesne, and there is still the heath land. There were now thirty-one tenants, twenty-three of them with one virgate, that is somewhere between thirty-five and forty-five acres (the Gloucestershire virgate was usually about forty acres), three with two virgates, and five with from one and a half to three acres.

The rents given were probably average for the time. For a messuage (a farmyard with a small house and usually a half-acre close), with a

49

virgate of land, rent was 15/- a year, a few tenants paying less—13s 4d˙ 6s 8d., or 7s. Two tenants as we have seen hold their land freely. Beside money rents almost all tenants owed also 'bederips' i.e. work on the demesne in the rush time of corn harvest. But now they owed few or no other services. In earlier times the bordars, the smaller tenants, had owed service on one or two days of every week, and the villeins too had other service dues. There has, then, been a large change in the direction of money rents.

But there is another, more recent change. The usual way of referring to holdings or houses was by the names of their tenants—a natural way when son followed father and mother, generation after generation, and one in use in the country even now—'Holdoms' farm,' 'Stows' house.' Thus in the rental the name of the tenant suffices unless he and his family have entered on their holding recently, and then it is identified by the name of his predecessor. We find that no fewer than thirteen holdings are in the hands of families succeeding tenants of another name. Making allowance for the fact that a difference of name may be due to the succession of a daughter or re-married widow, still in 1355 there was a special reason for a new start, and therefore for stress on recent changes. We also note that some virgates have been in the hands of the Lord, i.e. the Abbey, and are now, or have recently been, distributed among the tenants. Some other tenants' holdings and parts of holdings are still being farmed with the demesne. Of 12 cottages listed, the names of former tenants are given in every case, together with the names of present occupiers, a fact suggesting rapid changes.

It seems probable that of some 24 householders, 23 have been robbed of their head, and of anyone of his name who could take on his work, i.e. wives and sons have also died (it was common for widows to succeed). We cannot arrive at anything approaching a precise figure, but whatever deduction we may make to allow for some unknown circumstances it is reasonable to conclude that not fewer than one in three Bledingtonains died. The rental is a succinct document; not a word is wasted, or indeed a letter—there are many abbreviations. An economic aspect of the village situation is completely isolated. We learn nothing of the villagers' thoughts about the plague. The story of health in English villages is as long and as interesting as that of, say, literacy. It hardly begins yet; the plague seemed an 'act of God' like a whirlwind, and a punishment for sin.

Langland, writing perhaps thirteen years after the plague, expresses this point of view and puts it forward as that of Reason itself:—

> He proved that the pestilence were purely for sin,
> And the south-west wind, on Saturday at even,
> Was plainly for our pride, and for no point else.
> Pear-trees and plum-trees were puffed to the earth
> For example to sinners, to serve God better.
> Beeches and broad oaks were blown to the ground,
> Turning upwards their tails, as a token of dread
> That deadly sin, at doomsday, would condemn us all.[1]

The failure of harvests was seen in the same way as other catastrophes. Bread was a very uncertain thing. Harvests were often a partial failure; months of food might be in hazard. It has been shown[7] that two centuries later than this the seed corn (a third of the corn had to be saved for planting) would sometimes be in part consumed, so that a very poor harvest could affect life for two or even three years. Disease and starvation were bad hazards, but recovery was helped by the smaller population and by the fact that a greater proportion of the population were of the years between childhood and old age (very many infants died). When the Black Death passed, needs were acute. There was as much work as ever and fewer hands to do it. But life surged up in the survivors. They saw that the vacant holdings were their opportunity. The Skeyl family, for example, seem to have been fortunate in the epidemic; five of them took on virgates that had been others'; (they did not become one of the longest family lines; their name never occurs in the registers, which began in 1603. Yet it is not quite extinct in 1969. There is still a field called Skeys' Thorns, on the right just past the turn to Icomb). The highly respectable family of le Kentys had re-established themselves after the death of their founder, the steward, in 1310.[8] His childrens' wardship and marriage and the management of his property had been granted to the new steward, William de Bladenton. Now le Kentys' son or grandson farmed two virgates as freeman and freeholder, and was locally known as Kynch or Kench, though in documents the old name was copied. But this family kept sound traditions though not high status; they remained here till modern times as small farmers and craftsmen, highly respected.

The Bithbrooks (by-the-Brooks) have taken over land which has been in the hands of the Hankins family and of 'Roys Croys'; Rudolf Jordan's land has been divided between John Colynes and William Brown. The latter has also land of the Forel family. Nicolas Shepherd has land from 'John of the Chapel' (the church seems to have been known as 'the Chapel' and the lane past it as Chapel Lane) and of Rudolf atte Burwe. On seven occasions we learn that 'the rest is in demesne.'

A few other facts about the village may be deduced. The total rent is £16.3s.4d; this does not include the value of the demesne or of the parson's glebe or tithes, or the value of the land held 'libere.' Nor is the real rent of the mill given; the miller pays an annual rent of 9 pence, but later he pays also 'twelve quarters of toll corn,' and we may infer that he already pays a proportion of the tenants' corn which he takes for his services.

Who, one would like to know, inhabited the landless cottages? One or two, as Hugo Skeyl and William Kitte, are probably older members of tenant families. Two are women. Others may have been labourers on the demesne, receiving money wages. But the cottagers were certainly not the poorest inhabitants; labourers slept in the out-houses of the messuages, or in huts on the closes.

There was here as elsewhere a reeve as well as a steward—John Colynes, whose name comes first in the short list of tenants, who apparently bore witness to the correctness of the rental. It was usual for the reeve to be one of the tenants, chosen by themselves. It was his duty to know the services owed by his fellow tenants and their manorial dues in such matters as the scouring of ditches, and hedging. The other names given in this preliminary list are 'le Kentys' or Kench, Wylkoks, Hulles, and Hobbes. The last two names will recur in the fifteenth and seventeenth centuries, a Hobbes having already been named in 1327.

From the record of the manor court two years after the Rental,[9] in 1357, we learn of other changes. Since after the plague there were too few labourers a man might better himself by going elsewhere. especially if he were a serf. The steward of another manor, desperate for workers at ploughing or harvest might give a better wage and ask no questions, and if a man were free for twelve months he gained a legal right to his freedom. John Hankyne a 'native' or serf had gone away and was supposed to be somewhere in Buckinghamshire. Two other serfs were also absent, no one knew where. It was probably not difficult for serfs to put Wychwood Forest between themselves and their servitude. The whole 'homage' i.e. all the manor tenants were reminded that by custom they were responsible for the absentees, but that would not bring them back and we do not read that the homage were penalised. As for other faults, one tenant has a plough, though to use one is beyond his rights. Another has failed to come to the court to do homage. Wylkoks the reeve has himself failed to do his carting—his bederips—on the demesne.

Feudal customs must always have been felt as a restraint. The appetite for freedom was always present and now became for the more energetic serfs and villeins an acute hunger. It was not easy for lords of manors to insist on the old terms. They needed to keep their demesne tilled and the manorial holdings tenanted, and so consented to some modifications. But at this time a primitive radicalism gew among the poor; it seemed to the lords that they did not know where to stop and must be curbed.

But the homage in Bledington at this time were not on remarkably good terms with each other, it seems. They allow their animals all too often to trespass on their neighbours' arable, as well as allowing them to graze in the lord's 'park.' The reeve John Wylkoks presents Richard by-the-Brook for concealing that his five little pigs had murrain. This unneighbourly deception recurs. William the Beadle is fined for a false presentment—an untruth about a neighbour. John Warre was also in mercy because he had not done his share in marking the boundary between Gloucestershire and Oxfordshire. He should have carried stones to the edge of Bradenham, one of the open arable fields where Bledington and Idbury parishes meet.

Among the suitors in the Court John the Rector appears more than once. He is accused of allowing his cattle to trespass: he has a quarrel with a neighbour. In the court he had no special dignity: he is a husbandman and tenant among others.

From these court records we get the impression of a rather mean, small community of neighbours in grudging relationship, though sharing resentment against the lord. From whom should leadership to a better state have come? The steward is certainly better off than others; the demesne is large (between four and five hundred acres, temporarily increased by the plague). His direct access to the monastery assures him privileges: he could and did reserve a good reach of the river for his private fishing; other men fishing there risked great severity, possibly ex-communication. Also the steward was allowed to dig himself a fish-pond in which to keep his catch alive. When he wants a cottage for a servant he is allowed to choose one near his house. But he was not popular around this time; he represented the lord of the manor. The reeve, chosen by his fellows and approved by the Abbey, held two virgates, being among the more prosperous folk. But he figures as a delinquent in the court.

The Rector was better off than other tenants: his glebe was now among the larger holdings and he was also in receipt of all the tithes, paying only an annual one pound to the Abbey. But whether he used the tithes generously to help the poor, or how villein and serf responded to him or to the services he conducted, we do not know. The qualifications of rectors were not high: one we know to have been a sub-deacon, the most modest possible qualification, one that it was not uncommon for Bledington boys to achieve, though the privilege of becoming rectors probably was not theirs. Yet as we shall see one rector towards the end of the century seems to have done his work with some enterprise and with support from his parishioners. (A curious fact, unconnected with our present topic, is that some rectors exchange cures with clergy of other dioceses, e.g. one with the rector of Shobury in the London diocese, another with the incumbent of Mordeforde in Hereford; a fact which suggests the growing frequency of movement).

No doubt the court roll shows the community at its worst. The main agricultural customs held in spite of the disturbed relations of lord and homage. Those customs were co-operative. The work of the husbandmen's own ancient officers, the Oarsmen, was never interrupted.

After 1355 our township re-established itself in a modified way. Some gain for the homage appears in changed customs. Villein-tenants continued to improve their position. The custom of paying fines on the marriage of daughters when not arranged by the lord died away. No one would again assert that serfs could call 'nothing their own but their bellies.'[10] Villeins gained the right to bequeath their personal property. The first Bledington will we hear of was that of Richard atte Brooke made in 1410. There is no reason to suppose that Richard was a freeman, and certainly his executor Richard Skeyl was not. The will itself is not extant, but we read of the executors taking steps to secure payment of debts to the estate. That also is significant;

villeins were able to defend their kind by recourse to lawyers and to the courts. Also, a new custom had spread by which the terms on which tenants held their land came to be recorded in the roll of the manor court and the tenant himself had a copy of the entry; he became a 'copyholder.' The record related to rent and to the terms on which successors should enter the holding. Further it had become customary for the widow and a son of the tenant to succeed him on payment of a sum of money, but in ordinary cases with no more than formal permission from the lord. But all that came slowly.

With improvements in status went slow modifications of the villagers' homes. They grew and were improved rather by inherited contrivance and building than through any great change in the productivity of the fields and consequent increased income. Our sources of information are meagre; legend supplies a little; a few ancient remains can be interpreted and there is a good deal of negative inference: what we know to have been added later, we deduct.

The rental of 1355 shows us that there were thirty-eight messuages and cottages. To these we add the rectory, the miller's and the steward's dwellings, to get a total of forty-one homes. A careful count shows us today some thirty very old houses; wills, mortgages, and the Enclosure Act confirm the observation. A few other old sites are known; across the road from the old rectory stood two old thatched cottages, demolished only fifty years ago. Some five other cottages stood just off the south-west corner of the green. Three of these, mentioned already, were pulled down nearly a hundred years ago as uninhabitable. The legend of them continues because of their remarkable style. Their walls stood only three or four feet high and their long steep roofs were of deep thatch. They had consisted of one large room, with an ill-lighted little room in the thatch. In their early days they almost certainly had no inserted floor, and earlier still, no chimney but only a smoke-vent in the roof. Patients in all illnesses, including the plague, lay on straw bags or mattresses among the household tasks, but let us hope within the fire's warmth. Almost certainly all these houses, except possibly the steward's, were thatched. In a house of ground-floor only, a rough untorched stone roof would have been intolerably draughty and cold, while thatch is a friend in cold and heat alike.

Nor were the walls yet built of stone. Oak was a common timber along the Evenlode and there were thousands of oaks in Wychwood. In the Home Farm an interior wall, erected about 1550, was recently taken out; it consisted of oak posts set only a few inches apart, covered with split-oak laths and plaster. Outer walls had earlier been built of such materials. In the ancient 'wing' of one of the old farmhouses ('Little Manor') the end wall is of different construction from the sides: it was probably built of stone in the early fifteenth century to take the hearth and chimney while the side-walls were still of wood. Stone walls ousted wooden ones while roofs were still thatched, but the oak posts were not burned. Pull to pieces any very old stone house-wall, and you will find in it old posts laid along, as if they were a means of bonding.

Thatch only gradually gave way to stone. It wore well: I myself have known thatched roofs that had not been renewed for fifty years and were still weather-proof. When an ancient thatched roof is pulled to pieces here you may see a layer of rushes (though there are only stray rushes in the parish now) and above that very old layers of stiff rye or wheat straw obtained by cutting very near the ground. Another advantage as compared with rough stone roofs was that they do not require to be supported by such massive timbers. But there was one great obvious disadvantage: in hot dry summers it occasionally happened that almost every house in a village was consumed by fire.

The skill of splitting stones so as to make slates not requiring immense timbers to support them developed slowly, but by the late fourteenth century it was an established trade at certain quarries. Many families in the Cotswold area still bear the name Slatter, and the bearers may carry on the work—now chiefly of repairs. For larger and better-furnished houses stone roofs were a valuable insurance. As thatch decayed every family of aspiration wished for stone. The Cotswold style of building was already developing elsewhere and would be followed here. But the craft of thatch was not lost: cottages erected as late as the seventeenth, eighteenth and nineteenth centuries were thatched, beside here and there a barn or shed.

Time came—not till the middle of the fifteenth century—when improvement was rapid. Most houses came to have two rooms on the ground floor. The miserable size of the modest farmhouses was presently mitigated by the use of rough kitchens in the yards or attached to their walls, used for cooking on great occasions when a sheep or pig was killed, and some day for household washing, but not yet by a long while: little washing of any kind was done.

We cannot be sure that any substantial part of a house remains from the fourteenth or early fifteenth centuries: part of the King's Head looks ancient. The oldest part of Town Banks farmhouse has stone walls and stone roof, and is a complete house, though tiny. It must go back to the early fifteenth century, though then thatched.

The steward's house was the largest: it was one of his customary dues to be ready to provide food and bed for the Abbey's officer who might come to take down a record of the manor court's proceedings or the reeve's annual account of what the tenants paid in goods and services. It was no doubt still thatched, but would be a longer, larger house than any other.

All the houses were in close contact with the yards: pigs and fowl might wander in, weakling pigs or lambs shared the heat of the fire. One room might shelter both animals and humans at night. Not even the steward's house was apart from the yard.

The church was the exceptional building. By 1300 it had stood, an object lesson in building in stone, for about a hundred and thirty years. Windows in the houses resembled the oldest in the church, the narrow Norman slits—sometimes between two upright mullions, occasion ally hacked out of a single stone. In the poorer houses these were closed by oak shutters, perhaps stuffed at the edge with straw: rather better houses might have openings covered with waxed linen, and that was a great advance. Church windows were early glazed, and a visit to church had thus much of luxury, though there was no fire.

In the thirteenth century the chancel had been well lighted by its three-light East windows. In the early years of the next another new window 'with two lights and square hood-mould' had been inserted in the south wall of the chancel. In the aisle the window just east of the porch was of similar design and date. Late in the century two beautiful windows of Decorated style pierced the west wall, one being in what is now the base of the tower. The head of these windows is a pointed arch, filled with interlaced stone-work—'reticulated tracery.' Such windows carved on the spot were costly—a sign of care for the church and activity in its service. The nave was much used by the laity and for purposes of government connected with them, e.g. for the review of the weapons they were compelled to possess, and it was therefore the custom for them to maintain it. Bledingtonians valued their church and saw reason why it should so outstrip their houses in comfort and beauty. But in such works they needed the leadership of a good rector.

The general picture, then, of the village is of a rather wide-spread group ot small houses, with chimneyless roofs, thatched and shaggy, often surrounded by mud, owing to the undrained, clay-based ground. Heaps of farmyard manure stand about the houses. Cattle and pigs being few and small the heaps are not rich and large, not yet neatly built, with the liquid drained thriftily away into small wells as one may see them still along the streets in rural villages in Luxemborg, but running away in foul streams, sometimes to the annoyance of neighbours.

Set above all this the church rises in the dignity of relatively high stone walls and moulded lofty windows. The quality of mental life, though no doubt ultimately dependent on material sustenance, has no constant proportion with it. Indeed, above a level of starvation and foul disease there may at times seem to be an inverse ratio. A separate enquiry into thought and feeling would have to be made, had we but the means. We are at present only able to infer that life here was much as in the villages around us.

Reference has been made to the teaching given to the illiterate congregations in the churches through stories, told in words but also through paintings in the churches. They may still be seen as has been said at Oddington Old Church, at the end of a walk through the fields and woods, and at Shorthampton. At Broughton and Horley near Banbury others remain. These include representations of the Annunciation to the Virgin, of the Last Judgement, of St. Christopher carrying the Christ child across a stream, and sometimes even—a favourite fourteenth century subject—as at Shorthampton—of Christ as a child at play with doves. At Broughton the paintings once showed a traveller kneeling in homage at Bethlehem, and the Madonna throwing her girdle to a saint as she ascended into heaven. St. Christopher at Horley was (or used to be, for the pictures fade) watched by two anglers standing by the stream, each with a landed fish.

The windows and the paintings could never give the full stories. Here in the villages there were no miracle plays to give them in words and action: they must have been narrated. It has been noted that both windows and paintings show chiefly saints, much less often the crucifixion. Nevertheless Christ was the centre and the outlying legends depended on the gospel stories. The effect of the central story when well told to simple uneducated folk was illustrated for me in 1942. The place was a club in a south-coast resort, for women bombed out from the east end of London. A devoted cultivated woman told the story of the crucifixion in words of one syllable. The audience sat entranced and awed, and at the end exclaimed 'We never heard that! Why did no one tell us before?'

When religion reached the people at all it came often in charming guise. Beside the pictures there were the carols, as for example *The Holly and the Ivy*[11] collected in our country:—

> The Holly bears a berry,
> As red as any blood,
> And Mary bore sweet Jesus Christ
> To do poor sinners good:
>
> The Holly bears a prickle
> As sharp as any thorn
> And Mary bore sweet Jesus Christ
> On Christmas Day in the Morn.

Religious pictures, carols and stories showed a poetic affectionate relation to small objects of daily life, as did lay songs, and the names given to birds (Robin Redbreast, Philip Sparrow, Molly Heron) and the carvings of leaves and flowers round the capitals of pillars and of musical instruments and animals in the frieze at Alkerton, another village near Banbury. Thus some mediaeval art touched our remoteness, though only as yet in a thin stream.

Whether solid religious fare was provided we have to doubt. Subdeacons or deacons such as our rectors could not say mass, still less did they preach. Without exposition and with the use of a dead language and the difficult symbolism of the mass when it was said the people could rarely help themselves by thought to a fuller understanding. A parish might be fortunate: sometimes the clergy had a surprising knowledge of parts of the Scriptures, never of the whole.

At the time two streams of religion flowed parallel—one poetic and popular, the other ritual and institutional, the latter impressing on the folk the need for acceptance of teaching and for submission to authority. All this was linked with the social structure of the time which had come to seem to the people a prison and to the more highly placed a tower in danger of falling. The two tendencies were driving on and must collide.

Meanwhile the Bledington folk had another means of emotional and aesthetic if not spiritual kind. They had still their communal arts[12] which lightened labour and expressed, notably in the springtime, joy in youth and life and work and pleasure in the community. This we know because these arts lingered for centuries, partly in uncertain remnants, partly in a living tradition modified to express and console in varying circumstances. There were work-songs for the ploughing and the haying, games of skill and strength on the green for ordinary holydays, and for Whitsuntide old and curious pastimes, and for Christmas what became the 'mumming play' of St. George and the Dragon. Notably at Whitsuntide, but not only at that time, there were two sets of dances. One was the long procession dances in which men and women joined, whose dignity and slow measure showed them to be by nature religious even though they were no longer headed by priest and emblems; the other the strenuous, complex morris dances for the men alone. That all these were felt as a basic inheritance and possession cannot be doubted. Nor could thay have seemed in any way barbaric. The attitude of the church to the old arts and festivities varied. Leaders of the early church had tried to repress the pagan idea of the old dance and drama and at the same time to use their festivals and some of their ritual. The services of the Church offered another drama 'the procession of candles in early February, the darkness of the church at Tenebrae in Holy Week, the bright lights and flowers at Easter . . . the churchyard service at All Souls' Tide and the Crib on Christmas Day.' In the fourteenth century some bishops, including the Bishop of Lincoln (in whose diocese were all our Oxfordshire neighbours) endeavoured to make their clergy repress the old drama sternly, but his diocese was vast and our neighbours outside his effective supervision; they retained their ancient arts. In later days we find a Spelsbury dance performed on the church tower[13] and the church wardens of Churchill (as of other parishes also) helping to pay for the morris men's accoutrements at the village Whitsuntide feasts.

But after all the folk arts were chiefly a pleasure and consolation, no longer in vital connection with the developing thought and imagination of the day. It was natural that it should be felt that access to the Book which was the source of the religion that all were taught might lead to enlightenment and reform, and heal the rifts of society. The psalms had been translated into English and there were Anglo-French versions of parts of the Bible: indeed by 1361 the whole Bible might be read in that tongue by rare persons. It was for feudal dependents, and for remnants of the feudal system itself, that the Bible had rightly seemed dangerous. But now English was the easier language for almost everyone and to refuse one class was to refuse all ranks, in town and country alike. There were always, also, some clergy who felt for the laity and the poor, like the north-country cleric who thought that the congregations had 'as great need to know what the gospel at Mass means as learned men for both were bought with Christ's blood.' (We should note this last clause: it occurs in socio-religious literature from Anglo-Saxon times and is the recurring basis of a claim to equality and fraternity). He translated the French gospels early in the fourteenth century.[14] More and more of the clergy contrived to see some parts of the Bible in English through, for example, translations of sections made in monasteries and universities, and the published psalms.

Meanwhile events in daily working and social life continued to unfold. The Black Death had passed but was to return with reduced virulence more than once. Nor was bubonic plague the only one; there were cholera, dysentry, and influenza at times, besides infections that touched chiefly children. The failure of the corn crops, when not so severe as to mean starvation, could still mean death through lack of resistance to disease. The French War was ruinously costly and was going badly. In 1380 the Poll Tax, the tax per head, was levied the country over. In Bledington sixty-seven persons, almost two to every household, were assessed: nothing could have been more likely to act as a last straw. There was resentment everywhere and resistance in several areas, but it was the Kentishmen who revolted. The strong religious movement combined with a strengthened social resentment. The poet Langland writes of the Bible as 'the Book;' this it was to be for many generations of intelligent peasants. So it was for John Ball, a homely priest of Kent who addressed audiences of villeins and serfs every Sunday, outside his church, applying Bible teaching as he saw it to the problem of their lives In the beginning of the world there had been no serfs. There should not be vassals: all were descended from Adam.

In 1381 Ball was with Wat Tyler and Jack Straw at the head of the peasants who marched to London, were there received kindly by the boy-king and then defeated by the nobles. The three leaders lost their lives dying for their views—or for their wicked rebellious actions as the Chronicler reviewed the matter.[15]

The Black Death had spared three young men who were to become great writers in the English language—Chaucer, Langland and Wycliffe, all living and in their earlier or later prime in 1370, all to be of importance for the study of English villages. One of them, Wycliffe, would in fact deeply affect their development. He was a great student of theology and of social affairs, a politician and University leader. He gathered round himself in Oxford a group of scholars to translate the Bible into English. They finished this work in the very year of Tyler's failure and death. Wycliffe then proceeded to organise a body of 'poor' and 'simple' preachers who were to teach the importance of knowing the Scriptures. The Lollards, as they were called, carried with them sections of the Bible. They could not often be robbed of these for many of them knew the gospels by heart and could recite them to the people. They also preached, of course, and were presently accused of having taught extravagant and untrue doctrine, rather than the Scriptures, as who could doubt that some did. But only their enemies' accusation, and not their defence remains. Did any Lollard preach in Bledington? Lollardy had been born and bred in Oxford; naturally the villages round were visited. It was natural that when the young, strong King Henry V, very orthodox in religion, started a campaign against it, he and his Archbishop decided to root it out from the University. Further, the county of Oxford was presently divided roughly into sections, in each of which some prominent person was given the duty to hunt out Lollards and imprison them. At Hook Norton this mission, in 1401, was laid on the lord of the manor one Thomas Chaucer.[16] Lollards continued to be severely persecuted. The burning of heretics was given Parliamentary sanction: all office was denied to learned men who shared their views. Even highly placed persons who had been attracted were forced to flee from the country. With no support from learning or high place Lollardism came to be confined to craftsmen, husbandmen, and the like. But it was never extinguished and perhaps by being confined to lower ranks became the more inclined towards political reform. Religious texts, including parts of the Bible, were incriminating documents,[17] and became very rare indeed. But the demand for the Bible in English (with often the dislike of a foreign and unknown tongue in worship) would never quite die away till the craft of printing began to be practised in London (in 1470) which made inevitable the scattering of copies of the entire Bible over England, like grain in seed-time. Many fell of course on stony ground. How slowly the Book spread may be illustrated from our village: a hundred and seventy years (in 1551) after the completion of the Wycliffe Bible, the Vicar of Bledington[18] showed almost complete ignorance of the gospels; and the first Bible known to be possessed and cherished in a lay household here was bequeathed in a will dated 1683.

Not only was the Bible disseminated slowly: it was interpreted in a hundred strange ways, but that was a disadvantage it shared with all literature. The saving fact was that all the main literary deposits of a nation were gathered within the covers of the Bible under the same protection of sacredness. If as many had similarly cared for such a large selection of texts from Greek literature it would have had importance in somewhat the same way. But the Hebrew and Aramaic books had originated with a small pastoral and hard-pressed people and in parts with lowly folk, shepherds and the like. Much of it spoke directly to the minds of rural folk of later days, as to Langland's in the fourteenth century. The book was read by adults, heads of families and households, members of an agricultural and a 'neighbourhood' community.

Of the two fourteenth century poets mentioned as of importance for village history, both show that by this time the townsman has come into existence and so, by contrast, have the relatively slow, old-fashioned ways of the countryman. Both show the good husbandman as the salt of the earth. Chaucer with his beautiful rhythms and descriptions and his high spirits was more important for poetry. But Langland's passionate concern for the well-being of ordinary folk and knowledge of rural life makes him unequalled in another way. With a little boldness we may claim him for a neighbour. His father lived 'as a gentleman at Shipton under Wychwood'; Langland was born, however, near Malvern, an illegitimate son, but not entirely neglected. He was sent for instruction in Latin, probably to Malvern Priory, and became a sub-deacon or possibly deacon. He earned his living as a singer at funerals and other rites and possibly in part as a clerk of accounts, taking down statements for stewards or reeves of manors. But his chief work was poetry. Though never a priest he had a great mission, which he discharged through his long poem, Piers the Plowman,[19] parts of which he wrote over and over in the course of thirty years. He was concerned with the life and spiritual condition of the whole country and its people. As he walked from Malvern to London, perhaps taking the road via Pershore and Chipping Norton,

63

he saw little to make him happy. His humour (he saw much that made other men smile) was submerged in his sense of England's ill-condition. His poor birth, some experience of labour in the fields, of hunger sitting 'meatless and moneyless on Malvern' and the hardship of his life in London probably inclined a nature not of the happiest to a complex attitude to wealth and privilege. When he was about fifteen he had seen the terrible sickness which, as we saw, seemed to him a punishment for inferior and sinful living. Being an initiate into the life of clergymen he deals early and often with his colleagues. Village clergy clearly neglect their duties; they

> '. . . complained to the Bishop
> That their parishes were poor since the pestilence year
> Asking license and leave in London to dwell
> To sing there for simony, for silver is sweet.'[20]

Some men, trained for the Church's work, have given it up for the pleasures and trades of lay life. They love hunting, can cast accounts but read no religious works and have forgotten the Latin so necessary for a churchman.[21]

Often to be seen on the roads and in villages and towns was the pardoner who hawked round indulgences for all kinds of sins and faithlessness. These proceeded from the Pope but had been counter-sealed by the Bishop of the diocese the pardoner is working in. Such men were seen at every church porch, on every village green. Once the poor friars had preached simple and practical sermons there, but now—

> 'There preached too a pardoner, a priest as he seemed,
> Who brought forth a bull, with the Bishop's seals,
> And said he himself might absolve them all
> Of falsehood in fasting, or vows they had broken.
> The laymen believed him, and liked well his words,
> Came up and came kneeling, to kiss the said bull;
> He blessed them right bravely and blinded their eyes,
> And won with his roll both their rings and their brooches;
> Thus they gave up their gold for such gluttons to spend,
> And lose to loose livers their lawful gains.
> If the Bishop were wiser, or worth both his ears,
> His seal ne'er were sent, to deceive so the people.'[22]

At least half of the *Vision of Piers the Plowman* is devoted to the condition of the Church—naturally, for Church claimed pre-eminence over State, and her men and her works were everywhere. How bold Langland was: the very Pope, he says, is poisoned by greed, and 'holy Church is impaired' by 'love of gold.' Once hermits and anchorites

'All for our Lord's love lived strictly and hard,'
but now there are
'Hermits a huge heap, great lubbers and long,
That to labour were loth.'[23]

Such men might be seen in our area, so says legend, in old small quarries near Stow, or in the holes under great beech roots from which tempest had washed away the soil—near the roads where men must pass and beggars could thrive. Pilgrims and palmers were to be met, with shells on their hats and 'hundreds of vials' (that is, little bottles of water or wine or oil, purporting to come from Sinai or Galacia) with crosses on their cloaks and beggars' bowls and bags in their hands. They had been to shrines in Armenia or Alexandria, so they said, but they had never sought out St. Truth or met any palmer who had.[24]

All around him Langland sees superstition, greed and riches, together with poverty unrelieved. Pope, priests, bishops, have all failed the people. Greed is the basic cause of evil, affecting not only the great folk, but merchants and tradesmen, and in even greater degree lawyers, those flatterers and sycophants. Langland says clearly what he means by greed. He contrasts 'measureless meed' with 'measureable hire.' Here is a more than Marxian touch. The longing for unearned increment is in all men; 'capitalism' is only one of its results.

Langland's answer to the question, how a better state of affairs can be brought about, is complex. It is largely religious, as we should expect, but he also has his political insights: the relief of villagers' troubles will come in part through the growing and developing towns:

'The poor have no power to complain though they smart'
but
'Ye macemen and mayors that are midmost and mean
The King and the Commons have power.'

Langland does not look to rural knights or to the lords of lands for help. In this, and in looking to the towns, he is prophetic. The nineteenth century saw terrible need for help and saw the towns indirectly give it.

Just as greed is a universal natural vice there is a virtue which all men may cultivate to balance it—industry, the will to work. And the basic work was farming. There is a large sense for him in which every worker is subordinate to the Plowman, the peasant.

The ploughman working on his little field, his 'half-acre' is ready to employ the rest of the world. Ladies are to 'sew up the sacks' against shedding the wheat; only after that may they sew 'sendal and silk' for 'chasubles for chaplains.' Wives and widows are to spin the wool and flax the farmer grows. Thus they will

> 'All manner of men that meat earn and drink
> Help them to work well, that win you your food.'

The very knight must serve Piers by hunting the animals that plague him. And also he must 'o'ertax no tenant'; if he imposes fines on tenants in his court he must let 'Mercy be taxer,' and 'though poor men should proffer' him 'presents and gifts', he must decline them.

For religious help he did not turn directly to the church of his day; it was too full for him of superstition. 'Patents and pardons a peashell are worth.' Though the nobles and rich ones buy years of prayers for their souls, 'what thou didst day by day the doom will rehearse.' It is to the Scriptures he turns for guidance, quoting from them time and again—from the Gospels and Epistles and Psalms, the Book of Proverbs, and Job and Isaiah. He suspects the use of Latin by the Church is due to the wish

> 'that laymen might fail
> To object or to judge or justly to doubt
> But suffer and serve'.

The priest of his time did not greatly value the Bible. 'Rude wretch; little reads thou thy Bible' he exclaims. From his Bible Langland learns—as John Ball would do a few years later and Joseph Arch and his fellow Methodists in the eighteen-seventies—a certain radicalism:

> 'Beguile not thy bondsman, the better thoul't speed;
> Though under thee here, it may happen in heaven

66

His seat may be higher in saintlier bliss,
Than thine, save thou labour to live as thou shouldst;
"Friend go up higher" (Luke 14, 10)'

and

'In the charnel at Church, churls are hard to discern,
Or a knave from a knight there; this know in thy heart.
And be true of thy tongue; all tales shalt thou hate
Save of wisdom or wit, that may workmen reprove.'

But if Langland was a Christian radical he was hardly a political one. His Utopia is not brought about by struggle. Reason and conscience and love of kind are his revolutionaries. All the same these virtues can be stern and practical.

'Let all runners to Rome, to the robbers therein
Bear no silver o'er sea, that shows the King's image.'

and Langland would

'Punish on pillories and penitent stools
Brewers and bakers, and butchers and cooks;
Such men, in this world, can most harm work
To the poorer people that piecemeal buy;
For they poison the people, both privily and oft,
Grow rich by retailing, and house rents buy,
With profits that else would support the poor.'

Yet his advice to the poor is stern—to work, to be sparing, not to 'munch over much' and 'for livelihood labour,' for so our Lord ordained.

Langland is, then, partly idealistic and utopian, but there is a realistic base for whetever he writes. He has eaten the food of the hard-working husbandman and tells us exactly what it is:

'I've no penny, quoth Piers, young pullets to buy,
Nor bacon nor geese, only two green cheeses,
Some curds and some cream, and an oaten cake,
Two bean-loaves with bran, just baked for my children.
And I say, by my soul, I have no salt bacon,
Nor eggs, by my Christendom, collops to make;
Only onions and parsley, and cabbage-like plants;
Eke a cow and a calf, and an old cart-mare
To draw afield dung, while the drought shall prevail.
By such food must we live, until lammas-time come,

67

I hope I may then have some harvest afield;
And I'll dight me a dinner, as dearly will please me.'[25]

He knows how classless is discontent and opportunism, and lack of foresight. It only required a good harvest and workmen become over-confident.

'Then would waster not work, but would wander about
Nor beggar eat bread wherein beans had a part,
But flour of the finest, and wheat of the whitest;
Nor half-penny ale would in anywise drink,
But the best and the brownest the borough could sell.
Then labourers landless, that lived by their hands,
Would deign not to dine upon worts a day old;
No penny ale pleased them, no piece of good bacon,
Only fresh flesh or fish, well fried or well baked,
Ever hot and still hotter, to heat well their maw.'[26]

For more of Langland's realism we can follow him into the 'local', seek the mixed company there, and learn of the trades of the time:— a shoeseller, a tinker, a needleman, a fiddler, a rat-catcher, a rope-seller, a wafer-man, a dish-seller, 'and a heap of upholsterers,' besides weavers and spinners. Some of these were women and some men. There were also present in the ale-house Clement the cobbler, Bat the Butcher, and Hickey the Ostler, and the church was represented there by a priest and a clerk. Only some of these would be seen in a Bledington ale-house, and perhaps none of the lawyers, and leeches, jugglers and jesters.

Note: In 1319 occurred what seems to have been, for Bledington, only a shadow event, though it is often mentioned. The Abbey wished to acquire the manor and rectory of a parish near Winchcombe which was owned by the Abbey and Convent of St. Evroult at Ouche, (St. Ebrulph at Utica) in Normandy. (Since the Conquest there had been close connections between some religious houses in England and Normandy). The Abbey offered to St. Evroult an annual rent of £20 for the desired manor and advowson of Rowell this sum to be charged on two of the convent's manors. In addition it seems that the full annual value of the Bledington manor was to be part of the rent or hire-purchase. There is no sign that our affairs ceased to be administered by Winchcombe's servants and it it likely that the tenants never knew of the arrangement.[27]

The condition of the Abbey after the Black Death had been—as we saw—very poor; its income had slumped and the number of monks was low. Gifts and legacies almost ceased for a time and the convent was deep in debt. It was for these reasons no doubt that at the end of the fourteenth century an active Abbot, William Bradley, returned to an old method of raising income: the appropriation of rectories. For example, after a long, dour and undignified struggle between Convent and Town regarding the rectory of St. Peter's at Winchcombe the convent was at last successful in gaining the right to nominate a vicar in place of a rector and to take some two-thirds of the tithes. Three years later, in 1402, the Abbot applied to Pope, King and Bishop for permission to appropriate the rectory of Bledington. These dignitaries had their different interests and policies in such a matter and the process took time. The monks already drew twenty shillings yearly from the Rectory—had done so for nearly two hundred years: they now hope to draw 15 marks or 200 shillings. This was a sum well worth having: presumably it was in addition to the earlier sum. Together with the monetary income, they hope for the right to appoint a monk or a lay clerk of their choice and to remove him at will: thus the Vicarage would be thoroughly subordinate to the Abbey. The Pope's permission was readily given, in 1402, but not so the King's: his agreement was not given till 1405, and then on condition of a fee of one year's value. The Bishop also had objections to the arrangement. In 1406, no doubt with the assent of higher authorities, he required that Vicars within his diocese should have security of tenure: without this, they would hardly be under his authority. He also required from Bledington an income of ten shillings per year for himself: it had been the Bishop's right to receive a fee each time the rectory was vacant but convents, it was thought, never die. Thus, without a new payment the Bishop would lose. The Bishop also demanded that something should be done for the poor: half a mark was to be distributed among them at Lent (But there exist no signs of this having been done). The Vicar's income was to be ten marks, or £6.13s.4d., but he would have (and would need) also the petty tithes, the value of which would depend upon weather, murrain and to some extent on the parishioners' good will.[28]

The original purpose of tithes, never quite forgotten, was to provide for both priest and poor, and this they had been adequate to do. Now the poor were left unprovided for. The duty of charity was left to neighbours, but the payers of tithes were naturally slow to adopt it. In the course of time royal pressure was brought to bear upon them but their response was small. Parson and poor remained unfortunate.

Another result was that Vicars tried to supplement their income and to that end asked for and often obtained a second cure. They then employed an unlucky deacon or sub-deacon to serve one parish for a portion of the stipend. During many decades of later centuries Bledington parish would be so served. Whether it had Vicar or sub-Vicar, the 'curate' (the cleric in charge of the parish) would be an impoverished man, not able to keep pace in standard of living with the two-virgate or eighty-acre tenants. Only exceptional quality of mind and presonality could sustain so poor an officer in mental and spiritual leadership.

From equality with the steward of the demesne the parson becomes poor and often ignorant, a state of affairs which would last a long time.

It should be said that this treatment of the Bledington living was not rare in the diocese. Out of some 350 villages in Gloucestershire there were, early in the fifteenth century, 52 parsons receiving not more than 10 marks. And in the Deanery of Stow, out of 30 livings, 10 were Vicarages, and 13 livings were of the value of 15 marks.

While the negotiations for the appropriation of the rectory proceeded Abbot Bradley paid a visit to the manor—the only visit by an Abbot of which there is record. In 1404 he was present at the manor court. We try to imagine the meeting. Perhaps it was held in a rough room kept for the purpose on the Court Close, very near to the church : in early times the headquarters of the manor were often in such a position and might remain there. We imagine the room resembling one sometimes found in nineteenth century farmyards, having a rough fireplace on one wall, furnished—for the court—with benches and a board on trestles, and on this occasion with a single chair brought in for the Abbot. Of the business transacted we know something : some serfs who had gone away were to be summoned back to their manor. If they did not come their relatives would suffer : their goods would be taken. (In 1970 restrictive governments threaten their subjects in the same way). There is great uncertainty as to where the men have gone. No one says 'It is useless to threaten' : tongues were tied no doubt by the great presence.

70

During the same visit the ancient ceremony of homage was carried out: Thomas, son of William Fifide (Fifield)? did homage to Abbot Bradley 'in his chamber there,' no doubt for his freehold, in the presence of tenants and of Lawrence the Rector.[29] (Did the Abbot stay the night in the steward's house? Maybe, for it had been improved about this time).

That other old manorial customs continued hereabouts at this time is clear. In the next year Abbot Bradley was called to Shipston on Stour, one of the manors of the Prior of Worcester. The tenants there had rioted because heriots had been demanded—the handing over of 'the best ox,' on the death of some of their fellows. The Abbot's arbitration rather naturally went in favour of his fellow lord:[30] we may infer that his own tenants still paid this due. Heriots would have to be paid for a very long time yet, but the sense of injustice in this and other manorial arrangements was now felt and expressed.[31]

'About the dawn' of the fifteenth century there had been something of a transformation of the church: a 'good Perpendicular tower was built,' says one authority. Another writes that it is 'simple, lofty and imposing.'[32] We may add that it is given charm and visual interest by a rectangular towerlet, containing the stairway, attached to the 'imposing' tower. Before the tower was built the church must have looked like a long Cotswold farmhouse; sloping stone-tiled roofs covered nave and chancel, the nave rising somewhat the higher. By 1400 a church without a tower lacked an almost essential feature. The long, low St. Leonard's needed the new structure to renew its dominance over the improving human dwellings.

Since the church was more than large enough for the population, the tower was built within the nave, resting at the west end on the old west wall. It cut through the nave roof, and some of this remains as 'lean-to' on the north and south. This plan suggests economy, but in fact the tower is in beautiful proportion with the length of the church. Fine narrow arches connect it with nave and aisle. As to who initiated its building, there are no signs. There is a temptation to suppose that the Abbey sent its masons to make monkish compensation to the parishioners for the appropriation of the rectory. In fact the evidence for the date of the tower lies entirely in the building itself. The events we have reviewed show the monks of the Abbey proceeding as if there had been no changes in the consciousness of ordinary rural laymen—no Piers Plowman, or Wat Tyler or Lollards. Later they will

71

profess anxiety for the beggars at their gates, having shown little for the poor on their manors, remaining in their own communities.

Later events here in the century, as well as the gradual changes that are always going on in the contents and outlook of minds, would be much affected by the national condition. There were still the French wars till 1471, with shorter episodes later. Within England the struggles of families and individuals for the Crown, and of powerful nobles for a maximum of influence and control, went their rough way—they are known by that inadequate name, the Wars of the Roses. The King had found it convenient to encourage the nobles to lead contingents of his army in mock-feudal fashion to the French Wars. They had recruited men in their own areas, to some extent on their own estates. They also bought up the horses and fodder. To do all this, they raised the rent on village holdings. There were for example the Earls of Oxford under whom the Pastons—whose letters of these years give a vivid notion of the condition of the disturbed areas—took service and the Earls of Warwick, one of them the famous Kingmaker; both of these families being landlords of vast estates; the Dukes of Norfolk controlling much of eastern England; and the royal Dukes of York, still wealthier and naturally of still greater ambition; England felt the disadvantage of excessively powerful, irresponsible subjects, an evil the Norman kings had striven to avoid.

Familiar facts come to mind: Henry V, in part perhaps to distract the nobles' attention from his imperfect title to sovereignty, pressed the claim to the French throne, winning the great battle of Agincourt in 1415. Unfortunately he married the daughter of the 'lunatic French King,' and his infant heir Henry VI was to prove of unreliable sanity—a condition to tempt ambitious relatives. The French rejected the infant King of England as their sovereign and presently Joan of Arc led them in their effort to throw the English out. The English had conducted sieges of towns with cruel persistence and had demanded excessive ransoms. They further blackened their reputation by burning Joan, the young heroine; long wars for largely personal objects had hardened hearts.

The same brutality was seen at home. King Henry V had gained the favour of high churchmen by persecuting Lollards with a new ferocity. The use of spies and the burning of accused persons were both unusual, and the latter inconceivable in some earlier periods of English history. More unexpected, a contumacious Archbishop of York, captured by royal forces, was 'promptly beheaded.' Nor did the high classes keep to themselves the new violence; towards the middle of the century sailors at Portsmouth lynched a Bishop who had brought them their pay, but not all of it.

It was during the long tenure of the throne by Henry VI, the king of weak mentality, that the Wars of the Roses came to a climax. In 1453 his only son was born. In the next year the King became insane and his brother Richard, Duke of York, became Regent. When the King recovered the Duke clung to the Regency, taking the King prisoner. Then came the struggle between the Queen, Margaret of Anjou, on behalf of her husband and the young prince on the one hand, and the Regent York, with his supporter, Warwick, on the other. This struggle between legitimate claimants and those who wanted strong government drew a good many partisans to both sides. First one side and then the other gained strength. York and Warwick were both slain in battle in 1460 but their heirs were ambitious men and took up their fathers' swords. In the very next year, 1461, they defeated the royal cause in the battle of Towton. Henry VI was deposed and Edward, Duke of York, became king as Edward IV. There was now an interval in which the country began to be pacified, under a King who reigned with some firmness and success.

Serving on the side of Henry VI and his queen and son, that is, the Lancastrian side, there had been a priest or deacon John Maleyn (Malyne or Malen). We do not know in what capacity he served—possibly as a kind of chaplain, with the soldier-followers of some noble. He was important enough to think it worth while many years later, when fate had made Edward IV a legitimate sovereign, to ask that his opposition should be forgiven.

At this time, between about 1461 and 1466 at a reasonable guess, the vicarage of Bledington became vacant and the Abbey nominated John Maleyn to it. Possibly he had sought retirement or even asylum in the Abbey and then thought it wise to proceed to a quiet parish which had remained undisturbed. Our end of the county had remained peaceful: husbandmen and other villagers had not felt themselves closely concerned in the wars unless as followers of magnates or sufferers from their demands. It was always to the interest of even a temporary victor in the struggle, to keep going as much of central and county government as was possible; landlords and tenants alike, in such disturbed times, were glad when manorial customs held firm enough to ensure that the one could work in peace and the other collect his rents and dues.

The new Vicar seems to have entered energetically into the cure of his new parish. By 1470 he had begun a great work: our church was being transformed. In Maleyn's time it achieved the beauty of stone that it has to this day, with added richness that has been very largely lost. It was brought gloriously up to date, setting—as not many achievements here have done—a fine example to its neighbourhood.

The tower had already been built. The chancel was not touched: that was in the care of the rector, i.e. the Abbey. Only the nave, the responsibility of the parishioners, was rebuilt. The sloping roof was removed, the walls raised and a new timber ceiling laid on them, with a lead roof above, presently with parapets. Ranges of new windows were inserted and these fitted with glorious new stained or painted glass. There are many signs that the great effort was communal. It was not unique, unless in detail; some other villages and small towns enlarged and enriched the naves of their parishes, for example our neighbour, Chipping Norton, but whether in the same decade I do not know.

Beside the magnitude of the work by so poor a manor and parish one must be struck by the care spent upon detail. Excellence of craftsmanship was the basis of the achievement; thought and knowledge added elegance and richness to it. No one, surely, could have had the knowledge of the arts, the 'know-how' to command the services of artists, and the force of leadership except the Vicar; he had had experience of a wider world, had doubtless known many men, and seen churches and abbeys.

A walk in the churchyard round the church shows the scale of the work and its architectural nature. The north wall of the nave rises cliff-like, with a row of four clerestory windows and four larger but otherwise similar ones below. At night with lamps within, it is a glorious wall. In the day, the detail of building is seen: the windows are regular, all with square, not arched, heads with hood mouldings, ended or 'stopped' with portrait heads. On the south side the windows under the clerestory are less regular. The fine thirteenth century porch was retained and in the east and west walls of the aisle two delicate windows of the fourteenth were too fine to displace. But one window, west of the porch, resembles those of the north wall, with its hood moulding and mask-stops. Near this window, at the south-west corner of the parapet above, a cubic sun-dial is fixed, still capable of telling the time to those few who glance up to read it: it is a detail most suggestive of delight in elegant completeness.

The charm of the south side of the church in contrast to the rich, sheer cliff-wall of the north, is due to the large number of planes, the light and shadow sun or moon produces—like a Cézanne picture of buildings. Beside chancel and nave there is the tower with its stair-turret, and the porch—low and broad, but graceful—and finally, the last work of the fifteenth century, the tiny chantry built out in the angle of chancel and aisle. One notes the absence of ignorant fervour in the changes: mere symmetry and modernity are not the aim. Good older windows are kept and the parapet of the roof is broken to retain unchanged the ancient bell-cote, of Norman origin.

The portrait heads are the only external feature conveying suggestion about how the work was done. On the north side the eight portraits are of ordinary working village folk. The faces are homely, the heads rough. But the mask-stops of the south window show a man and a woman, sleek and neat, with shapely head-dresses. One infers a number of village supporters whose work should be commemorated, and a single family of higher status and greater wealth. But if there was one such contributing, we shall learn no more of it.

Within the church, more inference is needed, in order to grasp what was done at this time. After the stone frames and mullions of the windows had been set in place, came the oaken ceiling. It is a fine one—having been thought worthy of having its picture in a work on church roofs and ceilings;[33] it is elsewhere described as 'flat-pitched, with principals, intermedials, purlins, ridge-rafters and plates all more or less moulded.'[34] Now the timber is black with age but at first it was painted in patterns of green and red, remnants of which could still be seen in 1876.

The greatest work was the windows, not only their glass, but also their stone framing. The style was 'Perpendicular,' marked by strong, close-set vertical lines. Mullions and jambs of windows were more or less standardised and could be prepared at the quarry instead of being carved on the spot. Economy in labour and carriage helped the speed of building. But in St. Leonard's windows some of the carving is work of the highest skill. Looking up to the clerestory windows, one sees them finely and deeply cut, but comparatively simple. The windows below in the north wall have large hollow jambs and in those are pedestals for statues, with canopies above—clear-cut, delicate and ornamented, in the words of the expert, 'double-cusped, projecting canopies, with crocketted finials.'[35] The intention to have exquisite small statues together with stained glass indicated that the aim was richness—overloading, another age would feel. No remnant of statue remains and vandalism has been bewailed, but only in one window are there even doubtful signs that figures were ever secured in place. The most beautiful of the canopies and pedestals are not in the north wall but in the window at the east of the aisle where also the busts under their pedestal shelves, of a Bishop and some other dignitary, are most delicately cut.

But eyes turn quickly from the stone to the bright glass. Still to be seen are many remnants, all of the last third of the fifteenth century.[36] The larger lights of the north clerestory windows were once filled with memorials of villagers. Eight family names occurred under portraits or 'effigies' of persons, a few of which may still be seen. Those remaining enable us to imagine the whole range. In the three lower lights of the second window from the east are now shown three pairs of spouses, all kneeling, all robed in purplish-blue. Under them are the legends (omitting abbreviations) *Orate pro animabus*) (pray for the souls) *of Willi Water and Agnes his wife*; from the second some words are missing (doubtless 'pray for the souls') *of Thomas Andrews senior and Agnes his wife A. D. MCCCCLSSVI* (1476); and under the third *Orate pro bono statu* (pray for the good estate, or the souls' health) *of Thomas Smyth and Agnes his wife*. In 1476 these 'effigies' were not all in one window; they were re-set together in the nineteenth century.

A figure and legend commemorated Thomas Eyre, and another window bade us pray for the 'good estate' of Henry Byschop and Margareta his wife. These were dated 1470, the earliest date we find for the re-building. There was another window of 1470: one light of it was an earlier memorial of the Andrews family and a second showed a figure of *Sir John Maleyn, Vicar of Bladynton* with the usual bidding, to pray for his soul.[37] In one of the windows below there was in 1676 an inscription to Nicholas Hobbes and his wife, and in another three figures from which inscriptions were missing. Eight or nine families contributed to the glazing and decoration by presenting these memorials.

The contents of other windows are of more vivid interest in themselves. The glass in the smaller lights, not being set entirely in lead, but supported partly by stone, has suffered less by the lapse of time. In the north clerestory we find a notable small picture of St. George and the Dragon, the saint wearing full armour of the time; St. Mary Magdalene is seen with her pot of ointment, and the Risen Saviour, 'pointing to the wound in his side.' Scattered in tracery lights nearby are beautiful small insertions—'a boy carrying a chrism-box,' perhaps once accompanied by other members of a procession, full-faced lions of Judah,' a slip of a tree, with a scroll bearing the words 'in Gadis Hay,' a mysterious expression even to scholars. One may also identify a chalice and host and, touchingly natural, an eagle with wings outspread over nestlings. Vicar Maleyn out of prudence, perhaps, but also maybe of gratitude for his peaceful asylum here, inserted a number of 'suns of York.'

The finest pictures shone in the large lights of the lower windows. There was St. Christopher with a babe on his shoulder,[38] wading through the stream with his stout staff; and 'a female figure in blue under which is worn a sleeveless robe or surcoat, trimmed with ermine' holding a sceptre in her right hand and a rosary in her left. She is often called the Virgin, but when the picture was whole, she might have seemed some other saintly Queen. These two windows had decayed and in a nineteenth century restoration their fragments and those of others were gathered together in a single window. Here are remains of the architectural settings of some of the figures—elegant finials of buildings rising high, and fragments from the backgrounds of figures, white and and gold pomegranates.[39]

In the aisle to the south was also stained glass. Some lingered in the east window till fairly late in the 19th century, remnants of a Crucifixion with an exceptionally notable painted head of Christ, the leading of which was found vacant after the visit of a 'gentleman', about 1890.

The chantry at the west end of the chancel, a tiny bay not visible from the nave, was the last item in the re-building. It is thought to date from about 1490, which is after the end of John Maleyn's cure. But it accorded beautifully in stone and in glass with the new nave. A narrow altar stood under a fine square-headed Perpendicular window, spanned by a carved ceiling, terminated by 'a fine and light double-cusped four-centred arch supported on angels, the main cusps terminating in good foliage carving, and the spandrels filled in with tracery.' Only in this technical language can the facts be stated: it

77

can be followed as one looks at the work and afterwards serves to keep images of the stone clear in one's mind.

The large lower lights of the chantry window contained a repressentation of the coronation of the Blessed Virgin with passages celebrating the sacraments: in a good light the Words 'presthood' and 'wedlocke' may still be seen. In the smaller lights above the Coronation there was and is a series of Christ's disciples—figures of St. John, with chalice, St. Matthew, with money box, St. Andrew and his Cross, and also St. Bartholomew, St. Matthias and St. James. The window once bore witness to the fact that Nicholas Hobbes and his wife had built the chantry. It was usual to endow these tiny chapels, if only by the profit from two or three farm animals, so that prayers might be said for the souls of the founders and a few children be taught to read. It is likely that such provision was made here, but if so it was of course very insecure. Some members of this family, possibly the same couple, had already provided a memorial window. No tenants at this or any time for a century yet had a large holding. It must have strained the resources of this family of husbandmen to build the chantry and endow it, however modestly. But it did not ruin them. They had been in the village since at latest 1355 and are to be met as late as the seventeenth century, respectable but not prosperous.

The work on roof, walls and windows was only part of what was done. The south doorway was renewed and the oak door set in it is still in its position and in use, though now in a modern frame. Its old hinges remain and these are 'studded with Lombardic As (i.e. letters A) in sunk squares.' 'Did the As,' one writer speculates, 'stand for the name of Andrews'; did this family contribute the door as well as a window? Possibly an Andrews forged the hinges' and possibly also a local craftsman made the square-topped bench-ends, which may still be seen (encased like the door in new oaken frames).

The work must have been more or less complete by 1478. Many of the village families had made special contributions: there were most probably also church rates so that the whole parish was involved. The leaders of the enterprise had had the services of the best craftsmen and artists. whose stained glass was of the finest quality in the period when this art reached its highest development. It resembles some in the Beauchamp chapel at St. Mary's, Warwick, known to have been made by Henry VI's chief glazier, John Prudde of Westminster. Prudde would hardly be living by 1476 but his workshop no doubt remained.

To understand the work as the villagers saw it in the late fifteenth century one must imagine visiting it with the masonry clear-cut and pale with newness. One would step inside the church into a realm of colour, bright, rich, with meaning from a great religion, and great humane traditions, stories of courage and self-sacrifice. However many times one entered, the light from the sun, at different times of the day or reflected from clouds, would show up a new head in the carving, a new form of branch or bird or holy object, in the glass. Not only to right and left and behind one was there beauty: in front across the chancel arch was the rood loft with the cross upon it and probably figures of the Virgin Mary and St. John to right and left of it, and with its ornamented doorway in the wall above the pulpit. Beyond it was the quiet-coloured chancel, the triple east window filled with the old grisaille glass—even the plain glass at that time was beautiful.

We wrote of the church as in the fourteenth century something of a pattern of building, encouraging improvement in the homes. Now it had transcended all that, and must have been associated in parishioners' minds with other worlds than that of the fields and yards. The Vicar, to carry the people with him as he did, must have made the services of the church very meaningful. We rightly imagine him narrating the events and the stories depicted in the glass, encouraging an understanding of the ceremonies of the festivals of the church, stressing doctrines as well as duties. His leadership had been talented and the villagers' response noble: how painfully they must have gathered the pence to pay for it all. Parson Maleyn may well have been one of the many clergy of the time who read to their congregation English translations of the psalms, thus encouraging here a desire for the Word on which Christianity is based, in their own daily language. Christ here, it would seem, was lifted up and drew men unto him— with an effect very different from the compulsions and threats of Tudor times, a few generations later.

Maleyn appears to have left the village by 1479. By that time Edward IV had been on the throne, with a brief interval, for 21 years. His rivals for the throne were no longer living; no one had a better claim to it. He had built up his position financially and fostered the central government so as to be independent of the great landlords, who settled back into a more peaceful life. John Maleyn might well make his peace. In the brief entry in the state records[41] relating to his absolution he is described as 'late Vicar of Bladyngton': on that one word 'late' we base the assumption that he had gone—a mysterious figure, yet standing in a high light for us.

Four years after this, King Edward died. His brother Richard Duke of York became Regent; Edward's two young sons were lodged in the Tower and after a while were seen no more. Richard III is said to have been a talented and cultivated man but the deaths of too many persons whose lives might impede his ambitious plans caused great distrust and fear. Henry Earl of Richmond, a Lancastrian, a descendant of John of Gaunt, claimed and fought for the throne. He had good support. Richard III was defeated and lost his life at the Battle of Bosworth and the Earl, Henry Tudor, became King as Henry VII. Wisely, he married the eldest daughter of Edward IV thus uniting the lines of the white rose and the red. The only further qualification he needed was success in maintaining peace and a reasonably just government. He and his Queen were the founders of the Tudor line, parents and grandparents of the famous sovereigns relatively familiar to us all—Henry VIII, Edward VI, Queen Mary and Queen Elizabeth in whose reigns much happened in our village and more was recorded than hitherto. It may reasonably be said that in 1485 our country entered upon a period which would not end until after the First World War. Social and religious problems would take their rise and flow on as recognisably the same throughout that time. Many and great changes would occur in agriculture, in transport and overseas commerce, and in education and literature. They have been called revolutionary but they were gradual and visible: revolutions since the Second World War, determined in laboratories, have set a new scale of change.

Meanwhile, especially in those parts of the country little disturbed by the Wars of the Roses, social development had continued. There was, for example, the spread of literacy, which was needed by craftsmen and traders of the towns and desired by country people. Boys continued to learn a little Latin in order to qualify as acolytes, and sub-deacons, but also schools for frankly lay purposes were being founded. About 1440 lands at Lyneham, some two miles as the crow flies from Bledington church, were given to set up a well-endowed charity, including a 'freschole' at Chipping Campden[42]—the school to which in 1969 many Bledington children proceed at the age of eleven. From late in the century Stow and Chipping Norton had chantry schools. As we have seen there may have been a little—and

80

The Church: porch XIIIth century; tower, early XVth century, nave
rebuilt and glazed 1465–1500.

Stained glass in the north wall of the Church, *circa* 1476.
left: St. Christopher and the Babe, above a medley of fragments
right: The Virgin or a figure of a saintly Queen.
Photograph by Mr William Ashby

temporary—teaching of children here. Such schools sprang up in a very widespread way.

The basic status of the lowliest villagers had so far improved that serfdom was ceasing to set impassable barriers. By 1452 Winchcombe Abbey had accepted one man of illegitimate birth and one serf to be monks and was asking Papal recognition for them.[43] Further afield the Pastons of Norfolk, who as lawyers and royal servants gained money and lands, were taunted about their recent unfree ancestors and cared little more than might President Kennedy of the United States, if reminded of his poor Irish immigrant forebears.

There had been unsuccessful attempts on the part of landlords to hinder the decay of social and economic bonds by preventing lowly folk from learning to read and by regulating their wearing apparel. A more successful attack was made on one privilege of relatively poor husbandmen. All freeholders had been able since the thirteenth century to shout their accord or to withhold it when Knights of the Shire were nominated for Parliament. The Kenches and de Bladentons were likely, given their traditions, to ride to Gloucester to use this right. In 1430 the qualifications for the election was raised: only those whose freely held land was worth forty shillings annually might vote. In 1355 the usual rent for one virgate here was 15 shillings and our freeholders held two. By 1430 their holdings may well have been worth 40 shillings and their heirs' and successors' rights have gone uninterrupted. But we must note that there would come to be something of a doctrine, held even by reformers, that property rather than status was and should be the basis of political rights and responsibilities.

There was one rising of peasantry in the century, Jack Cade's in 1450. It bore a resemblance to that of 1381. Kentishmen, supported by men of Surrey and Sussex, marched on London and held it for three days. But the *Complaint of the Commons of Kent* struck new notes. The rebels demanded better statesmen, freedom of the royal and other courts from the influence of landowners, and the restoration of the wider suffrage for the election of Knights of the Shire. The rebellion was unsuccessful but it had shown the interest of "the Commons" in the administration of justice and in the new laws and had given notice that attempts to thrust them back to earlier conditions or to impose new restrictions would meet with resistance.

Social change was more general than is conveyed even by important events: it was due to changes in deep-flowing economic development.

There was slow improvement in agriculture, in building, in the crafts of weaving and metal work, and with those a growth in commerce between England and the continent and in the use and accumulation of money. The interests of landlords and successful townsmen had something in common. Landlords could buy produce easily, and no longer wished to draw it from demesne lands: it was easier to let them than to appoint stewards: thus they ceased to have an officer living on the manor and the tenants were left to more self-regulation. They became so secure of the right of appointing successors on their holdings that they were able to make a charge for entry—practically to sell or exchange rights. Those husbandmen (and others who rented the large demesne lands) became well-to-do and their children might marry into the gentry. Religious houses, unlike lay lords, were not quick to lease demesnes or to relax control of manor courts. But presently they would cease to exist and change would come rapidly on their estates.

[1] Still to be seen in the orchard at Banks Farm
[2] Landboc I p. 14
[3] Ed. Sir Thomas Phillips, Gloucester Subsidy Roll I, Ed. III 1327 (privately printed, no date)
[4] Victoria County History, Gloucestershire, Vol. I Religious Houses
[5] G.R.O. D 678 Winchcombe Abbey Manor Court-Rolls
[6] Langland *The Vision of Piers Plowman*. Ed. Skeat, Kings Classics, London 1910, p. 66
[7] W. G. Hoskins *Harvest Fluctuations*. Agricultural History Review 1964, Part I
[8] Landboc I, p. 316
[9] G.R.O. D 678, 65 Winchcombe Abbey Manor Court-Rolls
[10] C. G. Coulton *Mediaeval Panorama*, Vol. I, Ch. VII. Cambridge 1938
[11] The English Carol Book. Music edited by Martin Shaw, words by Percy Dearmer, 1938
[12] See Chapter I, p. 30–31
[13] Hon. Elsie Corbett *History of Spelsbury*, Cheney & Sons Ltd., Banbury 1962 p. 239
[14] Margaret Deansley *The Lollard Bible*. Cambridge University Press 1920. pp. 149, 150
[15] Froissart *Chronicles of England, France etc.* (1388). Everyman edition p. 207
[16] Margaret Dickens A.R.C.O. *A History of Hook Norton*. Printed at the office of the Banbury Guardian. Chapter IV, p. 15
[17] A. R. Myers *England in the late Middle Ages* 1307–1536. 1963. Chapters III & IV

[18] James Gairner *Bishop Hooper's Visitation of Gloucester*. English Historical Review, Jan.–Oct. 1904. p. 109

[19] Nevill Coghill *Visions from Piers Plowman*. Phoenix House, London, 1949. p. 127

[20] William Langland *The Vision of Piers Plowman*. Ed. Skeat, Kings Classics, London 1910. p. 7

[21] See Ibid. pp. 84 & 85

[22] Ibid. p. 6

[23] Ibid. p. 5

[24] Ibid. p. 90

[25] Ibid. p. 110

[26] Ibid. p. 111

[27] Gordon Haigh op. cit. p. 104, note 6 Landboc II. pp. 121–3
Calendar of Patent Rolls 1317–21. no. 322

[28] Landboc II, pp. 42–3, and Calendar of Patent Rolls Vol. V, 1396–1404, p. 497

[29] G.R.O. Winchcombe Abbey Manor Court Rolls. p. 678

[30] Noakes *Monastery of Worcester*

[31] Landboc II XXVIII p. 90

[32] Anon: *St. Leonards' Church, Bledington*. The Church Builder Oct. 1876

[33] Reference lost

[34] Anon: *St. Leonard's Church, Bledington, Gloucestershire*. The Church Builder, Oct. 1876. (Said to be by Rev. David Royce)

[35] As above

[36] S. A. Pitcher *Ancient Stained Glass in Gloucestershire Churches*. B.G.A.S. Vol. XLVII, p. 925

[37] Bodleian Library MS Wood c10 anno 1676. B.G.A.S. VII (1882–83) p. 86

[38] See Herbert Read *English Stained Glass* p.149

[39] J. D. le Couteur *English Mediaeval Painted Glass*. S.P.C.K. London 1926

[40] The Church Builder. op. cit.

[41] Calendar of Patent Rolls 19 Edward IV pt. 2, m. 29

[42] Christopher Whitfield *A History of Chipping Campden*. Shakespeare Head Press 1958, pp. 63, 64

[43] Gordon Haigh op. cit. Calendar of the Papal Registers, Letters. Vol. X, 1447–55, 592

chapter four

THE SIXTEENTH CENTURY

I   Change in the Church
II   Change on the Manor
III   Life in the home

THE TUDOR LINE of sovereigns, starting with Henry VII, stood at the political and social apex of England during the initial period of her modernisation, when she first began to be a close-knit nation. This family was gifted for the profession of kingship. Henry VII ruled firmly over a country which had lately been deeply divided and brought it to some degree of firm goverment and unity. Henry VIII (1509–47) carried through an ecclesiastical, though not a religious revolution. A majority of the nation had been ready for great changes in the government of the Church in England and accepted Henry's settlement, but also many were keenly interested in religion, some adopting new views—puritanical, presbyterian, congregational—while others were devoted to the catholic outlook.

The short reigns of Edward VI (1547–53) and Mary (1553–58) saw governments which, first, pulled the Church and the country in the direction of puritan protestantism, i.e. to a profound revision of the Church's outlook, and, second, returned England forcibly to the fold of the ancient Catholic Church of the Pope.

After this interval of eleven years, Queen Elizabeth's self-appointed great task and that of her administration was to bring the country into a middle way and thus to unify it. While discouraging extremes of dogma, ritual and conduct she had also to keep the nation safe from formidable foreign enemies and thus to give it the peace in which the people's work on the land, in workshops and in trade and all peaceful activities of family and civic life could proceed. She was the last Tudor sovereign, only successful in the typical Tudor policy by means of constant struggle.

Between 1485 and Elizabeth's death in 1603 immense changes were seen—in the teaching and government of the Church, in the growing towns, in transport and in schooling. Some of these changes, especially those in the Church, were very subject to force exerted at the centre by the government and these would be felt not only in every parish but by all individual villagers. Other changes were also very widespread but took longer to become all-pervasive, or to be seen to be so. The great struggles and developments of this period would continue and remain recognisably continuous through more than three hundred years, until the First World War in 1914. Villages would undergo changes apparently revolutionary, but never so thorough that many old patterns ceased to throw up problems, at least one of these, the relief of the poor, growing more acute and tragic for centuries and until 1918, never solved.

In spite of wide agreement that the Church in England stood in need of change there was much difference about how far and in what direction to go. The wish on the part of the simpler people, shared in a more doctrinal way by some instructed and studious folk, for the Bible in English and for the general intelligibility of church services had been, in the fifteenth century, first vigorously repressed and then pushed aside by the struggles of dynasties and nobles. But slowly growing literacy and increased movement within the country to-together with the inherited religious devotion of a few kept alive the conscious wish for such changes and these would come to be accepted temporarily by Henry VIII's government. The use of English would naturally lead to discussion and differences and the growth of dissidence within the Church was greatly feared as likely to divide the nation in an uncontrollable way.

There was widest agreement, probably, in the view that the Church had come to own and exercise power over an excessive proportion of land, without justifying her tenure. On a rough calculation it was believed that the Church held a third of the land, and of this the share of the monasteries approached a half—or a seventh of the total area of the country. Also some bishops held immense estates. But the dioceses were essential organisations, affecting and serving all the parishes. Monasteries in the general view had long since ceased to be useful in any important way. The life within them did not serve the lay

85

community and had in almost all cases lost the devoted and austere quality to attain which they had been founded.

Our immediate neighbourhood affords three examples. Chipping Norton had a close view of one of the numerous small monasteries. Cold Norton Priory, just outside the town, had at one time served vagrants, beggars and other travellers on the road to Oxford and had maintained a small hospital for sick and aged persons. In early days the Prior and monks were very poor but in the fourteenth century the Priory was given the lordship of one large manor and owned property in some twenty other parishes. The Priory did not increase its work but on the contrary an idle and wasteful life was lived there. In 1417 the Prior, held responsible by the Bishop, had been forced to resign, but no reformation followed. The community lingered on but in 1496 not only was the Prior of the day forced to resign but the property of the house was confiscated, apparently by royal action: King Henry VII's minister Empson became its owner. In such small religious communities there was often rumour of more flagrant ill-living, but sheer inefficiency, neglect, and idleness sufficed to bring general contempt.

Nearer to Bledington, under two miles from our church, there was Bruern Abbey a small Cistercian house of about a dozen monks In the Cistercian way it had long since turned its smaller manor of Bruern into a sheep farm. To that end the brethren had reduced the number of their tenants, never numerous. There was consequently no village there, no ordinary families for Bledington folk to intermarry with or holdings they could inherit or enter on in any other way. When in 1536 it was one of the smaller religious houses to be closed there would be no great interest here in the changed ownership of a manor-sheep farm, more perhaps in the feat, when it presently occurred, of carrying a great 'decorated' window from Bruern to Chipping Norton to be inserted in the south aisle chapel of the parish church.

In 1539 came the expected dissolution of larger, richer monasteries. There is no sign that Bledington folk had a great attachment to their landlord-convent, but certainly Winchcombe Abbey was a different case from Cold Norton or Bruern. The most notable of all its Abbots, Richard of Kyderminstre (Kidderminster) was, rather curiously, the last but one. He had reigned there for thirty-seven years till his death in 1525. A scholar of Oxford and a notable preacher, he was known to Henry VIII and Cardinal Wolsey. In his time there were twenty-seven monks and he and they together lived a strenuous life of learning which he himself described.[1] 'It was a fine sight to see how the brethren devoted themselves to sacred learning, how they made use of Latin even in their familiar conversations . . . brotherly charity was so honoured that you would have said that there could not possibly be another such family, so united, so harmonious and yet so small, in the whole of England. The good God alone knows what it was then for me to be immersed in my sacred studies with my brethren in the cloister. There day and night I passed the time at my books in a little study I had constructed . . .' (It was Abbot Kidderminster who collected what remained after a fire, long before his date, of the Abbey's documents and the legends concerning its past, to which we owe some light on the early history of the Bledington manor).[2] But of this studious life it is likely that Bledington had no notion, and it must have been difficult to persuade the laity that so few monks needed vast landed estates and splendid buildings.

The Abbey had been a mild landlord for seven hundred years. Its rents had been about average, the tenants secure in the old customs, not subject to any special exploitation or experiment, except in the appropriation of the parish's Rectory. Folk memory, though some times extremely tenacious, is capricious and it seems likely that the last had been quite forgotten.

There had been no special tenderness to serfs. It was said earlier that many of the monks were of local and lowly origin but no serf did or could join them till within a few years of the closure. The monks or their stewards had not abandoned the rights of fishing and hunting.

The relation of manor and convent was approaching its end. From what they had already seen Bledingtonians must have almost known that the greater monasteries would be closed, and must have feared the changes that would follow.

The closure was in fact being prepared. In 1535 Thomas Cromwell, Henry's minister, had had made a survey of all ecclesiastical pro-perties—the Valor Ecclesiasticus. Information concerning every manor was collected. Bledington was roughly worth an annual £37.11.2, allowing 26s.8d. for expenses. Of the total revenues (£38 17s.10d) customary tenants paid £28.17s.10d; the rent of the demesne 'at the present time' was £10– it had already been let and would shortly be divided between several of the tenants.

Our manor was of less than average value. Of the convent's

Gloucestershire manors only Snowshill had a smaller rental. The sums of course sound tiny in our ears. If we multiply by a hundred we shall not reach the modern equivalent. We have to think rather in terms of produce, of families and institutions supported. Of the latter there had been the parish Church and contributions to the monastery, and to the government of the country.

One new arrangement with more than one important aspect of agricultural and social importance was made by Winchcombe between the Valor Ecclesiasticus and the closure. In 1537, as we briefly saw, there ceased to be demesne lands: the farm, probably by this time of about 350 acres (judging by its value relative to that of the 28 virgates held by ten customary tennants), was divided among sixteen tenants, their farms being enlarged. The expression 'demesne' ceases to be used: the substitute is "the site of the manor and farm.' Thus there was no longer a steward in the village—a man of some economic dominance and perhaps of social dignity, representing the Abbey and rewarded for his charge of the demesne and certain other duties on a higher scale than the income of any single tenant.

However, another arrangement made by the convent in the same year ensured for a few years one relatively well-to-do tenant. The rectory had been leased by the Abbot and Convent to Thomas Freeman, Yeoman, of Campden for thirty years. From Henry VIII's confirmation of this lease after the closure, we learn some details of the Rectory. It comprised tithes and offerings, a cottage, one virgate of land (the glebe), a very small wood near the mill, a small plot of ground in Foscote Hayes, called little Woodnam, meadow land in Horsham, Whiteams, Densham and Claydon (that is along the Evenlode in our own parish), and pasture for 300 sheep (a surprising number). Freeman was to pay annually £15.5s.8d. Of this rent £6.13s.4d. went to the Vicar, and to the monastery till 1539, later to the account kept for the King, £8.13s.4d. In addition 'the cottage called Cotelande' was valued at 7s.32d, Woodnam at 13s and 'the rest' at 66s.8d. Thus the whole would appear to be worth £19.13s.72d. —to have the same monetary value as when it was appropriated by Abbot and Convent a hundred and twenty years before. (In this document there is a mysterious reference to the Rectory having 'belonged' to the Preceptory of the Hospitallers at Quenington. Possibly they had a lease of it before Freeman).

The lease to Freeman, a man of no ecclesiastical standing, with no qualifications to judge between possible vicars seems irreligious: it shows that the Rectory is already mere property.

Freeman seems to have put his son in charge of the Rectory lands. The latter settled here, a husbandman like his neighbours. He was a churchwarden in 1563, and was followed in the village by a brief line of descendants. But the original Freeman had not bequeathed to them the right to appoint the parson, the advowson.

In 1539 the Act of Parliament for the dissolution of the Greater Monasteries was passed and action long and thoroughly prepared was taken. At Winchcombe Abbot Kidderminster had resisted some changes Henry made, but had gone as far as he could in accepting the King's schemes, not opposing his wish for divorce from his Spanish Queen. The monastery lasted Kidderminster's time, but ten years after his death the new Abbot and the monks had been subjected to enquiries, followed by many indignities and the seduction of some monks from loyalty to their Abbot. Under these threatening and humiliating circumstances the Abbey continued till 1539. It seems curious that after Cromwell's mean, low-style treatment the closure was effected without great personal injustice to Abbot and monks. They were pensioned not illiberally and most of the monks became parish priests, some in local villages. The Abbot himself became Rector of Notgrove and a Canon of Gloucester Cathedral—itself though an ancient building, a newly created institution. The closure was devastatingly final: the land was disposed of—we shall see how— and the buildings were torn down till within comparatively few years scarcely a wall bore witness to their form or their past use.

The closing of the larger religious houses was of great economic and social importance but was only an incident in the changes desired, sanctioned and controlled by the King.

For many centuries England had been linked closely with Europe by the fact that her Church was a part of the Catholic Church. For the people the Pope had been a central and for the pious among them a revered figure. But also there had been papal taxes on every parish. Bledington tenants paid an annual penny per virgate. Now in the fifteen thirties a sense of national interest was growing fast, accompanied by mild nationalistic feeling. The King's and the country's need of a male heir and Henry's desire for a new marriage, thwarted by the Pope, or by those who influenced him, led to the King becoming in 1534 Supreme Head of the Church in England—an event not unexpected by the well-informed but surely a great jolt for villagers. We shall see in wills of a much later date how Catholic expressions and surely sentiments lingered in the minds of our villagers. Meanwhile under the new regime of the King's headship of the Church changes began to be made in the services. The Church was the only source of a world view, of form and ceremony at birth, marriage and death, and often the only consolation in dire trouble available here. Outside it the families had only the manor court, the meetings of tenants relating to husbandry, and the remnants—vague and sometimes superstitious—of paganism. The regular services and the more occasional ceremonies were central to life for all but a few individuals (there are always some on the fringes of a culture).

Unhappily for simple people changes followed changes—a few of them wished for, some not at all understood, others resented. Sometimes there was a bewildering reversion to earlier days. What wonder that villagers lost some of their reverence for services and priest and that some ceased to feel the sacredness and necessity of services, and presently had to be compelled to come in.

The Puritan and rational influence was at first important. Henry VIII and Thomas Cromwell (not as is popularly thought, Oliver!) first attacked 'images' in the village churches (in 1538) because they were superstitiously regarded, as was doubtless the case, but in very varying degrees. Where there were local Puritans some action was taken under this ordinance but in many churches including our own stained glass and statue went untouched. In 1536 and again in 1538 it was ordained that the Bible in English should be placed in every church. The Wycliffe translation had lacked literary quality and at times exactness but the great translator Tyndale, born a villager on the other side of our county, knew the religious poverty of villages and that access to the Bible could defeat the extremes of ignorance. 'Ere many years' he had declared to another learned man 'I will cause a boy that driveth the plough shall know more of the Scripture than thou dost.'[3] That day was to be far off but Tyndale finished his beautiful translation before his matyrdom in 1535. In any but the very last of the great editions of the Bible we are reading largely the words he chose and the rhythms he evolved. Unfortunately, the notes and summaries he attached to the text showed his own Protestant interpretation and his work met with official disfavour. In 1538 Coverdale's version, ordered by the King and Council, was ready and the order went out that it should be placed in every church. For some Oxfordshire churches near to us copies were acquired but Bledington did not have one for a long time yet. Soon the King feared that clergymen whose thought was more Protestant than his own would encourage dangerous conclusions from the text; they were instructed to read it without comment, Henry not realising perhaps the stimulus the bare text might afford. Again a few years later (in 1543) a fresh edict, going back to a view which had receded in and since the fourteenth century, went forth: only clerics, noblemen, gentry and substantial merchants might read it: it was not for servants, apprentices and 'base people.' Hence our church wardens acquired no Bible. But at least there was no withdrawal from the position that parts of the Scriptures might be read or heard and that services were not less holy in the people's own language: the use of English had proved too popular to go back upon. Three years later a helpful book was published containing in English the Apostle's Creed, the Lord's Prayer and the Ten Commandments with a few Collects and Articles. This came to be widely used. Some recollection of the contents of this appears to have been the equipment of our parson of the time, John Cooke, as we shall see.

The Tudors were ambitious rulers, intending their edicts to be carried out in every parish, but the conditions of the time hindered this. Bledington and neighbouring parishes had been within the huge Worcester diocese till 1541 when the civic county of Gloucester became also the area of the new Gloucester diocese. A great monastery had been closed in Gloucester town and its wonderful church became the Cathedral.

It was not too far off to come in time to mean something to Bledington folk. They visited the county town on both lay and ecclesiastical errands—churchwardens to report to the Consistory Court, freemen to vote for members of Parliament and to attend the King's Courts of Justice. Orders would come via Archdeacons concerning changes in the Church some of which seem to have been very unwelcome. But as the years went on Bledington men felt warmly enough to leave in their wills small sums to the 'Mother church of St. Peter at Gloucester.'

In 1547 Henry VIII died and his son Edward VI, a boy of ten years, came to the throne. Henry VIII had not completed his programme of confiscation of ecclesiastical property but Protector Somerset acting as Regent carried it forward almost immediately, by suppressing all chantries. We have no documentary evidence as to the amount of the property belonging to the chantry built by the Hobbes family, or of what became of it, but it is certain that prayers ceased to be said at its altar not later than 1548. Now the chantry became nothing more than a beautiful small recess in the chancel.

The two Protectors who acted on behalf of the boy-King were more genuinely Protestant than Henry had been and further changes in church interiors and services took place. In this same year 1548, the Privy Council ordered that all imagery should be removed from churches, and two years later an Act of Parliament ordained the removal of any that might remain. In 1550 if not earlier, the screen in Bledington Church between nave and chancel, with the Holy Rood or Cross above it, was torn away and possibly also some statues removed. We must imagine villagers coming to church the Sunday after the removal seeing a great, unexplained, undesired gap before them.

The stained glass still remained: reluctance to remove it would be reinforced by the thought that it would have to be replaced by new glass and new leading. The glass had been paid for by fathers and grandfathers of the congregation: now from the church's glory it had passed—in the eyes of great ones and strangers—to be merely a sign of the villagers' ignorance and idolatry.

Meanwhile some Protestants felt that stone altars kept alive the primitive idea of blood sacrifice and the Real Presence of flesh and blood in the bread and wine in the sacrament of communion, whereas they believed or 'knew' that it was commemorative only. In 1550 the Council instructed the Bishops to see that all altars were removed and replaced by simple tables to be used in the nave at the 'Lord's Supper.' At Bledington the High Altar had been respected and cherished by parishioners. In 1546 and '47 men were remembering it in their wills, leaving small sums to provide 'tabors' or candles for it and also to the 'roodlight.' There were two altars, the High Altar and the one in the chantry, a stone extension of its window sill.

The care of the fabric and furniture of the church had been the duty of two churchwardens—always two husbandmen—since the fourteenth century. From then to the present day there has been no long neglect of their charge, no censure of their conduct except in relation to this order. They obediently removed both stone altars. The great High Altar stone was, it seems certain, carried no further than a few yards from the south door of the church, where it lay till a few years ago, overgrown with grass. They also provided a 'plain table' for the Lord's Supper. But dumbly they refused on several occasions the further step of making good the floor of the chancel. where the supports of the great altar stone had stood. As late as 1576 it was reported to the Consistory Court in the Cathedral that the gap in the floor had not been filled. Did the churchwardens leave it to the Vicar? Yet there was a conscientious Vicar at the time. Although there was no Vicar for a year about 1563 there were always dutiful churchwardens, fully capable, we fairly infer, of doing such a job themselves at little cost. Maybe they expected an order to replace the stone altar but it did not come and the table was so far accepted that in 1572 Agnes Andrews, widow and husband-woman left a table-cloth for it in her will.[5]

In 1550 a new Bishop had been appointed, John Hooper. He was a Protestant, protesting indeed about many things. He strenuously administered the new diocese, trying especially to stir up his clergy to improve their knowledge and to follow promptly the enlightened lead of Protector and Parliament. To learn the condition of his field of work he sent a commission to enquire into every parish. An eighteenth century copy of its report remains. Every clergyman was asked the same three questions: the first concerning the Ten Commandments, the second the Apostles' Creed and the last the Lord's Prayer. The questions were put in Bledington to Sir (or as we should say the Reverend) John Cooke. From wills we infer that Bledington was his native village; he was the son or brother of a husbandman and himself a copyholder. Already he had been Vicar here for 14 years. Because he answered the questions with freshness and simplicity Cooke came to be quoted and mis-quoted, having thrust upon him a wide and probably unjust fame[6] e.g. asked by whom the Ten Commandments were given, he replies that he does not know, 'unless by the King's Majesty.' Human forgetfulness and unkind fate ensured that later generations should hear of a country parson who said this of the Lord's Prayer, a very different matter. Cooke did not know where the Ten Commandments could be read, nor did he know them by heart. He repeated the Apostles' Creed but could not say how it is derived from the Scriptures. He could recite the Lord's Prayer: it was the Lord's because it has come from Christ but where it is written he had no idea (peritus ignorat).[7]

Cooke's ignorance was by no means startling at the time: almost all the parsons of villages in the same deanery—Broadwell, Little Compton, Wyck Rissington, Westcote, Oddington, Upper Slaughter —gave very similar answers: only the Vicar of Temple Guiting is well-informed. Thirty-one clergy of the diocese did not know the author of the prayer.

In his fourteen years as Vicar up to this point in time Cooke had seen all the changes in the Church of which we have written—the closure of monasteries, the banishing of the Pope's authority and name; in his own church the pulling down of the rood loft, the removal of the altar. It seems likely that he had a copy of the King's Book.[8] He must have heard in 1548 or '59 of Cranmer's Book of Common Prayer in English. An Act of Uniformity had sought to impose its use in all churches but it had seemed to many Puritans to depart too little from 'Romish' practice and it had been withdrawn for revision. Now the demand upon Cooke himself was that he should know his Bible. Section by section it is easy enough reading, and lively, but approached as a whole, how daunting.

Under Edward VI's Act of Uniformity it had been decided that all public services in the English Church should be in English. Three years later the new Prayerbook was revised and its regular use in every church ordained. But before the Prayerbook had reached remote churches like our own, the young King had died and a Catholic Queen had mounted the throne. Queen Mary, coming to the throne in 1553, used her royal power as we all know to restore the ancient services in the Latin tongue and re-instated the Pope as Head of the Church in England. She punished heretics in a number of ways and with a severity and frequency so far unknown in this country. Though many of the sufferers were comparatively lowly folk, Bledington may not have known much of their exacting experiences and painful fate. But they could not help knowing about their own Bishop. For thirteen years this strenuous Puritan had done his best to stir up his clergy to follow the lead and the instructions of sovereign and Parliament, to reformed practices. Now he was tried before a London court for heresy and found guilty. Like hundreds of humbler people he refused to recant. No doubt it was precisely that his diocese should feel his fate that he was brought down to Gloucester and burned just outside his Cathedral gate.

For five years the Bledington congregation was thrust back into the "unreformed" Catholic church. Then Queen Elizabeth, a Protestant but not a Puritan, came to the throne and again withdrew the Church in England from the Pope. One provision of Edward VI's second Act of Uniformity had remained in force under Mary: everyone must attend church on Sundays and Holy Days on pain of ecclesiastical censure.

Elizabeth coming to the throne in 1558 also passed an Act of Uniformity, one of whose first requirements was the regularity of attendance of all parishioners at church services. A fine of twelve pence was to be levied for Sabbath absence. So much diversity of guidance from King and priest had shaken faith in authority, robbing the services of their sanctity and therefore of their attraction. Queen Elizabeth was determined to force the nation into a middle way, to re-establish peace and unity. She reigned for 45 years and in that time had some success.

The fortunes of the Church in Bledington were affected by its new Rector. In 1546 Henry VIII had given to the Dean and Chapter of Christ Church, Oxford (i.e. to the combined Cathedral and College which had been founded by Cardinal Wolsey) a score of rectories in Gloucestershire, Warwickshire, Oxfordshire and further afield. Among these was that of Bledington, carrying with it, as in other cases, the advowson—the duty of nominating vicars.[9] The same details are given as in the lease to Freeman. The Vicar's stipend is specified as £6.13s.4d.

The relation of Christ Church to Bledington illustrates the fact that rectories were by now all but divorced from all idea of religious duty. Christ Church would make a practice of leasing the Rectory to laymen from 1559 to 1860 and until the 19th century the lease included the advowson. During that time the Dean and Chapter felt little or no responsibility for the welfare of the village.

In 1553 the manor had been sold (as we shall presently see) to Thomas Leigh, mercer, of London. To him Christ Church leased the Rectory in 1559 for a period of ninety-nine years. Leigh, though a conscientious landlord, failed to tend the Rectory adequately. In 1563 the churchwardens, William Hathway and William Freeman, with John Guy and Robert Hathway, report that 'their parsonage is and hath been void this yeare.'[10] More than a hundred 'houselynge' people (communicants) had no shepherd. Nor was this the only failure of the patrons. It was their duty to appoint competent clergy

95

but in 1576 when John White was Vicar it was reported that no sermon had been preached in Bledington church for fifteen years, though the rule was that there should be one at least every three months; nor had the catechism been taught.

The standard of the clergy's duties was being raised. Edward VI's Council had published a book of homilies to be read in churches and in 1571 Elizabeth published a second. The Queen's Majesty ordained that the contents should be 'read in churches by the ministers diligently and distinctly that they may be understanded of the people.' The book was commonly possessed by village churches: there were homilies on salvation, sacrament, and on good works; exhortations against swearing and perjury, against the fear of death. The homily against whoredom and adultery was not superfluous. Our own churchwardens found little under such headings, to report to the Consistory Court (though in 1633 a member of a Bledington family already established for at least a hundred and fifty years, more than respectable and still respected to-day, was reported to have got his niece with child).[11]

Elizabeth's moderate settlement of the church did not meet with any party's complete approval, but it lasted and it had a means of regaining the affections of simple people: the open Bible in English and the Common Prayerbook. The ability to read was becoming more common. Bledington Church had now its copy of the Bible (the covers and chain are still retained). In the houses built in the half century from 1550, the chamber (that is, the one bedroom above the hall) contains a small doorless cupboard made by inserting thick oak blocks, below, above, and at the sides of a space about a foot square—big enough to hold a couple of the large books of the time.

How much reading of anything but the Book of Common Prayer was in fact done is doubtful indeed: in all the wills of the reign not a single book is bequeathed. A Vicar who feels incapable of the most modest, most occasional sermon can hardly have read much. But Bledington Church is small enough for every sentence in collect and prayer, psalm and gospel to be heard. Week in week out the people here and in every parish in England not only heard but recited Cranmer's terse and realistic but verbally harmonious phrases, with their full recognition of the weakness and sinfulness of all men both great and small, and of the dangers moral and physical that lie around all men and women too. The phrases stayed in the mind to keep

Banks Farm House
on the village green,
near the ancient
Town Banks and the
Roman farm.

The Manorial Steward's House (note the new window).

thoughts and self-estimation true. Who can doubt that Morning and Evening Prayer did much in these early days to affect men's relation to each other, keeping so clear in honest hearts the fact that mankind is basically one, thus helping to produce some of the novel attitudes of mind so potent in the next century.

We may see something of what the Reformation meant in Bledington minds from the wills made between 1546 and 1615. There is scarcely one among them all whose first legacy is not to the Church. Perhaps the formula used indicates that to remember the Church was part of propriety. The Vicar was frequently a witness to wills but the Cooke vicars were husbandmen among husbandmen, married to neighbours' daughters with little influence from prestige. There is real feeling for the Church, especially for the altar and the bells. In the first will (1546), William Wright leaves 8d. to the bells, 2d. each to the 'hey auter' and the rood light: Bedowe, a commoner of a few ridges of land in the open field, leaves (1547) 2d. each to bells and rood light. Often the poorer folk leave money only to the bells; they are the favourites. It seems that there were three of these, for legacies are sometimes to the three ringers.

In the earlier wills we have the picture of 'our lady and the company of heaven' praying for the soul of the dying testator. This gives way to references to 'a hope of salvation through the blood and passion of our Lord.' But we must not hasten to be sure of a change to Puritanism. The sacrifice of the Son is alluded to in a rare early will: it is after all a fundamental doctrine of the Church of Rome.

Nevertheless, there is change. The little grace of reference to another language in such expressions as 'Sancta Maria,' 'Gloria Dei' dies out. The oaken altar-table is accepted.

A change comes with the legacies to the poor and to the whole community. The first to remember the poor in her will is a woman, Alice Grayhurst. In 1571 she leaves them 4 bushels of corn. In the next year, Agnes Andrews is very generous, 'every poor man' receiving a bushel of wheat or 'mong corn,' every almshouse in Stow-on-the-Wold two pecks of maskelyne (at this time a mixture of wheat and rye). Down to 1595 it was not unusual to leave corn to be distributed; after that money is more frequent. By 1615 or 1620 a usual sum is 13s.4d. but there are larger amounts. Few wills at this time but contain legacies either to the poor or to the 'poor chest in the church.'

One must belong to a very strict school of history to doubt that the

Sermon on the Mount and the Book of Common Prayer had something to do with this charity, but its form and its frequency owed much to government direction. In 1542 Henry VIII reminded his subjects that part of the tithes had been intended for the relief of the poor and should even at the time he spoke be devoted to them. But when he bestowed the Bledington Rectory on Christ Church it was an outright gift with no such stipulation. Even a Tudor sovereign had not the power or the popularity to put back the clock so far as to give back tithes to the poor.

For a long time past the problem of poverty had grown more acute and more pervasive. It was now like plague or the failure of crops—more acute in some areas than in others, but spilling over from one into another, tending to severity everywhere.

During the sixteenth century there were added to 'God's poor' (the aged, the blind, the lame, the widow and the orphan) great numbers of destitute persons who were young and even, when not starved of food, able-bodied. The population was growing and on the other hand corn-land was here and there being reduced in favour of sheep-farming. Flocks required few labourers: husbandmen and cottagers were turned from their homes and holdings and the latter were amalgamated into sheep-runs. Many other workers had ceased to derive their living from the land and found work as weavers, largely of cloth for export. When this trade was suddenly reduced, through war and other causes, terrible hardship fell on the workers. It was a natural impulse to go in search of a better fate than unemployment and starvation. Thus numbers of men, and often women and children too, took to the roads. At times cruel fate further sharpened the problem: the harvest failed and the price even of barley or ryebread rose beyond the power of the poor to buy. Other causes could work with these, as in 1527 and 1528 when Henry VIII's policies not only closed the continental market for cloth, but, the King being short of money, took precious metal out of the coins, which of course sent prices higher still.

There was an attempt to treat the problem of able-bodied vagrants as fundamentally different from that of the 'impotent poor.' The theory that a man who wanted work could find it, therefore that idleness was a crime took centuries to die. Thus, at this time no simple, charitable relief was provided for the vagrants. Some towns tried the plan of providing work and forcing vagrants to do it before food or shelter would be given. But often the work was unsuitable and the

vagrants recalcitrant. Punishment—whipping as a rule—followed refusal to work, but much more dreadful pains and penalties were also
tried and were a failure.

They were, besides, clean contrary to the Christian and human
impulse to charity which Tudor governments fostered for the relief
of the stationary, helpless poor. The responsibility of a community
for its own folk was recalled and vagrants for whom work could not
be found were given instructions to return to their native homes: no
one must give them food or shelter unless they could show that they
were going back as directly and as fast as might be.

Re-settled in their own parish, what could be done for them, and for
other folk in need? In 1540 the clergy had been bidden to exhort
parishioners in their sermons, at confession, and when making wills,
to be liberal to the poor. Somewhat later it became the law that alms
should be collected by the churchwardens 'and two others' (later
called overseers of the poor) every Sunday. A 'poor's box' was to be
placed in every church.

From 1552 householders were to be called together to nominate two
collectors of alms: thus the responsibility is brought home to the
whole community in a way to which an open-field parish is accustomed. It was the collector's duty to ask each man what he would give
weekly for the poor and the promised sums were to be entered in a
book. But it is difficult to make voluntary alms systematic, let alone
just, as between one contributor and another. From 1572 overseers
were required to assess householders for poor rates: compulsory
payment was not far off. But in the form of legacies in Bledington wills
some voluntary charity continued to be customary.

From the wills we learn that these injunctions relating to the poor
were obeyed—overseers were appointed and a poor's box placed in the
church. Many villages find lively information in churchwarden's and
overseer's accounts for the last decades of the century; but if ours were
literate and wrote down their disbursements, the accounts have been
lost. We may summarise gifts of testators between 1572 and 1625.
Money legacies in definite sums range from 3s.4d. to 10s; in some cases
we cannot tell how much money is involved; the poor are to have
'three pence apiece' or 'twelve pence apiece,' or 'every cottager 4d.'
It seems that 'apiece' means 'to every head of a poverty-stricken
family.' But we never learn how many sums are paid out.

Nearly half the legacies to the poor are in corn—often a 'peck of white corn,' 'mong corn,' 'mill (or myle) corn,' 'grist corn,' or just plain 'corn' to each. But in two cases each 'poor' was to have 'two strike,' that is, two bushels or eight pecks. The value of the gifts is not easy to arrive at. A 'peck loaf' presumably made from a peck of flour or somewhat more than a peck of corn, was substantial: it was expected to weigh over 17 pounds and bread was good for strong, adult digestions. How much bread would 3d. or 4d. buy? Perhaps in good times a quartern loaf.

Some Bledington folk became vagrant and were sent back here by other parishes, to their 'settlement'—a proceeding that gave much trouble and work to everyone concerned and involved great waste— waste that went on for centuries. But vagrants from other parishes and counties and towns affected us less than most parishes. Bledington was on the direct way to nowhere: there could hardly be said to be a road through it. The ancient road past the church was a mere roundabout lane still. Bennet's Lane, the old name for the road past shop and vicarage, was a muddy narrow track onto which some neighbours threw their household rubbish and filth. Four miles away, at Stow, roads branched off through Oddington and Kingham to Chipping Norton and Burford, and the Fosseway passed through Stow to Cheltenham—all hilly and, at least in parts, well drained roads. They acted as 'by-passes' for Bledington. Our whole county seems to have had fewer vagrants than some. In 1560 the Sheriff reports to Queen Elizabeth's minister, Cecil, that Gloucestershire is quiet, though the cost of everything has risen owing to the decline in the value of money. In 1571 the county Justices of the Peace, upon whom much responsibility for vagrants was being laid, replied to the Privy Council that 'in certain Hundreds' where they had made enquiries, the only vagabonds were 'such beggarly persons as are not thought fit to trouble their Lordships with.' But in nearby Oxfordshire Hundreds there was trouble. In the same year, the Constables of Chipping Norton and Chadlington forwarded 'certificates of the rogues and vagabonds arrested, whipped and passed on.'

But the duty to whip was not always discharged. In very many villages householders were reported to Hundred Courts for mercifully allowing vagrants to sleep in their hay or—and not infrequently —for 'harbouring a woman in his house with child.' How difficult it must have been to decide upon one's duty when softened on Sunday by the Vicar's admonitions on the duty of charity, by the prayers of the liturgy, and the parable of the Good Samaritan—and then to meet on one's path, or in the 'backside' of one's house, a poor starving unknown wretch. Such problems the countryside would have at any time, always, between 1526 and 1834 and hardly less for many years beyond.

In the last years of Elizabeth's reign it was one of her numerous troubles that the harvests were poor[12] and in the end almost ruinous. West Gloucestershire had been reported discontented in 1586; ten years later there were riots in Oxfordshire villages..[13] Even rye cost 44/- a quarter—a ruinous price for the poor. The expedients that were tried show how far the country was from knowing how to act effectively. Those who had corn to sell were punished for holding it back and an attempt was made to force sellers to take a low price from the poor. In short, many expedients were tried and at length reviewed; the use of the most successful was ordained by Acts of Parliament. One was passed in 1597, somewhat revised by that of 1601, which remained in force, without fundamental change, till 1834, intimately affecting every village in England. Under the Act the relief of the parish poor was again placed in the hands of the churchwardens and two overseers. When adults were out of work it was the overseers' duty to see that they were provided with materials for spinning or weaving, or with wood or iron or other raw material. Children in need of relief were to be apprenticed. Vagrants had to be sent on their way, being relieved only if they were proceeding to their own parish. Between 1550 and 1600 new and difficult duties had been laid on the parish.

Exactly who were our Bledington 'poor' and what were the conditions under which they lived? As for the children and the very old they might belong to husbandmen's families. Beyond our present period we shall find evidence that orphans of the Baker family (some members of which are always fairly prosperous) are relieved and that aged folk of the name of Tidmarsh, also husbandmen, would be helped. Time would come when the term 'labourer' applied to a man placed him in the class of 'the poor,' liable at the slighest misfortune to need relief. But in the late sixteenth and seventeenth century a labourer might have money and goods to bequeath, might marry a husbandman's daughter, slip into some holding, or be apprenticed to a trade. A shepherd might be a skilled, valued and rewarded man with a close attached to his cottage where he could keep animals. But there was another class or worker, the 'servant.' On the larger holdings

—Andrews', Wrights', Guys', Halfords'—there seem to have been two or three. In all, in 1608[14] 'there were nine men servants' of military age, three of whom were too young to be family men. There must also have been some over sixty years of age, as well as one or two women heads of poor families. Thus we may infer some twelve or more householders who were 'servants' or poorer still. ('Servants' could be temporary, young sons of husbandmen, but there was also a permanent class).

In 1355[15] there had been 39 habitations. Two centuries later in 1563, it was said that there were '20 households,' yet in 1638 a list of the men in the village, due to pay or exempt from tax, gives 47 individuals' names, 31 family homes. It seems likely that the word 'house' in 1563 meant a unit of building which might contain more than one family. it was not at all uncommon for the poor to be 'destitute of habitation'[16] Agnes Wright's 'servants about the house' slept in her lofts. Till recently there stood in a little Bledington backyard, just behind the house, a small building that appeared to have been a dwelling, and one has seen elsewhere in farmyards little primitive cottages long uninhabited. Such attachments, part of a messuage, may sometimes have been omitted from lists. It seems generally speaking that if 'servants' had for dwelling a room with a chimney and a door they were not relatively unfortunate. As to possessions, in the middle of the seventeenth century it would be true of numbers of poor folk that they 'could carry all they possessed on their backs.' It was however, recognised that the poorest families should have houses. By a statute of 1589 it was ordained that no single habitation should be shared by more than one family. This was optimism: in Bledington one or two cottages would be shared as late as the early twentieth century. A quite idyllic provision that no 'cottage' should be erected without 4 acres of land was made in Elizabeth's Poor Law. Whatever the motive of this provision time would come when it was used in this village and elsewhere to prevent the erection of small habitations for poor folk who might presently have to be kept by the parish. In the poor thatched dwellings of one room on the farmsteads a rather wretched and short life must have been lived, but not brutish: the inhabitants belonged to a community; they worshipped in a still lovely church, and they had still their arts and festivals. We might hazard a guess that there were fifteen or sixteen poor households.

The first legacy bearing witness to a concern for the community and even the public as a whole comes in 1595. John Wright then leaves money for the repair of the highway; seventeen years later his widowed daughter-in-law a similar sum for mending Smenham (or Smettenham) Bridge (over the Evenlode on the road to Kingham and Churchill); again in three years' time Anne Andrews remembers the 'King's Highway between Bledington Cross and Thomas Guy's wall.' Women were not so confined to their houses that they did not know the needs of village and wayfarer.

Roads, of course, were becoming more important. More goods were being carried on them: people were travelling more frequently. But in this matter too, as in some other, even agricultural matters, the church organisation was being used, instead of the manorial, which was now everywhere in decline. The duty of surveying the roads and allotting duties of repair had been laid on churchwardens. Roads and bridges thus became linked with the poor as objects of true charity.

II Change on the Manor

Alongside changes in the church our villages were to see slow changes in land tenure and agriculture. King Henry VIII gradually sold his vast newly acquired landed property. It would not do to "unload" so much land on the market within a short time Before the process was completed he died and it was in the next reign that preparation was made for the sale of the Winchcombe estates. The values of manors had been roughly assessed in the Valor Ecclesiasticus of 1535, but before a manor could be sold it had to be thoroughly surveyed, the terms of all tenancies clearly stated, and the legal position of all tenants ascertained. In 1550 a thorough-going 'extent' of Bledington was drawn up. This survey is the most detailed we have. It seems to have been compiled on the spot, the surveyors walking over the open fields, seeing every furlong. They ascertain not only the number of selions or ridges each tenant has in each furlong of the open field, but also the name of the holder of the selion on each side. There has been practically no grouping together of a man's selions. Some holders have ridges in every furlong, that is to say (for the furlongs follow the lie of the land) on every varying incline, with every aspect and soil. Perhaps no one had yet seen reason to change this careful and ingenious distribution. The furlongs are far from being alike in acreage and the same is true of the ridges: One man with a virgate has

46 selions and another over 70. There was enquiry as to the 'fines' due, i.e. the fees to be paid on entry to a holding, and as to heriots (the forfeits of money or cattle on the death of a tenant). Each man's word is taken as to the custom of the manor by which he holds, though no doubt there was some public occasion when the surveyors met the tenants, as a body, and presented the 'extents' to them.

All but two of the tenants are copy-holders. Each one gives the date of his 'copy,'[17] the years ranging from 1524 to 1549, a year before the enquiry. There are, as centuries earlier, only two freeholders and curiously, their holdings now are amongst the smallest. They share a single messuage and each holds one virgate. It seems likely that Tidmarsh and Hathway have each a half of one of the old 'free' holdings? but since when? Possibly for a long time: Hathway was an old name here. There is reluctance to admit their full right: they 'hold free,' but 'by what service is not known.' They pay a rent, but only three shillings each. For the others rent varies a good deal but averages about fifteen shillings a virgate. the rents for the manor totalling £24 (without the demesne land).

'Fines' paid on entry to holdings vary between 33s. and 6s.8d. but three holdings pay none, beside the true freeholders whose holdings are not due for fines or heriots. The amount of the fines is not related to the size of the holdings. The heriots are generally 'the best ox' or the 'best animal'; the sum of 3s.4d. is due as heriots on some messuages and 3s. on one cottage. A cottage is valued at an annual 3s.4d.

There are in all 20 commoners. The smallest holding is that of a member of the Hathway family who has a cottage and 4 selions; the largest is Joan Andrews' of 2½ virgates, but she has two messuages, in effect two holdings. One of these is what is now Banks Farm, which contains the Roman site and whose orchard includes the old town meeting place, the Town Banks, and the butts. Banks Farmhouse in Joan's days did not include any of the present front but contained only the two oldest portions, at right angles to late sixteenth, seventeenth and eighteenth century portions. Joan Andrews is one of three women who hold by 'free bench,' that is, as widows of tenants. These pay rents, fines and heriots just as other tenants. Ellis Ovenell is the other tenant with 2 virgates. Thomas Rooke holds 1½. Thus we can trace 23 holdings, almost the same as two centuries earlier, in 1355.

Considering the account of a representative holding—R. Tidmarsh's, of one virgate—we find that he has 57 selions; two of these are meadow-land: he is also entitled to half an acre in the 'lotte mead,' which is not divided into selions His 'allotment' in this mead is determined annually by the rough justice of chance. We do not know just how he drew his lot: in nearby villages a marked ball was drawn from a bag. His 53 arable selions are distributed in all three arable fields and in 23 different furlongs.

Tidmarsh has the right to pasture 30 sheep and 4 horses on the common land. As to the last item his rights are unique: all the other tenants have pasture for oxen, but horses are not mentioned again. No doubt the plough teams are all oxen: Tidmarsh's holding may have provided horses for traction on the roads. Or perhaps the ratio between horses and other livestock, for grazing on the common lands, had already been settled and was in use, Tidmarsh's being the only holding that had permanently settled for horses. At all events in 1539 John Cooke had left to his son his 'teme of horses.' The Cooke holding has a small special interest. The Vicar, John Cooke, supplements his stipend of £6.6s.8d. by tilling half a virgate. He holds by copy of 1527. He is a relative of a family settled here a good many years and to remain at least another century and possibly until today. It provides the village with at least three vicars. John Cooke signs many of the wills proved between 1539 and 1550. (It is he who was examined and found wanting).

Altogether there is, on the manor, pasturage for 870 sheep and 124 oxen, beside Tidmarsh's 4 horses.

The crops grown we have to infer from wills of the time. They are very limited: wheat, barley and pulse, with a little hemp for spinning. In one or two wills the mixed crop, maskelyne or maslyn, is mentioned.

A fact worth pondering on is the extensive nomenclature of the parish. The men knew by name every pole or perch of ground; the names we find of field and furlong and lane and brook and meadow and group of trees can hardly be numbered. Many of them are ancient: in these days scholars are tracing their meaning, so that we can see how and when the tilled fields were extended and how vegetation has changed.

Does this command of detail indicate one advantage of this old style open-field farming? It is already at the beginning of the sixteenth century subject to attack as wasteful and old-fashioned, being compared to its great disadvantage with 'several' farming in which the old fields are broken up and enclosed in separate farms. The old system was not incompatible with the use of every foot of ground and grain of corn, whereas its successor wasted land on useless dividing hedges, on undue multiplication of draught animals and ploughs. But there were many poor harvests in the sixteenth century although it is likely that the yield of corn (3 and 4 grains to one in the middle Ages),[18] through more attention to manuring, more frequent tilling, and increased planting of peas and beans, was higher in good seasons.[19] Still, when there was a second and perhaps third poor harvest some of the seed corn would be eaten and another harvest endangered. Of the quality of cattle here we have no evidence but the sheep were 'long-necked and stocky with large bodies and broad buttocks; their staple was deep and thick and even the forehead was tufted with good wool.'[20] There was something to be said for such sheep, and the market for wool was at hand. In Bledington our handsomer houses were not built till after the wool-trade had declined. But though sheep brought no great wealth, they were useful and reliable as a source of money and goods: probably it is from wool that the farmers built up the small sums of money they left to their children and sometimes lent to their neighbours.

The impulse towards the separation of individual and family fortune from that of the village did not come from within Bledington, but from Henry VIII's masterful re-organisation of land and from urban and commercial life. It began perhaps when individuals were given the opportunity to lease demesne land. It continues with the advent here, as landlord, of Thomas Leigh of London. Our land and our farmers were now to move out of a long period of slow, small-scale change into more or less crowded hours. The survey or 'extent' having been drawn up in 1550, the manor was offered for sale, with others, by the government. Thomas Leigh (not yet a knight), Mercer and Alderman of London, is ready to acquire it. He is a typical figure of the time: he and his like, anxious to purchase for himself and his family the advantages of 'landed estate', will affect Bledington and many small rural communities for centuries. In 1553, Leigh was a man of forty-eight years or so. As a boy he had been apprenticed in London to a mercer and by the time he was 21 years old he was a Freeman of the Mercers' Company. In trade with the continent he found a field for financial ability. Through his success he was able to lend money and in other ways make himself useful to Henry VIII and his minister

Cromwell. Meanwhile he strengthened his position in the City of London, becoming Warden of the Mercers' Company. It was in 1553 that he purchased several manors hereabouts; but he continued his career in London, becoming Lord Mayor in the year Elizabeth came to the throne.

Leigh had two spheres of eminence open to him, as a Merchant and Alderman in London and as head of estates in the country. He chose to continue his life in London but he went on buying property, acquiring Stoneleigh Abbey and the manors of Adlestrop and Longborough a few miles from Bledington. We must suppose that he bought to provide financial security and dignity of life for his children; he established one of his sons at Adlestrop and another at Stoneleigh. He was, with some family vicissitudes, successful after death as in life; Adlestrop is still possessed by a Leigh and the Baron Leigh of Stoneleigh is his descendant.

Bledington's association with the Leigh family was brief. There was no attractive site for a house and no society here. The village 'street' was liable to flooding and for a good part of its course in our parish the river was often inaccessible. The manor was bought as an investment, as others must have been.

The final indenture of the sale of the Manor to Leigh was signed in 1553. The price was £897.13s.1½d. i.e. 25 times the value of the customary rents with two small extras included generally in the extent of 1550, but now specified as the value of twenty cocks, (i.e. 3s.4d. at twopence each) and Peter's Pence paid by customary tenants at 1d. per virgate, 2s.4½d. Fines, heriots and reliefs were valued at £1.0.4d. The tenure of the manor was by Knight's service—already obsolete.

We learn more from the 'extent' about the disposal of the demesne— the homes of the sixteen tenants, and that their leases were for ninety-nine years. All the tenants were described as 'free men'; their services had all been commuted and they were free to leave the manor, to apprentice their sons or to send them to school. Mediaeval social relations were giving way to modern ones.

Leigh would not be able to raise the rents of customary tenants. Even when a tenant died it was not usual to raise rents and to do so would have disturbed the homage. Assuming that Leigh's income from this manor would continue to be much the same as the convent's his return would be about 4% net. But Sir Thomas who had lent money to Henry VIII and Cardinal Wolsey and shared in commercial enterprises must have had much experience of high risks as well of higher returns. Now he was investing his gains to produce a secure income. However in general it was to be expected that the value of good land would rise: increasing population, growing towns and successful commerce like Sir Thomas's own, brought a greater demand for corn. The income from this manor seems to have improved very soon. In time Sir Thomas's family would benefit greatly from his investments in Gloucestershire and Warwickshire manors.

The rectory aside, the manor was now the possession of a family. Presently the relation between landlord and manor would come to an end at the will of the family heir—though perhaps also with the warm approval of tenant families. The claims of family and individual in all classes were growing, change coming slowly till about 1600.

The central institution of the manor, its 'court baron,' upon which we have had little information for some decades, continued to be held though at longer intervals by Sir Thomas Leigh's visiting bailiff. In the old days courts baron had been held more than once a year; now it seems that the Bledington court meets no more often than every two years. There are records of the first five meetings: in 1553, 1555, 1557 and 1560.[21] In 1554 four officers were chosen by the homage to be entrusted with 'the good order of the fields,' 'the ordering of the number of cattle' turned by tenants on to the heaths and common pastures, and also for 'contentions,' and for 'easing land and all other controversies.' Those who would not accept their ruling were to be fined. Clearly they were a substitute for some meetings of the court. Whether they included the 'oarsmen' or whether these continued to be appointed as in times past, by their predecessors or sometimes by all the husbandmen, we do not know: but there were oarsmen still.

Simon Wisdom was the chairman and more. It is for him as representing the Lord of the manor to decide on matters left in doubt. Wisdom is for us a new remarkable character—one of the most remarkable to play a part here. He came from Burford where he lived in a substantial house (now become a cottage, by the size of more modern houses) still standing at the foot of the hill, down which the main street descends. He has been some sort of merchant, but now holds land and is settling his sons on large holdings in the neighbourhood. In 1530, when he was young, the Bishop of Lincoln had sent investigators about the diocese to unearth heresy. At Burford they discovered that Wisdom had three books in English, the Gospels, the Psalter and 'the Summ of Holy Scriptures.' He professed his regret and was not required—as some other, more active 'heretics' were—to stand on the steps of the market cross with a faggot of wood on his back. Eight years later he was employed by the government as collector of a 'lay subsidy.'[22] Later he was an Alderman of Burford, steward to the Burgesses, and in that capacity he induced them to allow him to change their method of recording their decisions. In 1571 he was helping to found Burford Grammar School. He gave property for its support but his greatest gift to the school was his arrangements for its finance and government and for the appointment of its headmaster. It may well be that these account for its survival till the present day.

Sir Thomas Leigh would recognise him as a born administrator, a man of affairs—not unlike himself—and one alive to chances for himself and his family but also public-spirited. Such men leave functions for finer spirits but how useful they are.

The records of the Bledington court meetings are neatly written in a leather-covered book.[23] They must be Wisdom's summary of notes or of his memory. The first item is always a statement that the two freeholders were present or one of them excused. In larger manors where there is sometimes need of a jury, the freeholders are its members. Here they seem to have no special function, but it is very much their duty to be present, perhaps as having a useful impartiality in some matters.

The major work of the court is making and recording changes in tenancies. A man dies and his widow applies to the bailiff to become tenant in his stead. This is her right, her 'free bench,' and is therefore always recorded. In 1557 Wulfstan Steyt has died and his widow Agnes is 'granted seisin.' Similarly Alice Kench and Alice Greyhurst are given 'copies.' Sometimes a copy is given to a widow for her life, and for her sons after her. When tenants die leaving no widow or son the holding comes 'into the lord's hands' and no custom controls whom he shall admit: but it seems that the customary rent is not raised.

Whether a holding is vacant by death or by retirement (Alice Greyhurst, for example, leaves her messuage to become tenant of half a cottage at a rent of 10d.) a 'heriot' is due to the lord—usually the tenant's best animal. With one exception in these records this is always a horse, more valuable than a 'rother beast.' In the exceptional case in 1553 the 'heriot' is a 'cowe colored red': its value is ten shillings, whereas the horses are worth from thirty to forty shillings, usually the latter. The animals are specified always by their colour, 'bay' or 'black' or 'red,' not by size or breed, and that is no doubt significant: care in breeding is not great. The heriot is paid from the estate of the ex-tenant and the new tenant pays to the lord a 'fine' for entry. This payment appears not to be rigidly governed by customs and here the lord has his opportunity to gain if the demand for land is rising. Fines are always money.

Women are never members of the homage but they attend court when they apply to be granted a copy-hold, when they have complaints to make or if one is to be accused of misdemeanour. One of the greatest offences to be dealt with is that of Margaret Freeman who turns her cattle on to the 'ground or common of the lord's tenants where she has no right to do so.' She is fined the enormous sum of £1 (twenty-two shillings is here the annual rent of a messuage with a yardland and a half). Two years later Margaret is still offending: now it is not only 'rother beasts' in question: she is also turning too many sheep on to the common. She is to reform 'on paine of £4.' Margaret would hardly be so difficult if the 'homage' were her near neighbours: she lives at Blockley.

A woman copy-holder with a complaint to make in 1552 is Joan or 'Jone' Andrewes. John Guy has encroached upon her land in Claydon Field. Two years later 'the homage present' that they have 'made agreement' between the two, and more, Simon Wisdom has recommended that the ground in question should be 'merestoned' and it has been done. This is the first reference to a modern way of marking the limits of a selion. In the seventeenth century merestones could be seen in numbers over the arable fields—fine large stones standing nearly a yard high with a handsome letter carved on the face—the initial of the tenants' name. They were set between one ridge and another, defining the correct widths—a more economic method than leaving baulks of turf between, as was done and still is to this day at Westcote.

One function of the court was to keep the manor in sound agricultural order. In 1553 the homage are bidden or agree to plant each of them ten trees (oak, ash or elm) for each yardland held. In 1555 they are to plant six and to 'defend them from danger of cattle.'

Custom is strong and a great defence for tenants but a certain adaptability is of use to them also. Widows are permitted to yield up their copy in favour of a younger relative of their choice. The old Vicar (he who was ignorant in 1540) is allowed to share his tenancy with a younger man, no doubt because he is no longer strong enough to work the land: he dies two years later. On one occasion licence was given to a copy-holder to 'take an under-tenant.'

Detailed records of the manor court cease in 1560, but we infer from a rental that it met on July 18, 1570. The last reference to the court occurs in a document drawn up in 1583. There has been a dispute about the 'profits of the manor' which has involved 'disturbance' at the manor court. ('Profits' here seems to mean some or all of the income from the court itself, penalties etc., not the rents of the holdings).

Some light on Sir Thomas Leigh's income from the manor is thrown by rentals from 1553 to 1563 and for 1569 and 1570 At first these strictly record only rents due and paid for holdings with the addition of the total annual payment of one penny per yardland, once known as 'Peter's Pence,' then as the 'Roman fyne' and in the last years as the 'common fyne.' This was originally, as its name shows, a contribution to the Roman see, but it has become merely a part of the annual rent to the lord. Another small sum is added after a year or two. Ten couples of 'hennes' have been due from the manor 'at the lordes pleasure'— but only once a year. This due is paid in kind in 1563, but is shortly converted to money, a hen being valued at twopence and it is paid at Christmas. How tenants share the payment of this annual 3s.4d. we do not know.

When Leigh bought the manor the 'fines, heriots and reliefs' were valued at an annual £1.0.4d., but either this was an under-estimate or soon rose in value, especially it seems the fines. In 1557 Robert Kench's fine on entry to his holding was £12.17s. He takes three years to pay it, but even so it alone raises the lord's income. Joan Andrews' son, when she goes off to her half-cottage, pays a fine of £10 and in the same year Thomas Guy pays £5. In 1556 five heriots were received to a value of £5.10s. and in 1558 £2.10s. In that year the sum total is given as £40. 9s.6d.—an increase of £4.10s. upon the income Leigh has been led to expect. A final item of income was the 'amerciaments'—the payments, usually small, made in court when a commoner was convicted of some offence in the common fields. These amounted in 1554 to 3s.4d. in 1558 to 11d., in 1562 to 7s. and in 1563 to 2s.8d., finally in the last rental for 1570, 2s.5d. The totals are not easy to ascertain, but that the manor increases in value cannot be doubted.

Returning to the manor court we find that when tenants die without immediate heirs 'Copies' are granted, but leases are given or sales made and the land concerned passes out of the view of the court. Gradually the court loses its importance. It is hardly worth while to send a bailiff.

But yet the working of the open fields has to be regulated or there would soon be confusion. The ancient office of oarsman continues to be filled: there are two oarsmen each year. But a court is needed to receive their reports and enforce decisions. It seems that in the next century the Hundred Court of Slaughter comes to the rescue. It had always been the court leet for Bledington, dealing with offences against the King's peace and against criminal law; now manorial offences are reported and dealt with there.

'No court, no manor.' The reigning Leigh becomes gradually a modern landlord and the former copy-holders modern tenants or owner-husbandmen. When the Leighs sold land in Bledington they began with the demesne leases, offering freehold. The first tenant to buy was Baker and the date 1608; others followed his example soon. In the course of the seventeenth century there came to be a score of freeholders. The husbandmen in their wish to be owners learned to borrow money: here begins the career of that potent and dangerous document for farmers—the mortgage.

III   Life in the home

What of the more intimate details of the lives of Bledington families? Our evidence is the wills that have survived in the Worcester and Gloucester diocesan records. Unfortunately none of these till 1611 has an inventory attached. The usefulness of the wills themselves is limited by there being usually a residuary legatee; specified legacies are small, and at first few. We have heard already of a Bledington will dated 1420.[24] It was not till about 1520 that husbandmen in general began to feel it proper and even necessary to make a will.

Copyholders had of course no right to leave land or houses. They could dispose of farm gear and the contents of their houses, of sheep and pigs and minor stock. It seems to have been usual to allow the likely heir of the copyhold to have the plough team and the cows and often the plough (if one was owned) and the harrow. But all money was at the testator's disposal.

Money was not as basic as other property but as a topic it is more easily dealt with: we may despatch it now. Early in the century monetary legacies are small—two pence to the high altar, the rood light, the three bells or their ringers, or 'my ghostly father.' By the middle of the century such legacies are larger. A member of the Andrews family leaves 4s. for the bells. In the next year another Andrews leaves money for his three sons to be given them when they marry—20 marks (a mark being 13s.4d.), 10 marks and £4—twenty pounds in all.

Evidently the amount of money that can be accumulated grows, but its value does not increase in proportion. Early in the next century another Widow Andrews leaves £40; Agnes Wright in 1612, £34. In 1606 John Grayhurst leaves £25. Most of these testators have lent money to neighbours, in three cases about half as much as they bequeath. The three families last named are among the most prosperous: they live at Banks Farm, Harwoods Farm and perhaps the 'Home' Farm, re-built about 1550, or at the house which became the Five Tuns Inn.

One thing that the wills certainly show is that inside all the husbandmen's homes domestic comfort was growing. Coffers and chairs and tables once made were inherited again and again; blankets and sheets spun at home and woven nearby lasted generations, as much as a century. Thus by accumulation, decency and convenience grew, independently of great increase of produce.

The highest comfort the husbandmen's families had (we should think it their only one) was in their beds. By now, the beds in the two chambers had wooden frames, criss-crossed with rope, straw palliasses on this, and wool mattresses—not feather ones as yet—on top. Feathers have to be hung up to dry for months and then each must be cut (it was quicker to wash wool): then, one must have beeswax and thoroughly line the hempen container with it. There was little time to spare from cheese-making, bacon-curing, spinning—the utterly necessary occupations. Nevertheless there were a few elegancies—table cloths and napkins and bed-covers, and at the end of the century one woman even had a painted cloth in her hall—a fashion that had crept out into this remote village—for wall decoration, smaller and less costly than tapestry. To summarise before passing to further details: the husbandmen's homes make progress, the skilled labourers hold their own, but the fortunes of the poor are the worse for the decline in the value of coins.

We learn more from the wills about the minor farmyard and indoor gear than about the larger implements because of a sex difference. When widows die they arrange in great detail for the disposal of the objects they have used or worn, but men are more summary. The names of household objects given by women are legion. There are sieves and barrels and presses, and small vessels galore, and for many purposes. All these are greatly cherished. One might think that the crafts of using the products of the field are ahead of the practice of agriculture—more progressive and ingenious. Possibly housewives were less hampered by custom and prescription.

But there are crumbs of information about farm vehicles and implements; they include ploughs and plough-gear, carts and trows (one of which 'will take 15 strike (bushels) of corn'). There are also harrows, an occasional dung cart and a number of 'rewles' or rolls: were these last a recent arrival? Between the larger objects and those used exclusively by women come the farmyard tools—ladders and bill hooks and axes. These are kept in the small 'hovels' in the 'backsides' of the houses. Here, in the yards (but the word suggests too much space) are the tool sheds, the sties and the fowl. Here, to the 'backside' the cows are brought for milking, and in the close beyond it the calves graze, small hay ricks are built and the corn is threshed. We have to banish from our minds all images of high, prosperous-looking barns; even modest ones if well built belonged to the seventeenth century or after. A few larger ones belong to the early eighteenth century. Even small barns show an old roof-line; they had once half their present height.

As to stock there figure among the legacies cows and calves and bullocks, but no bulls; the bull is common property and a special pasture is kept for him. Horses apparently few in 1550, became common towards 1600: some husbandmen own four or five. Sheep are a favourite legacy. Giles Wright in 1599[25] leaves a total of 160 sheep, chiefly by tens: he shared the farm with his mother and probably bequeathed the whole of his share of the sheep. Some testators leave one sheep to each of quite a number of children, grandchildren and godchildren. Giles Wright's neighbour Thomas Andrews leaves a sheep and a lamb to each of his two shepherds. Many folk keep pigs, most have cocks and hens, one has ducks, but only one mentions pigeons. Several have bees. We learn little of monetary values: but one girl gets 'ten shillings to buy her a sheep'; in the very early years of the next century 'kine' and 'young beasts' are worth £2 each, horses between £3 and £4, and a 'stock' of bees, five shillings. The rarity of monetary legacies is partly due to the fact that sons and daughters who have left the village have gone only to a neighbouring village, and are still in the farming business: they can easily take home whatever it is convenient to leave them.

Wills are legal, and rather conventional documents relating chiefly to property, yet perhaps we get as much light on the conditions and even the psychology of family and household life from them as from any source we have—on the relations between men and their wives, and between parents and children, mistress and servant, self and community. Some of the wills, though firstly economic documents, are highly civilised, careful expressions of duty, not narrowly conceiceived. Something of this quality pervaded the little community: we hear little of cruelty, nothing of witchcraft, much of responsibilities well discharged.

Family relationships depend largely on the fact that the family lived very directly on the produce of the farm and of the manor, and that the women had to turn the raw produce into food and clothes and bedding. Not only that: they tended the small stock. A woman needed ability and enterprise as well as a liking for hard work; and if she had all these they brought her some regard: she not only was, but was recognised as, an equal partner with her husband. It is well known that a man of tyrannical spirit might learn from Bible-reading to think a woman's sphere narrow and subordinate: a farmer might subscribe to such a view in theory. In practice when he surveyed his affairs before he made his will, he came to the conclusion that he had better make his wife his executor (or co-executor with one of his sons.) John Wright (1595) supports his wife's authority: his son is bidden to give her no trouble; if he does it shall be the worse for him. He is 'not to make or meddle with anything save that which is appointed to him' and is to 'order himself as he has done hitherto.' In another case a son's legacies depend on his being loving and diligent to his mother's interests. Husbands sometimes allot their wives formidable tasks—tasks they themselves have failed in. They owe money which their widows must pay and also they must invest money for their children. Thomas Cook (1614) has mortgaged certain lands and hopes his wife will redeem them. Thomas Cury (1616) dying worth no more as to goods and chattels than £125 calls upon his wife to pay a debt of £74, almost certainly a mortgage, beside smaller debts, and also to save a further £80 to give his daughters on their twenty-first birthdays. She is also to conduct the holding so that his son and heir, who will meanwhile be a royal ward, shall receive it in as good condition as it had come to the testator. This may be the madness of a household tyrant; it is not that of a Victorian husband of a wife he considers incapable.

Daughters too, are quite handsomely treated, in both fathers' and mothers' wills; their legacies are usually equal to their brothers' except where one of the latter is going to carry on the farm with his mother. The lives of spinsters are very tolerable: Anne Andrews (1615) has a well-furnished house and good clothes: her neighbours—commoners and shepherds—are in debt to her to the tune of sixteen guineas.

The number of sons and daughters varies very much. The Grayhurst families are for a while very large, in two cases twelve children, but others are mostly small. Yet heirs are often many, for grandchildren get a share; and also, it is interesting to note, godchildren figure in many wills: they get at any rate a token of love or recognition.

One of the most humane of the wills is that of a bachelor, Thomas Andrews (1588) who leaves money to his brothers and sisters, uncles, nephew and niece; his residuary legatees are to maintain his cousin Anne all her life. No doubt she suffers some disability: she is to do what work she can for her hosts. A Bledington girl of to-day who had to go back to some earlier era would not make a mistake in choosing Elizabeth's reign.

An important difference from other times and classes may be noted; it is often the youngest son who carries on the farm: the older ones had been hived off to farms or crafts in other villages.

The occasion of will-making is of much interest. A lawyer must have been required to provide the rather elaborate framework—including the full title of the sovereign (Philip, husband of Queen Mary, rules half the world it seems!) and to act as amanuensis. Surely only a professionally trained person could marshal all the detail of some of the wills. Like much else of life at this time, the will-making is very public. There are often half a dozen witnesses. Two executors are named and also two overseers, who may or may not be among the witnesses. The function of the overseers is to survey the execution of the will, seeing that all is fair, aboveboard and complete.

An example of the discharge of duty by overseers is seen in the case of a young man's will. On his death-bed he is so far childless but his wife is pregnant. He provides that money shall be saved for his child, on his sixteenth birthday. But this was not done: we find his will embedded in the papers of a lawsuit brought by an overseer against the son's mother and step-father more than 21 years later. Overseers are sometimes called upon to put out money for the benefit of orphans, their responsibility continuing for a very long time. How they invested funds remains something of a mystery. With no bank and no public stock to buy what could they do? By the early seventeenth century and perhaps a few years before, mortgages could be bought but these were usually for larger sums than the legacies. One supposes that overseers sometimes took the sheep or cattle with their own stock and paid a rent for them.

It is very noticeable, how the husbandmen depend upon each other. The clever Grayhursts, soon to rise somewhat in life, the solid Andrewses and Wrights make poorer Hulls and Guys their overseers and even executors, and are willing to serve them in their turn.

All this neighbourliness among the husbandmen matches the communal decisions they still make about the planting and harvesting of crops, the choice of officers, the regulation of the use of the common pastures. We should remember too, that they are still choosing their tithing man, and briefing him for the meetings of the Hundred Court. The young men have still the duty to practice their archery together at the parish butts: the churchwardens have many a civic duty. Some-day separate farms will give fine scope to a man's individual force and intelligence: produce from the land will increase. But meanwhile Bledington men might agree with Mr Krushchev's assertion that a man's joy lay not merely in the fact of living 'but in living consciously in the collective and for the collective, and this is the happiness and the reward.'[26] Even if this power has not been totally lost by our villages, it is now difficult to conceive a great degree of it,

For lack of letters or diaries to indicate personal experiences and affections, of accounts to tell us of the business aspects of farming, and of inventories to give us details of implements and furniture we may make the most of a single detailed will. Agnes Wright's will made in 1612 affords us a view of some intimacy into one home and family. We have no date of birth for her, but a study of her husband's will and her own leads to the conclusion that she was at least 60 years old in

1612. She must have been born some years before Elizabeth came to the throne and was on the youthful side of middle age when the Armada came. She was thus an Elizabethan woman. Her father and brother were husbandmen in Bledington throughout the sixteenth century: only in 1599 does one of them take to himself the title 'yeoman'—by then a fashionable term. The line of Wrights continues into the middle of the next century.

Wrights are established folk, able to make pretty substantial bequests, and good folk, remembering their shepherds, servants and the poor in their wills. We cannot tell for certain in which house Agnes lived. There are two possibilities: Harwood's and the old steward's house, the only houses large enough, at her marriage, to contain parlour and spence (larder-storeroom).

Agnes had reared three sons and two daughters: when she made her will she had forty relatives to remember, beside four godchildren. Her husband had made her executrix of his will, with her son Giles acting as co-executor and taking on the work of the fields. The parents had had, it seems, a little trouble with their eldest son William. He is bidden—it has been mentioned—in his father's will[27] "not to make nor meddle." Giles, her youngest son, continues to live with his mother, never marries and when he dies in 1599 she is left his sole executor, and after a few legacies to his relatives and his shepherds, sole heir to his rights to the house and holding.

Agnes was fully equal to this charge. When she makes her will she has efficient and well-loved assistants in her house and on the land. These are a married couple, daughter and son of neighbour husbandmen, never referred to as servants. There are servants of lower status 'about' (that is, roundabout) 'the house.' She has lent money to no fewer than 23 of her neighbours in Bledington and Kingham and leaves an account of their debts: the sum (£34) does not sound impressive. Few of her legacies are monetary: these amount to £34.

In 1612 she has living in the house with her a grand-daughter Mary Wright as well as the couple, Jane and Richard Hathaway. Richard 'guides' her workmen and Jane is her right hand in the house, Mary being but a 'maiden.' Agnes loved the 'worldly goods which the Lord of his great goodness had lent her.' She knew each—the red stripe in the blanket, the band round the mended kettle, the seam in the towel, the use of every barrel and every sieve, the contents of every 'copper.' These are the nearest and dearest things, but she is the owner also of crops in the fields, of cows, pigs, cocks, hens and pigeons; she assumes that her will may control the house for a winter season after her death, but she does not leave house or land, horses or oxen: they are not entirely hers and to whom they pass we do not learn, for her son and partner has died.

Her chief concern appears to be for Joan Midwinter, her daughter, and for Jane and Richard Hathaway. Her care for the latter is partly prudent care for her own affairs: their legacies depend upon the continuance of their work for her. Joan Midwinter and the Hathaways are to share the crops that are growing at the time of her death, or 'guided to be sown' (by the oarsmen and other senior commoners) 'in the dead year next after' her decease. Her daughter Joan is perhaps like herself, a widow and husbandwoman. At any rate Agnes's first and most important legacies to her are agricultural—four bushels of winter corn, four of 'mault' and two quarters of barley, beside the winter corn growing on Dunstall or the Owres (Oars) the pulse growing on Hangasson Hill, or within Fromdon Hedge, or on Brad-mid (Broadmead) Hill, and some hay. The Hathways are to have the white corn within Fromdon Hedge or on Bradnam (Broadenham) Hill, and the hay growing in Chief Meadow and Dole Meadow. They are also to share with Mistress Midwinter the wood in the woodhouse and yard.

Daughter Joan is to have in addition a goodly hamper of the house-hold implements and articles of furniture, and Jane Hathaway a substantial though smaller share. There are enough of these together with linen and Agnes's garments for forty other relatives to share. The will gives us much more detail than many an inventory; for Agnes has used every implement and made and mended many of the small things. Many tools and vessels have been used in making and pre-serving food and drink. There are lidging barrels in which the barley lies to germinate for malt, a varge or verjuice barrel, presumably for pickling, 'powdering tubs' for preserving, a cheese press and cheese blankets. Cheese is made on a scale; eighteen cheeses are specifically bequeathed and there is a remainder to be divided between two heirs. Mustard and spice are ground at home in mill and mortar. Agnes has at least two 'dowe coypers' or dough kivvers,[28] one 'broche' for great baking, and a small one, in which she kneads bread, and a 'new churn' for butter. She has many uses for salt: there are two salt barrels in the spence, beside bacon and beef already brined. Two ale benches show another activity: one has been promoted to some use in her bedroom, the other is where it belongs in the spence. Does Agnes make some sort of barley wine? She has a 'wyne seve.'

Not only food is made. There is a 'linen tourne' or spinning wheel, and much hemp about the house. Hemp is grown in the fields, and where Agnes does not specify that her sheets are of linen, they are almost certainly, like her neighbours', 'hempen.' Shoes are made or mended at home, perhaps by Richard Hathaway: at any rate the 'irin foot and wedge' are left to him.

Many implements and vessels are of general use. 'Pantens'—which I take to be the great red or brown pottery vessels, 'Pansions' that still stood about old-fashioned farm kitchens forty years ago—stood about the spence, to hold cream, or ale, or vinegar. There are numbers of sieves and 'barke' and 'joyne' (wooden) shovels. Outside the house, in some shed or woodhouse there are ladders, a long one and a shorter 'elmen' one; 'stonnen' and wooden pig troughs a winnowing sheet, beside bags she needed for many purposes; there are 'two strike' (or gallon) and 'three strike' grist bags, a 'lethar' grist bag, a one strike bag filled with malt.

A 'great new pail' and a 'water crocke' stand at the back door. Empty' barrels are ready for use—'lidging' barrels and drie barrels and a clothes barrel; was the family linen steeped before being washed in the brook?

The animals in the yard and close are Agnes's to leave; cows (six are bequeathed), pigs, 'my cockes and hens and pigeons.'

Of the house we learn something, because objects are identified by their position in the rooms. The 'chamber' is over the hall or general living room; stairs lead up to it and there is a stair-head on which stands a demi-wake—if I but knew what that is!

In the chamber Agnes sleeps and so, in the 'maiden's bed,' does her grand-daughter Mary Wright. Between the two beds is a window and under it a small coffer. The mistress's own bed is left to Jane Hathaway, with 'all the furniture that is about him'—sheets, blankets, coverlid—together with more sheets 'of the best' and a blanket with a red line. Mary's bed is left to herself and is not described.

Jane and Richard Hathaway sleep in the house on one of the 'second best, beds, made of wool; the mistress's and the maiden's may have been of feathers. There is no indication as to where the second bedroom was—possibly off the hall, at the opposite end from the spence.

The hall is never clearly referred to, but we gather that it was old-fashioned and bare. It contains no 'joyne-table,' but 'table bords' with frames to lay them on, and 'formes' for seats, but there are 'quissings' to lay on these. There is one 'cheyre' only and one stool. In 1572 Agnes Andrews had a 'painted cloth' to bequeath, but Agnes Wright, th ugh as well to do as she, had nothing of this aesthetic kind. (The only oevi-dence of a special feeling for colour and household comeliness is the description of the 'coverlids' of the beds; they are 'green' and 'red and white'). At the fireplace in the hall are the usual fire-shovels, pot-hooks and links and andirons. On shelves (which themselves are bequeathed) are pewter platters, wooden trenchers, and brass candlesticks, with a little pot (a 'posnet)' and spoons—nothing it seems of silver. Together with her other linen (a good supply of sheets and coverlids) Agnes leaves 'bord cloths) and table-napkins, used at meals.

At one end of the hall is the spence. From this she leaves the shelves to a nephew. Here, no doubt, were the cheeses, the butter, the salted beef and bacon, together with the barrels of salt and some of the malt. It must have been commodious.

Agnes, like other women of the time, values her clothes and be-queathes them with care. The sole legacy to her sister Grayhurst is her 'best medley apron'—made, no doubt, of the 'linsey-wolsey' that Shakespeare mentions. (How long did this stuff wear? How long did it continue to be woven? I wore a remnant of it when I was a child in 1902). Other aprons are of linen and holland and one goes undescribed She possesses three suits of 'appell' (apparel?) her best being made of 'baphet' or taffeta. She has also two smocks (to cover her when she wears her best clothes?), a partlett[29] and a carchon.[30] But she is not a great lover of clothes: sixty years earlier her husband's mother had left almost as many—kirtles, kerchiefs, neckbands, petticoat, smock and cap, beside aprons.

All these objects are bequeathed with much consideration, it seems, of individual claims and needs, and with great precision. If a daughter is left sheets they are 'best' or 'second-best.' A grand-daughter's kettle is the mended one with 'a band round it'; the destiny even of a patched towel is specified. But certainly there is no meanness here. Barring accidents, cloth wore indefinitely long and the patch had been put on we may suppose by the mistress's own hands. She knows though, that she has set great tasks in all these detailed assignments. Perhaps no one—certainly not a male executor or overseer—would carry it out but Jane Hathaway. It will take her many weeks: she is allowed to remain in the house a whole winter.

As we would expect, Agnes has not forgotten the church or the poor. Her gifts to these are generous, as such bequests go—18 pence each to the bell ringers, to 'the poor of the town' twelve shillings. It is Agnes who leaves a shilling for the repair of Smenham (Smettenham) Bridge. Her 'servants about the house' are to have sixpence each. But there is also a special bequest to the poor: at her funeral twelve shillings are to be spent upon penny loaves for poor folk and children. Further, on that occasion, one pound is to be 'otherwise bestowed in meals.' This is comparatively a lot of money, but if all her 44 heirs are to be fed, it is not too much.

Her executor is not a relative but a member of the Pegler family, living in the old part of what is now called 'Hangerson House.' Agnes also appoints four overseers, all husbandmen-neighbours.

She understands the workings of the open fields, and has a feeling for the needs of the community and the wayfarer.

We remember her numerous loans to neighbours: one notes too, her use of the word 'guide.' The oarsmen 'guide' the seed-sowing and Hathaway 'guides' her men: it is not the word a tyrant uses. Perhaps there was a little exuberance but hardly egotism about her arrangements for her funeral. Agnes had lived more than half a life-time under a great Queen. We have seen Bledington affected throughout the centuries by the visions and theories and drift of the central government. Was the husbandwoman affected by the example and the character of a Queen at once princely and practical, who could declare[31] that if she were turned out of the realm in her petticoat, she were able to live in any place in Christendom, and who is not loth to imagine herself a dairymaid;[32] and who is known to be willing to listen to speeches on farming in the Cotswolds?[33] And who perhaps recalls that she had (as I read somewhere) a yeoman ancestor, a Boleyn. At any rate both held their own as heads of their households, and liked to rule 'with their loves.' Perhaps the Queen was the more plagued towards the end of her life by men who think women divinely ordained to be inferior. Agnes was fortunate to live in an economy and a community where such a view could hardly grow up.

Elizabethans, excited by the advance of their time, felt themselves to be at the growing tips of life and Agnes Wright was a moderm woman, master of the newest women's skills of her day. Probably no farmers' wives would surpass her in the skills of house, kitchen, still and dairy till they atrophied for lack of usefulness.

[1] Dom David Knowles. The Religious Orders in England. 1959. Vol. III, p. 92
[2] i.e. the Landboc
[3] Dictionary of National Biography
[4] G.D.R. Hockaday Abstracts Consistory Court 1576
[5] G.D.R. Bledington Wills 1572
[6] Stephen Neill. *Anglicanism* Penguin Books 1958 p. 666
[7] James Gairdner, *Bishop Hooper's Visitation* 1551. English Historical Review, Jan. and Oct. 1904, p. 109
[8] Issued 1543. Contained the Creed, Seven Sacraments, Ten Commandments, Lord's Prayer
[9] *Calendar of Letters and Papers Foreign and Domestic* Henry VIII Vol. XXI, Pt. 2 (1546)
[10] (i) G. D. R. Hockaday Ecclesiastical census 1563. (ii) G.D.R. 20/75 Hockaday Abstracts. Churchwardens' Report 1563
[11] G.D.R. Hockaday 181 (1633)
[12] W. G. Hoskins *Harvest Fluctuations.* Agricultural History Review 1964 Pt. I
[13] In Winter 1596 a rising was planned in the Witney area. Enclosures as well as very high corn prices were widely resented. V.C.H. Oxfordshire Vol. I pp. 194–6
[14] J. Smith *Men and Armour.* 1608
[15] G.D.R. Winchcombe Abbey, Rental 1355
[16] Wilmot *Gloucestershire* 1590–1640. 1940 Oxford, p. 262
[17] The custom of recording a tenant's terms of holding in a minute of the court and giving the tenant a copy of it was much older on some manors
[18] W. G. Hoskins *Harvest and Hunger.* Journal of Agricultural History Vol. XII Pt. I
[19] Edited by G. E. Fussel *Robert Loder's Farm Accounts* 1610–1620 London 1936
[20] W. B. Willcox Gloucestershire 1590–1640 Yale 1940 p. 9
[21] Leigh documents. Shakespeare's Birthplace Trust, Stratford-on-Avon
[22] Subsidies were exceptional taxes, levied at varying intervals
[23] Leigh documents. Shakespeare's Birthplace Trust
[24] Hockaday abstracts, *Fifteenth Century, Bledington.* Reference to the will of Richard atte Brooke. G.D.R.
[25] List of Wills G.D.R. p. 106, No. 30
[26] The Times. April 18th, 1964
[27] John Wright, 1595
[28] Wooden trough-like vessels in which dough was kneaded
[29] Neckerchief or ruff
[30] Meaning unknown
[31] J. E. Neale *Elizabeth I and her Parliaments* Part III, p. 149. Cope London 1965
[32] Ibid. Part IV, Ch. V, p. 366
[33] (i) Sir Egerton Bridges ed., *Speeches delivered to Queen Elizabeth . . . on her visit . . . at Sudeley Castle.* pp. 8, 9
(ii) W. B. Wilcox, *Gloucestershire* 1590–1640 Yale 1940, p. 8, 9

chapter five

THE SEVENTEENTH CENTURY

QUEEN ELIZABETH HAD seen many changes in the intellectual and religious life of the nation as well as in trade and daily life. Skills in iron and pottery making had developed; London was using coal from north-eastern mines; textiles were being developed. Cargoes of spices and cottons and silks were coming from the East. England had trade with her colonies in America and some traffic with many European countries. There were by 1603, when the Queen died, large classes of active business people—merchants, manufacturers, shopkeepers, owners of mines and ships—all that is covered by such vague expressions as 'development of industry and commerce.'

There was an associated development of village skills. Woollen textiles had made great strides in our locality: the master blanket weavers of Witney were laying the foundations of modest family fortunes and were interested in trade with distant foreign lands. Even in Bledington and Kingham the means of livelihood had become more varied. The apprenticeship system was not often applied in villages, though craftsmen trained in towns found their way to them. Farmers had been in a rough way their own carpenters if not smiths; they possessed apparatus for coopering. A man of natural tendency to skill could earn a living by a self-taught craft. By 1608 Bledington had a shoemaker, a tailor and a butcher. Later—in 1670 and 1679—a blacksmith and a weaver made wills. More women were spinning.

The professions were growing in knowledge: even medicine was throwing off superstition; the knowledge and practice of hygiene grew slowly. The clergy were expected to be better informed as to their church's doctrines and were—conformist and dissenting alike—well able to read and write and fairly well-read in the Bible. The most developed profession of all—or so it seems to a reader of village documents—was the law. Attorneys and solicitors could earn a living in every small town. The extent to which their services were understood and used by small copyholders and free holders and even labourers of the superior sort is surprising. Many who could not themselves read and write sent for a solicitor as for doctor or tailor.

Craftsmen and tradesmen found it necessary to keep accounts, to do which they needed to read and write a little. By half way through the century husbandmen also felt the need of letters for their business. Up to now they had little need of reckoning as they were still farming largely for subsistence, but they were accumulating some cash and often possessed some money or had debtors. Mortgages of land have already been mentioned. Not so far away Robert Loder of Harwell, though an open-field farmer, kept careful figures of his sales and purchases and was as keen on the financial results of his business as a twentieth century member of the National Farmers' Union. Habits of counting have effects on minds. They lead to a liking to sum and to save. Miserliness can exist in every degree and the possession of money leads to social ambition. Accounting was a factor in the immense changes in village living which came about in the next century.

Literacy for practical purposes was accompanied by the spread of religious literacy. Surveying the reign of Elizabeth's successor, James I, the publication of the Authorised Version of the Bible was its most influential event. It was a complete, scholarly edition based on Tyndale's work, employing his rhythmic and truly English phrasing. It gave a great impulse to the desire for the Bible, which had been long widespread. Of course only active and intelligent persons read it but these were not rare: there had been no 'brain-drain' from the villages. So began the love for literature that would be the solace and art of many country people, poor and less poor, for centuries.

Those who read the Bible when it was a novel thing to do were forced to think. Some thought passionately and crudely, others with more balance. So there came to be numbers in the countryside who could not honestly conform within Archbishop Laud's very authoritarian Church. In our own area there was a fairly large proportion of dissenters.

To this rapidly changing people came a new dynasty. The Stuarts were a very different family from the Tudors. James I who was welcomed in 1603, his son Charles I, and his two grandsons Charles II and James II—Kings of England with an interval till 1689—shared with variations a single outlook. They claimed immense powers through their 'divine right', going so far at times as to declare that it was presumptuous in subjects to question the actions of the sovereign, that it was within the royal prerogative to suspend laws and to levy taxes upon subjects at their own discretion. There were continental countries where such a claim to absolutism had been asserted with a high degree of success but in the early seventeenth century in England, growing as it was in wealth and in political and religious interest, it was unlikely to be so easily accepted. Some sections of the people were as doctrinaire as the sovereigns, but holding different views. Just when some means of tempering minds was most urgent, the King's claims prevented Parliament from playing in this role. In less than forty years a physical struggle had become inevitable—one that would involve every village in England.

Of religious strife, if not of political, Bledington must have known something. James I meant to favour neither Catholic nor Protestant dissenters from the Church. Before he had been on the throne two years disappointed Catholics excluded from all power appalled the country by their Gunpowder Plot. They had aimed at disrupting the government by destroying King and Parliament together. In common with all England, Bledington rang its bells—four small bells—with fervour, and surely called 'Amen!' with one voice when the special service of thanksgiving was read each succeeding year on November 5th. The service was printed in the Book of Common Prayer and together with the custom of bonfires celebrating the plot, strengthened the popular attitude to the Pope and his Church which was to last so long.

Towards Protestant dissenters James showed no more toleration than to Catholics. Those who would not conform should be—in words believed to be his own—'harried out of the country.' The Puritans were not a single party. Some continued to struggle within the church; Presbyterians, followers of Calvin in his clear-cut logical views had a foothold in Elizabeth's Articles of Religion and hoped to capture the whole Church and insist in their turn on uniformity. Independents did not object to a national church but claimed a larger freedom for each congregation in various matters. Since under James and still more Charles I there was less and less of accommodation within the Church, they tended to split off into small independent 'congregational' churches. This was an indirect way to toleration: they expected others to be free to do the same. Later in the century (from 1648) there would be Quakers, developing their doctrine of the Inner Light, the direct illumination of the individual soul.

The great opponent of all these was William Laud, Archbishop of Canterbury from 1633 but influential long before. He had a vision of a united and all powerful Church-cum-State. He believed that he cared for justice but tried to impose his chosen, somewhat mediaeval pattern of society by arbitrary and primitive methods of enforcement upon a people moved by powerful tides of change.

Our own vicar in 1603 at the accession of the first Stuart was a relative of Sir John Cooke who in 1550 had shown himself so inadequately instructed. In 1606 Parson John Cooke II was called upon, like other clergymen, formally to accept all thirty-nine Articles. Hitherto it had been sufficient to subscribe to those concerning faith and sacrament. We shall find him conforming to requirements— wearing a surplice, for example.

The laity were also subject to discipline. It was the duty of church-wardens to report offences to the diocesan Consistory Court. From its records we draw a short story concerning our parish.[4] David Rylands was 'presented' to the Court for carrying corn on St. Bartholomew's Day (August 24th) in 1604. (Puritans wished to pay less attention to Saints Days and more to Sundays as holy sabbaths but orthodoxy wished still to celebrate the saints). The churchwardens had ridden the thirty miles to Gloucester to report him to the officer in the little Court Room in the south-west corner of the Cathedral. David was ordered publicly to confess his fault and to pay a fine. This he refused to do and was later excommunicated for several months. The term of this sentence wore away and on Sunday morning, February 3rd, the day after Candlemas, in 1606, Rylands went with his wife to church. They arrived after the service had begun while the Vicar was reading the prayers. Mr Cooke (so he is called in the evidence recorded) saw the two Rylands enter. He ceased to read and asked David whether he had with him the certificate of discharge from excommunication. 'No,' replied David: he had served his sentence and that was all the discharge he had. The parson then bade him leave the church: he dare not, he said, read prayers with an excommunicant present. The Rylands couple made no move to go out, so the Vicar ('curate' is the word used, but the sense is not what the word bore later) left the 'chaire' or 'pewe' where he had been reading and took off his surplice. The altercation continued till David went out, threatening the parson. Elizabeth, Ryland's wife, followed her husband, repeating his threats: the parson 'would have to answer elsewhere' for what he was doing. Unfortunately she saw Cooke 'laugh': perhaps he smiled from relief of tension. 'Sir John,' Elizabeth threatened, would soon 'laugh in another place' —a classic type of expression in brawling!

The account of this disturbed service was given in the Consistory Court in much detail by no fewer than four persons who hade been there—Loggan, Stayt, Mince and Hathaway. Unfortunately the entry lacks some essential detail, as well as its ending. Had David Rylands seen a shortage of bread ahead of his family—for these were years of disastrous harvests—and felt innocent and resentful? We do not learn whether he was tactfully given his discharge, which seems to have been due to him, or whether he was required to accept a further punishment. And if he refused would he have to leave the village—not an easy thing for a poor commoner to do—to begin life in another diocese?

It is impossible to imagine such a scene in the church during the fifteenth century. Much of the effect of the sacredness of the service, the beauty of the building, was not felt as it had been: there had been too many drastic changes. Perhaps the husbandman-parson lacked impressiveness though a worthy man. At all events, the scene is one to remember when, presently, other changes originating with the heads of the church, are insisted upon.

There are three other references to Bledington's shortcomings and misdemeanours in the records of the Consistory Court. The church-wardens report that the bells are out of order in 1633,[3] and in 1634 that William Lord has broken the Sabbath. But Lord defends himself. One Sunday in Lent his man had stopped a hole in the thatch of his barn 'because the wind was extraordinarily great.'[4] Anyone who has seen the wind tearing away old thatch will think that there may have

The ancient stone fencing (See p. xxii). The house, a happy example of conversion; once farm buildings, then two cottages since about 1930, one house.

Air photograph of Bledington, April 1946. (By permission of The Ministry of Defence (Air Force Department). *Crown Copyright Reserved.*

been misdemeanours of tale-bearing or that churchwardens render a too formal obedience to the duty of reporting. But if we turn to the presentations for other parishes we find many examples of Sabbath-breaking—shearing sheep, and travelling, for example, and 'railing against a preacher.' Another type of case, of which examples are not infrequent, is adultery. Here, again, Bledington's record is not frequently blotted, but its one case of trouble of this kind is severe. In 1633 a member of an ancient copyholding family, honourably knitted into the fabric of the community for centuries past and to come, was presented 'for incest with his own sister's daughter'—a rather circumstantial story. The girl 'being near her deliverance' had been sent to Temple Guiting. In such a case as this, villagers could be cruel: it is as well for the girl to leave. One likes to think that the rarity of crime, petty and great, on the part of Bledington people was due to the strength of bonds within the community—the intermarriage between families of varying acreage, the large number of small public offices calling for responsibility and efficiency, the co-operative and neighbourly nature of open-field farming. Even the 'servants' were often members of old families and subject to the same firm public opinion.

Village Arts

The most serious religious outlook due to the reading of the Bible led to a desire to convert the English Sunday to a Holy Sabbath, a day of rest and contemplation and purity. Many were attracted to this ideal beside the Puritans guyed at Banbury in the couplet

'He hung his cat of a Monday
For killing of a mouse of a Sunday.'

It had been usual for various sports to be practised on Sundays as on other festival days of the Church. There was everywhere the official, prescribed practice of archery at the village butts, part of the duty of all able-bodied men. This was gradually losing its military usefulness but continued out of custom and as a sport. In our area on Sunday evenings there was the game of Aunt Sally, in which a bow-shaped 'pin' was thrown at a highly-coloured doll: great skill was required to hit in one. There was putting the disc on the green: one of the discs can still be seen in the King's Head. The Morris Men would practise outside the church while the bells rang and leave service promptly after Morning Prayer to dance again. All these sports were quiet enough but there were rougher games, shin-kicking and the like, and some drinking.

Before this period, and long after it also, in our nearby villages and over much of the country the church made use of the Morris and other dances at annual Church Ales, often at Whitsuntide, when money was collected for church maintenance. Our own churchwardens' accounts begin too late for proof but it is safe to assume that the practice held here. Often churchwardens bought bells and other equipment for the dancers. Thus, the local churches were identified with folk dance and song and defended them when Puritans attacked them as desecrating the Sabbath.

The controversy became political: Parliament adopted the Puritan view, forbidding Sunday pastimes by statute, while King James and his Court identified themselves with the Bishops in defence of the old Sunday. In 1617 he issued for the use of certain magistrates his instructions that archery and other innocent sports and merrymaking were to be permitted on Sundays: these days were not the Jewish Sabbath but a festival of the Church. The next year James ordered that the Book of Sports should be read from every pulpit. Perhaps the reading in Bledington did something to sustain the Morris and country dancers.

It so chanced that in 1611 or 1612 Robert Dover, a local lawyer and steward of estates, visited the Whitsun Ales at Campden (now known as Chipping Campden) and Weston sub Edge which were jointly held on Kingcombe Plain, part of the high 'edge' between the market town and the small village. He was enchanted by what he saw. The hill faces the great valley of the Avon and the Severn, the Plain being a small plateau interrupting a long slope. Dover saw it as a wonderful site for a great gathering. He was a man of enthusiastic temperament who had studied at Gray's Inn and made acquaintance with poets and scholars in London. His numerous friends in the country included some who had access to the royal Court, where the King enjoyed and encouraged music and musicians.

When Dover first saw the 'Ales', games and sports were more prominent than Morris dancing. 'Cotsall Games,' says Mr Whitfield[5] 'were of a rough, manly and plebeian nature'; they included wrestling, vaulting, pitching the bar, leap-frog and shin-kicking. Dover took his friends along to applaud and they offered prizes and began to take part in the more elegant fun, such as archery and handling the pike. At this time 'gentry' were becoming more numerous in the countryside, because of the free market in land, large estates being broken up (as here in Bledington) and on the other hand farms or holdings gathered into one by ambitious local men. From sixty miles around small landowners and farmers brought their ladies each year to the festival. Dover's jovial, friendly and picturesque presence (he is said to have ridden around in fine clothes from the king's own wardrobe) made a focus. The London visitors brought choirs to sing new songs and to show dances collected around London. In fact as at the Aldeburgh and Edinburgh Festivals today artists were brought together to stimulate each other and the public enjoyed and tested, and incidentally supported their work.

It has been suggested to me by Mr Rolf Gardiner that Dover's Games may provide a partial explanation of the quality and persistence of popular art, especially dancing, in a wide area hereabouts— and explanation is certainly called for. But there was evidently a plentiful local basis, not only of the famous dances and mumming plays but of song also. There were beside the ancient inheritance we have already noted[6] many songs if not dances which had arisen in Tudor times. The Gloucestershire Wassail, said to be especially associated with Stow, was ancient:

> Wassail! Wassail! all over the town
> Our toast it is white and our ale it is brown;
> Our bowl it is made of the maplin tree;
> We be good fellows all. I drink to thee.

Very old also was the song of the painful plough:

> Come all you jolly ploughmen
> Of courage stout and bold
> To clothe the fields with plenty
> Your farmyards to renew,
> To crown them with contentment
> Behold the painful plough.

There was an old song of Henry VIII's time a phrase or two of which recalls the terms used in Manor Courts:

> Quoth John to Joan wilt thou have me?
> I pray thee now, wilt? And I'se marry with thee.
> My cow, my calf, my horse, my rents,
> And all my lands and tenements:

131

Oh, say, my Joan will not that do?
I cannot come every day to woo.

These songs were recorded early and sung widely. Bledington had its own May Day song, very similar to those of many villages:

Gentlemen and ladies
I wish you happy day.
I'm come to show my garland
Because it's first of May.

The courtly song of Greensleeves was too elaborately and 'sumptuously' worded (that was one of its own expressions) to become a rustic song but it was heard hereabouts. It is parodied in the Idbury version of the Christmas Mummers' Play:[8]

Greensleeves and yellow lace,
Get up, you bitch, and work apace
Your father lies in an awful place
All for want of money.

The last two quotations show songs in degeneration, but originally the words, though sometimes coarse, had quality. Dance and song, ballad and play were hardly separate arts. Shipton under Wychwood had a play apparently based on Robin Hood ballads. Sometimes as in at least one of the Bledington dances the team sang as it danced: accompaniments to songs provided the music for most of the dances. Songs alluded to and even described the dances, and plays made use of them.

In the merry month of June
In the prime of the year,
Down in yonder meadows
There runs a river clear
And many a little fish
Doth in the river play
And many a lad and many a lass
Go abroad making hay.

Then joining in a dance
They jig it o'er the green;

> Though tired with their labour
> No-one the worse was seen
> But sporting with some fairies
> Their dance they did pursue
> In leading up and casting off
> Till morning was in view.[9]

Shakespeare, in his eclectic way, seems to have had this haytime song in his mind in his invitation to a harvest dance:

> You sunburned sicklemen of August weary
> Come hither from the furrow and be merry.
> Make holiday, your rye-straw hats put on,
> And these fresh nymphs encounter everyone
> In country footing.[10]

The Cotsall Games were an annual event till 1643 and had seemed likely to continue indefinitely but the Civil War broke out and the Campden area was traversed by troops again and again. Young men had to join the militia or became officers on one side or the other. The Games were never resumed.[11]

After the War folk sports, dance and song suffered some general decline. Renaissance and Italian styles at Court made them seem rustic though the dances survived there. Puritan villages became deserts of such arts and in others like our own they came gradually to be confined to the poor, all but totally unknown to other classes. Yet in some parts of the country very many old and lovely songs continued to be inherited. In our own area dances still survived in numbers and in fine style. Even here the 'country' or social dances—though Bledington has still its Maypole round which they were danced—died away; it was the Morris and the jigs, danced by men only, that remained. The teams or 'sides' of Morris Men met in small festivals and competitions of their art in neighbouring villages. There came to be emulation in journeys to Oxford and London, when the dancers gave evening displays on village greens en route. The joys of exacting techniques and the social pleasures of the meetings were for the 'sides' the highlights of life.

Before the Civil War folk dances, both ancient and newly composed, had been published in book after book in London. Earlier the dances had been pictured in tapestries and mentioned in literary works, but after the War they never appear in novels, country newspapers or

133

parsons' village histories. They disappear from view till the late nine-teenth century, almost till the twentieth. But it is necessary in our thoughts of the condition of Bledington still to remember that games and more especially dances continued to be the pleasure and solace of some labourers and through the worst times must have served, though unseen, to reduce the stresses in the community.

The End of the Manor: changes in Land Tenure

In the course of the seventeenth century our husbandmen's lives were to change in many ways. They would hold their lands on new terms; they enlarged their houses and perforce conducted operations on the open fields without the supervision of a manor court and a land-lord's steward. For them the Civil War was an interruption: it brought no immediate revolution to any class in Bledington, though the even-tual settling-down after it would in time have dire results.

Our sources of information are few but in addition to documents we can read something in stones and mortar. The most numerous writings are wills, with a number of inventories, the latter, with one exception, dated after 1676. Inventories afford us homely information giving us a view inside the houses, but seem to be defective in that they minimize change: there is reason to think the husbandmen's literacy and outlook and the value of their possessions change more than wills and inventories indicate. There are also mortgage deeds and these will always be important in the history of our farms till the golden days after the Second World War. The records of the Consistory Court have been referred to: there are also those of the Slaughter Hundred Court. Some papers of the Leigh family throw light on, first, changes in the manor, and then its disappearance. Copyholders cease to exist here.

The manor had become, as we know, the possession of a family, an investment destined to serve its purposes and to change with its varying circumstances. Sir Thomas Leigh who had acquired the manor together with others in 1553, made various dispositions of his property in 1571, the year in which he died. He gave a lease of the Bledington manor with three others to three gentlemen of the City of London—a member of Lincoln's Inn, a mercer. and a haberdasher, all business-men of substance and, like himself, landowners also. The lease was to terminate on his son's, Rowland's, death, or on the twenty-first birthday of Rowland's heir.[12]

134

Clearly, Sir Thomas's heir, Rowland, found some fault with the lease. He laid a claim to the 'manorial profits' of Bledington, not to the copyholders' rents but to income from the Manor Court. He appears to have sent his own representative to hold the Court: the leaseholders of the Manor were in the habit of doing the same. The two deputies met, it seems, and there were 'disturbances' as to which should hold the Court. The leaseholders secured peace by an acknowledgment that Leigh owned the reversion of the manor and an undertaking that he should receive a half of the 'profits'—i.e. of the customary heriots and fines levied by the Court.[13]

In 1587 occurred an arrangement in itself small, but of a new and important kind. With the consent of Rowland Leigh, the City gentlemen grant a lease to Robert Hathaway of a 'cottage called Snowes' together with the 'Court close' which we know to have been a small old enclosure in Chapel Lane very near to the Church, possibly where Church Cottages now stand.[14] This transaction indicates a willingness to grant leases: it can hardly have stood alone. We may take it that other leases of more important holdings were being arranged. When a lease was given the Lord of the Manor was able to break away from the customary rent and impose one at a modern rate. For the tenant there was gain: for the period of the lease he was independent of the Lord and the Manor. He could leave the remainder of the lease in his will, and no heriot would be payable at his death.

One document dated 1590[15] shows Rowland Leigh giving a 'quit claim' for the manor of Bledington; that is to say he makes a legal statement that he resigns all interest in the property in question Whatever the true meaning of this document may be in 1598 Leigh again becomes, by 'bargain and sale' the owner of the manorial rights.[16]

From about 1600, probably earlier, the reigning Leigh has a settled policy, not to lease holdings but to sell the manor piecemeal. To do this with fair rapidity the purchasers must be tenants, since they have customary rights, The dates when the sales were made are only known in one or two cases: we learn incidentally, chiefly from wills and morgages, that a holding has become the property of the one-time tenant, but only rarely the year of acquisition. Those tenants whose predecessors had, in 1538, rented parts of the demesne, acquire those lands as well as their copyholds. In these cases, it is usual in documents to describe first the old copyholds, and then to add an account of the section of the demesne which has been acquired. For example in mortgages of the Lord family from 1690, and in John Rooke's or Rucke's will of 1677 we read, after the account of the "messuage and tenement", of "petty farms" and "berridales". Both of these terms are restricted to ex-demesne lands. It is thought that the word "berri-dale", which is confined to this district, may be derived from "bury" or "borough", signifying the central settlement.[17] (If this suggestion implies that settlements were from the beginning manorial in organisation it might raise difficulties). As a measure "berridale" is the equivalent of about half a yardland, the latter term itself not being a precise measure of area, but rather of agricultural value. The earliest date we have for one of these purchases is 1611. A deed of the early eighteenth century reviews the history of the Baker holding from that date, when Thomas Baker bought from Leigh.[18] The will of Thomas Cooke dated 1614, shows that he owns the freehold of his messuage and tenement and also that the Ivinge family possesses land which they have leased to him. Thomas Guy making his will in 1616 writes of "my messuage lands and tenements". In 1624 William Leigh of Adlestrop, the owner of the remaining Leigh properties, sold to "William Lord, yeoman", "the water grist mill", with cottage and land. By 1649 the Hulles family had had the freehold of their messuage and close long enough to rebuild the house. Thomas Stayt's will (1625) shows that he has a long lease of his land. In addition, the Victoria County History referring to Chancery documents tells us that "in the early seventeenth century" Thomas Loggins, Andrew Phillips, Thomas Holford and John Rucke (or Rooke) have bought land.[19]

The monies possessed early in the century by the makers of wills were small: debts owing to them were £10, £20. And even the Holfords, relatively well to do, leave tiny monetary legacies. How then did copy-holders contrive to buy land? The answer can be given in one word: mortgages. Thomas Cooke dies in debt for £324. In 1611 Baker had to produce £146.

The history of mortgages and law relating to mortgages has its importance for Bledington. From the middle of the century, or in some cases earlier, farmers would be always in debt, using their holdings as sources of credit for their purposes. Always there were folk ready to lend money on land—London merchants recommended by solicitors, a Stayt of Kingham, who had been a sutler during the Civil War, a clergyman prospering in an office at Gloucester Cathedral, the widow of a collar-maker of Stow who had sold her husband's business, all canny folk refusing to risk money in the companies, then common, trading adventurously with the East Indies and other distant parts. In mortgages the great risks were at first the borrowers'. Interest could be as high as ten per cent. (When a Grayhurst lent a small sum to a neighbour Cooke he charged six per cent). A failure to pay interest on the appointed date might mean that a farmer's land was sold at the will of the lender, even if it was worth much more than the loan. Bledington men must have escaped these dangers, or they would hardly have followed each other in buying. One is tempted to suppose that at first the Leighs allowed gradual payment: they appear to have been usually just and reasonable men. Presently, interest rates settled down to a reasonable 5% or 4½% and in the main court of equity, the Chancery Court, the mortgager received full protection. We shall see that in the eighteenth century defaulting Bledington farmers receive tender consideration.

There is, then, evidence that ten families have freehold land early in the century. In addition Grayhursts appear to be owners of property in this village and elsewhere. The Gloucestershire historian, Atkyns,[20] tells us that there were in 1721 twenty-one freeholders in Bledington and that these were "lords of the manor". There is literal truth in this statement. Every purchaser of copyhold and demesne land shared in the "site and farm" of the manor, that is, had purchased the full lordship of what he bought. Practically nothing of the lordship was eventually left. There ceased to be a manor court ("no court, no manor"): the manorial records remain with the Leigh family. It is true that one farm, Bledington Grounds, when put up for sale has in the past been advertised as carrying with it the "reputed" lordship and that a single small manorial due was paid for a few years to one of its owners. Also documents are extant[21] which appear to suggest that members of the Leigh family have sold the manor to various indiviuals but scholars who have examined these find other meanings for them or doubts as to their meaning. Bledington had swung into modernity in respect of land ownership if in no other way.[22]

But the purchase of a freehold did not at all mean that a man had land in his exclusive control. We have a very full account of the Baker holding in 1710[23] from which we see how little change came over agriculture here in this century. Baker held 250 arable strips distributed in 207 locations. No more than three of his strips lie side by side in any furlong and the great majority lie singly between strips belonging to fellow commoners. Even the laying together of strips, let alone of larger areas, had hardly begun. Consequently there was still the need for communal regulation and to call miscreants to account.

Before considering how this was done now that there was in effect no manor, we may turn aside to the freeholders' homes, for the messuages were a different matter from the fields. A man's house began to be his castle. He could add to it or rebuild it without asking permission or for materials; he could sell it; he could leave it to whom he and his wife chose. Today when a poor old cottage is bought by its tenants it is soon transformed—bathroom and porch added, roof attended to, new windows put in, a fine 'Cotswold' wall built round the garden. Similar changes took place in the freeholders' homes.

It is not possible, as a rule, to find exactly when a house was enlarged. Documents only tell us that it contained certain rooms by the date of the document in question—not how long it had done so. Information from the buildings themselves can be misleading: for example, country practice in building may lag behind that of towns, but probably all but rough re-building here was carried out by masons from Stow, and the style of details might not be greatly later than contemporary practice. It may be well to remember that building must have almost ceased during the Civil War.

The first example of re-building takes us back well into the sixteenth century. On the holding known in the nineteenth century as the 'Home Farm' a brand new house was built on an ancient site, possibly after a fire. It was a model house, with the features that are still often reproduced in our area. It was built according to a plan frequently used, the pattern being exactly followed, although in varying sizes, so that an almost precise picture of the original Home Farm House may be seen in books on architecture.[24] It was not impressive by size: no room in the house was large. It had and still has (though incorporated now in a larger house) mullioned windows of decreasing proportions on its three floors. Within was one good room on ground and first floors, with finely chamfered fireplaces of stone brought from the west side of Cotswold. (How beautifully the firelight played upon the chamfering!) Beside the single room on the ground floor there was a space for general storage: and at the head of the narrow stair was an open space which would take a big bed, and beyond it the fine square chamber with two windows and its chamfered beams making a cross.

138

From this floor good stairs led to an attic stairhead and chamber. The walls of this house are of rubble thirty-three inches through.

The Home Farm House shows that comfort was understood fifty years before the seventeenth century. There are sufficient windows, designed for glazing without great expense, and fitted with shutters; the two main rooms can be easily warmed. No room within the house was suitable for large domestic operations, but a small barn-like building on a parallel line with the house, set a little further back, contained a rough kitchen and another room, spence or dairy. Like all the good sixteenth and seventeenth century houses it had a steep roof made handsome by the great overlapping stones. Experts have dated it as of 1550, by the moulding and chamfering of stone and wood and by the lettering of the name JOHN carved on a small window (suggesting literacy in the builder). It was a small but comely house and may well have served to some extent as a model when other houses were rebuilt. At the end of the sixteenth century nearly all the husband-men's houses still contained little more than hall, a small "parlour" opening from it, used generally a a "chamber" or bedroom, and a chamber over the hall, reached from it by a narrow stairway. The first improvement had been often to add a spence, or to build outside it a kitchen, separately or as a lean-to. As late as 1696 the Ivinges' house had a hall, with a chamber "below". i.e. off the hall, and one above. Ivinges had been described as yeomen earlier, but Thomas in 1696 is a tailor. We shall see that the craftsmen are less well off than those who follow agriculture: most of them lived in small houses, little improved. In 1659 Richard Buswell, a weaver, left in his will[25] a cottage he had very recently built, attached to the one he had bought from the Hulles family, built just before the Civil War. Each of these houses consisted of one room below and one above, with hovels in the backside for domestic purposes. The Hathaways' house had been well built in the early sixteenth century, with a hall and chamber and tiny stone-framed windows and so it remained till lately, always inhabited. But in the seventeenth century its interior was improved: it came to have three hearths[26]—in hall, chamber and kitchen—where once it had only one.

The more well to do husbandmen made more considerable changes in their houses. In a few cases we can be sure that this occurred before the Civil War. A house improved to a middling extent was that of Thomas Guy, who died in 1677.[27] The house had then its hall and "the lower chamber within the hall", and chambers over both these rooms. So far it is the old house but now there had been added a kitchen, "with a chamber over"; here the house itself has been extended. There are also a "buttery", probably opening from the kitchen, and a dairy house, entered from the yard.

Two houses had seen exceptional development before the Civil War. The old steward's house had reared its present high front over the "Yate" or street since the late fifteenth century. Then its roof had been raised and good chambers made. At that time or in the sixteenth century carved stone hearths had been inserted in two of the chambers. And in the early seventeenth century its owners decorated its ancient hall and parlour with a plaster-work frieze whose remains to this day are the most exotic decoration in the parish. Which family had such high taste remains a conundrum, but most probably that of a late steward of the manor.

The old steward's house remained, as it still does, our most impressive domestic building but it was surpassed in size by another house, which from being the messuage of a modest holding had passed to a relatively well to do family early in the sixteenth century. Their name was Lumbard, showing their Italian origin. They had entered this country through the wool trade, having bought wool in the Cotswolds in the fifteenth century. They not only enlarged the house: they introduced a new comfort by planting the first orchard in Bledington on a close at the back of the messuage, which continued to be known as Lumbard's Orchard when every vestige of the trees had vanished. This house (now known as Manor Farm) passed to the Loggans, another family of distant origin. They had come south from Scotland, members of the tribe buying land in Butlers Marston and Great Tew. Here the family settled down to become true Bledingtonians, marrying a son of the house to a Hathaway girl, acting as churchwardens, witnessing neighbours' wills and acting as "overseers" of them. In 1625 a Loggan was an overseer of the poor.

Although they became true village neighbours they retained some connections with the outer world and some prosperity. A member of the Idbury branch was a student of New College and when the Warden and Fellows visited their manor of Kingham in 1674 he gave them refreshment at his home.[28] We shall find reason to suppose them active royalists in the Civil War and in that exceptional.

Very early in the century they rebuilt their house, a little later in style and more spacious than the Home Farm's new building. Until 1956 this house still had its original front of singular harmony with an elegant though simple doorway, flanked by deep-moulded and mullioned windows. In 1662 it had no fewer than ten hearths,[29] reduced by 1672 to six.

We have seen that the comfort and the enlargement of houses have become an object with the yeomen and husbandmen. The exteriors of the new and rebuilt houses are very comely indeed. Was this beauty consciously admired and demanded? Or was it an incident in the search for light and improved shelter; or due to the wish for social status and prestige? No doubt motives were mixed and much was left to the masmasons: but certainly some features rise beyond the realm of pure utility and must have pleased eyes and minds. The improvement of the houses would be resumed after the Civil War and Bledington would become a village of some beauty. The contents of the houses seem to have undergone less development than the buildings themselves. From wills dated before 1642 we find that Thomas Guy in 1616 has only one chair. Ellis Grayhurst in 1635 is able to bequeath five chairs, a fine bedspread and a "chest with a spring lock". Tables continue to be formed of a "borde" and trestles; sheets are "hempen" still. No book or musical instrument appears—no evidence of literary or musical culture or of the visual arts. Even after the War such objects are strikingly absent. Yet it is as early as 1614 that Thomas Cooke, dying young, makes some provision for the education of his children till they are 14 years of age.

Open-field Farming after the Manor

With no lord or steward chairing the manor court other changes followed. From about 1600 commoners held their own meetings to arrive at decisions about their farming. There must have been a good deal of unofficial leadership at first, but two officers were available, the Oarsmen. When more than neighbourly discipline was needed, appeal was made to the Hundred Court of Slaughter, from time immemorial the court leet for Bledington. (It was not a novel thing to refer manorial offences to it: Great Rissington had still a manor court, but it stood in great need of disciplinary support and appealed to Slaughter for it).

The Slaughter Court was still formally known by its ancient name of Salmonsburie though it was very long since it had adjourned to Slaughter. It is described in its records[30] as "frank pledge, Hundred

Court and Court leet". A "bailiff" or "steward" deputed by the Sheriff of the County presided over it, with a jury to which each parish sent members. Each village still sent also to the meetings (held in April and November each year) a constable and a tithing man, the latter chosen by the "inhabitants" or the "commoners". These pay into the court at every meeting a certain fixed sum—e.g. Bledington 6s. 8d., Rissington Magna 7s. 9d. The earlier records of the meetings are fairly full, written in a fine script, and properly headed by the names of officers and jurymen. Later the writing is poor and only special items of business are recorded. Some fourteen parishes or manors report to the Court, with also a few tiny hamlets or farms which are, or have been, manors. The meeting would be one of perhaps fifty people, with bailiff and jury facing the village officers and any villagers who have accompanied them. It seems likely that the room was small: often the village deputations follow each other in, for the presentations from various villages preserve each its own style and each has its own selection of sins of omission and commission. For example, Bledington is the only village which reports (year after year) that its butts are out of order.[31] It does not seem likely that all others were well tended.

The Bledington officials report at first in a very impersonal way: the offences are regarded as communal—it is the whole community which is being "presented" as at fault. Sometimes "the brook" or "fence" itself is presented. The fine is to be paid by "us". Many of the offences are obviously in fact communal—the highway needs to be patched with stones, or the footbridge between Bledington and Foscote (the road still went through the brook) is broken down or the stocks on the village green need repair. (The last cannot have been often used: there is to be no fine if they are mended within six months, when the Court meets again).

But in 1632 some individuals are presented for failure in their duty to the highway. John Grayhurst although he was way-bailiff did not do his service, and Messrs. Lord, Hathaway and Holford have failed to carry stones. There are more personal misdemeanors. William Wright, the elder, has shed the blood of Thomas Pilmore "our town servant". Richard Tidmarsh has thrown "the excrement of his household into the street, to the annoyance of the highway". John Cooke has turned the stinking water from his yard, to the annoyance of Thomas Ivinge; a man whose name is illegible has dammed up the water that should serve John Cooke's messuage.

These are Bledington offences but it is fair to say that they are the only ones of this nature in the course of more than twenty years. Rissington Magna has its scallywags, stealing silken objects from a house, and often taking wood from the common, though a good deal grows on their own holdings. Windrush and Rissington have to have their affairs regulated on a great scale: merestones have to be set to show the limits of every commoner's ridges and the whole jury must go down to see it done. But Bledington for the most part is peaceable to dullness.

The great majority of presentments concern the common fields and give an insight into the difficulties of open-field farming at this time. The Bledington constable and tithing man almost always report ditches unscoured and hedges at the limits of the parish that need mending. Over and over it is the same hedges; the same lengths of ditches. The one long hedge is that between Oddington parish and our own, but there are shorter ones. The problem of their routine maintenance is not solved between 1624 and 1647, and possibly not till 1769 when the fields were enclosed. Other offences—but not for a number of years in Bledington—are failing to fold the sheep at night between May and harvest, turning too many sheep on to the common, leaving mares and foals tied up on parts of the common which belong to other beasts, doing much harm to the common by turning pigs on to it unringed. In Bledington, the pound is in frequent need of repair, and on one occasion, William Wright "rescues" a sheep of his which is being taken to it: that is he takes it by force or strategem, to escape a fine, or show resentment. (Is this Agnes Wright's son who had been difficult within the family circle long before?).

It is clear that there is some indiscipline on the manors, but certainly not more at Bledington which has lost its Manor court than at Rissington Magna which has not.

For the year 1647 a notable document was carried by five Bledington "men of the Jury" to the Hundred Court. By that time the Civil War had gone on for five years. The first engagement, the Battle of Edgehill, had been fought twenty miles from here, on and below the ridge that runs from Stow via Chastleton to Sunrising and Knoll End Hills, and looks over the Vale of the Red Horse. That was in 1642; in 1643 royalist soldiers were quartered in Oddington and Stow was the scene of a contest between Lord Essex the Parliamentary leader and Prince Rupert. Essex had heavy guns which must have been heard in Bleding-

143

ton. Civil customs and events were disturbed: Dover's Games, we know, were halted. But as in the Wars of the Roses, much of local government continued hereabouts in its accustomed way. Whichever party, Royal or Parliamentary, held sway sent bailiffs as usual to hold Hundred Courts, and the ancient customs of open-fields farming could not be dispensed with. Yet doubtless disturbance and failure of authority in the national sphere favoured division and indiscipline in small communities. Certainly Bledington had its disharmony. The absence of a manorial court had left commoners with only their own ancient meeting which alone had no power to compel. Men had been breaking the old rules—ignoring the dates for turning rother beasts on to the common and sheep on to the stubble. A new misdemeanour was turning sheep on to the common and baiting them there on the way to and from Stow market. Meetings of commoners had discussed these matters but the miscreants defied their fellows. There were only four or five of them against twenty one. The majority decided to appeal to the Hundred Court. They drew up a summary of the rules— mostly ancient, but with a few adjustments e.g. provision for growing oats. The duties and rights of fieldsmen and oarsmen were also set out. Finally this long clear document provided that the fines for dis- obedience would be the property of the Hundred Court.

It seems likely that those who would not agree were poor common- ers, for one rule struck a note of charity which might have soothed them: every one who had as much as two yardlands of copyhold or ex-copyhold shall let half a rother-beast's common at a reasonable rent (8d) to those who 'lacked to keep their family.' In the end comes the question of those who have refused 'to subscribe to the said orders.' If these can be by any lawful means persuaded or compelled the regulations are to continue in force for six years; otherwise they are to remain but for one year, and then be frustrate and void.

The twenty-one signatures to the document include the old names— Guy, Baker, Ivinge, Grayhurst, Pegler, Lord, Hathaway, Cooke, Rooke, Andrews and Dodford, beside some already named above, and a few more recent ones—Winter, Dalby, Taylor and Ellems, Cornwell and Young.

One is struck by the competence of this village parliament: the rules are clear, the penalties definite and reasonable. How did it proceed? Did the members manage alone, or did they in the end employ a solicitor to write down their decisions? If the latter, the competence

John and Elizabeth Hall at the Point-to-Point Races, Bledington Grounds 1920. (By permission of Miss Mary Hall).

Charles Benfield by A. van Anrooy from the first issue of *The Countryman*
1927, by permission of the Editor.

of the proceeding still seems remarkable: it is the commoners who have considered the whole situation and have a clear plan for meeting their difficulties. Today we have public spirit, but could we discuss a plan, say, for new housing in Bledington with as much grasp and balance?

Were the regulations destined to be "frustrate and void?" No other written agreement seems to have followed this one, nor is there any recorded comment by the Court upon it. Perhaps the Court had no precedent for accepting or rejecting it.

The old method of co-operative neighbourhood farming was to continue here for another hundred and twenty-two years. Common sense and common interest must have helped commoners to find solutions to difficulties. But the rules of 1647 show how irksome open-field farming could be. Differences had been acute among the villagers. The two warring camps in the nation made it easier to conceive of a deeply divided village. Was the struggle here between haves and have-nots or between the well-disposed and the egoists?

Toward Civil War

In all our thoughts of the early seventeenth century the Civil War or Great Rebellion looms ahead. While it lasted Bledington lay in a pocket off the roads. And yet to a backwater the stream is everything. Indeed almost every village in the southern half of England would pay some physical toll in the struggle, while on other levels every class and person would be in vital ways concerned.

In earlier wars villagers had had duties, the majority of them involving obedience to the call of superiors. The lord of the manor had the feudal obligation to attend the king in his wars with a specified number of horsemen. Bledington had been on knight's service, with Winchcombe Abbey due to find one soldier for this manor. In form, Sir Thomas Leigh had accepted the same duty, an undertaking then a matter of legal form, long out of date. But another ancient service survived. All able-bodied men had been liable to serve in the militia, for home defence only.

In readiness for a call, men had been expected to become proficient with bow and arrow. It seems however that they no longer practised shooting. From 1631 to 1636 the constable and tithing man at Bledington report at the Hundred Court that the village butts are out of repair.[32] After this confession, a date is fixed by which they must be amended, and also the amount of the fine to be paid if they are not.

But all that happens is that they are again reported as defective: the reports are a matter of form and routine. Men had practised archery in the Town Banks for hundreds of years but by now it was the prevalent view that the day of bow and arrow was over, though professional soldiers did not always think so.

The duty to serve in the militia remained however. The Lord Lieutenant of the County had the duty to gather, equip and train all inhabitants who were able to bear arms, to lead them against the enemy, whether rebel or invader. There had been a long peace in England from 1588 to 1642, with little interruption, and the militia's training had become perfunctory, but the framework was kept in repair. In the early years of our century Lord Berkeley, the head of the great landowning family of West Gloucestershire, was Lord Lieutenant and he had a most efficient servant and officer, John Smith,[33] himself a lord of manors who drew up for the Lord Lieutenant in 1608, with the assistance of Hundred courts and village officers, a list of "Names and Surnames of all the Able and Sufficient Men in Body fit for His Majesty's serivce in the Wars". In the Bledington list thirty-five men are named, of whom ten are already "trained". Something of what this term meant we learn from other sources. The men were summoned[34] once a month in summer to spend a single day in some convenient place where they met men from other villages for "drill". By 1608 the weapons whose use was to be practised were pikes, muskets and calivers, the last being short, light muskets. By the time the men had reached the rendezvous, on horseback or on foot, and their arms had been "viewed" it was dinner-time. After the meal there was a little practising of positions and a charging of muskets, so as to cheer their captain with a volley. Then it was time to ride home. Naturally a day out was an occasion for enjoyment. Sometimes it was said that what the men learned was to drink. But no doubt the practice varied: the proportion of Bledington, and probably of all Gloucestershire men, who had gone through the drill was much above the national average: the training may also have been relatively good.

The weapon a man should learn to use was determined by his strength and stature: the tallest should be pikemen, men of middle height musketeers, and those somewhat under average, "caliver men". Other men of "meanest" stature, but nevertheless strong, were "pyoners" or diggers. In Cromwell's Army later these last did whatever was beneath the dignity of others. We do not learn in what category the trained men of Bledington are placed. Of the others, 2 are pikemen, 19 calivermen, and there is a single "pyoner". Perhaps in this area men were not trained to use the ordinary musket. The twelve young men of "about 20 years", and those in the second age class, "about 40", are untrained. The age groups of the trained men are not given.

When, at long last, armed resistance to the King by Parliament began the trained men must have expected to be called up by the party locally in power: that was one reason in remote parts for awareness of the rising discontent and enmity. Parliament was able, before war had actually begun, to seize control of the militia in most counties.

In our own, Parliament was strong and the call to the militia was a call to support its cause. But it was not the only one to be heard. In most areas, local leaders called for volunteers, as did the lord of the manor of Maugersbury on our borders—a Royalist. There were also press-gangs, but there is no sign that these reached out to the eastern borders of the county. It seems likely that Bledington men would be recruited to fight in the militia, few being anxious to be among the first to risk all. Rural youths, except the very poor, are reluctant to go soldiering unless the call is exceptionally clear.

The full reasons of townsmen and merchants for fearing the policies of King Charles I would not be clear to our villagers, but they were affected by two of them. First, in the church: Charles' first Parliament, the "Puritan" in 1625, forbade Sabbath sports but his new Archbishop, William Laud, in 1633 ordered that James I's Book of Sports should be read again from every pulpit. Laud was known in our county for he had been made Dean of the Cathedral in 1619. In that capacity he had incurred his Bishop's wrath by removing the Cathedral's altar to the east end of the choir. As Archbishop one of his first actions was to give detailed instructions to his successors as to how to put the Cathedral in order; he appeared locally as a wilful and interfering administrator.[35]

Laud had a great interest in order, ceremony and regularity: he knew of many incidents such as the brawl in Bledington church. First came his order that everyone must kneel at communion. Soon followed the decree that the altar must be removed to the east end of the chancel, its ancient position. More than this, a rail must be erected setting apart the altar from the rest of the chancel. Here was work for

147

the Bledington churchwardens. If today, one lifts the draperies of the altar in our church we see the heavy, comely late Elizabethan carved oak table which had stood in the nave. Now the churchwardens moved it back to where the altar had stood anciently and in Queen Mary's day. Laud might have wished to order a return to the old stone altars, but too many had been thrown out into churchyards, and used for other purposes, or broken up by frost. This time, the churchwardens' obedience was fully given: they also erected the altar rails— those still standing. It has been thought, on what grounds I do not know, that a remnant of the old screen of the Holy Rood still stood in the church and was put to this use. This return to old ways expressed a determined opposition to Protestant attitudes now themselves long established.

About this time (1636) the line of our Cooke vicars came to an end and John Nant was appointed Vicar. He was an ex-student of Christ church and had a poor smattering of Latin which he occasionally used in the church registers, to the puzzlement of readers. He settled down in the village for life and he and his family became, it would seem, as homely as the Cookes. He accepted the changes being made and was to prove amenable to many others. He lay low during the Civil War; under the Commonwealth he was licensed as a preaching minister and in 1662, after the return of Charles II, he would again subscribe to all the Articles and be recognised afresh as "curate". It sounds like the Vicar of Bray, but maybe he served well a parish which, at that time, developed within itself no great religious talent or impulse.

Certainly John Nant was no negligent priest: during his time church affairs went well and parishioners continued to leave small (sometimes tiny) sums to the church. The old families were loyal: Hathaways, Grayhursts, Guys, Holfords, Stayts, Hulles and Rookes continue to act as churchwardens, not to the exclusion of some later recruits. During his time, the good work of improving the peal of bells went on. All the bells that survived till 1930 were cast in the seventeenth century. The earliest of these—the "ting-tang"—dates from 1630: "Humfre Keene made me", he still announces. The Keenes were a Woodstock firm: it is thought they cast all five of the peal. The next two were made by Humfre's son, just before the War began. A fifth was added by Parson Nant and his churchwardens in 1651. That was after the execution of King Charles (1649) in times still troublous. The Puritans, disapproved of many things but bells had a way to almost all hearts.

In other villages around us certain individuals and groups were less acquiescent than John Nant and his flock. The parish church did not meet their felt need and they held supplementary services in their own homes. Presently they would have ministers (sometimes former parish priests) and an organisation of their own. But usually a community must be rather larger than ours to generate the enthusiasm and force to favour a minority movement.

A second aspect of the troubles of which Bledington had knowledge was financial. Charles I was in great straits for money throughout his reign. To grant taxes was a privilege of Parliament and the source of its power. When Parliament approved the King's plans it granted various taxes including subsidies, and these last brought in more money than any other. Without subsidies a sovereign was hard put to it; they had in times past been paid by all but the poorest. Three centuries before, in 1327, eighteen Bledington men had been assessed, for between 2s. 2d. and 12d. each. But by 1608 the number of "subsidy men" had been reduced. John Smith's list in "Men and Armour" named five: Hathaway, Guy, Andrews, Loggan and Pasham. Four of these have more than one yardland and probably the fifth also. So when Parliament ceases to grant subsidies to King Charles, Bledington men knew that something must be wrong: no government can manage without taxes. Charles had resorted to "free gifts", and later had assessed the well to do for "loans", which were in fact heavy taxation without Parliamentary sanction. Naturally, many refused to pay: a monarch independent of Parliament was the greatest of dangers, for most Englishmen; and where would it all end, they asked? By 1634 the King had discovered a tax which had been levied without any reference to Parliament—ship money. Gloucester and Tewkesbury, both river-ports, had paid the tax of old: they had for example contributed a vessel to fight the Armada. In 1634 they again responded to demand. For other communities this was a new tax. Pay once, pay always, that was the fear. But when "forced loans" had been refused the King's Privy Council had ordained that men who refused to pay might be "pressed" and made "to serve on foot in our wars". Worse might happen to those who refused ship-money.

Ordinary yeomen and copyholders were required to pay it, and free-holders were given the "duty" to act as assessors: constables and tithing men were to collect the money from their neighbours. In this way the men of this village who met to decide about the planting of the fields and the dates for opening the stubble and who went to the Hundred Court were all concerned in the struggle of King and Parliament: the pockets of the meanest and the hearts of the best were touched to some effect or other. No wonder, that, as Clarendon wrote "The common people in the generalty and the country freeholders would rationally argue of their own rights and the oppressions that were laid upon them". By 1636 resistance was general: there was trouble in our own Hundred. The Sherborne freeholders seem to have assessed their parish, but £21 of the assessment could not be collected, and that must have been nearly the whole. In Slaughter village the constable, himself named Slaughter, refused to pay his own tax or to collect others.[36] Presumably Bledington men paid what appears to have been a small assessment, in that and later years. At the April meeting of the Hundred Court in 1638 a list was presented of the 47 men of the village, six of whom had been assessed for some tax, doubt-less ship-money, and the rest are "E", exempt. Thus ordinary folk here and all over England received a painful prick on the skin: taxa-tion had served to rouse villagers in earlier struggles.

Another of Charles' modes of raising money touched two Bleding-ton families: the old feudal dues of "wardship" of orphans, long for-gotten, had been resuscitated. Thomas Guy's will dated April 1640 sets aside a third of his messuage and holding "to descend unto John Guy my son and heir-apparent according to law", so that the King and his heir may have "their wardship, seizure and livery . . . as law requires".[37] It was expected that payments would have to be made for twelve years. Leonard Mace a young tailor who died in 1641 left to his daughter £12 and to his unborn child £5 to be paid to him or her at the age of 16. His wife is to be his executor, but it is expected that all the spare produce of his house and land will be required to pay the wardship dues if his unborn child is a son.

A further stimulus to interest in national affairs was Parliamentary elections in which freeholders elected two County members. Often there was no contest: the candidates were accepted by acclaim. But in 1640 and 1641 there were two elections. At the first, two supporters of the King were elected—by a ruse, so a well-authenticated story goes. Yet a few months later the two men elected had both been punished for refusing to pay ship-money, one of them, John Dutton of Sherborne, by imprisonment.[38]

To men accustomed as even villagers were to live and speak with considerable freedom and responsibility in much of life, to say nothing of electing members of Parliament, some of the teaching they now met with must have seemed provocative. The clergy were bidden to preach to the people that "the persons and goods of subjects were at the absolute disposal of the Crown", and that it was "a fatal error to suppose that authority derived from the people". This teaching came up against old assumptions and some knew of Old Testament kings who certainly had "divine right" but were as much subject to law as others. What had the royal side to offer to husbandmen? On the whole, country tenants who joined the King's standard did so as followers of their own landlord, often as a tribute to mild and customary ways.

While the War was waged the solid but often unenfranchised yeomen and tradesmen were wanted in both armies. In Cromwell's Ironsides and later in his New Model Army as a whole younger members of these classes found opportunity to test their own qualities against those of men of other traditions. Also, they had talk and discussion with their fellows from other parts of the country, often of politics and religion. The acute mental movements and excitement of the wartime resemble but surpass those of the fourteenth century. With the countrymen there came to be strong views and even fanatic ones about the land and who should profit by it, and how.

The Civil War or Great Rebellion

The King made Oxford his capital and Gloucester was held for Parliament; the latter lay between him and Wales where he could count on gathering supporters. The route from one city to the other lay through Chipping Norton, Oddington and Stow; and Stow was also on the route to Worcester. Gradually, by both forces marching through, lodging in, and fighting battles over it, the entire county of Gloucester is said to have been reduced to miserable conditions, "ruined by free quarter". As early as the last day of December 1641 before any blood had been shed in the struggle Stow had troops quartered on it. Some Welsh regiments under the Marquis of Hertford were there from Saturday to Tuesday, on their leisured way to Oxford. The case of our landlord-neighbour, Mr John Chamberlayne of Maugersbury, shows how a single household and family might suffer in the War. Accused when the struggle was over of being a "delinquent", of supporting the king and enmity to Parliament, Chamberlayne drew up a statement of his involuntary contributions to both sides. On forty-five occasions men had been quartered upon him or had taken quarters for themselves, Royalists and Parliamentarians alike, sometimes three or four times in a month, as the tug of war went on. He was called upon to send provisions to the armies; they turned their horses into his corn; seventeen of his plough-horses were seized; he lost above a hundred sheep taken by soldiers. In the famous confrontation of Essex and Prince Rupert, he had "corn upon the ground" "spoyled by the two armies", forty pounds worth of it. Famous men on both sides had occupied his beds—the Earl of Lichfield, Ireton, Rainsborough.[39]

Bledington had its personal connections with the fighting. Young men were in the militia, fighting for Parliament though of how and where there is no evidence. One family, the Loggans, were royalists: a connection of theirs helped to build the King's fortifications round Oxford. In 1906 the family living in Manor Farm noticed that the ceiling of their room was bulging. They detached the plaster and down came an old leather bag, full of silver coins minted in Oxford in 1642, 3 and 4. This was no miserly hoard: it was the king's money minted from College plate, some of it from Christ Church, sent for a royal purpose.[40] In the second week in August 1643 the King's drums were beaten on Kingham green. They would be heard, like the church bells, across the fields in Bledington. Men were urged to "come in", to "serve for the king". On that occasion recruits were promised that they should "only keep garrison at Buckingham", to defend the town against "the rebels"; but some thought they would be "carried to Gloucester". It was natural and easy to find it necessary to break such promises to simple village youths. Maybe Loggan of Bledington on that and later occasions encouraged recruits with the silver and when times grew dangerous in 1644, hid what remained.

It is worth remembering that village families had relations in many neighbouring villages: Andrews and Maces in Gawcombe, Westcote, Icomb, Barrington—the last in Oxfordshire and Royalist-led. Tidmarshes had dissenting cousins in Adlestrop and Chipping Norton and were likely to hope for Parliamentary success.

There was one group of villagers who would certainly have some precise knowledge of the war and the way it was fought—boys. Their gift for obtaining information had great scope; they could slip up to Stow or hide behind the long hedge between us and Oddington. One morning in April 1643 when Royal troops were quartered in Stow and Oddington and in Lower Slaughter they were roused at break of day. Parliamentary dragoons had attacked the king's men billeted there and then rushed off to Oddington to surprise a troop still asleep. Knowing the royalists in Stow would be rousing they doubled back to Slaughter and then were themselves pursued all the way to Andovers ford.

Four months later there was a more serious affair. It was not a time of success for the King's enemies. Gloucester was besieged: if it fell the King's way to Wales and reinforcements would lie open, and London itself might not be safe. London Train Bands, five thousand strong, marched towards Gloucester via Aylesbury and Buckingham soon to be met by Essex, the Parliamentarian general with fifteen thousand men and forty guns, some of them heavy. He paused in Chipping Norton and from there sent the Red and Blue London regiments on to Oddington. By the time they reached the village it was nightfall. The Blues were fortunate: they turned into the houses and farm buildings for a night's rest but the Reds were set on the watch. They went forward half a mile towards Stow, and were turned on to the great open field, and "drawn up on guard", "without bread or water", "nor daring to light a fire". In the morning the folk of Oddington saw a man coming on horseback, bleeding from a wound, calling out that the king's forces were half a mile behind him. Meanwhile Prince Rupert was on the other side of the Parliamentarians, on the hills by Stow. He divided his 5,000 cavalry into three parts—one to face Essex's men down the hill from Stow, another to go round by Adlestrop and take them in the rear, and a third to make a smaller semi-circle in the Evenlode valley and attack their right wing. But Rupert had to retreat before Essex up the Stow Road. He faced the enemy again in Stow and then was chased through the town and three miles along the Cheltenham Road. Here again he turned. "It was a brave champaign country", the Royalist reporter says, "with no hedges, high and dry, and the Parliament men marched a thousand abreast and six deep—a broad broom indeed". "All the Roundheads in the country were there", Prince Rupert swore. There was not much Rupert's small force could could do: they put on all speed and rode away.

By 1644 the War was not going well for the royal side: the last serious engagement before the fatal battle of Naseby was fought on the Donington side of Stow, in March 1645. Sir Jacob Astley, for the King, was totally defeated. Many prisoners were taken. A Parliamentary officer wrote to a friend "We know not at present how many but the church is full of them".[41] (Perhaps it was at this moment that Thomas Loggan thought it better that the King's money should not be found in his house).

Two months later on May 7th, the King left Oxford as he had long been trying to do, to start on the journey that brought him to Naseby and to the end of his hopes of victory. He stayed the night of May 8th in Stow, "at Mr. Jones's". That was the last opportunity of Bledington's direct knowledge of the war.

But it was not the last or saddest war-drama our area saw. That took place at Burford: everybody concerned was Parliamentarian. The discussions in the lower ranks had led to some conclusions. For them religion, politics and daily bread went together. Every man they had decided had rights and dues simply as a man. Every man who paid rates ought to have a vote for Parliament and he should exercise it frequently: Parliaments should last only two years. The countrymen amongst them expressed their sense that landlords had too much power. The common lands belonged to the people: lords of manors were the successors of invading Normans who had brutally overcome the free Englishmen. They were, in brief, "Levellers", in a more modern word, egalitarians.

A group of radicals had settled on land in Surrey to demonstrate the rural and agricultural community they approved of. The point of view of Levellers and Diggers seemed anarchic to officers coming from more prosperous classes, who held that a man without property was necessarily irresponsible. The senior ranks grew impatient, but the men were embittered by suffering, by the never-ending marching, and by the fear of being sent to quell rebellion in Ireland. At last, their lack of pay (officers' pay was never so far in arrears) brought them to the point of mutiny. There was trouble in Banbury, Gloucester, Salisbury. Cromwell and Fairfax had been patient but army discipline was now urgent. They marched with loyal troops towards Salisbury and the mutineers chose flight. They sped away through Wiltshire and Berkshire, swam the Thames, crossed the Isis and finally arrived, horses and men dead-beat, at Burford. In the middle of the night the Generals caught up with them—and then came the last act of the tragedy. The men were driven into the church and watched over there, while a court martial sat in judgment on their leaders. It condemned four men to death. There were plenty of witnesses of the final scene:

the men in the church were sent up to the roof, overlooking the church-yard. There three men were shot—a cornet and two corporals (of such lowly rank were the leaders). One was "repentant", the second merely desperate, but the third—the last in fact to die—met death like a man of deep conviction—"without the least acknowledgment of error, or show of fear he pulled off his doublet, standing a pretty distance from the wall; and bade the soldiers do their duty; looking them in the face, not showing the least kind of terror".[42] Not even the King with all his reasons, all his spectators, died more bravely. The Levellers were indeed fellows "whom it hurt to think". Five hundred of the rebels are said to have scattered themselves in the villages near Burford. That was the end of them.

Bledington could not have heard of the trouble at Burford till it was all over and Cromwell and Fairfax had ridden off to Oxford to dinner at Christchurch. It would be centuries before ideas such as those of Diggers and Levellers broke clear upon ordinary villagers.

There had been much justice in the Rebellion and Cromwell brought good intentions, strength and devotion to the ruling of the country. But for lack of foundations, of an accepted body of law from which everyone could work, Cromwell's Protectorate foundered. In 1660 confusion and fresh violence were prevented by the invitation to Charles I's son to the throne. He came from the Continent with the acquiescence of the entire country and the enthusiasm of those who might hope to profit by a return to the old régime. The events of the time between 1649 and 1660 do not much concern us, but one should be mentioned. The Army could not be paid through taxation: the only way had been by confiscation of the lands of royalists or "delin-quents", sometimes entire, more often partial. Even offenders of modest estate had to be sought out. Our neighbours Chamberlayne of Maugersbury,[44] the Walter family of Sarsden and a mere yeoman's widow, Mistress Hacker[45] of Churchill, all suffered. Some of the arrears of pay were received, not in cash but in "bonds" or shares in the proceeds of the confiscated land. But cash was what the men in the ranks needed: they parted with the bonds to officers who could afford to wait and bought out the men at low prices. This was honest enough before the law but to him that had was added. Soldiers in the ranks went home with little or nothing. Neither they nor the folk they had sprung from had made any economic gain or progress, nor as it proved, any-thing else except the likelihood that royal absolutism would not return.

The new king made one broad condition for his return: there were to be no fundamental changes in the Church of England. The Parliament on its side made none, but one thing was clear to all: it was for Parliament to vote supplies. True, it squandered this advantage by voting liberally for Charles's lifetime, but still the king kept his memories of early pain and trouble and a healthy fear of returning to his "travels".

The new Parliament elected was—as Parliaments always had been—composed of landowners. It had been strengthened by recruits who had made their position from trade and had still mercantile interests. Nothing turns minds more firmly towards stablity than the possession of lands, broad or narrow. Even the sons of Parliamentarians became willing or anxious to repress the modern movements whether social, political or religious.

Charles II reigned for twenty-five years. Politically he leaned to absolutism and the Catholic Church but he was cautious and much concerned with his personal life and pleasures. He was not vindictive to his enemies and did not ask for religious persecution, but Parliament nevertheless passed a series of laws to be known as the Clarendon Code repressing nonconformity and blocking other ways to change. All nonconformists including Catholics had a troubled life under the Act of Uniformity of 1661 and under the Code. Conscientious Puritan clergy who had remained within the Church were forced out e.g. at Chipping Norton. Nonconformist ministers must not be found within five miles of their one-time churches: the Baptists of Stow and Moreton—strong churches both—met weekly in the open country five miles from each town. The Baptists of Oddington were heavily fined in 1664,[46] one of them a Tidmarsh. Tiny Idbury had always Catholics for the next hundred years, with at times a chapel in the Manor House or in another farm house.

Bledington was peaceful. John Nant was Minister till 1669. A poor and peaceable man, his more Puritanic neighbours would be little provoked. Seven years after his death an "ecclesiastical census" (1676)[47] was taken which shows five dissenters here—by inference the Tidmarsh family, with Baptist cousins in Adlestrop and Quaker relations in Chipping Norton. But dissent faded out here: fifty-seven years later (1733) there were no dissenters and no "papists". There was not quite always peace within our church congregation but we hear no more of Nonconformists till the nineteenth century.

Chipping Norton was a community just large enough to support a number of small religious bodies. The evil effects of the Code on a local community was seen clearly there. One loyal Baptist was "twice arrrested by the County troops who rifled his house and took away his goods", and spent ten years imprisoned in Oxford Castle. Quakers had no Ministers nor did they sing: there was little sign of them. But official persecution made use of neighbours' spite and vindictiveness; a group of informers gate-crashed their meetings and reported their names to the magistrates. But of one of them it is told that when his goods were set out for sale in the market-place the whole town abstained from purchase.

Nonconformity was not altogether defeated: there are still Baptist churches in Stow and Bourton on the Water, Quakers in Burford, Banbury and Oxford. Its folk were all excluded from office and education and continued to be so when active persecution ceased. Fortunately for village life of the future the free churches relied largely on laymen's work. As stewards and trustees the "chapel folk" bore responsibilities as great as the civil duties withheld from them for the next two hundred years or so.

Charles II was followed in 1685 by his brother James II who in four years contrived to outrage both Scotland and England so that he had almost no friends. He was determined to force his kingdoms back to the Roman Church and in general to manipulate the constitution and government to his own revolutionary end—absolute monarchy.

In 1689 the throne was offered by a powerful group, with general approval, to William of Orange and his wife Mary. She was a daughter of the now exiled king but also a Protestant and granddaughter of the Earl of Clarendon, a statesman and historian, royalist, but moderate and humane. William came from Holland where absolutism was unthinkable and was the leader of continental Protestants in the war to resist Louis XIV of France. He had been offered the throne by Parliament and his claim and that of later sovereigns depended on "a particular clause in a particular Act of Parliament". Revenue was voted to him annually.

All this was of direct importance to villages. Wealthy landowners for long shared with royalty not only power but prestige, culture and social influence. One tyranny ended and large classes were freed from certain threats but for the lower orders a far more searching tyranny took its rise.

Meanwhile William and Mary had a great welcome. In villages a usual mode of celebrating their arrival was the planting of an oak tree. None was planted here but a few years later (1695) when a new bell was hung it was inscribed with William's name—the only bell in England, says a learned campanologist, to bear it.[48]

The public and popular welcome to the new sovereigns was a sign that though before 1642 no one of lower status than a freeholder had been regarded as part of the "people of England", others had begun to regard themselves in that light. And one amelioration of life came to them: religious persecution ceased under the Toleration Act of 1689, though the civil handicaps of dissenters remained and they came to be the object of much social exclusion and disrespect.

The growing power of landlords was seen in various ways. The feudal courts were becoming obsolete in many parishes through enclosure of open fields and the break-up of manors by sale of land, as here. Courts leet, such as Slaughter Hundred Court in one of its aspects, remained for a while but their functions were taken over rapidly by magistrates' courts—minor cases by petty sessions often held in landlords' houses, more important ones in Quarter Sessions, the justices of the County meeting in the county town. In the feudal courts there had been juries: a man's equals and neighbours heard evidence and influenced judgment. Magistrates acted alone: they were all landlords, joined in the next century by prosperous clergymen who were often dependent on them and echoed their views. It was symptomatic that when Charles II in the Act which abolished all such feudal tenures as still affected landed persons[49] the dues of copyholders such as fines and heriots were left untouched.

The Village Society: (a) The Farmers and craftsmen

By 1660 there was scarcely a copyholder left in Bledington. Means of livelihood were becoming more varied and to look at village conditions we must classify the heads of families—best, perhaps, into "yeomen" or farmers, small ex-copyholders and craftsmen and two classes of labourers.

Though the term "yeomen" was used by solicitors employed by our group of freeholders, none of them held more in 1660 than 2½ virgates —the equivalent with common land of 120 acres more or less. It is better to describe them usually as farmers, though the term had hardly arrived at its modern meaning. The chief source of our information about this group is documents relating to property—wills, inventories and deeds of sale and mortgage; we gain a little information from a list of houses with the number of their hearths, made in 1671–2, for purposes of taxation.

Few wills are available between 1640 and 1670, but after that they are plentiful.[50] Inventories should have been and perhaps were made for the probate of every will but except one for 1616 they are lacking till 1677, after which till 1701 we find a good many. In the course of a century wills have changed their character a good deal. By 1677 the pious introductions never omitted in the sixteenth century have become much fewer and shorter and with two exceptions charitable legacies have ceased. Up to 1641 everyone leaves at least a small sum to the church, and almost always another to the poor, beside sometimes a small sum to the cathedral, or for a highway or a bridge. Charity to the poor did not cease because there were no poor: it is thought that their numbers had everywhere grown. Two causes almost certainly affected minds. Taxation, constant during the Civil War and heavy, though less frequent, since, must have taken away the husbandmen's sense of a margin. Together with this factor there came the view that the poor rates must take the full burden of the poor. In the first forty years of the century this had not been felt; the overseers were used as a channel of personal charity, of corn or small sums of money added to relief from the assessed rate. But the charitable impulse promoted by the Tudors had largely passed.

The two exceptional legacies to the poor were both notable for generosity. Mary Guy in 1676 leaves 30/- where earlier gifts had been such sums as 3/4d. or less frequently 10/-. In 1685 William Andrews left £5 for the poor. This sum was to continue to be "stock" for ever and the poor were to have the annual profit from it. But again, as is the case when money has been left in the same way for the profit of young children we do not learn how the money is to be invested.

From 1690 there would be a simple means of safe investment. One of the administrative reforms made under William and Mary was the founding of the Bank of England to carry the burden of the King's debts, which then became the national debt. Interest on loans was guaranteed by the nation. From that year when, say, an orphan girl had a legacy the executors knew what to do with it till she came of age.

The most remarkable difference between the wills of the seventeenth century and those of the sixteenth is that messuages and lands, or leases of lands now figure as legacies, as a result of the purchases that had taken, and were taking place. Some nine villagers leave houses and lands between 1677 and 1701, while others leave personal property only. Properties owned are large and small: Guys, Maces and Rookes are "yeomen" with two yardlands, in one case two and a half; Barnes is a poor blacksmith owning little more than a cottage; Bussell or Buswell leaves cottage, garden, orchard, barn, cowhouse, but these are all small; Ivinge (1696), a member of a family who have appeared hitherto to be among the more prosperous villagers, leaves only his "apparel", furniture, and debts good and bad (for his work as a tailor). That the farmhouses had been and were being rebuilt with fine windows and doorways as well as more rooms we already know. From the hearth tax list 1671-2 we learn a few facts about interiors. One house, William Lords, has no fewer than six hearths, others have three, but clearly most still have only one—and indeed would continue to have only one till the nineteenth century. We must note that a house with three hearths could have quite a number of rooms. The Mince family has, beside kitchen and parlour, three chambers, two butteries, a dairyhouse, and a cheeseroom. Their house is the first, judging by the wills, to boast any silver. It is a sign of prosperity also that John Mince (1691) is the first of the yeomen and husbandmen to have a wagon.

Three was a rather usual number of hearths. The truncated hearth tax list shows that of the twelve houses mentioned five have three hearths, one six, one five, and five others one. A house with a small number of rooms and hearths may show some sophistication: the Andrews family (inventory 1690) have only four rooms, and no doubt fewer hearths, but have nevertheless a "dynning room". John Maunder (inventory 1700), with three rooms and a buttery, has a "chimney front", probably over his only hearth, regarded as removeable, worth 6s. 8d.

The two largest houses, early in 1672, are those of the Lord and Herbert families. Lords had succeeded Loggans at Manor Farm as it is now called, where the number of hearths had been reduced from ten to six. The Herberts must have lived in the old Steward's House. There still exist, in the two houses into which it has been divided, four sixteenth (possibly earlier) and seventeenth century fireplaces. In many houses the ancient "hall" is still given that name but in a few cases it has become a "kitchen" or "dinning room". It was round a single hearth that many a village family carried on all their ploys, including reading and music, for centuries to come. But social rank is raised when domestic assistants become "servants", eating in isolation.

It is strange that the increasing beauty of farmhouse exteriors, and the height and number of their rooms, appears not to be accompanied by much change in household equipment and furniture. Most of the sheets are still "hempen", there are a few "boxes of drawers"; there are still many "table bordes" with "frames", though also an occasional "joyne" table and even a joined bed. "Joyne" stools are still being used and in inventories for some houses no chairs are mentioned; but in others there are four or five. A novel piece of furniture is a "round table" (probably an oak pedestal table); two families possess these. That sophisticated household, the Minces', possesses a clock as well as two "salts", two silver spoons, and a little silver cup.

A notable change in interiors is the paving of floors with stone slabs. The farmhouses have few earth floors, and the rushes have been swept out of doors. Houses in Stow had floors of yellowish stone, looking like marble and as hard: a few of these are seen here but less fine stones than these have lasted centuries. The floors were sometimes washed or swilled: this is a great hygienic change. But earth floors could be found in cottages in the nineteenth century. Fewer domestic implements used are mentioned in seventeenth century inventories than in women's wills of the sixteenth—no doubt because the makers of the inventories were never women. But one useful object is mentioned for the first time—a clothes horse.

It has been puzzling to find no spinning wheel in wills, but they figure in two inventories: Thomas Ivinge, tailor, in 1696 possessed two, one "woollen", and one a "linen whiele": Hathaways had one wheel. One family possessed a quern.

A new word, in the last quarter of the century, in the list of contents of rooms, is "trunk". In 1677 the Guy family has more than one, filled with linen: later, Hathaways and Andrews each have one. It seems likely that these witness to more frequent travel, more conveniently provided for.

Of garments, men's or women's, we now learn little. The inventories often begin with a rather formal item, "his wearing apparel", with sometimes "his purse", or, in the case of a woman "her apparel, purse, and girdle". The value of this item varies in most cases between £3 and £1, though in the case of Thomas Cooke, yeoman, (1701) it is five shillings only.

Agnes Wright had made her own malt but by the middle of the century, malting has become a trade, carried on in two houses, Stayts' and Hathaways'.

In the fields a few merestones, with fine-cut initial letters for the owners' names are marking the width of one commoners strips, where difficulties have arisen. Among implements in the "backsides" we find two innovations. A number of holdings have "wheat-rick staddles". "Staddle" seems to be used as a collective name for the stones on which a stack was raised, to keep it free of rats: they are, it seems, a seventeenth century invention. Until this time there has been no mention of ricks although the barns have been small. Another innovation is the wagon. Rookes and Minces have each one. There had been carriers' wagons between Stow and Burford, and Stow and Oxford via Chipping Norton for a good many years. These latter were known as wayne-carts they appeared some time before this on Bledington farms. We do not know where Rookes' and Minces' wagons were made—possibly, like the church-bells in Woodstock, for "Woodstock wagons" are sometimes mentioned in nearby villages. Certainly they were not the fine "Cotswold" wagons with spindle sides, arched top-rails and half-locks now to be seen in museums (those belong to the next century) but they were an improvement on the "long carts" with only two wheels. It is notable that several farm yards contained "coopery ware", but no one is described as a cooper. Someone must have been able to make buckets if not barrels

Crops have changed very little as yet since mediaeval times, but a small quantity of vetches is being grown by John Mince in 1691. There is no certain sign that hemp and flax are still grown: the housewives have many "hempen" and "flaxen" sheets, but then, they could be in wear or in chests for a hundred years.

Among farm animals oxen are rarely mentioned. Husbandmen with a yardland or more have 4 or 5 horses. Most also have about 5 cows. Bulls do not occur at all: the parish bull or bulls are kept in a small close near the mill. Every "backside" has its cock and hens, but geese are not mentioned in will or inventory. However there are poor families who never make wills: maybe they had geese.

The total value of farmers' personal goods as shown in their inventories from 1682 to 1692 is, roughly, between £90 and £120. This is less than the value of Thomas Guy's in 1616—£135, but his inventory is more detailed than later ones and the total may be nearer the true value.

Monetary legacies in wills might shed some light on farmers' profits and margins, but comparison is not easy. In 1640 Thomas Guy had directed his wife to pay £120 each to his daughters. It seems likely however that she is to save these sums from the produce of the farm during the twelve years she will hold it. The largest monetary legacies of all are those of John Rooke or Rucke whose will was proved in 1677. His house was the one above the present Vicarage: to it were attached two yardlands (the original copyhold) and also a part of the demesne lands—a petty farm and two berridales. When John died he left all his possessions to his "loving wife Johane" for her life. After her death they are to go to his son Thomas, on one condition—that within two years he pay to his brothers and sisters sums amounting to £700. If he does not, the overseers of the will are to "let and set" the messuage and land for fifteen years and take the rent. (The Rookes' farm would probably be the equivalent of 120 acres. Thus, the rent would be about 6s. 8d. per acre).

Altogether it seems safe to conclude that Bledington farmers in the latter half of the seventeenth century are making more profit from their land than their predecessors, not altogether because of changes in farming. Other possible explanations are an exceptionally long series of good seasons, or good prices for corn.

There is reason then, to think that communal farming did not prevent our "yeomen" from prospering in a modest way. They naturally profited incidentally from legislation passed by a Parliament of landowners, by which the importation of corn was discouraged, and from 1689 its export favoured by bounties, except when harvests were very insufficient for our own population. (But too much must not be credited to the bounties: Bledington farmers' prosperity had grown before that year).

Reading the wills of farmers and of their widows one finds striking differences between those of the first and second halves of the century. At first one is in a world of wide family connections and affections, a valuation of persons and also of objects, of goods: charitable bequests are frequent. The wills are in fact similar to those of the later sixteenth century. After 1675 the family recognised is the immediate group of

163

parents and children, charity is absent and money is prominent, and in larger amounts.[50]

There are a few wills of craftsmen; their estates, without exception, are small compared with those of farmers. Some of them are sons of farmers, whose farmer-brothers, whether younger or older, inherit the home fields. (But now it is becoming usual for eldest sons to inherit). Also, since none of the craftsmen prosper, opportunities of gain must be few.

Thomas Ivinge, tailor, in 1696 has goods valued at £11. 15s. in all. His shop tools are worth £8. His is the house with two spinning wheels: perhaps wife or daughter earned money by spinning. Francis Barnes, blacksmith, dies possessed in 1670 of a cottage with a backside, orchard and garden. His estate is valued at £19 of which £8 is the estimate for his "household goods and shop tools", and £10 is money owing to him. John Maunders, also evidently earning his living by a skill, has debts of which £12 are "good". Thomas Ivinge's ''goods'' include an amount of £5. 16s. for debts, "sperate and desperate". Farmers are often creditors for small amounts of money, but their debts are never indicated as "desperate". They appear to be neighbourly loans to friends. But craftsmen serve rich and poor alike and no doubt find it difficult in business to make distinctions between just and unjust, solvent and insolvent.

A series of documents dated from 1647 to 1888 throws light on the lives of tradesmen, craftsmen and superior labourers.[51] They relate to two cottages one of which was built somewhere about 1630 and the other twenty-five years or more later. The history of these cottages could be fully known from 1647 to 1969.

They stand, attached to each other, in Bennets' Lane. The second remains to this day much as it was built, the house in the village which is nearest to its seventeenth century condition. It still consists of the old "hall", and the "chamber" above, with some frail partitions. Each of these has its original stone-framed window, though the bedrooms have had others wedged into the deep thatch. Both cottages, when they were built, consisted of these two rooms—not mean, because fairly large, with solid, wide stone hearths, with recesses to right and left. When later generations preferred privacy and smaller rooms, they were big enough to be divided.

The first cottage was built by the Hulles family, belonging to the group of commoners who intermarried, employed one another's sons and daughters, lent one another money, witnessed and executed each other's wills and served in public offices. They sold their new house in 1649 to Richard Bussell or Buswell, a weaver. It had been built upon a small close called Mattocks in which apple trees had been planted. Buswell built himself a weaver's shed on one end of the house and about 1659 built the second cottage which, in his will, he called "the other part of my house", though it was almost immediately occupied by his married daughter. From this time till 1850 the cottages would be tenanted by weavers, "cordwainers" (shoemakers who have gone through apprenticeship), coopers, and by chapmen and two labourers. The first of the labourers rescued the property from debt for the third Buswell weaver, and the second bought one cottage for the no-mean sum of £60.

Twelve years after his purchase Richard Buswell made his will, leaving the older cottage to his son-in-law Bennett and his daughter (the position of wives and daughters is not what it had been fifty years before: Bennett becomes the owner and master of this cottage). The second cottage was left to two spinster daughters, the first to marry to have the cottage and pay her sister twenty pounds. The orchard was divided between the two cottages and they are to share the pump which Richard has installed over the well. The pump will figure in the deeds for a hundred years: it is still there and in use for gardens. Presently the second cottage was sold to a chapman of Hook Norton for £36. Four Charlwoods, all chapmen, will live in it. Members of this family work in the district from Hook Norton to Stow on the Wold and Burford. We never hear what they sell: no doubt their wares were any and every portable commodity. In 1678 the first Charlwood's son married a Bledington girl and received the cottage as a gift from his father. Mary Cook belonged to the old family of husbandmen and parsons. Her relatives see to it that her future home is settled on her for life: probably she brought a small dowry to the marriage. The husband did not do well: fifteen years later he mortgaged their home to an Evesham "boddice-maker" at 6%. Charlwood's son became a "yeoman" and later paid off his father's mortgage and became himself the lender of the money.

The first cottage by 1703 is in the occupation of another Richard Buswell, weaver. His news is of his mortgage. But interest rates had come down: he paid 4%. His son Samuel, also a weaver, married Elizabeth, a daughter or ward of Thomas Baker, of an old-established and relatively prosperous family of husbandmen. Baker gave his ward a small dowry; probably he paid off the mortgage on the cottage. Buswell draws up a document, not an agreement, but subsequently treated as if it were binding. He and Elizabeth are to have the cottage as long as they, or one of them, survive. But Samuel's father lives with them: he too is to have the right to remain as long as he lives; not only that, but Elizabeth is to be "serviceable" to her father-in-law throughout his lifetime, providing him with meat, drink and firing and all his domestic needs. For her small dowry Elizabeth got a roof over her head and extra unpaid work for her lifetime. Her husband died and she married again but though her new husband paid off a mortgage on the cottage, the old Buswell's right to stay was recognised. Elizabeth was to be "serviceable" "as heretofore". Here is confirmation of the decline in the status of women.

Not one of the four weavers could write, but their illiteracy did not connote the ignorance that usually accompanied illiteracy in the nineteenth century. A man might know the name of every furlong and group of trees, be able to recite Morning and Evening Prayer, be a fine dancer and freely command the services of professional men to safeguard his property and yet make a clumsy mark at the foot of a deed.

Other events in the cottages' story take us too far ahead but already one sees the usefulness of such small properties. They provide bases for all sorts of trades: there will presently be carried on here, beside the crafts already mentioned, spinning, farriery, wheel-making, carpentry, coopery, not to mention the use of the close or orchard for cows, poultry, cider-making. A small possession makes for self-respect: it may also encourage a retentive rather than an adventurous spirit. These two cottages have remained to this day (1972) the possession of superior workmen and their womenfolk.

Labourers and the Poor

Our cottages on Mattocks have shown us the relation of craftsmen to a class perhaps a little below them. The "labourer" who was not one of "the poor" had often a sound cottage, with a good garden or a close. He had not been apprenticed or succeeded his father on a holding or in a trade, maybe because the family was too large or had met misfortune. Not having any one skill he might be able to turn a capable hand to many jobs. He had sufficient independence for his good sense or his charm to make itself felt: he might marry prosperously and apprentice his sons. We find examples of the kind of sum he might invest or bequeath—forty, sixty pounds.

The poor labourer, though referred to in documents by the same term, was in a very different position. He worked for a single employer for wages held at the old figure by the magistrates, though prices had risen. He and his family still lived about the farmhouses, families in one-roomed houses, young men any and everywhere. Though there would be very thin times, food would sometimes be plentiful, with gleanings at harvest, nature's occasional bounty of wild fruit, sorrel and mushrooms, a share of pigs' chitterlings wives had helped to clean or of some beast that had had to be killed.

But their numbers were increasing. Some became casual workers, and vagrants and then destitute. This was an old problem. Henry VIII's government had tackled it with some success, providing a parochial machinery and stimulating charity. Elizabeth and her Parliament had passed experimental legislation and checked its results. Frequent reports had been received from counties and even hundreds. But after the coming of James I these practices were discontinued and during the struggle between throne and Parliament the poor were left to the parish officers.

The Restoration brought no return of systematic thought or planning. All the radical thought of the Puritan army and of Diggers and Levellers died away out of sight, for the most part out of existence Those who could have spoken for the poor were silenced and depressed; the idea of allowing or encouraging the poor to speak of their own condition was totally absent. On the contrary, under the dominance of the wealthy landowners who, now, in Boswell's term "possessed" Parliament, and of industrial entrepreneurs and merchants there grew up an attitude to the poor of unheard of brutality and insolence whose development and spread would continue through the next century.

Meanwhile some action in this sphere had to be taken. There was much confusion owing to the growth in the number of vagrants and to the idea that a person with no resources should be sent back to his own parish. There was often no certainty as to which was that parish and as to how a pauper, possibly old and weak and often recalcitrant, could be induced to go there. The Act of Settlement passed in the first year of Charles II, 1662, provided that once a poor person had been permitted to stay forty days within a parish, he gained the right to stay and to be relieved there. But the overseers could, within that time,

167

refer the case to the magistrates, whose duty it was to determine where he had his "settlement". He could then be despatched home with a license to beg, if he could go alone and was likely to do so, or he could be conveyed thither at the expense of the parish wishing to be rid of him.

Conveyance was likely to be very costly; the expedient would tend to set parish against parish and be often cruel to the poor. Yet it is possible to sympathise with overseers who feared that ill-fed, unskilled, weakly men (and women and children too) might become permanently unemployed and a life-long burden.

The records of the Gloucester Quarter Sessions show Bledington overseers "presenting" persons under the Poor Laws. Two men, a yeoman and a labourer, were taken there in 1664 and 1667 for erecting cottages with less than four acres of land attached, contravening the Act of 1589. No one had thought of "presenting" the craftsmen who built the cottages on the field called Mattocks, a site of about one acre: there is no doubt that this Act was meant to be used with discretion.

A rather curious case occurred in 1679. First, the Court ordered the Bledington overseers to pay Thomas Cook, a native, two shillings per week till they found him a habitation. At its next meeting it licensed him to build a cottage on a small piece of land that he possessed (we may be sure it was far smaller than four acres!). Cook did not in fact build and in the next year the churchwardens and overseers were ordered to give him five shillings a week till they had found him a house. Cook acted with persistance, confident of his rights.

Cases of settlement occur before the end of the seventeenth century. Donnington (near Stow) and Bledington were in dispute in 1677 about Thomas Smith. Two local magistrates decided that Donnington ought to relieve him, but that village appealed to Quarter Sessions, which ruled "that he be settled at Bledington". Many such contentious cases occurred but there is an example of one settled in neighbourly fashion. Our overseers acknowledged to their confreres at Kingham that George Phipps, residing there, had his settlement in Bledington. If he should ever be destitute they will receive him. Phipps would have no choice but to come: but a member of the Phipps family—sturdy men, small-holders or skilled labourers—was not very likely to become so poor as to trouble overseers for a long period.

There are other cases in which the judgments of village officers are set aside by Quarter Sessions after appeal as in Thomas Cook's case. In 1681, four children named Baker appeal to the Court to order their maintenance. The Court was of the opinion that the children ought to be relieved: it commissioned two magistrates to decide on a weekly payment. Knowing something of the prosperity of the Bakers, one thinks it likely that overseers felt that the children should be supported by their own family and that the Court was generous at the village's expense.

The suffering from the Act of Settlement is belittled in some works of social history, yet it often made the poor prisoners within their own parish, or threatened them with starvation if they could not accept this condition. It could divide families, for parents and children could have different "settlements", and it was most wasteful. But like much else, it went largely uncriticised.

The wills had come nearer to being purely economic and legal documents, but that fact seems to indicate that something had been lost or was being lost from social life. Agnes Wright's will of 1612 had shown how life throbbed between herself and her family and assistants, herself and the church and her community, and even her feeling for the communal farming. Other wills, women's and men's, had expressed something of the same feeling.

In all the wills and inventories only one book is mentioned and no musical instrument. We know however that the Morris dancers had their whittles and dubs: did not the prosperous families share in that activity and was music totally lacking from their houses? Perhaps not: perhaps the instruments passed always into the possession of the young.

Education

There was now general need for knowledge of letters. The frequent and precise recall of custom as in the manor court no longer occurred: reliance on the community's memory has ceased. It was by this time essential for all business transactions to be recorded: a husbandman's sons, if not himself, must be able to read freely if not to write. Clearly, they were learning.

Schools were becoming numerous in the area. Burford School had existed for a century, having been founded by Simon Wisdom and his friends. In 1910 Kingham boys were daily cycling the ten miles thither:[52] earlier it would have been easy to ride a pony. A school at Stow was endowed in 1604. In Churchill there was a school suitable for boys by about 1700 and perhaps earlier. Trespassing on time ahead, about 1738 Warren Hastings, son of the ex-Vicar of Bledington, attended it. One need not give the reins to imagination to suppose that Pegler, Herbert or Grayhurst boys sat beside him. Indeed for two and a half centuries—till 1876—Bledington parents would have to seize on such chance local provision as they could for their children's instruction in letters, boys riding to school when weather permitted and girls being taught by anyone who knew how to read. As time went on a few girls had fair teaching. Possibly a few went to inexpensive boarding schools for a short time and we know that a few received lessons from local teachers of music.

But in the latter part of the seventeenth century two families knew how to get education for able boys. The coroner, Grayhurst, had no doubt been taught but we do not know how, nor where he sent his son to school, but the latter matriculated at Oxford in 1685, when he was sixteen and in 1691 gained his degree.[53] (It was surely this family who added the late seventeenth century portion to Harwood's farmhouse, with its ovolo mouldings, fine fireplaces, and numerous windows. This was surely "architecture" due to the stimulus of contacts outside the village, not mere "vernacular" building).

Another family sent a son to Oxford: the Herberts, who lived in the village only for two generations. William graduated and became "clerk and minister" in his native village from 1697 (probably somewhat earlier) till he died in 1708.

The Lord family who bought the mill from Leigh in 1624 acquired Loggans' farm about 1670. In 1689 William Lord, Junior, married a young woman of established family. These transactions involved mortgages and elaborate legal provisions. Later events show this family straining after gentry status: they undoubtedly gave their children some conventional education.

The Clergy

John Nant's successor was the Reverend Griffith Jones, appointed by the Dean and Chapter of Christchurch in 1669. (That other expressions are succeeding the word "minister"—the "Reverend", the "clergyman", the parson—to describe the parish clergy is not without

170

significance). We know from the census of 1676 that Parson Jones inherited a peaceful parish with only one family of nonconformists.[54] A little is learned of the Church's material conditions from information given to the Archdeacon in 1677. The chancel was "greatly out of order"; the paving and the seat needed repair. The responsibility for the chancel had been passed by Christchurch to the lessee of their tithes, together with the payment of the Vicar's stipend: the lessee's widow was negligent. The Archdeacon found that a Common Prayer Book was wanting in the Quire and that there was no terrier of the living. The churchwardens were admonished to repair these lacks and to provide a pulpit cloth, a cushion and a Bible. It appeared that the churchwardens had kept in order their part of the building, the nave and the tower.

In this century and the next there are gaps in the line or the service of incumbents but never in the double line of churchwardens. Christchurch might forget its duty as it appears to have done in 1689, and later would pass even the appointment of ministers to lay tenants of the impropriation but the nave was always fairly tended and routine reports made.

We do not learn much of a more private piety. Only one Bible appears in will or inventory (1683) but that is not proof that there were not others.

Like some of his successors Griffith Jones felt able to absent himself awhile from his parish. In 1689 the transcript of the register was sent to Gloucester by the churchwardens who write after their signatures, "no minister". In thinking of the quality of service rendered at this time and later, the Vicar's income should surely be borne in mind. A terrier of the living drawn up in 1704 stated that the income from the tithes, paid by Christchurch or their lessees, was seventeen pounds, and that was the sole income. The labourer is worthy of his hire but there is a tendency for him to be worth no more.

Jones' successor William Herbert, son of the Herberts, was a far better priest: he had a special, natural interest in his native parish's well-being and proved a vicar of conscience and education. During his eleven years of duty (1697–1708) he wrote all the transcripts of the registers in a careful old-fashioned hand. Long after his death in 1708 a tribute was paid to him by his widow in a verse inscribed on her tombstone, richer in sentiment than any other inscription in church or churchyard:

Languet ut infelix abrepto turtur
Sic moriens vixi fata dotens vidua
Nuncius ecce Dei tandem immedicabile vulnus
Contrabit omnipotens angusto limite vitam
Sed nova post obitum verag: vita manet.[55]

Englished by a later Vicar, Dr. Stephen Liberty, it reads:

Like hapless turtle-dove of spouse bereft,
Pining, mere death in life to me was left:
At length a careless hurt, at God's behest,
The fruit of sorrow, speeds me to his rest.
Brief is the span th'Almighty here provides,
But after death the new, real life abides.

[1] G.D.R. (Consistory Court Books) 97 folio 106
[2] Hockaday Vol. 40, 116
[3] G.D.R. Hockaday 181, (1633). G.D.R. 186, 634
[4] G.D.R. Hockaday 186, (1634)
[5] Christopher Whitfield *Robert Dover and the Cotswold Games*. Distributors: Henry Sothern Ltd., London 1962
[6] See Ch. 1 pp. 12, 13
[7] *A Handful of Pleasant Delites*. 1584
[8] R. J. E. Tiddy. *The Mummers' Play*. Oxford 1923
[9] Nettell *Sing a Song of England: History of Traditional Songs* 1954
[10] Shakespeare *The Tempest* Act IV, Sc. I
[11] They have been revived recently
[12] Leigh documents. Shakespeare's Birthplace Trust, B 1578, 1571
[13] Leigh documents. Shakespeare's Birthplace Trust, B 1578, 1583
[14] Leigh documents. Shakeapeare's Birthplace Trust, B 1582, 1587
[15] Leigh documents. B 1071, 1590
[16] Leigh documents. B 729, 1598–99
[17] V.C.H. Vol. VI, pp. 91, 110
[18] G.R.O., D 1375/3–5, (Thos. Baker, title and terrier, circa 1710)
[19] V.C.H. Vol. VI p. 28
[20] Atkyns *The Ancient and Present State of Gloucestershire*. London 1712, Under *Bledington*
[21] e.g. P.R.O. C. 25(2)/1016/8 Geo. I. East
[22] However the lordship had not been tidily disposed of: the question of the lordship of the village green—a mere nuisance and possible expense to any claimant—has been perhaps unnecessarily a hindrance to its full use by the community

172

[23] G.R.O. D 1375/3-5
[24] M. & A. Potter *Houses*. London 1948. p. 16
[25] Papers, Mr Cecil Acock
[26] G.R.O. Quarter Sessions Papers, pp. 28-31
[27] Thomas Guy's Will, 1677
[28] Lainchbury, op. cit. p. 62
[29] (i) G.R.O. Hearth Tax List, 1662
(ii) G.R.O. Hearth Tax List, 1672
[30] G.R.O. M. 16. Salmonsbury Court
[31] G.R.O. D. 45. Salmonsbury Court 1631, 1633, 1634, 1636
[32] G.R.O., D. 45. M. 14. Salmonsbury Court
[33] John Smith *Men and Armour*. 1608
A. J. & R. H. Tawney *An Occupational Census of the 17th Century*. Econ. Hist. Review, V, 1934, pp. 25-64
[34] C. H. Firth *Cromwell's Army*. London, 1902, p. 8
[35] H. R. Trevor Roper. *Archbishop Laud*. London 1965, pp. 45, 46
[36] W. B. Wilcox, op. cit. p. 125
[37] G.D.R. Bledington Wills 1640
[38] (i) Williams *Parliamentary History of the County of Gloucester*
(ii) Wilcox. op. cit. pp. 36 and 119
[39] H. P. R. Finberg *Gloucestershire Studies*, Leicester 1957, p. 184
[40] Lainchbury *Kingham: the Beloved Place*, p. 325
[41] Sir Samuel Luke *Journal*, Oxfordshire Record Society, Vol. XXIX, 1950 & 53, p. 136
[42] Thomas Carlyle *Oliver Cromwell's Letters and Speeches*, Edinburgh Edition, 1845, Vol. I, p. 124
[43] R. H. Gretton, Burford Records. Oxford 1920 p. 233
[44] Finberg, Gloucestershire Studies, *John Chamberlayne and the Civil War*. Leicester University Press. p. 188
[45] Lilian Rose *History of Churchill*. Brackley, 1934, p. 38
[46] V.C.H. Vol. VI p. 97
[47] V.C.H. Vol. VI. p. 32 Compton Census 1676. G.D.R.
[48] H. B. Walters *Miscellaneous Notes on Gloucestershire Bells*. B.G.A.S. Vol. 42
[49] e.g. knight's service and wardship
[50] Wills: Gloucester City Library (Diocesan Records)
Bledington Wills Guy 1640 & 1676, Andrews 1685, Barnes (Francis) 1670, Barnes (Francis) 1697, Buswell 1679, Ivinge 1696, Mince 1691, Andrews 1690, Maunder 1700, Cooke 1701, Rooke 1677, Johnson 1690, Mace (Leonard) 1641, Mace (Francis) 1700, Hathaway 1683
[51] Papers, Mr Cecil Acock
[52] E. J. Lainchbury op. cit. p. 200
[53] Author's Papers (from Rev. Stephen Liberty)
[54] But in the eighties the heads of three families were presented in the Consistory Court for not attending church
[55] Bledington church, in floor near east end of south aisle

chapter six

THE EIGHTEENTH CENTURY (1702-1815)

Introductory; the Church; the Husbandmen before
Enclosure; Enclosing the Open Fields; Craftsmen,
Tradesmen and superior labourers; the Poor Labourers.
A retrospective note: How many Villagers?

Introductory. During the years 1702 to approximately 1815 village
life tends to a greater separatism between classes and to increasing
differences between families and in individuals of the same social
group. Outside forces affected the village more promptly than in the
late seventeenth century. The movement from age-old communal
agriculture to individual and family farming of enclosed holdings
affected more than farming life. The great question, then seldom
asked, was whether the sense of community could survive it. There
was some beneficial change, nationally, in the church but this was
countered by the supposed interest, not only of the landed class, but
also of industrialists, in the subordination and the poverty of the poorer
classes. Village labourers—a growing class—had few means of communication beyond the boundaries of their parish and no means of
self-defence against tendencies very harmful to them.

The tendency to differentiation in the life of classes and families
followed the growth and change in knowledge and skills. It was
inevitable: it might conceivably enrich the communal life but it had in
fact strong tendencies to disrupt and impoverish it.

Meanwhile, in the world outside villages the life of industry and
commerce—textiles, mining, transport—changed; the population
grew; and by adventure and exploration the world was in effect
enlarged. In the latter development an English villager took a great
part and much later it would have vital importance for some of our
farmers and labourers. The new techniques and organisations of

industry had most pervasive effects on all classes and all localities.

Only the briefest outline of dynastic changes and of reigns is necessary. Sovereigns, though very important at times, were so chiefly in relation to the governing class of landlords and their Parliament. King William III was succeeded in 1702 by Queen Anne, younger daughter of James II, sister of William's wife, Queen Mary. Their Catholic half-brother and his descendants had been legally excluded from the succession. Anne was the last Stuart on the throne. Her reign was internally quiet but she inherited King William's struggles against the ambitions of Louis XIV of France, waged on behalf of England by the Duke of Marlborough. Even great wars fought by their country did not till the end of the eighteenth century immediately affect such villages as ours, except through taxes and those largely indirect. Presently, the great Duke's home would be built for him by the Queen and the nation at Woodstock between us and Oxford.

Queen Anne was a conscientious ruler and in a time of little religious feeling she cared for the national church, setting on foot a practical reform to which she made a great contribution from monies legally her own—the better payment of poor clergy. By this, the parsons and thereby after a time the parish of Bledington would benefit from her day to ours.

The first two Hanoverian sovereigns who followed Anne were Germans by language and extraction; as such and as reigning Electors of Hanover, they tended to be more interested in continental politics than in English and failed to attract the affections of their English subjects. But they were Protestants and the best hope of a quiet life.

The Stuart heirs made two attempts on the throne, neither of them very threatening. The small events hereabouts in 1715 and 1745 illustrate the scale of the uprisings in support of them. When George I came to the throne, some few officials loyal to the Stuarts refused to take the oath of allegiance, among them the non-resident lord of the manor of Idbury; in Oxford, the Second Keeper of the Bodleian Library was kept out of his post. Some Colleges affected to despise the new dynasty. The Jones family of Chastleton House looked back to ancestors who had rendered services to Charles I, and maintained a tradition of loyalty to his descendants. But the Jacobites were defeated at Lancaster.

The second attempt took place thirty years later at the time of the War of the Austrian Succession, when the Army was on the Continent.

It is said that Lord Cornbury had in the meantime secretly entertained the Stuart claimant,[1] the "Pretender", presumably on a visit seeking support. It was a Charlbury barber who later told of the visit. He was summoned to shave the guest and noted the extraordinary respect shown to him by his host. The Jones family had planted "Jacobite" fir-trees in their small formal garden and drank loyal toasts from rose-engraved glasses to the "King over the water" and to the success of the next attempt. This second time Charles Edward, the Stuart prince, led his Scottish supporters as far south as Derby, being joined by a few Englishmen. Some enthusiasts from Devon and Cornwall marched to meet him, only to find he had been defeated by troops hurriedly called back from Europe. Turning homewards, the men from the West broke into inconspicuous groups and made their way nightly by woods and along lonely roads. Wychwood lay in the way of one group. At Cornbury Park they hoped to be helped by the Clarendon family and were in fact sheltered there. Bread was hurriedly baked in Burford and carried to them in the darkness and the next day they vanished.[2] Thus passed Stuart loyalty and from England the danger of civil war.

In 1760, the third George came to the throne. During the two previous reigns, the power of Parliament had grown, through the dependence on Ministers of Kings who had little English and who, being absolute heads of state in Hanover, did not know well the more complex constitution of this country. Ministers were members of Parliament and in their turn dependent on its favour. Notably, the King's patronage—the power to nominate to the Civil List and to appoint to offices—had passed to the Prime Minister. George III, grandson of George II, was a thorough Englishman. At this time an interest in agriculture marked the intelligent landowner; the King earned the title "Farmer George". He was determined to regain some power for the monarch and in fact did so by reclaiming the royal patronage. Through his deliberate effort to have a corps of M.P.s ready to support him, it became more than ever common for members to receive with one hand large, even immense, bribes in the form of well-paid offices and sometimes unearned incomes without pretence of office; with the other hand, they paid small bribes to voters in boroughs near their homes—as Lord North bought votes in Banbury and the Churchills later in Woodstock. This state of affairs was usual, but honesty was known: the first William Pitt refused a sinecure.

King George III having gained influence, used it particularly in overseas affairs. These were very important in his reign for the development of national commerce and power and would also greatly affect the future of village folk.

France was our great rival in foreign trade. Her commerce and our own with India had grown and there was a great field there for further enterprise. In North America, the English colonies occupied much of the East coast region. Emigration to these from both England and Scotland was proceeding. France had a settlement on the St. Lawrence river and forts west of the New England colonies, along the Ohio and Mississippi Rivers. It looked as though the English colonies would lose their chance of expanding in the vast lands beyond the rivers. A great event in the war that began in 1756, the Seven Years War, was the taking of Quebec and consequently of Canada. The great St. Lawrence River was surveyed for the assault by James Cook[3] who had been, not so long before, a common sailor. His work made possible Wolfe's heroic and successful landing. So, in brief, occurred the conquest of perhaps the favourite colony for our rural labourers in the nineteenth century.

The French were also ousted, by the joint work of the Army and the colonists, from the area of the Ohio and Mississippi. Thus there was, for many years to come, the chance of farmers from New England and Old England also, to acquire cheap fertile land.

In India also, the English overcame opposition. If there are successful wars, the Seven Years War was one for England. Yet, twenty years later, its greatest gains were lost. The American colonies, except those north of the St. Lawrence were united into one independent federal country, the United States of America.

The colonies had been by the motives of their foundation devoted (in varying degrees) to religious freedom and by their circumstances settlers were accustomed to great family and individual scope and freedom. During their struggle to gain from the government of the mother country some control of their own affairs they developed political experience and views which would encourage the revolutionary ideas of Frenchmen. These in time would cross the Channel to affect Englishmen, though perhaps they brought more fear to rulers than hope to the ruled.

The new American country kept its doors open to English immigrants and never lost popularity with them. We shall see Bledington folk cutting free from their problems here, and even gaining the wherewithal to return in some prosperity.

Meanwhile, voyages of discovery were adding in more peaceful fashion to British dominions. The sailor James Cook—the title of "Captain" denied to this low-born hero till very late—directed the most famous of these. He explored the oceans and charted the coasts of New Zealand and East Australia—countries which would play a fateful part, for ill and then good, in the lives of English farm workers. In almost all references to Cook, we are told that he was the son of a farm labourer, but it should be noted that his background was not that of labourers late in the century: his father was a skilled and able man who became a farm manager. What Cook's life shows is not so much opportunities open to the humble, as that among such men there was an almost untapped reservoir of talent and character. Cook had shown learning as well as seamanship and most just and patient leadership and administration.[4]

In about a dozen years after Cook's exploration, the first British settlement was made in Australia (1786–87). Convicts could no longer be sent—as had been done for decades—across the Atlantic to to colonies, but the new vast, empty Australia, half the world away, could be used. Adventurers, farmers and free labourers followed the convicts. Through the call of the new lands, there came about the strange condition in which it was easier for hard-driven English villagers to conceive of themselves in a new far-distant home than in the back streets of a town a score of miles away.

From 1789, the end of the century saw in France the breakdown of society, owing to the unbearable suppression of her lower classes and the severe limits set to the developing energies of her professional and trading folk. The Revolutionary and Napoleonic Wars followed— waged first in defence of the changes and later for reasons partly obscure but including the aims of conquest and empire. The sympathies of many Englishmen everywhere had been with the revolutionaries, but Napoleon's direct threat to our own soil, combined with his overweening personality set every simple soul against him, no matter how little reason they might have for patriotism. Scattered villages formed volunteer defence groups, like that at Shipton under Wychwood. From every village, farmers and labourers were drawn by lot for the militia. Many poor unemployed men, not drawn, took money to serve instead of those who were. And when they had gone, their villages had to support their wives and children by the poor rates. Every village would rejoice after Waterloo and grieve when presently maimed and diseased men returned from the Armies. From this time the consequences of all major wars would reach down to every village and every class.

Perhaps the oustanding fact of England's situation after the Restoration, in highest degree from about 1714 to 1760 but continuing with little qualification till 1832 and beyond, is that the wealthy landlords were the governors of England. They "possessed" (James Boswell's word) not only the House of Lords but through their control of elections in many constituencies, the House of Commons also. On their own large estates and in the small towns on which they bestowed trade their power was very great owing to their economic whip-hand over farmers, shopkeepers and inns. In addition to power they had immense prestige for they lived in magnificent houses, (some of them very beautiful, others too elephantine for beauty) employed many skilled and trained people from lawyers to housemaids. Their very animals—horses, cattle and dogs—were fine creatures. They drove in most elegant equipages. Among them palatial architecture flourished, portrait painters were required to decorate great rooms and to minister to their sense of family and quality. A few made a hobby of science and some cared for music. Their outstanding achievement lay in the art of spending leisure pleasurably—an art never practised more successfully. In many outdoor sports, in dress, talk, and elegant social gatherings they excelled.

One curious cultural result of the dominance of this class will presently be seen to have affected our village. They were much influenced in the arts by the tours in France and Italy which were part very often of their higher education and social initiation. Mediterranean art came to be so much to them that they were not well able to recognise that of their own country in some matters; it was during this century that English music was gradually ignored by court circles and omitted from concerts. This country became a byword for the lack of a national traditional music. Not till we recovered our heritage could we become again a musical nation.[5]

The great prestige of families in this high situation ensured that the pattern of their life was envied and imitated and even felt to be very admirable by many far removed from the possibility of sharing it. Their stress on family claims, their exclusiveness, their manners and

179

education and their sense of the superiority of the clay from which they were moulded led to absurd consciousness and cultivation of "class" throughout the social spectrum even where differences of income and education were not remarkable.

It was an anti-communal influence. Numbers of villages, of which Bledington was one, were outside the immediate power of great landlords but not outside this subtle, divisive influence which was reinforced by other very great developments. Their exclusiveness went far. Brilliant, well-informed men with strong and generous motives for political work, were hindered from office or successfully kept out of it; e.g. Samuel Whitbread, the son of a brewer, and George Canning (who did however become Prime Minister) because his mother was an actress. It was significant, though not typical, that Benjamin Franklin[6] representing American colonies in London was mocked and taunted as a mere trader and editor.

As legislators, the distance at which they stood from the populace and from modern circumstances meant that they could not have insight into the needs of the moment or into the future. Of course there were exceptions: some were interested in agricultural progress and some in new inventions and plans for transport. Lord Shaftesbury (the seventh Earl) gave a lifetime of work to the reform of factory life: but that was in the nineteenth century and he had been touched by the evangelical movement and other modern influences.

Among the new developments which were to make political and legislative changes imperative, were inventions in the textile industries. In country districts, from about 1750, as hereabouts, weaving was leaving the small village houses: looms were gathered in barns and later in factories. Spinning machinery was invented and cottage women lost the means of supplementing the family income and teaching their children to help. Presently, in some parishes e.g. Kingham, the women put their idle wheels on bonfires so that overseers could not refuse them parish relief.[7]

For other reasons conditions in villages were changing. Another of the great events, not much noticed in government circles, was the application of steam power to machinery—first in the mines, then in cotton factories and later still in wool manufacture. Mills could be built wherever labour and coal were available. Small factories on streams were abandoned (though one survived at Chipping Norton) and the towns expanded. Production grew and the population of the towns increased, both through the concentration of industry and the absence of some of the great plagues. There was no planning, often no regulation of house-building. Even in small towns like Banbury, where a few factories were built, the new housing was crowded and insanitary. In larger towns, whole sections had no provisions for disposal of waste and no streams were led or water piped to them.

Fortunes were being made in the towns by factory owners; landowners under whose ground minerals were found, added greatly to their wealth. Beside these fortunate ones there were many smaller men hoping to make money by similar means. They naturally developed points of view which justified and favoured their objects and these became very important. A second class outlook was evolved, not unrelated to that of the legislators. Competition was the bugbear— that of neighbours or neighbourhood, of other towns, of other countries. France and Holland were, at the time, our great national rivals. International co-operation hardly existed outside the military sphere, where it was related to temporary needs. Every country's trade—so went the mercantilist theory—depended on the protection of armies and navies and these must be paid for by trade. England must, it followed, ensure her dominance by underselling her neighbours: the country must prosper; it must be on top. The easiest way to keep down or lower costs, was through low wages and long hours, whether of men, women or children. (Nor were such views subconscious: they were constantly expressed in numbers of books and pamphlets). The poor in their poverty were at the basis of society. It was their function to uphold the ranks above them. All that they needed or should have was food and shelter to ensure survival and reproduction. The majority must be kept in poverty that the whole might be rich—a view as conscientiously held no doubt as many another cruel theory whether to the "right" or "left", in other days.

The work of the towns and the wretchedness of the countryside cried out for constructive government. An age-old theory stood in the way: the basis of rights, of citizenship, was property: without it men were outside the nation. Many were losing their modest possessions and also the skills by which property might be gained; with these, they lost all.

Yet the propertied folk (the nation in their own eyes) were growing in numbers and in the variety of their means of livelihood. There were more doctors, more lawyers, more builders, more shopkeepers, more large lease-hold farmers (and fewer of smaller acreage). To grow in numbers was what the wealthy landed class could not, in the nature of things, do. Some power in time must pass to the middle classes. London was full of life. Dr. Johnson found there everything to stimulate and enliven—libraries, clubs, discussion groups and bookseller-publishers most eager to develop their sales and publications. In his talk we see the variety of outlook to be met in his circle. "The time has come", he said "when every Englishman expects to be informed of the national affairs and in which he has the right to have that expectation gratified".[8] Yet he set a very high value on "proper subordination in society", therein agreeing with those whose high status or profits depended on cheap service. On the other hand, an aristocrat who treated the Doctor coldly till he was successful and then flattered him, received a most courtly but scorching letter.[9]

Another famous writer and talker who loved the life of London, but who brings us also back to the country, was Sydney Smith—the Reverend (1771–1845). Like Johnson, he owed prosperity and security to the Establishment (it was a contemporary term). And though Smith's heart (I judge by his letters) was always in his own charming life and the income on which it depended, he kept his vision clear. He was rector in turn of two parishes, one near York, and the other in Somerset. On entry successively to these, separated by twenty years of his life, as well as by two hundred miles, he describes the majority of his parishioners in one almost identical sentence: "The people are starving,—in the last stages of poverty and depression".[10] Was his church, then, content with this state of affairs? with the deadly towns? with the outlook on the poor? Such questions must often occur to those who have followed the story of religion in earlier centuries. Sydney Smith is brief and cogent on this point. "In England I maintain that except among ladies of the middle class of life there is no religion at all. The clergy of England have no more influence over the people at large than the cheesemongers of England have". And in his next letter, "You may depend upon it, my dear Madam, that my observations on the Clergy are just. Religion is . . . much like Heraldry, an antiquated concern; a few people attend to one and the other, but the world laughs at them for engaging in such an antiquated pursuit".[11] In 1809, there had been no resident rector in Smith's Yorkshire parish since Charles II.

As to other churches, dissent—repressed and despised—had settled down into quiet acceptance of things as they were. Within their own communities they maintained high moral traditions and good preaching, but they were scarcely more missionary than the Church of England.

However, the New Testament was always available and was sometimes read. Dr. Johnson, though his talk was of the classics, was in private devoted to it and lived a life of great charity. He was also well acquainted with John Wesley, finding him a well-informed man, of interesting conversation, and admiring his power of speaking so that the poor understood. As early as 1729, the Wesley brothers, Charles and John, sons of a Lincolnshire parson, who himself inherited a spirited outlook from dissenting forebears, were concerned in an Oxford group for daily, methodical religious exercises. John became its leader—leading those who would follow to missions in the Oxford prisons and presently to the benighted poor of England.

Wesley never taught resentment of economic injustice, nor sought means to political or social reform, and for this he and the movement he started have been criticised. But one thing he did: he made straight for individuals and their immortal souls. It was their own value that was being denied to the poor and he restored it to them. His movement, and the Methodist Churches presently based on it, trained a body of men to read and speak and to organise their fellows, thus equipping them to serve in such social directions as they chose. The Wesleyan Church's theory was less democratic than that of the seventeenth century foundations, the Baptist and Independent Churches; but in practice it reached and taught humbler classes than they had done.

Wesley's evangelical outlook had great influence in both the Church of England and the dissenting churches. It led the latter to modify their Calvinist élitism and the "clergy" to reconsider their teaching and showed them a way to extend their work and influence. This broad evangelical movement had a great share in promoting the generosity that so greatly—though so slowly—leavened politics in the nineteenth century.

Evangelism had allies. From the middle of the century books and newspapers lubricated the minds of men, and women too, of the middle classes and of the more fortunate wage-earners. In the towns, intelligent working men discovered each other and discussed their own condition. Men of philanthropy, variously stimulated, were shocked into action by the maiming and exhausting of workers in factories and mines and by the death rate in the new towns and urban districts.

At the same time, social and political theories were the result of the growth of professional and intellectual groups. One view that seems to reflect the harsh outlook of the time on the place of wage-earners in society is that of Malthus: the increase of population—by 1789, unquestioned—would exceed the supply of food, the fecundity of the human race having been kept in check in the past only by apparent catastrophes, such as starvation and plague. The systematic relief of the poor was in his view a mistake. Other thinkers concentrated on injustice to labour, arguing that, as the source of value, it should be better rewarded: rent tended to absorb all gains from higher productivity. It was calculated by one writer that, for seven eights of their time, labourers worked, not for themselves or their families but for others! Bentham's view,[12] printed earlier, became popular after 1810. The aim for politics and private endeavour as summarised in the phrase "the greatest happiness of the greatest number" seemed practical and humane. Though it stressed pleasure, it was not selfish but social and could reinforce evangelistic Christianity. In the agricultural sphere, Thomas Spence expounded the community's claim to land ownership.[13] Greatly disturbed by enclosures and by the distorted social conditions of the time he argued that land should be returned to genuine village communities of cultivators, with provision for fair apportionment of produce in a modern way, including education for the young.

Meanwhile throughout all the century and before and beyond it, there was the legend that England's life was "happy and free", that her "glorious revolution" and her inheritance from long past ages had given her a constitution that could scarcely be improved upon, that her laws were equitable and her citizens "equal before the law". But conditions towards the end of the century grew worse, through fears of radicalism and of a tendency of working people to combine. The law, that persons must not be taken into custody without being charged with an offence, was suspended: public meetings must not be held without permission of magistrates, every person attending an unauthorised gathering being liable to severe punishment. Combination of workers to raise wages was also illegal. More than a hundred offences could incur the death penalty and, in fact, did often lead to transportation to Australia.

Was there then no basis for the legends of freedom and justice? Visitors from foreign countries, seeing chiefly London and comfortable circles, thought there was, for in some countries absolute monarchs still ruled, the use of torture was known and there was religious intolerance of a degree long unknown here. The jury system was certainly a safeguard for the middle classes and, since members of juries valued it, for the freedom of printers and the press. The legend and the truth can be reconciled if we remember that the poor were not, in fact, citizens of what for some was 'no mean city". They had the very negative right not themselves to become property even to save their wives and children, and remarkably little else.

ii The Church

In Bledington throughout our period the parishioners were so far united, with the exception of one family for a time, as to be all undissenting members of the Church of England. The ecclesiastical census of 1676[14] showed only five nonconformists. In 1733 there were none and no papists. The village was exceptional in this. Most parishes in the Stow deanery had larger numbers of nonconformists though Roman Catholics were rare. Stow had a fairly large Baptist community, of 55 members. Chipping Norton, in the seventeenth century exceptionally lively in religious matters, had Presbyterians, Baptists and Quakers. Tiny Idbury always had Catholics, with at times a chapel in the Manor House or in one of the other farmhouses till 1738. As late as 1768 the shoe-maker and his wife were Catholics and a priest visited their house to hold a monthly service.[15]

Our neighbour Kingham[16] had also little dissent, though there were a few Quakers, later some Methodists and for a time a small meeting of "Anabaptists". There were also (1738) some "who commonly absent themselves from church, thro' no Principle but negligence". This one may take to have been true here also, as very generally. There is a greater difference between the clergy of the two parishes: the contrast has its significance for the Church of England as a whole, and for hundreds of villages. The Rectors of Kingham are Archdeacon Grantlys,[17] for all that Trollope did not write till the middle of the nineteenth century. They make a good background and contrast for Bledington. In 1652 William Dowdeswell, son of a landowner, bought the advowson and became himself incumbent. His family and the similar and closely related Lockwoods provided

Kingham with rectors, except during a few short intervals, till 1911. The living, in the eighteenth century, was worth £760 a year. Several rectors of the two families are described as "of Christ Church, Oxon"; they were M.A.s of the University. Even their women were well-educated. They were generous folk, rebuilding the chancel of the church and endowing a charity with liberality. In their routine work they were men of conscience. In response to questions they write to their Archdeacons such phrases as "I reside constantly in my own Parsonage House", "I have resided upon my cure except for two weeks". In 1738 when only four parishes in the Oxford diocese had two services on a Sunday, Kingham was one of them.

But also they loved the good lay life: in 1688 they built a fine rectory house in the latest architectural fashion; some of them hunted enthusiastically; they bought the latest books (I saw some of them sold in 1958 and read their inscriptions). Their estate in the Rectory was not their only financial resource: they lent money to their neighbours the Lord family of Bledington and cannily transferred the mortgage[18] to others, (but not, be it noted, to men poorer than themselves) in time to avoid loss. Perhaps like Archdeacon Grantly, they were genial and tolerant and fairminded rather than spiritual: they make it very clear that they do not intend their charity to "relieve the landlord" in any way; one of them calls some early Methodists "ranters", but it is the only sign of disrespect for those who had different views from their own. In any century before the twentieth they could be accounted good rural clergy. They are a local proof that in the eighteenth century there were pockets of humane culture. Perhaps the circumstances of Kingham in part explain them: the Lord of their manor was New College, not a personal landlord secluded by wealth who might have demanded their allegiance to narrower views, and the advowson was the property of the family, usually of the Rector himself.

The circumstances of our own parish priests were very unlike those of the Dowdeswells and Lockwoods. The sole income of William Herbert, the good parson who died in 1708, was "£17 and a cottage house". By the most diligent enquiries the churchwardens of 1704 could find nothing else. Nine of the thirteen vicars appointed between 1708 and 1800 were graduates and had they served here might have been efficient, but they frequently paid substitutes—of course only part of the stipend—who were evidently ignorant men. (They must have supplemented their official income, but how? One or two of them could hardly have acted as scribes: did they do occasional manual work?)

During two periods of uncertain length there was no Vicar. How baptisms, marriages and funerals were then provided for there is no sign, though registers were kept and churchwardens carried on such duties as they could without a vicar or a substitute.

Some particulars of the parsons can be given. John Nicolle M.A. was Vicar from 1711 till 1716, but the transcripts are ill-written and— with all allowances for lack of convention—very ill-spelled. In 1722 Henry Lamb was Vicar: he took a wedding that year, but in 1724 the living was "vacant by the absence and negligence" of Lamb and the Chancellor of the Diocese sequestrated the income of the living. The Vicar appears to have employed a substitute for much of his incumbency before leaving the cure unserved.[19]

How the parish was tended from 1724 to 1730 is not clear, but in the latter year the Rev. Penniston Hastings, member of the family once of Daylesford and father of Warren Hastings was presented "by the King" which indicates that the parish was then neglected. He lived at Churchill, within two miles of his cure, and appears to have served the the parish himself for three years, after which an attractive script and literate spelling give way to poorer hands and to such spellings as whife (wife), Agost (August) and Dacamer(December). When Hastings left the country for the West Indies in 1735 (or possibly 1736)[20] he doubtless left a cleric in charge, but if so his substitute departed and there was no minister here and for a while the Bishop sequestrated the profits of the Vicarage.

In 1738 a new Vicar was appointed. The Rev. John Ingles B.A. was Vicar till twenty years later when he died and was buried here. But from 1740 to 1758 his handwriting is absent from the records, except for one occasion in 1754 when he signs the register.

Of the next three Vicars (1758 to 1799), one (Brown) was an elderly and soon a sick man, the second a bird of passage, and the third (Paget) was never resident. His registers were for several years signed by "T. Haynes, curate" and fairly well kept. Later there were again illiterate entries, names oddly spelt—Hannameriah, Cathern (for Catherine) and Write (Wright).[21] Crude ignorance in our parsons never recurs after 1799, when Paget's "ministry" ceased.

In the next year Christ Church itself nominated the Vicar—an ex-undergraduate of the college and a Master of Arts of the University.

But in that same year the new Vicar was apppointed Headmaster of the Grammar School of Crewkerne, a town in the Quantock Hills, too distant for him to have any oversight of his parish of Bledington. For John Allen during about forty years, the living was to be, quite simply, the source of an independent income, not large but growing. In 1800 its value was about £50.[22] No doubt Allen appointed a curate at once, but no such person emerges from the records till 1805 when William Jones took up the work, which he was to continue for thirty-three years—that is, until the Rev. John Allen returned from the headmastership of his school and desired to live on his cure. Even the curate in this case did not live in the village but lodged a few miles away[23] and rode a horse to and fro. Perhaps the condition of the parsonage house accounted for this arrangement. In 1778 the non-resident Vicar had written[24] of it to Christ Church that it consisted of two rooms, one below and one above, the latter having been divided into two: and at the end of William Jones' curacy, his Vicar described it as lying low and being "rat-infested". But resident or not, Jones did the work regularly and well, as we infer from the registers, which will from this time on be well and uniformly kept. Jones was not young in 1805 yet his work belongs typically to the nineteenth century and we shall return to it.

Meanwhile better days economically were on the way for Bledington vicars. "Good Queen Anne" had been urged, and made the plan her own, to use the money from "Annates and Tenths", (forms of tithe paid by the clergy themselves, which Henry VIII had taken for his own Treasury) to augment the salaries of ill-paid clergy.[25] The plan was adumbrated in 1704, but the income had been used to pay pensions to politicians and royal servants, some of which had been promised for two or three generations to come. However, information could meanwhile be gathered in all dioceses: hence the terrier of 1704.[26] Though our Vicar's income at that time was only the equivalent of a superior labourer's pay, it was more than the income of some parishes. After 1714, when the scheme began to be put into practice, the poorest had first to be helped. It was probably after 1735, when money began to flow in faster to the Governors of Queen Anne's Bounty that Werndydyr (or Werndidier) Farm in Nantmell, Radnorshire was bought with a grant from them so that its rent should come to the Vicars of Bledington. Property had to be found which could be bought for £200 and whose title was beyond question. Probably the advisers of the Bishop of Gloucester suggested Welsh farms: and thus is explained this, as it seemed, outlandish source of part of our Vicars' salary for some two centuries. Werndydyr consisted of about 50 acres (not 120 as stated in the terrier of 1829) and with some rights of hill pasturage. What rent was received in early days we do not know, but the stipend remained low. By 1769 the lessee of glebe and tithes was paying £20 instead of £17, and in that year, by the Enclosure Act, Christ Church gave to the Vicarage a close of between four and five acres. Presently the Government and the Governors of the Bounty urged impropriators to contribute capital of £200 to low stipends, promising to earmark an equal amount in the Bounty funds. It seems that Christ Church was moved to present to the living eleven acres just over the border of the parish, in Westcote. The rent from this excellent field came to roughly £10, while the Governors of the Bounty kept their promise, though the interest on their allotment was by 1829 only £3. 16. Thus, the stipend crept up. By the end of the century, it was worth some £50 and higher values would some day add to this improvement. Unfortunately the increase did not yet mean that the minister serving the parish was paid so much, though no doubt the curate profited somewhat.

By this time some influential folk had realised the effects upon the parishes of the practice of "non-residence" and some moves were made towards making it illegal to take the income of a cure without serving it, but patrons of livings valued their privileges and the intention to modify them legally was sure to be blocked in the House of Lords. Long after 1750 Bledington pastors could be ignorant men, unable to give much help or stimulus to a parish much in need of the latter. They were no longer husbandmen; it is difficult to see what genuine status the poorest of them could have had.

Fortunately the church and parish were not utterly dependent on the Vicars or curates. There was the Diocesan organisation, with the Archdeacon's annual oversight of the parishes, and the churchwardens' access to him. And there were the wardens themselves. They were an old institution, recognised from 1604 by the civil government as well as the church. The office had become a part of our village life, like that of constable or "oarsman", held mostly, like those offices, by the husbandmen.

The wardens were chosen by the Vicar and parishioners in the Vestry, and in later years one was chosen by each. It would be possible

189

to make (from various documents) a complete list of them from 1703 to the present, and to give the names of many for the century before. Sometimes wardens served for as many as twelve years (William Stayt); another (George Gilbert) was warden for three series of years, amounting in all to twenty-seven.

In 1730 the roof of the church was repaired and the two church-wardens left their mark upon one of the beams: E.S. and W.L., standing for Edward Stayt and William Lord. At this time the parish seems to have had no minister, for that was when Hastings was nominated by the King. With few intervals efficient service seems to have been given by the wardens. We have the churchwardens' accounts and vestry minutes from 1764 to the date of writing. The first book in which they were written was used for 150 years—1764 to 1916.[27] Thus is struck the note of continuity. Throughout the book all the wardens are literate, though some appear to write with difficulty. Having been appointed in the Vestry, they report and present their accounts to it annually. For many years they continue to refer to the Vicar as "the minister", though for himself he preferred and always used the other term. It is a striking fact that no minister was present at vestry meetings for seventeen years, from 1793 to 1810, although we know that William Jones was curate from 1805. Such business as fell to the wardens they could do alone, and with fellow laymen, in the vestry. One of their major duties was the care of the building, with the churchyard and its paths and walls. About once in three years a "gleasher" or glazier was employed to look over the glass; the pliabi-lity of the old lead made this essential; but for this care almost every square inch of the fifteenth century glass must have fallen out. There is no payment for the cleaning of the church for thirty years (till 1794); cleanliness was very far as yet from "next to godliness". Shortly after noting this lack I saw French churches, one with a floor inch-deep in dried mud, and another with the rotting plaster frames of fifteenth century pictures falling to the floor: but they were much frequented. Brooms might be far from essential to religious life.

Sometimes the wardens contributed to the lay needs of the parish. By the latter half of the century increasing emphasis on time and punc-tuality had put out-of-date the fifteenth century dice-like sundial on the south-west angle of the nave walls which is still in its place. A clock had been inserted in the tower which by 1792 required to be overhauled. Somewhat before this the wardens were noting the month and day, as well as the year, of the vestry meeting, but never the hour. They were not hurried even in re-imbursing themselves for their expenditure: sometimes they would draw on their own pockets for as much as two years.

For the first ten years of the accounts the average annual expenditure is just under £5. It mounts to six guineas in the last decade of the eighteenth century and in the early nineteenth century would rise by leaps and bounds: but then the Napoleonic Wars were rocking our world. The costs were defrayed by a "church" rate on the forty-six yardlands of the parish—1s. 6d. at first, gradually rising.

The Kingham and Bledington types of clergy would long remain numerous in villages, but a new, modern interpretation of village ministry took its rise in the first half of the century. From 1725 for several years a young ordained graduate of Lincoln College had friends among the clergy in some of our nearby villages and rode out of Oxford to preach at the churches of Witney, Shipton and Ascott under Wychwood.[28] The word "preach" is important: the young man loved exposition and credited his audiences with ability to follow his thought and to respond to his enthusiasm. But he was not devoting all the latter quality to religion. His favourite friends lived at Stanton and here the young man, "so neat and precise" but "romanticised by dark locks' shared picnics in the fields, read Gulliver's Travels aloud (it had just been published) and danced and played with the Vicarage daughters, cultivating romantic but carefully conducted friendships. They might have been Dowdeswell girls. The well-to-do, well-educated clergy were naturally attracted to the finer but less costly aspects of eighteenth century culture, not of great houses and display, but of literature and music. Before long John Wesley would be learning how many communities in his England, how many thousands of people, needed something at once more basic and more stirring than the formal services of the church. But he would always want to bring them into the church and always wish that the best books should be open to all their potential readers. It would be more than a hundred years (1846) before the movement he led touched Bledington directly: but his leaven was taken by many who did not bake quite the same bread: it may well be that Bledington owed to his influence some of the quality of the Rev. William Jones to whom we presently come.

Looking back over the list of vicars, we recall the special note struck by the name Hastings. When Penniston (or Penyston) Hastings was instituted here, the name was of no very great note. He had been an undergraduate of Balliol, but not a graduate. His son, Warren, was born in Hastings' home at Churchill, ten years after he left Oxford. Father and son belonged to a family of landowners (but not of great acreage) and clerics. It was Warren's career alone that put the name among the most famous in England. My predecessor in this essay, the Rev. Stephen Liberty, spent precious months on the distinguished association, but after all it concerned Bledington very little. Yet Penniston Hastings was one of the types of his century and a summary of Stephen Liberty's findings is of value. Penniston's father had been Vicar of Daylesford; though the family manor there had been sold, the advowson of the rectory had been retained, and would presently belong to Warren Hastings. Penniston is believed to have left Churchill and his cure of Bledington in 1735. It is certain that he married his second wife in 1737 in the church of his own parish of Christchurch, Barbados.[29]

In Barbados, Hastings prospered somewhat in a material way. He became the owner of "Williams' Plantation" there, and left it in his will to his Barbadian wife for her life together with the Plow Inn at Cheltenham and other property there. This was at a time when great fortunes were made in the West Indies and perhaps Hastings had hoped that even a clergyman might do better. He had left to the care of others in England his two young children, Warren and his sister, but they were not forgotten in his Will.

Later the pathos, drama and foreignness of the story of Warren Hastings stirred this quiet locality to wonder and curiosity and to generous if ineffective loyalty. Even now it gives colourful associations to Daylesford and Churchill. Fortunate residents may still find relics of the great man, as did Major Prosser of Kingham, (the top of a huge trunk painted with Hastings' name which had gone with him to India).

iii The Husbandmen before Enclosure

Early in the century there was scarcely any approach here to the separated farms which have made up rural England for almost two hundred years. When our Bledington fields were enclosed in 1769 there were still no enclosures here beside the small home closes except that one family had apparently extended its home close somewhat: Loggans had planted a small orchard beyond the original close and the same five acres was later planted afresh by the next holder: this ground is still occasionally referred to as Lords' Park. Nor was enclosure common in our neighbourhood. There were some old enclosures in Broadwell but no considerable area had been fenced in Churchill, Sarsden, Idbury, Oddington, Chipping Norton; also the villages "under Wychwood" all lay open and as for Kingham, not till Christmas Eve 1850 would its award be read to the villagers.

It is likely, however, that there had been some laying together of strips in the open fields. In 1711 Richard Baker's holding consisted of 250 strips, never in groups of more than three together, and only thirty groups of three and two, accounting for 66 in all. The other 184 strips lay scattered singly. The holding was represented in all the six major divisions of the "field" or arable area, and in 45 of the furlongs, beside some in picks and butts which composed the six. He had a few strips in meadows, beside his rights in the Lot Mead, the Twenty Lands and the heaths. This holding was almost precisely as it had been in the Extent of 1550. Presumably the other holdings had been similarly stable: change on any considerable scale must have affected a number of holdings.

But in a late meeting of the manor court in the seventeenth century when a difference about the boundaries between the strips of two neighbours had occurred, there had been a recommendation that the limits should be ascertained and then marked by "merestones". Such stones were presently used: in our farmyards we occasionally find large stones about three feet long, tapering to fifteen inches wide at a rounded top where they bear a single well-cut initial. Turning over the stone sill under a gate of my own, on a one-time Pegler farm I found one bearing an elegantly cut P. Three similar stones with the initials of other families were built into a barn on what is now the orchard at Hangerson Farm. An old man used to tell of seeing several such stones built into a bridge over the brook, when he was a child. The stones are weighty and of the very hard type of local stone, not easily moved or broken.

It seems likely that between 1711 and the mooting of a plan, half a century later, to "enclose" the parish, commoners had amalgamated the ridges they held in single furlongs and that the merestones marked the junctions between one man's set and another's. An infinity of discussions and adjustments must have been needed in the commoners' meetings.

Amalgamation of this degree would make it possible for a farmer to profit by his own industrious weeding and eliminate short journeys when tilling and harvesting, but it did not bring much freedom in cropping because the fields had still to be cleared by Lammas Day for the "rother beasts" to graze the stubble. Wheat, barley, and beans continued to be staple crops but more oats were grown. A small quantity of turnips were sown on the small strips in the Oars. Hop-vines still trail along a single hedge as in some other villages—possibly because at some time the parish itself made beer. The animals continued to be cows, pigs and sheep and the larger holdings had each a plough team of four or five horses. There were few draught oxen here by 1711, although they continued till about 1750 to be fairly common in the county. Sheep, too, were fewer, no doubt because their value had slumped from 10/- to 5/- or less and those sums were worth a good deal less than a century earlier. Seed was still sown broadcast on the settled sods—and would continue that way sometimes late in the next century.

It seems that the Bledington commoners were very slow to change. Stimulus was lacking: they were far from the growing markets; no good newspaper reached them till well after the founding of Jackson's Journal in 1753; the church was all but dead and nonconformity not born here. But the meetings of the commoners must still have been efficient in the old way.

In spite of all this continuity a change had come about. One sign of it is the erection of big barns, some half dozen of them. Roses' barn bears the date 1746; Peglers' (at Hangersons'), Harwoods' and Rookes judging by their style were built at about the same time. Wheat yields had been rising for many years, especially since 1650[30] and prices had steadied somewhat. Their size also suggests the retention of grain for sale at chosen moments. It is clear that these large and sound buildings were not due to the effect of enclosure on farming. They show that farmers were able before that event to invest more money and more labour in their farmsteads—an economic change with perhaps some psychological basis. They were now owners of their messuages and closes and of their rights in the open fields: they and their chosen heirs had had for periods of varying length a new security and some new freedoms; their estates had grown in value. Before 1700 the largest total value for an inventory,[31] that of a Guy, a member of an old local family, usually exceptionally well-to-do, was £135. The

194

Andrews' family property may be seen rising in value: in 1690 it was £109, in 1707 £222. In 1717 John Pegler's was worth £331, Peglers being still tenants but becoming freeholders before 1737. A rather curious change comes over farmers' wills. They are leaving their estates burdened by very large monetary legacies, to be paid by those who inherit the land. John Ruck or Rooke, late in the seventeenth century had required his heir[32] to pay legacies of £700. In 1737, John Pegler left his 1½ yardlands subject to £450 worth of legacies. (But in 1776, only seven years after enclosure, his son requires his heir to pay out £1,100. He is childless and his wife inherits. In effect she will pay a high rent for a good many years). Similarly, Christopher Rose in 1733, lays a burden on his heir, a lad not yet of age, of legacies worth more than £900; he inherits 75 acres.

Altogether it seems likely that the new buildings and new family customs have, in part, a common origin. Freehold makes all their improvements the farmers' own: it stimulates pride and the impulse to work and to build. The enclosure of fields was recommended on these same grounds.

The new powers of owners included naming their own heirs and disposing at will of the property they lived upon. The pattern they adopt in these matters is that of the owner of large estates in which e.g. the head of a family provides for widow, daughter and younger sons out of the receipts of a landed estate. The pattern of course had other variations and influence on other matters. If life had been excessively communal in the past owing to the need to hold together all forces to subdue the wild, there was now growing scope for family and individuals while there was still a strong village life.

There were changes inside the farmers' houses. There had been a slow accretion of furniture and implements, which could spell a much higher degree of comfort and some refinement of manners and of cleanliness. In many wills household goods are taken for granted or dismissed in a single general term but Thomas Andrews (1707) and William Saunders (1739) specify some of them: bell-metal pots, clock-jacks, bacon-racks, iron-dogs, chests of drawers, close-stools, hanging-presses, clocks, warming-pans, kneading troughs or "dough kivvers", beside much pewter ware. The homely kitchen vessels of these years are our cherished "antiques" of today, as the farmers' staddlestones, stone gateposts and here and there a merestone, are our garden ornaments.

Domestic skills and customs had also developed, especially in the direction of cleanliness. A scouring powder known as Calais or Calis powder was imported from France and widely sold. But Kingham folk found a similar sand[33] deposited in pockets over their fields. They washed and sieved it, selling the finer for scouring pewter and the coarser for whetting scythes and for floors. Pewter was still valued and used for some time yet, though it would give way to pottery and china, far easier to cleanse. Some have thought that this change alone was of great hygienic value. Soap could be bought for sixpence, later fourpence a pound, though there were several better qualities. The washday for clothes was less frequent than for floors but was tending to become regular.[34]

China, towards 1770, was usually acquired as decoration rather than as utensils. Most of the farm housewives had oaken cupboards or open niches in the walls filled, as now, with china, striking a new note of elegant and, be it noted, private gaiety.

Outside, the houses still rose from the rough greensward on the green or beside the road with no gardens attached to them, but farmers' wives had long been planting roses and periwinkles under the walls and lilacs in the fence of the yard. There was a small vegetable garden in some fertile nearby spot.

The term "farmer" began to be used instead of older words. It is not fanciful to remember that to "farm" is to exploit rather than to "husband". The new name indicates a possible new outlook. Socially and economically farmers are still the basic group. They produce food; they employ not only labourers but also the smith, the cooper, the wheelwright and later, the drainer and the domestic servant and supply some custom for pedlar and small shopkeeper. As wardens and payers of tithes and rates they support the church and it is usually they, though by the seventeen hundreds sometimes a craftsman, who carry on civic offices as overseers, way-wardens and constables.

In spite of this stability we cannot look at the good farmhouses and say with accuracy "That is the Pegler (or Andrews or Stayt) house". Family tenancies were often broken off. Orphans would leave the family home or a son might marry a girl heiress of a better holding or house. In spite of changes of domicile, a proportion of farming families remained in the village, even for a dozen or more generations. In this they were unlike other groups, especially the poorer labourers.

Families whose bread-winners were unskilled were even in the eighteenth century, a mobile group.

The revolutionary change in agriculture and in social life which was about to come was, like all such events, the result of deep and manifold developments. New pressures and allurements were affecting our old families and these will be more intense after enclosure. It is a good moment to consider their past.

Oldest of all the families were the Kench line, Bledingtonians for nearly six hundred years. The first le Kentys had arrived at Winchcombe Abbey in 1190 as a clerk in minor orders,[35] some kind of secretary: he witnessed deeds relating to property and enfranchising a serf.[35] He signed the agreement confirming the grant of a pension from the church of Bledington to the convent.[36] That was in 1215: by then he was possibly living here. Certainly seventeen years later when he (or just possibly his son) signs deeds at the Salmonsburye or Slaughter Hundred Court, he is a freeholder of this manor. A descendant of his signs more deeds there in 1288. The extent of their freehold was two virgates; only one other holding, probably that of the other freeholder, was as large.

In 1311 the le Kentys children were left orphans. Their "wardship and marriage" fell to the convent and were granted, doubtless for a rent to William de Bladinton, the convent's Steward. We imagine them joining the Steward's family. By 1327, one of the children, John, had come into possession of his father's holding. This is listed in the Abbey's rental of 1355: the next information comes 150 years later, from the first Kench will. In 1517[37] Robert Kench, after the devotion of his soul to "the holy company of heaven", shows his practical piety by bequests of 4d. and 2d. to "the Moder Church of our blessed lady in Winchcombe", and to St. Leonard's light in Bledington. The reference to Winchcombe is the only one in Bledington wills and seems to indicate that the family has not forgotten its original connection with the Abbey, 300 years before. Robert proceeds to leave his "best pot" and "best pan" to his son and his daughters; his wife, he puts in full possession of his house "to the behouff" of his "heyre till he be of lawful age". In the last phrases we hear the freeholder who can dispose of his land.

The next Kench will is that of his son John, 1546, in which he leaves money to the high altar of the church and to its rood light. To one son he leaves an acre each of barley, wheat and pulse, to another son and daughter 20/- each and to a second daughter a sheep, and all else to his wife who is his executor. From this time Kench wills are lacking.

In 1538 the John Kench mentioned above was among the tenants who had been offered and had taken a lease of part of the demesne and thus the Kench holding was enlarged. But by 1546 (date of will) or shortly after, the Kenches ceased to be freeholders. In 1553 John's widow Alice pays a "fine", the entry to her "bench". In 1557, Robert, her son, has, like other copyholders, to pay a fine on entry to his holding (£12. 16. 8),[38] Alice having removed to a cottage.

The change to copyhold is not necessarily a sign of social or economic descent: a man might sell a small freehold to gain entry to a larger copyhold, but the family's prosperity in fact seems to have declined. The name of Kench no longer appears in documents relating to land. After the late sixteenth century Kenches are never witnesses or overseers of other men's wills; nor are they constables or tithingmen or churchwardens. But they have not lost everything: when the fields are enclosed in 1769, two Kenches have gardens on which they pay tithes; that is, their homes are among the better cottages. It was not very common yet for cottagers to be literate: from 1755, when some craftsmen could still not write, we find their signatures here and there. They had carried forward some knowledge though not any land.

The last Kench in a parish register is of a baptism in 1798. One must suppose that they became labourers, but they never quite joined the ranks of "the poor", away from the heart of the community. The last of them to live out his life here served as parish clerk from 1764 to 1786. He may have written the early vestry minutes which begin in the same year as his clerkship. At the end of the century they appear to have gone to live at Lower Swell. Perhaps they mended their fortunes there: at any rate, they erected tombstones to their dead.

Our next most ancient family is the *Stayts*, here before 1420, when one of them witnesses to the default of an executor of an early will. Since they are with us still, their continuity almost matches the Kenches'. No Stayt shares in the break-up of the demesne land in 1538/9: they were not prosperous then. In 1553 Woolfston Stayt is paying an annual 30/- for his copyhold, indicating a holding of medium extent. In 1605 his son, Thomas, is one of those who travel to Gloucester to bear witness in the affair of David Rylands.[39] Three years later Thomas's young son is one of the nineteen caliver men in the village, enumerated by William Smith. Thomas died in 1625, leaving only £38 in money but making careful family arrangements: £30 is to be invested for his two daughters. If his son shall choose to leave his father's tenement, he must take his mother with him. Stayts are sharing in the modernisation of land tenure in the village: we do not know the terms on which he held his main farm, but he has some land on lease.

In the subsidy list for 1638, the Stayts are all exempt from payment, why, we do not learn: they are still husbandmen. They give in the late seventeenth and early eighteenth centuries striking services to the church, taking the office of churchwarden for long stretches of years between 1624 and 1722.

At the enclosure in 1769, Stayts are still commoners; one is awarded 45 acres and another 14, having no doubt held 1½ yardlands and half a yardland respectively in the open field. By 1722 Stayts are living in the house near the Town Banks, the old home of the Andrews family, having probably been there a number of years. An Andrews had modernised the house in the seventeenth century. In 1722 the Stayts rebuilt the Andrews' modernisation, giving it a new graceful front with stone-mullioned windows without drip-moulds, a lozenge containing husband's and wife's initials and the date, and making an elegant front door, opening into a large room. A fine stone mantel was put into this room and another in the best chamber above. So pleasant are these details that one inevitably thinks of a bridegroom preparing for a bride. After enclosure another Stayt enlarged the house adding to the length of its front in a later style, but carefully harmonised with the earlier section. These were the last great changes in that palimpsest of a house, dating from the fourteenth century and probably long before. We think of Stayts as a family of taste.

From 1731 a more prosperous line of the family are connected with the village. Thomas Stayt of Kingham lends money to our largest farmer of the name of Lord. The grandson of this Stayt, also of Kingham, buys Lords' Farm and moves into the messuage. They remained there till 1820, when they left the village.

But the original Stayt family had, by that time, two branches, one still at Banks Farm, the other at a farmhouse in Bennetts Lane, its representative a bankrupt in 1824. The status of the senior branch also declined. The family had shown taste in the eighteenth century: in the nineteenth and twentieth they serve through their musical gifts

199

and their loyalty to their Methodist church. And still today they play a good part.

The Andrews family was established here by 1450. In 1476 they provided one of the stained glass windows in the rebuilt "perpendicular" church and were commemorated in it. They had one of the largest holdings, of 2½ yardlands. For two centuries their home was the messuage, Banks Farm House, later the home of Stayts. Their original house was the back premises of the present one, which now suggest a small mean dwelling, but the Andrews women had elaborate clothes and one of them in the sixteenth century a "painted cloth" to hang on the wall. In the seventeenth century the head of the family built a new "hall", with a fine chamber over it, enlarging the house. Andrewses were among the tenants to take leases of parts of the demesne lands in 1538/9 and to purchase their share later, with their holding. They pay rent for a cottage, half of which Joan Andrews in 1557 let to someone else. Shortly, she moved into the other half, leaving her son in the messuage. (The elders of farming families often retired in this way). In 1647 William Andrews supports the move, in the absence of a manor court, to draw up new rules for the common lands. The Andrews menfolk are among the first to sign their names as witnesss to wills and the like.

About 1700 they remove from the Banks to a somewhat smaller holding of 2 yardlands, but maybe a better house. They do not lose caste: on the contrary they now appear in registers and documents as "gent" or "Mr." as no other copyholders do. A partial explanation of this may be that "Thomas Andrews, labourer" has come to the village and some distinction had to be made, but that is not all: they retain the appellation. Possibly they had some other source of income and so schooling and servants. At the enclosure John Andrews was awarded 56 acres. Now we learn which messuage they had moved to—that above the Vicarage, once Rookes' then Maces'. It had been rebuilt before they entered it: its good farm buildings, one dated 1646, with a sundial, are still to be seen. They had not so clear a record of public service as some other families, but in their wills they show generosity, constantly remembering the church and the Stow almshouses. There are Andrews entries in the registers as late as 1812.

When the *Grayhursts* first came here, in 1546, they conformed to the usual pattern, but in course of time they showed qualities rare among the husbandmen—more of the energy and thrust that takes people out of their customary life. They seemed to arrive in a tentative way—to a holding of medium extent, $1\frac{1}{2}$ yardlands and uncertain of their name—"Grayhurst Alias Sanders". John, who makes his will in 1605, makes his mark, an elementary scratch, at its close. Grayhursts hold village offices rather rarely but John was a churchwarden and in 1632 another John was "way bailiff": we know, because in spite of his office he was presented at the Hundred Court "for not coming to do his service at the time of the mending of the highway". The way-bailiff's brother, Ellis Grayhurst, must have been good at figures: he lends money to his neighbours, as many a copyholder had done before, but Ellis charged interest. One poor neighbour pays him 6% but later he charged only $4\frac{1}{2}$%. It would seem that it is with this Grayhurst that the family takes an upward turn in ambition and success. His son John was educated and became a coroner for the county. Son John sent his son Thomas to Oxford to graduate B.A. from Hart Hall in 1691. Probably Thomas became a cleric or teacher or both: he certainly left the village.

The Grayhurst name reached the modest eminence of a mention in Atkyns' history of the County in 1712. The coroner is mentioned as having "a good house and estate in Bledington and elsewhere". There is no reason to doubt that he owned property out of the village: here, his holding was never large, but his house (Harwoods') was fine inside and out with many windows "ovolo moulded" and hearths of the new elegant eighteenth century type. The family's first messuage and holding were sold by 1750 and in 1768 re-sold to a land-hungry newcomer. By 1769 no-one bore the name here: the family had migrated to Cirencester. They seem to have lived for self and family rather than family and community: a type which eighteenth century tendencies would encourage.

The *Hathaways*, who are still with us, represented by married women bearing other names, were established here by 1550: by that time three of them have small holdings here. The family's main messuage and home close were very near to the Church, their home being the beautiful small fifteenth century house at the angle of Church Lane, where the two Hathaway women of today were brought up— not alas, as farmer's daughters. The family had kept its home, though not its land, for 350 years, a remarkably long tenure of a house. The first Hathaway will available is dated 1570. From then, for a century, we learn something of them from their own and other people's testaments. They are charitable to the church and the poor and affectionate to each other: now and then their wills contain small distinctive provisions. A Hathaway woman makes her daughter-in-law her sole executor although she has sons: another Hathaway housewife (1682) leaves the first "box of draughers", (i.e. chest of drawers) and Edward Hathaway (also 1682) owns a Bible, his precious possession, the only book mentioned in a Bledington will.

Such details give the impression of lively minds. Their status is not exceptional: the copyhold is of $1\frac{1}{2}$ yardlands. The freehold owned by one of them is very small—a close of nearly four acres: it was, however, one of the first holdings sold outright by the Leighs, not later than 1584. Soon after this, we find young Hathaways earning their living in various ways. In 1608 Edward is a shoe-maker. Richard is a "servant" on the Pegler holding: on the other hand, Simon himself had a servant. In 1612 Richard and Joan Hathaway are the props and stays of the elderly Agnes Wright: Richard directs her servants on her farm and Joan is her right-hand in the house. In 1672 the Hathaway messuage is one of the few in the village to have three hearths.

Hathaways constantly serve in village offices. Again and again they are churchwardens (Richard in 1605 reports sad events to the Consistory Court); sometimes they are constables and tithing men. That they are personally liked and trusted is evident in the frequency with which they are called upon to act as overseers to neighbours' wills. In 1647 they are on the side of order and reform: three of them sign the proposed rules for the common lands. But alas! the only illegitimate babe whose baptism is recorded in the seventeenth century transcripts is the son of a Hathaway girl: there are pitfalls no family of generous disposition can altogether avoid!

From 1700, news of the family becomes scarce but it is clear that they become poorer. The enclosure award shows that the family had lost its copyhold: the only award for a Hathaway (John) is of three acres thirty-eight perches. Farmers no longer, they became carpenters, valued labourers and domestic workers. They will appear in our history later for one of them shared the fame of the last Bledington Morris Men and today the last representatives of the family contribute in the background to every good work. Never ambitious or thrusting, they have been throughout centuries neighbourly, genial, careful folk, contributing to the grace of life.

There are other families as persistent as these. Peglers, for example, arrived about 1590 and the last member of the family left about 1920: though none live here now, some still come "home" to be buried. They were relatively well-to-do for two centuries and later showed a gift for holding on to education and status in spite of poverty. Eventually they recovered their prosperity, some doing well in the United States of America; others remaining in England sent sons into professions.

Of Cooks we have long heard. Their holding was always small but time had been when they cared for education; three of them were clerics in their own parish from the mid-sixteenth century well into the seventeenth. One of them—this is a rare thing, but not unique—left money to educate daughters. They descended to labourer rank but had skill and earned respect.

This is a mere handful of families. Others, resident in this village for fewer generations had forebears and descendants in the near neighbourhood, who knows how long (Roses, Guys, Maces, Mihills, Gilberts, Wrights)? Their stability seems dull but in the days when the population was hardly increasing, there was little to thrust them outward from home and neighbourhood. Daily life was satisfying in a way we can hardly understand. The defeating of the seasons in the provision of food and fuel afforded triumphs: the need to use to the utmost every product of farm and yard and wild life engrossed men and women alike. Beyond that was a real community life—a large family connection in the district, the friction and accommodation of joint farming, a village to serve, a church to give a world view and sometimes a challenging code; song and dance to be shared or witnessed at festivals; all these together could hold even energetic young yeomen.

In some earlier periods there had been cultural or religious allurement to other scenes and experiences, but since the Restoration this was lacking.

Of course there were shadows: an illegitimate babe was conceived within the prohibited degrees; there were severe differences within the Wright family; and a woman and her second husband were careless if not worse with legacies to her first husband's children. Respectable families are human: skin one's eyes as one may, there is little evidence of crime or disaster.

The enclosure award (1769) affords us a list of commoners, of whom there were seventeen, members of fourteen families.

Six of these had been in the village since 1600, three of them much longer. The stability of families must not be attributed to the open field system, or to other old customs for eleven of the fourteen families continued here till the twentieth century.

iv The Revolution: Enclosing the Open Fields

The families so far reviewed continued in many old ways and changed their outlook slowly and only partially. But one family started a thread of a new colour in the village weft. In 1586 Edward Lord of Little Tew had acquired a small messuage and holding[40] from Tidmarshes who had bought the freehold from Leigh a year or two earlier. (The power to sell seems to offer an easy way out of difficulties). Thirty-eight years later Lord's son William bought the mill from Rowland Leigh (1624).[41] (This miller had connections in the Bicester area—farmers, carriers and the like, successful in their businesses; they took to buying land as did their Bledington relatives). Milling seems to have paid: by 1672 the son of the purchaser had removed from the mill to the Loggans' messuage, having bought their holding. This had been originally of a modest one and a half yardlands but in 1538/9 a share of the demesne lands had been added to it, equivalent to more than a yardland. By 1662 Loggans had had a large house: they were taxed on ten hearths. Lords reduced the number of hearths to six, their house being still the largest in the village. By this time they were on the look-out for other properties and in 1690 they added the Darby half-yardland to their estate and also one going by the mysterious name of Three Men's Yardland: altogether they had by 1770 nearly six yardlands; by far the largest holding was now attached to the largest house.

Lords never married within the Bledington group of husbandmen. The second William's ambition had been to own much land: his son had social ambition. He had taken his first wife from a Warwickshire village twenty miles away and she had brought some money with her, probably £800. A year after her death he married a young woman of Seven Springs, who presumably also brought some money, for her relatives exacted a rigorous marriage settlement. The whole Lord estate, her husband's and his father's, is assured to her in case of her widowhood, with the exception of £800, to be the inheritance of

William's daughter by his first wife. It was, it seems, this William who acquired a coat of arms.

Meanwhile they had unusually little contact with their neighbours. They do not act as witnesses much less as overseers of neighbours' wills. After 1649 when William the Miller acted as constable there is no record of any office held by them except that of churchwarden.

That the Lords' purchases of land and their ambitions exceeded their true powers is evident. By 1707 the profits from the mill were exhausted: William II borrowed £320 on the Mill property from Mary Lane, Spinster. In 1731 he died and his son the third William must pay his half-sister, Sarah, her portion of £800. This he does by borrowing of William Stayt, sutler, of Kingham and presently of Bledington. Further, in the same year, he borrowed £1,000 from George Dowdeswell, the Vicar of Kingham. In 1738, Dowdeswell is repaid, but not in reality by Lord: the mortgage is taken over by Mrs Asplin of Arlescote in South Warwickshire, and her trustees, Myster and Godwin. Both of the latter families were by origin prosperous London merchants, the odd name Myster or Mister having been originally Meister. They were building the beautiful small "manor" houses, of Arlescote (with its neat gazebos at the four corners of a square garden) and Hornton—"small" houses for the ambitious, but wealthy enough to dominate small villages. Such "manor" houses, multiplying at this time, are doubtless the origin of the legend that English villages were, at one time, each dominated by "squires": but they remained relatively few. It is such houses and such preeminence in a village, one supposes, that are the lure for such a family as the Lords: maybe they missed the point that Mysters, Godwins and others had not derived their money from land.

Mortgages were a great resource and also a great danger to borrowers and lenders. The Rev. George Dowdeswell, with his local knowledge, had pulled out in good time from the Lord estate. The Warwickshire folk had difficulty in collecting their interest and six years later, 1744, they passed the mortgage, now of £2,000, to the Rev. Dr. Daniel Newcombe, of Gloucester Cathedral. After a short while, no interest was paid to him even though Lord was now selling small parts of his estate. In 1746, Dr. Newcombe started proceedings in the Court of Chancery with a view to resuming his money, if necessary by the forced sale of Lords' land. Newcombe had two unmarried daughters whose portion the mortgage was to be. The law-suit lasted some five years, Lord again and again failing to appear or to be represented. (The Court seems not to have been dilatory, so much as very tender of the interest of an embarrassed landowner). At length the property, whose value was estimated at the amount of the mortgage, was yielded up to the Misses Newcombe, who presumably let it for the next sixteen years. The Lords did not at once leave Bledington, though they ceased to hold land here. Possibly they had some small house, probably Tidmarshes',[42] unmortgaged. At all events they did not consider themselves too poor to pay tax for the use of their coat of arms. It had made them "gentry" and that had been their aim.

The new note struck in the village chorus by this family is discordant. They are more ambitious than scrupulous and became pretentious. They made little contribution to the general welfare. They are representative of a new tendency to social discriminations. In the documents drawn up by the Leigh lawyers some commoners are still plain John and William and others invariably "Mister".

The next stage of the history of Lords' farm will bring us to our farming revolution. In 1767,[43] the Misses Newcombe sold the estate to Ambrose Reddall, a "clothier of Stonehouse", a small town in the Stroudwater valley, where, earlier in the century, "the finest cloths" dyed with the "finest scarlets" had been made. He is still further than the Lord family from Bledington's traditions: his ambitions are like theirs but on a larger scale and his methods more advanced. A strong urge had caused him to leave his business and the warmer, grander slopes of the Western Cotswolds for our cold clays and small trees. Already he had acquired land at Broadwell and he had soon or a little earlier another connection with Bledington: by 1768 he had leased the glebe and tithes from Christ Church (as we know because we find him paying the Vicar's stipend). This was of greater importance than his purchase of Lords': it brought him into contact with the Dean and Chapter and probably through them with the University which had bought a holding of one and a half yardlands here in 1756. From this group of owners sprang the move to enclose our parish.

The slow rate of agricultural change in our parish was not altogether representative of the district. There were changing practices in open fields not very far from us, notably in Oxfordshire villages which profited by the London market where, for example, ridges in open fields were planted from time to time "as the parish agree" with clover, sainfoin or improved grasses.[44] In some cases the agreement was that each commoner should plant in one of the arable fields, during its fallow year, a number of acres or ridges of "hitch"—légumes or temporary grasses—in proportion to the extent of his holding. But it was not only markets that could bring this about. Shenington (at that time in Gloucestershire), twenty miles from Oxford and with no access to London, was surveyed by 1732. I had a garden in that old-fashioned small village for many years and in war-time discovered that though the soil was not in itself fertile it was "warm" and light, and responded in a single season to fertilisers and manure. Profits from new crops and methods could be demonstrated quickly.

Backwardness hereabouts might be due to the physical handicap of difficult soil. Yet as our newcomer, Reddall, rode roundabout inspecting the small properties he continued to purchase, he would see some improvements. On the tiny, enclosed manor of Little Rollright, a mile or two North of Chipping Norton, Robert Fowler was improving the Longhorn breed of cattle, following on the work of Webster and Bakewell. Soon other farms in the neighbourhoods were converted to the breed and not only on enclosed lands. In the seventeen eighties, John Lawrence the Kingham blacksmith[45] would be making "cowknobs" to prevent the descendants of Fowler's Longhorn *Rollright Beauty* from stabbing and ripping each other with their fine, scimitar-shaped horns in the narrow quarters of Kingham copyholders' yards; while at the same time he made chains for hobbling horses on the commons.

Nor were new rotations of crops unknown around us. In the Witney area a rotation had been tried in which beans and clover were so used that the fields lay fallow only one year in six.[46] Sainfoin had been grown at Daylesford a century before this, though it had not become common. By 1768 small quantities of turnips were being grown in Bledington.

There was and had been enthusiasm for private farming on the part of agricultural experts and writers. As long ago as 1557 Thomas Tusser had eloquently dwelt on the virtues of fences and hedges.[47] Defoe in his *Tour* comments several times on the waste involved in extensive common land.[48] Arthur Young, the first great agricultural reporter was a propagandist for enclosure in his early writings and would later sum up the stimulating quality of outright posesssion in the well-known phrases "the magic of property turns sand into gold" and "the enjoyment of property . . . has clothed the very rocks with verdure".[49]

Beside the satisfaction of gain in produce or money, there were the more imaginative pleasures of ownership and mastery—of being lord of what one surveys and able to say to one "Go!" and to another "Come!" and perhaps to a third "Vote!" Plainly, profit of this order helped to bring about the relatively early enclosure of all but a small area of Bledington parish.

Sometimes it is said that the growth of the population of the country led to enclosures, but they were not advocated as a means of feeding the people: the absence of this motive is shown in the general absence of the wish to feed adequately even workers on the land.

There was in fact no adequate debate on the gains and losses from enclosures: exposition was one-sided. Enclosure would change the basis of thousands of communities but this fact was not to the front. One "social philosopher" and "warm-hearted philanthropist" gave much of his life and income in the last quarter of the century to expounding the one-time relations between English communities and the lands on which they lived and his view that, in a developed and modern form, such a relation should be revived. But Thomas Spence was jailed for publishing these views,[50] spending more than two years in prison. Bledington commoners had enough experience of communal rural life to have thoroughly understood his scheme for corporate villages. Had Spence had freedom, there might have been many-sided criticism and some experiments. Some of the agriculturalists who saw indisputable evidence of better crops and higher rents on "several" farms might have written of some losses resulting from enclosure—as Arthur Young did, but not till 1812[51]—and considered other methods of change. But the good men who, like him, reported on the counties, were appointed and paid through the Board of Agriculture, by the lords of broad acres, strictly to report on agriculture, not on human conditions.

The rights and customs of open-field farming could only be extinguished over a whole parish by an Act of Parliament. Fresh energy was required for every such venture. If the owners of two-thirds of the rights wished for enclosure, they could obtain it. Late in 1768, Parliament was petitioned to allow a Bill for the enclosure of Bledington to be presented. The petitioners were the Dean and Chapter of Christ Church, Ambrose Reddall, the Chancellor, Masters and Students of the University of Oxford and five other named commoners "and others". The named petitioners owned the equivalent of 1,020 acres while the unnamed commoners held 159, the Home Heath and Far Heath accounting for most of the remaining 360 acres. There was almost certainly some opposition or the petition would have been presented from the whole body. Of the smaller owners there were thirteen in 1769 giving with Christ Church, Reddall and the University a total of sixteen to compare with earlier figures. In 1355 there had been thirty-two freeholders and copyholders (already a small reduction) and in 1550, twenty-one. In 1721, there were twenty-one freeholders who were also voters but it is possible that one or two of these were not commoners: a house with yard and a home-close of good size would then be worth forty shillings a year. The Lord family had acquired four small family holdings[52] beside Loggans' large one and Reddall in the short period since his first connection with the village had bought four others[53] Thus we arrive at the figure thirteen.

Reddall was finally awarded 393 acres, a larger award than even that of Christ Church for the glebe and larger tithes. But he held a lease of the Christ Church interest, to be valued anon at 251 acres. Thus he was concerned with much more than one-third of the farmland of the parish. Even so, resistance might have been considerable but for the offer of Christ Church to link with enclosure the commutation of all tithes. For the larger tithes and the smaller tithes on old enclosures belonging to commoners they would accept an allocation of land— one seventh of the commonable area. Holders of land without common rights (mostly gardens) owing lesser tithes were to have these commuted for annual payments.

Small tithes (tenths of vegetables, apples, poultry, litters of pigs, etc.) were inconvenient for cottagers to pay and to the impropriator to receive. (How Christ Church had collected them does not appear). In many villages the lesser tithes were beginning to be detested. There can be little doubt that nearly all commoners would welcome the joint projects: and they secured recognition of at least one peculiarity of the village. The ancient Oars and Twenty Lands, the meadow associated with them, were always exceptions and the owners of ridges in them insisted on being compensated within that area: hence the tiny fields into which the Oars were later broken up.

The petition for the Bledington enclosure was granted by Parliament as a matter of routine, and five members of the House of Commons (Tracey, Harvey, Southwell and Barrow—none of them with any traceable interest in Bledington) were "ordered" to bring in a

Bill. This had already been prepared by a lawyer of Gloucester and was shortly law. The speed and technical efficiency shown in these preliminaries was to be maintained till the operation was finished: every legally proved interest of ownership in the common land, the variation in soils, the relative cost of short and long fences—all were provided for. The Act[54] set out in detail all ancient rights and extinguished them. There is no mention of manor or lord, of unstinted commons or of rights of the poor. We may take it that no legal case could be made out for these, though the poor had the custom of cutting furze and brushwood.

There were to be two charitable, voluntary allotments: first six acres from the Home Heath, which naturally grew furze, for fuel for the poor. This gift, for legally a gift it was, would come from the common pool of land. Detailed arrangements were made for it: one fourth of the field was to be cut each year; hedges and ditches were the charge of the owners of contiguous fields. The churchwardens and overseers were to be responsible for the Poor's Plot: the expenses they incurred were to fall upon the poor rates. The provision may not have compensated the poor for privileges they had enjoyed, but it was worth something: in 1966 "the poor", a list drawn up by the Parish Council, received each a sum worth having at Christmas. for which the final qualification is willingness to be "the poor". From the first the poor had no part in their inheritance, but to stand and receive.

The other charitable allotment was to be made, not from the common pool but from the land due to the Dean and Chapter. There was first in this connection the firm statement that the Vicar had no right to glebe land or to any tithe and that his salary was £20 per year. On this background, he was to be granted land of the value (at the increased rate expected after enclosure) of £4 and his little field (as it proved, of 3¾ acres) was to be "conveniently near" to the Vicarage. (It was in fact half a mile away.)

The Bill contained a provision that was rare if not unique: a portion of the parish, the Far Heath and the Cow Common next to it, in all 140 acres, were to remain unenclosed and to be divided into strips allotted to commoners proportionately to their holdings. Thus there was left a miniature open-field farm.[55] Why? The enigma remains.

The petition had alleged only one reason for the proposed change—that the petitioners' property "lay intermixed and dispersed in small parcels, very inconvenient".

Before any of these provisions could be carried out the great public need for roads and paths had to be met. Roads had to be marked out, sixty feet broad in all but one case, and the line of footways to all neighbouring parishes and hamlets and one bridle way indicated, so that presently the necessary sites of stiles and bridges would be seen. Finally, every commoner must be given compensation for his rights. This was not a mere matter of acreage: some land was more fertile or easier to work than other sections: land close to the clustered messuages in the village was very desirable. Hence every furlong and all "picks,' and "butts" had to be carefully valued.

All this work was to be the responsibility of five commissioners, named in the Act, local small land owners of Shipton under Wychwood, Guiting and Salperton and one from a more distant Warwickshire village, all "gentlemen", but ready to earn a modest recompense. They were in no way professionals: the Act also named the surveyor, who would measure and "quality" the land and report his survey in a map.

The most remarkable characteristic of the Award made by the Commissioners is its efficiency. The clarity of the document passes all tests. The verbiage of farm mortgages and the like is absent. The cumbrousness of the 24 sheepskins on which the Award is written is a stumbling-block to a modern reader but a typed copy shows its true terseness. No doubt the lawyer who drew up the Bill and registered the Award was able to use as patterns many previous documents. There were also the skills on an economic level of surveyors and valuers. These are all thrown into high relief if we think of the condition of our roads, the primitive quality of farming tools and the universal ignorance of hygiene. But landownership and therefore the management of land as property, rather than as soil for crops, was the ruling factor in English life. Fine skills had been built up to serve the legal processes of sale and purchase and of estate management, considered apart from the tilling of the soil.

To do the work at once speedily and peacefully called for another type of skill: to adjust and reconcile. It is a great mistake to suppose that all farmers were given quite convenient contiguous fields by the Award. Farmhouses on the edge of the village might be given much of their land nearby but this could not always be done for holdings with homes in the centre. A partial solution was to permit exchanges, so that something of quality or extent could be yielded up for better access. Thus Mary Coombs, a widow, made three exchanges, amassing a small holding starting at her own back door and extending in three fields, narrow but connected, to the unenclosed Cow Common where she had her rights. Eight of the thirteen smaller commoners made arrangements of this nature with the approval of the Commissioners. These were registered in the Award, as well as in separate deeds. By this means, the cost of sale and purchase was saved.

All but one of the meetings with the Commissioners were held at Stow on the Wold at the King's Arms where good meals and beds were available: but some settlements set out in the Award must have been made in private. Ambrose Reddall and Christ Church, for example, agreed that the former should continue to have a lease of all Christ Church land and that he would not only fence the fields, make ditches and maintain these for seven years, but would also pay all the costs of enclosure, so that neither cost nor trouble would fall directly on Christ Church. By some chance, Reddall was able to take over the farming of the University's holding in the year of enclosure, and by his agreement he was to fence this farm as well as the Christ Church property. We see here clearly the expectation that land would rise in value when enclosed. The rent of "Diggers", the University's land, from 1756 to 1769 was £57 or £58: the lease being granted to Reddall gave him the land at £58 for 14 years, the rent being fixed no doubt in consideration of his fencing and payment for enclosure; after that he was to pay £100 per annum, a rent approaching £2 per acre. (At the end of his lease in 1790, he took a new one at £93).

Only one meeting of a formal nature was held in Bledington, at Thomas Edginton's inn. Here, no doubt, matters relatively detailed and concerning everyone were discussed. Reddall thought it convenient to add the pound near the church to Lords' Farm and offered the village compensation where the pound now is—a lower, and inconvenient wetter spot. Perhaps the farmers thought their enclosed land would make it in any case useless. The question of roads must have come up. They had to be repaired in a hurry that season, before roadside fences could be planted and they would now have to be kept in better repair than ever before, for when the mud and the ruts grew deep, it would not be possible to drive vehicles or flocks of sheep on to the land alongside.

Bledington affords a curious insight into the roads of the time. Among the major roads confirmed and regulated was the "road to

Oddington", now known as Heath Road or Lane. It dries only in the hottest summers and loads of stone soon vanish as though they had never been deposited there. It is crossed here and there by ancient cultivation ridges, very wide and also high.

It is curious to note that the road to Kingham and Chipping Norton, now so much used, was still regarded as a lane: it was to be 30 feet wide, while all the other roads were of twice this width! Stow and Burford had been our usual destinations.

The poorer owners (usually occupiers) of farms had two anxieties; how to pay their share of the costs of the Award, and how to fence their fields? Reddall, we may assume, would order hawthorn plants from a nursery and have them set out by the nursery's gang. The smaller men might divide among themselves the common stock of hurdles that had been used to shut the animals out of or onto the open arable fields and would cut limbs from ashes and willows to make rough fences, along which, later, they would set hawthorn slips to grow while the rails rotted.

The last two entries of the Award are the "Schedules of Payments", first the sums to be paid to the commissioners, surveyors and lawyers who had done the work, the other of amounts due by the ex-commoners, now to be known as "farmers" and "small-holders", towards discharge of these costs. The total cost of the operation was (£955). Of this nearly one half went to William Lane, the lawyer, who had prepared the Act and finally registered the Award with Quarter Sessions. It seems a high proportion, but it covered journeys to London and doubtless much work by his staff. The five commissioners received among them £130—small pay, perhaps, but since three of them could act, they had not needed to attend all meetings. The surveyor and his assistants upon whom much detail fell, received £120. The only large payments then remaining are those to the host at the King's Arms, £110, and just under £10 to the Bledington victualler, in respect of the one meeting held on his premises. The cost of Act and Award to the proprietors was in the region of 16s. 6d. per acre, but the amount paid by each depended on the valuation as well as on the measurement of the land allotted to him. For example, Ambrose Reddall paid £278 in respect of 393 acres, but these included much of the Home Heath, of which the value was low: for the University he paid £65 in respect of 66 acres, Mary Coombs had 19 acres and paid £21, while John Hathaway's 3 acres cost 31s. Susannah Wallington was somehow lucky and paid nothing in respect of her 2½ acres.

Thus ended the enclosure. The original of the Award was deposited in the Church chest in charge of the Churchwardens, to pass more than a century later into the charge of the Parish Council, and again, after many decades, it has been deposited by them in the County Records Office. Sometimes, its importance has been forgotten and its guardians puzzled as to its meaning, but they are reminded when questions of boundaries and paths and other responsibilities arise, for these are sometimes shirked and avoided, such as the duty of landowners to keep in order the stiles on their fences, across the footpaths which were in justice awarded to the public. Old Bledington families made and long maintained good oak stiles, with smooth tops and a cross-bench for stepping upon: newcomers have provided sharp-edged timbers at the top, difficult rails below and no cross-bench, stiles that no child or lame person can use.

The anxieties of the allottees were not at an end: Ambrose Reddall, to fulfil his surely burdensome undertakings, borrowed £2 per acre on all the lands in his own possession, from the widow of a collar-maker of Stow, adding to the large mortgages he had already contracted. John Gibbs found he could not pay his "proportion of expense" and borrowed the full permitted £2 on his 17-acre allotment from a neighbour George Gilbert, who, we may note, received an allotment no larger. But on the same day that this arrangement was made, Gibbs sold 1½ acres of his allotment in the Lower Oar to Peter Brookes of Shipton for £53—a good price for the time: his problem was, it seems, more than solved. Some 3 or 4 small freeholders lost their portions gradually—Kings, Stayts and Hathaways—but there is no proof that this was due to enclosure. There was not, between enclosure and the end of the century, a steady decline in the number of Bledington farmers, for within 30 years Reddall's great accumulation was broken up again.

Yet there was an undoubted increase in poverty and misery. For a while there were still some prosperous labourers. Wills, mortgages and purchase deeds from 1712 to 1800 bear witness to their existence and survival but after that the genus gradually became extinct. The connection of this fact with enclosure may be explained in this village as elsewhere by Arthur Young's observation "Those of property benefited; all who hired were ruined". We know that in the seventeenth century common rights were hired to those who had none: at that time a reasonable rent was fixed and commoners encouraged to give this help to neighbours. This hiring may well have provided the lowest rungs of the social "ladder". Evidence from other villages shows that it was unusual for any land on an enclosed farm to be let.

On the other hand, it seems true that commoners who received even a few acres could survive, if not benefit. There was no marked reduction in their numbers: on the contrary, the failure of the projects of our land-collectors actually restored it.

In the matter of farming, change was slow. For drainage, farmers long relied on open ditches. One may even see a field or two still ridged, today, relying on the furrows to carry water off to a ditch. In the nineteenth century the large farm, (first called Claydon Farm and now Bledington Grounds), awarded to Reddall for his holdings other than Lords', was drained by means of large government loans, but that was long after the turn of the century. Certainly some land became more fertile. Of the Home Heath one field still grows bushes and weeds in the large hollows, but much of it proved after eighty years or so to be of fair basic quality.

As in other newly-enclosed villages, new farmhouses were later to be built—four in all—when outlying groups of fields were seen to make convenient units. A popular development was the planting of orchards usually near farmhouses; later Rudge[56] noted that this had been done without due care for aspect and soil: certainly they were never a commercial success. However, Bledington came to enjoy its cider-making much as do French hamlets their grape-harvests. A cider-press was used in the yards, turn by turn. Men and boys followed it round. The great variety of fruit is said to have given it a most distinctive flavour.

The results of the enclosure were not in the economic sphere momentous: there was never emphasis on mere exploitation until the twentieth century. But the system which had come to an end was communal.

The original tilling and extension of the fields had been a co-operative enterprise, continuing till the whole area had been incorporated into a village farm, communally directed, whose main use had been the sustenance of the village households. The detail and beauty of the system comes home to one as one walks over the fields today, noting the old ridges and furrows and their delicate adjustment to the rise and fall of the ground, and ponders on the familiarity and knowledge that went to the naming of every patch of ground that could be distinguished from the next. The system had to be served and regulated by oarsmen or fieldsmen to carry out public decisions, haywards responsible for fencing, poundsmen or pindars for animals not under control, herdsmen and shepherds and watchers as needed.

All this neighbourly knowledge and training came naturally to be used in civic spheres also. The community was subject, not only to the manor court, but to institutions directly representing the central power—the hundred court, and the county, with its militia, and the King's courts. The men of the village had to choose their tithing men and constable, discharging responsibility for each others' obedience to law and custom. Presently, they would be called upon to take up duties in the church and civic parish as churchwardens and overseers of the poor.

Village officers were supported in their work by officers of the Hundred Court and magistrates in Quarter Sessions: but equally, when these officials and institutions had their own lapses, the village men could fall back on their fundamental community and temporarily support "the sum of things" alone. The strong social aspect of the neighbourly relationship—intermarriage, inter-employment, executorships and trusteeships—penetrated the economic bonds with family feeling and friendship.

Co-operation began with and rested upon communal farming, but there was the lord of the manor in the situation. In early centuries the person or the institution concerned was restrained on the one hand by his fealty to his own lord, the King, and on the other by established custom. Gradually land lordship tended to be changed into land ownership: possibly in part through the influence of patterns coming from the world of industry and commerce.

Would co-operation and community survive without its early basis? For enclosure meant a form of anarchy, every family for itself. And our small anarchic group would be embedded in a similar larger one, country-wide, urban and rural. If old communal ways were based on some quality of men as basic as self-assertion anarchy might be halted and controlled. How far in fact it proceeded would be seen in the next sixty years. For a time the Church was to be the only institution in Bledington bearing witness to common human nature and the common responsibility of villagers. How soon, after this revolution and its own decline, would the church be hard at work again?

We have also yet to see whether the magic of property and severalty did in fact turn the clays and brash of Bledington into gold.

v Farms and Farmers after Enclosure

Before considering farms and farmers after enclosure, we must finish the story of our outstanding parishioner, Ambrose Reddall. He continued to acquire land, buying farms in some Oxfordshire and Buckinghamshire parishes; he also acquired an estate in Woburn. He seems to have kept his Bledington land under his own direction. Although he had no great interest in agriculture as such, he built a fine "manor" house or very large farm house, with spacious modern yards and buildings on Claydon Farm, about a mile outside the village. These were admirable, though perhaps too extensive. The house had fine dining and drawing rooms, "four large servants' rooms in Attic, Cellars, Brewhouse, Laundry, Dairy, Coach-house, etc." It had nearly an acre of garden, "walled round and clothed with fruit trees". More remarkable for the time were its two large farm yards, surrounded with "thrashing and other barns, Cart stable, Double stable (6 stalls), 2 other Stables (two stalls each), Dove House, Carpenter's Shop, Milking house, open Beast house, one Beast house (seventeen stalls for fatting oxen, with cistern and pipes to convey water, and passages round to feed them): Cart Hovel, Granary, Pig Styes and other convenient out-buildings erected at great expense and complete in every respect."[57]

From the Stow road all this still looked till 1968 like a great handsome French *mas*. When Reddall's estate fell apart, the house, barns and gardens would be unsuitably costly of upkeep for a farm of under three hundred acres. Yet, in itself, it seems logical and sound and shines like a good deed from among its builder's complex and unsatisfactory operations.

The Newcombe ladies had never been fully paid for Lord's Farm and similarly almost all the properties Reddall acquired were bought with the help of mortgages. At first, his creditors received full interest, but less and less as time went on. He must have presented himself as solid and trustworthy to Christ Church, with all its experience, and to those who lent him money. One of his creditors was Thomas Osborne, a lawyer and landowner of Tormarton in Reddall's native area, whose son Nathaniel married Reddall's daughter. Soon, the son-in-law took over from his own father the debt on his father-in-law's estate and also lent Reddall £10,000 and guaranteed some of his debts. Osborne's knowledge of landed estate and of money matters was excellent, but also his sense of family duty abounded. (All this one distils from a score of manuscripts).

In the course of time Reddall's debts amounted to over £40,000, on little of which interest was being paid. The expected rapid rise in value of enclosed land failed to take place, one supposes, where Reddall bought. Twenty-five years after he began to purchase land, his creditors became so anxious that they took their case to the Court of Chancery:[58] a single property in this small parish, Lords' Farm, thus came to figure in that court a second time within fifty years. The two cases seem to run a similar course: the motive for contraction of debt appears to be in both cases aggrandisement through possession of land. In this second case the Court again favoured the debtor, Creditors became frustrated and angry and in the end bitter towards one of their number—Nathaniel Osborne—for the trouble-maker escaped all his responsibilities before the end and Osborne was one of his executors. In this capacity Osborne showed his full quality. The case in Chancery went on until at last the Court ordered the sale of the properties. Osborne's own welfare and his family's were now at stake: if the sale went badly he would lose much of his own loans and have to pay the debts for which he had stood surety. Fears were justified. But Osborne arranged that land failing to make a fair price in the auction sale should be "bought in" by the executors, in effect himself, so that he could manage it till better times. A good deal of the land was so bought. It was never conveyed to him: he continued to administer it and to pay some interest to his fellow creditors. Suspicion arose and he was accused of chicanery in his buying and not-buying of property. The Court exonerated him and showed that as executor he had done well for his fellow creditors.

During this painful business, Osborne felt the threat of mortality, drew up his will, and shortly died. The will is a model:[59] he provided for his wife and daughter and also a small annuity for Reddall's incapable, mentally defective son. (There is a little side-light here on the extent of such a misfortune at that time even in a prosperous family: an annual £35 would suffice for his support).

Osborne believed that the eventual sale of the Reddall estate, at the right time, would enable all the debts to be paid, and a note on one of the latest documents states that this happened. But it still took time: not till 1810 were the affairs finally settled.

Reddall is an eighteenth century type and as such not altogether unsuccessful: it was his creditors who most suffered. His acquired status brought him the pleasures of ownership, invitations to county balls and the chance of fine marriages for his daughters, and final burial in the chancel of the church, like any squire. His enterprise was his sole claim to quality as a villager. The vestry minutes show him always late in paying the parson his stipend. Only once or twice was he present at a vestry meeting and he never served the village in any way except for a short spell as churchwarden, nor do we hear of public work in any larger field.

In 1798, land held by Reddall had been let partly to local men and partly to newcomers—Claydon (Bledington Grounds) Farm to a "gentleman" farmer, the first of a series attracted by the large rational house; the glebe and tithe land leased from Christ Church had been sub-let in two parts, one being added to Lords' Farm, and the remainder let to a typical Bledington family, recent comers but here to stay. The Reddall estate, owned and leased, was to be divided into its old component parts but not till 1807. Sir John Chandos Reade of Shipton under Wychwood, another land-collector, had bought Claydon Farm and it was henceforth usually farmed as a unit without further additions. Christ Church had leased its land again: a woman had invested her money in the lease and for a while paid the Vicar's stipend, but neglected the chancel of the church. By 1808 Christ-Church was managing its own farms and discharging the rectoral duties to the church.

In 1807, the 1,539 acres of the parish were divided into 19 holdings, beside some very small ones which did not pay land-tax. Bledington Grounds was the largest—291 acres: the others averaging somewhat over sixty acres. Of these Lords' Farm was the largest at 91 acres. Thus thirty-eight years after enclosure the number of holdings was greater than before.

Between 1775 and 1807, Peglers, Stayts, Gilberts, Roses and Wallingtons were all here and most remained far into the nineteenth century. Bakers were no longer farming: they had sold their holding to a Stayt and Trinder partnership, but they still thrived. Mrs Coombs had not long retained her cleverly consolidated little farm: it had been sold to another woman who put in tenants. In 1808, a Stow family

219

coming from Churchill took over the University's farm and probably also the small holding—Mrs Coombs'—next to it.

Lords' Farm was acquired in 1808 by a modest, careful Kingham family, the Stayts, (one of whose relatives had had a mortgage on it in 1730). They were not so well to do as to buy without a mortgage, but they paid it off. There then occurred a short interval, the only one between 1707 and 1900, when that farm was not mortgaged.

We learn something of the monetary value of the land in the last quarter of the eighteenth century. Evidence as to the University farm is available from 1769 until 1959. Thirteen years before enclosure £1,600 had been paid for its 66½ acres, (to use the post-enclosure measure) i.e. £24 per acre. The rent was 17s. per acre, just over 3½% on purchase money. This rent was continued after enclosure in return for the lessee's undertaking the expenses of enclosure. In 1790, a new lease was agreed, at £93, i.e. at very nearly 28s. per acre. Shortly after this (in 1792) the Napoleonic Wars began: in 1808 the rent per acre rose to 39s. The farm was compact; the river flowed beside or through its fields and made good pasture though parts were rather wet; the arable land had good natural drainage. The well-found homestead stood in the heart of the village. The farm did not contain the best land in the parish, but its tenants were on the whole fortunate.

The catalogue of the sale of Reddall's Bledington estate in 1798, together with a statement of the sums paid on that occasion derived from Chancery, affords some facts. The highest price paid was £57. 11s per acre (66 acres), the next £47 (115 acres). The large Bledington Grounds (291 acres) brought £39. 9s. per acre which may suggest too high a value for the land, but the large house and superb yards were no doubt attractive to bidders. A usual rent was £2 per acre: one small property was let at a little over £1 per acre.

The area of arable seems to have declined after enclosure at any rate till the Wars began. Of rather more than 800 acres in the Reddall sale of 1798, three-eigths were arable and the remainder grass land, with 30 acres of woodland. We find a similar proportion at this time and later on other farms: before enclosure heath and meadow had certainly not amounted to a half of the land.

Cropping shows no experiment or adventure. In 1798 there were some turnips and for the rest wheat, barley and beans. Greater variety, except for small plots would not occur till well into the eighteen hundreds. There may well have been more interest in stock: Bledington settled down to mixed farming, nor were large areas ploughed up even later in the war period.

From 1792, agriculture was of highest importance to the nation, especially corn production and the price of wheat increased. From 1785 to 1794, the average price for wheat was 47s. per quarter, from 1795 to 1804, 75s. and from 1805 to 1814, 93s.[60] This steep rise affected mixed farming less than corn districts but there was also some rise in the price of other products.

Although the farmers here appear to have been conservative, prices must have raised their incomes. Some building took place. A map dated 1770 shows Gilberts' Farm without its more modern section which is nevertheless of the 18th century. The third addition (since 1600) to the Town Banks farmhouse was made in 1784 by a Stayt. New rooms were added, a new broader stairway was put in and the one-time hall was panelled with red pine, its seventeenth century, or earlier, hearth being covered: it became a charming room.[61] A severely attractive small farmhouse (Beckley House) was built or rebuilt, changes took place at Harwoods and the front of Roses' (now called Little Manor) was completely taken out and renewed.

Conservative as our farmers were, some general stimulus was reaching them. Jackson's Oxford Journal providing novel reading matter grew rapidly popular. Founded in 1753, it was of interest to farmers from the first: it published prices for corn in local markets and the time-tables of the coaches or "machines" that ran from London through Burford to Gloucester and through Stow to London. About the time of the Bledington enclosure there was often news of the Oxford Navigation Society's canal which was to link Oxford with Banbury and towns beyond. This was of interest for different reasons to labourers as well as farmers. In 1770, ten miles had been completed and agreements made for twenty more: seven hundred men were employed. The news also appeared that four hundred weavers had gone to North America the summer before from Gloucester and Somerset; and that in January, a Dorchester (Oxon) labourer had stolen some fowl and been "ordered to be transported" for seven years—one for each bird—with no arrangements for his return. Advertisements must have interested farmers in 1769: they were offered, for example, *The British Farmer* in 50 parts at 6d. each. It was to expound "a complete system of agriculture and husbandry", including the "best methods of breaking up Commons and waste grounds, draining wet lands and planting quick hedges". Both the Oxford and Gloucester papers were used before the end of the century for notices of direct interest to Bledington folk, concerning farms and houses to let in the village and neighbourhood, and work available. No reading matter could be of greater interest for daily life than such a competent paper as "Jackson's". From now on literacy will be more important than hitherto. The newspaper is the result of the modern need for more information. and is itself an encouragement and incitement to reading. We can discover something of the literacy of farmers and labourers and the womenfolk of both from the marriage register. From 1755 brides and bridegrooms are required to sign it if they are able to do so, but not till 1837 is their "rank or profession" indicated. We are able however to recognise the names of farmers and craftsmen and the others are almost all labourers or labourers' daughters. The names of literate folk from 1755 to 1837 are chiefly of more prosperous families, of which many more are those of grooms, than of brides. Among the illiterate there are, then, some craftsmen's and farmers' daughters and those of both brides and grooms of labouring status. To give the figures: in the twenty-five years from 1755–1780 inclusive, there are 46 marriages: of 92 brides and grooms, 48 were illiterate. At this time, the proportion of men who sign their names was nearly double that of women. Of 46 brides 17 can write—almost 37%—while of the grooms, 31 sign—67.4%.

Pegler, Fletcher, Lord, Mace, Stayt are all known to our readers as established farmers; Blizzard had joined their company; Laitt, Kench and Baker were all above the line of sheer dependence on wage. Ayers, Whitby, Panton are names making only a brief appearance in the village: these mobile folk are labourers and the very temporary families are almost never literate at this time nor for eighty or ninety years yet. Members of a very few families men and women alike (Pegler, Baker, Guy) can almost always sign: others (Stow, Wilkes, Hathaway) are not often illiterate. Taking all the figures, the proportion of the literate is 52.2%.

The same calculation for the next twenty-five years (1781–1805) when sixty marriages are recorded, gives us 30% of literate brides and 47% of grooms. Thus the percentage of literacy is 38%. This is a very sudden drop from 52% and in the next period (1806–1830) the percentage will revert to the figure 52: there is probably a factor of sheer chance in the low figure; or perhaps some teacher left the neighbourhood and was not succeeded. We see again that from 1781–1805 men are more literate than women. (This sex difference has continued from earlier years as we inferred from signatures and marks on earlier documents. For the time in question, one's impression is that it was even more marked than that between social classes. But it was not in the nature of things: there was a reversal later when reading and writing had become more useful to women).

It is a reasonable inference that from midway through the century about half the "younger end" could read and write. Twenty-five years later, half of the whole village would be literate.

There was to be no charitable or public provision of instruction (not to use the word "education") till 1852. Early in the eighteen hundreds, the labourers of better background could get, as adults, some instruction not only in letters but also in figures and as young parents they cherished some hope, as we shall see, that their children might receive some instruction.

Some farmers' sons had had more than minimum instruction in letters, riding to nearby masters with a good reputation. Replies to archdeacons' enquiries seem to show that there were no schools in Kingham; Stow was further away than Churchill and there was schooling to be had in the latter village from 1700. It is known that Bledington boys were attending a Churchill school (as fee payers) during the last decade of the century and almost certainly earlier.[62] There was a small charity school for girls there also, endowed in 1716 to teach letters and housewifery but only to "poor girls" of Sarsden and Churchill.[63] About 1755, a small farmboy sat on the benches of the school for boys, whose career suggests that there was soundness in the education given there and perhaps some contact with the scientific urges of the time. His predecessor in that or a similar Churchill school, Warren Hastings, was more famous but William Smith[64] would leave a very deep impression on thought and work. Born in 1769, William was the son of a husbandman and "skilled mechanic"; his grandparents, the Raleighs of Foscote lived just beyond Bledington's boundaries. He may well have joined Pegler and Baker boys on their way to school. When his father died he went—still a small boy— to his uncle's farm at Over Norton. Draining was going on there and William collected fossil-stones from the cuttings, "pundibs" and "pound-stones" that the dairy-women—so it is said—weighed their butter by. Soon he was "mooning over" his collection and had to placate his uncle for his idleness by carving sun-dials on soft brown "oven-stones" and by helping with the schemes for drainage. He went on journeys to see the canal that was being cut from Oxford to Banbury and somehow came by a book on surveying. It so happened that when he was eighteen, Churchill parish was being enclosed. William attached himself to Mr Webb of Stow, the surveyor, and became his assistant. Long before William was born, the scholar, Robert Plot, had collected fossils from estates all over Oxford county and Sir Thomas Penystone, a local proprietor, had broken up specimens to discover the nature of their material. But William, beginning his researches, in his uncle's ditches, was the first to discover that "Fossil remains succeeded one another in regular order and that strata could be identified by the fossils they contained and thus the age of the rock could be inferred". Smith's career showed the contribution a man of basic practical experience may make to knowledge and, more to our purpose, shows how, by this time, once a boy could read and knew there were books worth having in his own tongue and at his price, he only needed a strong impulse to carry him through the gates of wide mental realms.

From now on the homes of reasonably prosperous village folk will vary in a new way—in the breadth and furniture of mind of their families. Folk arts and music would die out of all but the humblest classes and literature became the resource of the imaginative. Hathaways had lost their holding but they and their like could keep their books.

vi Craftsmen, Tradesmen and Superior Labourers

The number of crafts practised here had grown somewhat. There were weavers throughout the seventeenth and eighteenth centuries and also "cordwainers" who had served an apprenticeship to their craft, and "shoemakers" who had not. Sometimes there was a cooper, as once for a while at one of the Mattocks cottages, but two or three farmers owned cooperage apparatus and may have been able at least to repair their own barrels and buckets and tubs. Perhaps they could do some of their own ironwork too, for smiths seem to have come and gone. (Modern conditions obscure the versatility competent countrymen had and still sometimes have). Down to 1790 women to whom any skill was ascribed were all "spinners".

In 1709, Samuel Buswell, weaver, son and grandson of weavers, married a daughter or ward of Thomas Baker, a prosperous farmer, the terrier of whose land has been referred to. Baker gave her a small dowry and her husband acknowledged it by giving her some rights in his cottage,[65] weaver's shed and half-orchard. But Samuel's father is to live in the cottage with them and is to have the right to do so till his death, with Elizabeth being "serviceable" to him, providing him with meat, drink and firing.

It has been shown that, in the seventeenth century, craftsmen whose wills were available were less well-to-do than farmers. It continues to be true that farmers, except those with very small holdings, fared better, as is shown by the growing size and comeliness, not to say elegance, of their homes. We have seen two typical cottages, those on Mattocks Close, inhabited by weavers and chapmen in the late seventeenth century. In the eighteenth century these were inhabited by coopers and shoemakers and in the early nineteenth century by a wheelwright, while the line of chapmen continued to occupy the other. The weaver's loom was in the living room of one, the perishable stores of the chapmen in that of the other. Small outhouses were attached to both cottages, in which stores and tools could be kept and in one of which the shoemaker worked. How many purposes these small spaces served! But the men had always some work in the yards, and the houses though small, were not mean: each cottage living room had a big fireplace with recesses beside it and the original rooms were large enough to be divided later.

Craftsmens' and artisans' homes were sound and made a basis for many good things. In them, families were reared, well-trained and taught their letters. Sons stayed at home long enough to learn a skill in the village. If they were poor, their poverty was quite unlike the privation that would later come to some and would undermine communities and personalities like a disease.

The ownership of premises was important to the craftsmen. They resort frequently to legal agreements, borrowing money, making elaborate wills, even holding little ceremonies when a parent bestows property on son or daughter.[66] Perhaps the sense of possession, not to say pride, was rather obsessive and encouraged an unadventurous and uninventive spirit, more akin to that of peasants in Southern France than like that of later Englishmen who were attracted to the open doors of the U.S.A.

The usefulness of a small property in family matters is illustrated when one of the Mattocks cottages was sold to Mary Cooke, mother of an illegitimate son. The money for purchase, it seems, was not her own. The cottage was to be hers only as long as she remained unmarried. At her death or marriage it was to pass to her son, her two brothers acting as trustee for him. How differently this fatherless boy fares from illegitimate children of a later date! He became a cooper, following his uncle-trustees and owned the cottage till 1832, when he sold it to a labourer-cousin, who gave him £60 for it.

Unfortunately, it is very rare for light to fall on the detail of the work that craftsmen did, but we learn something of a smithy and of the fate that gradually overtook the weavers.

Sometimes there was a smith in Bledington and at other times not. We know, however, where some of the horses were shod. Andrews, Wallingtons, Hathaways and Tidmarshes rode them over the fields to Kingham to John Lawrence, who was smith there from 1764 to 1792, and all that time kept a single small account book.[67] His son or nephew married a Bledington girl and became blacksmith here, bringing the old book with him. It was subsequently given to me as a peace-offering after an apparent difference in a village meeting and was a valuable present for it shows much of life at a village centre of work and communication. Lawrence could read and write only in a limited way but he made his modest techniques serve many purposes. The book's measurements are only 6 inches by 3 by 1. Its calf cover and chased brass fastener make it still a pleasure to handle. Evidently, Lawrence likes to note not only his business transactions but simple aspects of his more personal life. On an early page, we learn of the furniture he bought for his wife on his marriage and find a list of the tools in his work shop. Both lists are very short—the first includes "bed", "bowster" and bedstead, "soltbox", three blankets, two "boules", three "powter" dishes, six "pleats", six "cheares" and an iron pot. His cottage was very small (it may still be seen) and many of his wife's further requirements he could make for her. For his shop, Lawrence acquired a "Shop Book", that is, the leather-bound note-book, a lock iron, a tew iron, a nail hammer, a rasp and file, a hand-vice, and a square. His anvil was, no doubt, already in place in his out-house.

In his small premises, Lawrence has many functions. Beside shoeing horses, he serves as "farrier" in the sense of veterinary surgeon: in a pocket, at the back of his book, are "receipts" for cures for "a thrush in a horse's frog", for salves for wounds and for drenches[68] for sick cows. A modern villager is struck by the number of strange substances he is familiar with: "black rozen" (resin), "nitre", "diepent", "Lequeresh Powder", "balsam of sulphur", "Barbados ter" (tar), "alycompane", "tumeric", "alph nut root", "moderoot" (madder root), "limey grig",[69] "blue viteral", "cuming seeds", "yellow asnick", "red prosepet powder", "roach allum",[70] "butter of antimony", "fistelo".

All the time that Lawrence's work continued, Kingham farmed its open fields. From his book could be deduced much of the equipment, not only in the commoner's own yards, but also that used communally. Lawrence makes shaffpikes and dung pikes (now called "shoppicks" and "dumpicks" where they survive), stock-bands for the hubs of heavy carts; he makes cow-knobs to prevent the Longhorns from hurting each other, "loggers" to hobble horses on the open meads. He makes thimbles for gates, "syvel trees" for harness, "cleats" to prevent ropes from slipping. He puts new hoops on every kind of pail or barrel, makes paddles for cleaning ploughs, for weeding and other purposes. For some folk, he makes holdfast nails, sneads for scythes, "tuckholes in a gun", fromards for handle-making, nebirons, "hapses" and "keyes". He "tusks a shear" or share and "steels an ax" and makes knives and press irons for chaff boxes. There are, it seems, few tools he cannot mend or improve.

The community goods include six ploughs, a cart, harrows and hames. Every year Lawrence cleans a gun or guns for the constable, or mends it, "lock", "stock" and "barrel". He also sells the constable powder and shot. One supposes the gun is used for keeping birds off the seeds. Another function of the constable's is that of town crier: the smith alters his bell-clapper. The parish's pound, its turn-stile and bridge and gate all need Lawrence's attention.

Beside farmers, the craftsmen need the smith's services. Kingham has spinners for whom he makes spindles and swifts, a weaver for whom he "noses a shuttel" and "slumps" the beetle and collars two pulleys. The shoemaker needed few tools: he comes to Lawrence only for "feet" and nails and hammers and a taw (or tew) iron.

Women come to the smith: for them, he makes pattens (clogs on iron rings to raise them out of the mud). He mends their warming-pans, their fire-grates, and jacks for cooking, puts hoops on the wooden bottles they fill with ale for the field. Flatirons, gridirons, tongs, brewing-kettles and tea-kettles are all brought for repair. (It is surprising to find so many references to tea-kettles at a time when tea was sold there by the half ounce. The pot with the long curved spout, own brother to the tea-pot, had won its way by general usefulness).

He makes lanterns for the yards, bolts and locks and keys for doors. Two larger houses require andirons and fire-dogs, for burning long logs. Once Lawrence makes a "furnis-grate" weighing fifty-three pounds for Newman the weaver, no doubt for brewing: the weaver also, was not a mere specialist. Lawrence was neither a reader nor frequently a writer: he spells by sound and writes illegibly. Many words remain mysterious in meaning.

All this making and mending did not exhaust Lawrence's usefulness. At one time he bought large quantities of worsted "graywhit", gray, and black and sold it by the "top". This may have been woven into rough cloth by cottagers: the weaver, no doubt, used more varied yarn. In the same way, the smith buys single and double Gloucester cheeses from farmers, of any weight from two to fifteen pounds. At times, he will buy a carcase of sheep or ox and sell that too.

Another craftsman who comes to him for supplies is the tailor who buys thread from him many times and candles almost as often. He must have sat up night after night finishing coats and waistcoats— perhaps embroidered ones for farmers' weddings.

There are other entries of interest in Lawrence's books but these suffice to indicate what scope and variety of work there might be even in a small village for a man of skill, and a craftsman's varied service to farm and household and to fellow craftsmen.

One hears, by chance, in our area, of barns in which once looms clacked. Some half dozen or so of weavers found it convenient to work for one of their number who could, better than themselves, organise the purchase of their raw material and dispose of their cloth. Our villages were at a distance from industrial areas but yet we find pointers here to the concentration and specialisation in weaving if not in other crafts, that was proceeding fast elsewhere.

In 1756, a young man came to Chipping Norton[71] who acquired soon the business of a man who employed local spinners and weavers. Wool was bought from farmers in villages around and woven in a barn where several looms had been erected and then sent across miles of country to be milled or shrunk at Swinbrook. Back at Chipping Norton, the cloth was dried on a rock-strewn bank. Bliss sold his cloth to tradesmen in Cirencester, Evesham, Tetbury and Banbury. But travelling so far, he began to buy wool from outside our district, becoming more critical of quality.

The Bliss business grew. Near the end of the century, the firm bought a flourmill on a stream and turned it into a woollen mill, where, extended and modernised, it stands still. Once a pioneer, unconsciously pushing forward changes in crafts and farming, it stands now in isolation, a reminder of a comparatively primitive stage of modern manufacture, surviving upon its very high quality goods. Gentlemen, reading this, who like good suits, may well be wearing Chipping Norton tweeds. Each day twos and threes of workers are comfortably conveyed from local villages, sometimes from Bledington, to their work in "Bliss's", and thus in a modern way, there are again weavers here.

Various wills and other deeds bear witness to the existence of a class we may call "superior labourers". For example, in 1719 "George Gilkes,, labourer", leaves £60, with some residue, to his nephews. In other wills we find that his son and grandson are yeomen. In 1749, "John Gilkes, labourer", sells three cottages in one of which he is living.[72] The labourer who, in 1712 married the widow of Samuel Boswell, weaver, rescued her property from debt and was therefore made heir to her house. Thirty-five years later (1747), he bought the second of the Mattocks cottages for £60.[73] He had seen to it that his son had a craft, apprenticing him to a cordwainer: his daughter married a blacksmith. The two Prudes, father and son, labourers, sold a piece of land to the owner of Lords' farm in 1770.[74] It appears that the Westcote brook had changed its course leaving a slice of their holding on his side: he bought it to round off his land.

Up to the time of enclosure, there is clearly a number of men who work for wages but have other resources: they save or have inherited money or have rights in common land or own small houses. They do not live on farm premises nor are they among those glad of penny loaves at a funeral.

Their number indicates that their relative prosperity is not accidental: it must be partly due to conditions. Of what these are, we have no proof. They cannot demand wages above the fixed maximum for strength or skill and are not craftsmen. Probably there was some access to land, if only by custom, the feeding of geese or pigs, the supplement of wages by permission to run a couple of sheep with a farmer's flock; and the earnings of a wife at spinning.

They had a certain scope in life, being able to make friends or marry in other classes. Modest steps up or down the social ladder according to their abilities or temperaments did not involve triumph or shame.

Deeds in which men of this status are concerned grow very few after 1770, but are not totally absent: in 1832, one of the Mattocks cottages was sold to a labourer for £60, the same sum for which it had changed hands in 1747. But, by 1770, conditions had greatly changed: labourers were, with rare exceptions, most impoverished. Superiority among them there sometimes was, but very rarely of an economic nature. Enclosure here had not reduced the number of farms but it was an important factor, acting in more than one way, in the decline of the labourers' scope, comfort and status.

vii The Poor Labourers

The changes that could help farmers to prosperity tended against labourers. While subsistence farming continued shortages and anxieties had been shared though not equally, and for the poor who lived in or around the farmhouses there had been windfalls of food—a share in the sheep that broke its leg or in the pig's "chitlings" the women helped the yeoman's wife to cleanse. When the poor—up to say 1760 and here perhaps later—appealed to the parish chest or to the overseers for relief, they were given help in kind to meet visible and well understood needs. Not too many asked relief and a certain fellow-feeling was present because labourers of the two classes and the poorer commoners were not completely unrelated.

But after the middle of the century hardship both grew and took new forms. The tendency of the better-off to stress the welfare of their families and to care for privacy, gradually drove the poor into tiny, gardenless cottages away from the messuages. Because the hazards of child-birth and epidemic diseases killed fewer mothers and children, families were larger and pressed more upon food and space; young people had to leave home and try to find work elsewhere. Failing, they became idle vagrants and started on a life of pauperdom. The increased exploitation of available land meant the reduction of woods and wastes where dead wood could be gathered. When parishes were enclosed more timber and brushwood were cleared away and moreover gathering wood from remaining woods and hedges ceased to be an approved custom or right and became stealing or at best was done by favour. By the end of the century, magistrates in our district were dealing with innumerable cases of theft of wood. The poor used the same word for suffering from lack of food and from cold—"starvation". If, in past times they had been "starved" on their hearths, that had been due to howling draughts: they had never been quite fireless. Now there were times when cold was as bad as hunger. Finally, women had ceased to spin in Bledington: weaving, in the first phase of concentration, came to be confined to Chipping Norton (tweeds and other cloths) to Banbury and villages around (plush and girths) and Witney (blankets).

Economic troubles were accompanied by social ones. The anti-communal tendency was gradually approaching its climax. Since 1693 it had been obligatory for overseers to keep a written record of their expenditure and by means of these and other documents it has been possible in some villages to trace changes from decade to decade[75] e.g. in the number of paupers, the parish's expenditure (which became incredibly large), the occasional experiments of overseers and the change in social attitudes. But sometime in the nineteenth century almost all the parish records at Bledington were destroyed. There remains very little[76] beside the vestry minutes from 1763, saved because the minute book was still in use. Odd brief legends remain however on the farms and in the cottages but these can only be interpreted through knowledge of our national condition and outlook.

Something has already been said of these. "Profit", once so inclusive a term, was narrowed to mean monetary gain; Cotswold towns show merchants living well; many country parts were administered and ultimately controlled by large-scale landlords. Maximum wages were controlled by the landlord-magistrates, but not the minimum. Combination of workers was difficult and was made illegal. The easiest way to reduce costs of production was by the lowering of wages and increase of hours. There was, as we saw, the view that all this was right, being divinely ordered: leisure for others was vicious idleness in wage-earners. Saints' days had gone but market-days remained to corrupt the wage-earners. Even the humane Arthur Young wrote that "Everyone knows that the lower classes must be kept poor or they will never be industrious . . . they must (like all mankind) be in poverty or they will not work."[77]

In sermons and hymns the labourer, in places where he must be part of the congregation, heard that the functions he discharged were his duty: rebellion was sin. God had ordained him his place. (In villages like Bledington where property was widely distributed not all labourers bore this, for not all went to church). Burke was sincere when he assumed such views as socially necessary and spoke of the cruelty of those who took from the poor their sole consolation "trust in the proportions of eternal justice".[78]—which appears to have meant their hopes of a compensatory heaven. This view became the commonplace of prosperous rectories and so remained till late in the nineteenth century. It took at times the galling form of individual instruction in the lowly bearing suitable in inferiors. Domestic workers of the early eighteenth century as portrayed in novels and plays have a free and cheerful bearing, being the sons and daughters of parents who have fights. Later when labourers with no status had multiplied, service of a domestic and intimate kind became servitude, the resource of those who had no other.[79]

Could this outlook[80] exist in a Christian country? Its prevalence is proof of the extent to which the national Church had identified itself with government and the dominant classes. But like all periods, perhaps more than most, it was a time of contradiction and confusion. England was extolled as the land of the free: Wilberforce thought it his mission to free slaves the world over, though he saw nothing wrong with the condition of Englands own poor, some of whom, could there have been bidders, must have sold themselves to save their wives and children from starvation.

But the poor were allowed souls. The one strong religious movement of the century was that of the Methodists. John Wesley saw great numbers of people in complete ignorance of religion and each of them for him was in urgent need of salvation. It was not too far from the soul to the mind: Wesley himself took that step. It was further from the mind to the body and if Wesley did not take that stride nevertheless his movement would one day assist the widespread revolt against evil conditions of living.

There was the voice of sublime commonsense. "Want of tenderness", Dr. Johnson said, "was want of parts and no less a proof of stupidity than depravity", but England would require most of the nineteenth century to learn the truth of that.

The prevailing fog of economic and social notions arose a long way from our area and took time to penetrate into it. For example, Burford farmers in the middle of the century resolved to sell their corn to local folk, rather than send it where it might make a higher price to strangers —an almost Elizabethan proceeding. Here in Bledington, curates were so ill paid as to share the poverty of labourers and to be troubled by low social status. The lack of gentry spared the working people the servile manners that were developed elsewhere and no great house mocked poverty with sunless small cottages under the high walls of its park.

Nevertheless, by and large, conditions were here very much as elsewhere. Of the earnings of our labourers we have a little evidence. Lawrence, the Kingham blacksmith, employing a man in 1764, paid him 5s. 6d. a week, probably to work on the smith's holding in the common field; the next year, he paid another man 5/-. An equally homely record from another Gloucestershire village 18 miles away, shows John Plumb of Shenington (now in Oxfordshire) paying five shillings at times and at others seven shillings, the latter, no doubt, for some skilled work, perhaps masonry.[81]

Lord Ernle's figure for Gloucestershire from 1768 to 1770 is 6s.9d.[82] but it should be remembered that the west of the county included districts affected by the weaving industry. A lifetime's experience of villages shows me that the most sceptical approach is necessary to statements that wages were supplemented by payments in kind. Certainly wages were higher in harvest: on the other hand, work not done was not paid for and sometimes "the rain it raineth every day". Drink was sometimes and food occasionally provided in the fields, but wages took account of these, as we see in the tables of maximum wages put out by magistrates. In these, the wages of women when they worked in the fields were often given as half those of men and sometimes much less.

As to what wages would buy, the question can largely be reduced to the cost of bread. The people almost lived on it and therefore consumed large quantities, usually of the second grade, called "household". The price of corn was rising steadily from 1715 to 1774 from an average of 34s. 11d. to 51s. a quarter. After that, the price fell again somewhat but never to 35s. From 1795—the wars with revolutionary France had begun in 1792—to 1804, wheat brought an average of 75s.[83] to farmers, who, therefore, prospered while labourers were reduced to destitution and pauperdom: wages rose by 20% but needed to be doubled to keep pace with prices.

In 1795, Eden[84] gives the price of bread in Banbury as 1s. 10d. per half peck loaf and shows the budget of a family of seven in which 9¼ peck loaves are consumed. It seems a good deal, but it was almost the sole food and the hours of labour, dawn to dusk. If we take the number of a family to be more usually five and estimate that they need 6½ loaves at 1s. 10d., then bread for the family would cost 7s.7d.—more than a man's wage. There are indeed many calculations and actual budgets to show that a labourers' wages would not keep a family in bread. But a labourer needed other things—6d. per week for rent, 6s.6d. (Shenington 1799) annually for a smock and the same for a pair of shoes. Cheese cost, at Lawrence's shop, 6d. a pound. Lawrence also sold meat but its price is hardly relevant to the life of a wage-earner.

Under these circumstances, a strange condition came about. When a labourer fell ill his family would starve forthwith if they did not apply to the parish for poor relief. From about 1725 it was frequently and as the century went on, almost always, the case that men in full and regular work had to apply for relief if their families were to be fed. They were often given it—just enough with the wage to buy bread. Some disgraceful cruelties and tragedies took place. Our own overseers probably saw in Jackson's Oxford Journal for June 31st 1767 a letter from a coroner concerning a boy of twelve who had been found dead. He had himself opened the boy's stomach and found nothing in it but small coal and ashes, confirming his sister's statement that he had had nothing else to eat. "Many poor people", the coroner ended his letter, "there is reason to believe, are dying of the same disease, starvation".

(We shall not find many memories or legends of such extreme kind in villages. Some are so painful as to be repressed, as pain is from the minds of individuals).

Of course, misery was accompanied by decay and perversion in various kinds, some affecting the poor themselves and others those who employed them or administered the Poor Law and other enactments. The imbalance of the times tended to corrupt minds and especially to thicken skins. Our local magistrates administered repressive laws with a matching severity, sending mere children to prison. Amusing incidents are more persistently cherished than painful ones: it was a local joke till comparatively recently that one magistrate whose sons were clever sportsmen said to a labouring boy brought before him "They tell me you can shoot, you can snare, you can fish; in fact everything that's bad".

We have a description of labourers' homes in our area very early in the nineteenth century. In 1807 or before the Reverend Thomas Rudge[85] made enquiries in the villages. He reported that few had gardens and "of those few none sufficiently large to effect any great advantage". He writes of the extraordinary effort labourers would make to cultivate gardens and of how a little land ministers to "a proper spirit of independence". But he was dependent for publication on subscriptions from "the landed interest" and added that "what size indeed of cottage gardens" is compatible with "the interests of agriculture can only be ascertained by long-continued experiments on a large scale". These must be governed, he says, by "considerations of time and labour, which are due to another quarter", a suave statement of the view that a labourer's status and even the feeding of his family are matters secondary to the welfare of other classes.

Inside the homes women could not afford to buy soap and other cleansers. There was little fuel for cooking. Skills were lost from the homes as well as from the fields. The poor lost much of their independence and the honesty of the poorest, the largest families, declined. Those who took to the roads and failed to find work or a "settlement" took, perforce, to begging which is said to have been for some "an occupation and a livelihood". When begging failed or pride made it impossible the fate of vagrants could be terrible as was well-known here. In 1773 a coroner's inquest was held at Shipton under Wychwood on a woman and her child of about eighteen months, who had been found dead on the road a few miles away. The jury found that they had both died of starvation: they had been turned out of one parish by the overseers so that the expenses of burial might fall on another.[86]

Others, when begging failed, fell back on stealing—watching the clucking hens to rob their nests by day or, at night, taking eggs from hen houses. (The Kingham blacksmith was not making numerous keys and locks for household cupboards but for out-houses). In some villages, there came to be so much pilfering that farmers and housewives could only keep it within bounds by vigilance and cunning: you could not take half a parish before the courts.

Some of the temptations arising from the privations of workers were of course sexual. There is little doubt that men on farms had, far back, some knowledge of family restriction, but in the eighteenth century cottages sexual relaxation was restful like drink. Cottage women had

235

annual pregnancies far more often than farmers' wives.[87] "Bad women" were usually widows tempted by money. Girls, earning as early as possible, could not have much parental supervision and could only with difficulty be instilled with the sentiments of respectability. The undoubted evil of illegitimacy grew with poverty and pauperism. During the four decades 1703–1742 (inclusive) there is only one case of illegitimacy recorded in our parish registers. From 1743 to 1782, there were 20, from 1783 to 1822, 15 and from 1823 to 1842, 9. Nor did the trouble cease then.

Infanticide is known to have occurred: in 1781, the parson made this entry in the register: "James Campion, Born April 8th, murdered May 11th". The connection of illegitimacy with poverty and pauperism is brought out clearly in the register of baptisms. With one possible exception (one family name is that of nineteenth century smallholders) the cases of illegitimacy all occur among the poor; and of the ten mothers of bastard new-borns from 1769–1778 inclusive, the names of eight are followed by the letters P.P., short for Parish Pauper. (Not all our curates cared, it seems, to write this addition). Some have thought that the expectation of an allowance for each child from the parish, influenced unmarried mothers—a reasonable view in some cases but not here a necessary one and false in some parishes, e.g. Tysoe.

Supplementing wages by poor relief having become general the proceeding was (from 1795) oddly regularised. The Justices of the Peace of Berkshire (showing the power of magistrates in Poor Law matters) met at the henceforth famous village of Speenhamland and resolved that this system ought to hold throughout their county. Magistrates of other counties subsequently adopted this "Act" for their own areas.

The payment of relief to make up wages had a corollary. If all employers were paying rates to add to wages so that bread could be bought, they should share the labour equally, skilled and unskilled, strong and weak. So labourers went the round of farms, spending a short period, sometimes only a few days, on each in turn. Not only men but boys, then girls and last very young children went "on the round". On the Stows' farm in Bledington the story is still told that eleven men were sent to be given work by great-great- (how many greats?) grandfather.

Was ever any arrangement so strange? Boys and young fellows were without teacher or master. Men had to work on land and with animals they did not know. The young and the lame went where their infirmities and capacities were not understood. There were other girding and humiliating practices. In many parishes when work was lacking overseers refused relief unless the men performed some set useless tasks or even actions that did not pretend to be work. It is a tradition in Bledington that men were set to lower the height of ridges in the fields by throwing soil into the furrows with spades: they might as well have been set Epimetheus' task of rolling a great stone up a hill.

As in all times, in so large a unit as a nation, there was a variety of views and of degrees of humanity. In the later years of the century a few friends of the poor appeared in high places. In 1796 Samuel Whitbread the rich brewer and humane man and statesman brought in a bill to the House of Commons[88] to end the fixing of maximum wages and to institute minimum pay. He wanted to free farmworkers "from slavish dependence", to enable them to feed, clothe and lodge their families "with some degree of comfort" and to give the man who ploughed for and sowed the corn a right to some of it. He also brought in a Bill to provide schools in villages. (Finally, greatly frustrated, he died by suicide). There were Sir Frederick Eden's three volumes, suitable for statesmen, on the State of the Poor.[88] To get statesmen to read them Eden had to show his full appreciation of the economic rights of landlords; nevertheless, his fact-finding was excellent. Dr. Davies, a rector of Berkshire, used a sharp pair of eyes, serving a system of christian values and drew a "simple, faithful and sincere" picture of the facts. His book, unlike Eden's, was small and might be read by many. He could afford to attack flattering myths such as that (as Pitt said when he answered Whitbread) a broad stream of charity flowed to bring succour to the poor. The rich, said Davies, were now spending their money in Bath and London and coming home, not to help others, but to economise'[89]

Arthur Young, always tending to genuine observation and humanity, had come to fresh conclusions. He had realised that everyone could speak of the duties and conditions of the poor except themselves. "May God of His mercy grant" he wrote (and how significant the phrase is) "that the Legislature, whenever they take into consideration the poor . . . may enquire into it" (—"this momentous subject"—) "fully and minutely; and receive their information from those who are best able to give it, from the poor themselves."[90]

237

Young himself had conducted a practical research into what made agricultural workers industrious, free of debt, honest and sober and had found that it was a little property, a garden, a cow of their own. Men without property might be "notorious rogues"; with it, they were honest men. "It is impossible" he wrote, "for a country to go on respecting (i.e. concerning) the poor as this does at present; the consequences must be fatal."[90] Nearer home, in our own county, Sir George Onesiphorus Paul,[91] son of an inventive and successful clothier, was in his youth—like many other heirs of wealth at the time—a gambler living in very extravagant fashion. Later he became a sound man of public affairs, a magistrate, Sheriff of our county and a reformer of local prisons.

Overseers are sometimes represented by social historians as very hard of heart, but they could not influence either the theories or the legislation of the times, and their shoulders bore the ultimate burden of administration. The rates they had to impose and to pay reached towering heights and the problem of employing the poor was a most perplexing one.

A source of future help for all the underprivileged was the growing custom of newspaper reading. Our farmers' weekly newspaper was revealing to the countryside widespread political sentiments of resentment. Its editorials supported the City of London in the matter of Wilkes' election, reporting the Mayor's speech in which he spoke of the Ministry paying "with the money of the people for the violation of the Right of Election";[92] and reporting also how, after receiving a petition and replying to it, the King "burst out a-laughing" to the courtiers at his back. On January 6th 1770, it reports: "It is given out that the Administration had adopted very coercive methods with respect to North America". There was surely intention in the choice of the speeches in Parliament to which it drew attention. Lord Pomfret, in the Lords, talked of "the swaggering and impudent behaviour of low citizens on their own dunghill" and on January 20th of the same year the editor reports on his own account: "We hear the lucrative sinecures of the Joint Vice-Treasurers of Ireland have lately been offered by way of Baits to two patriotic commoners to desert the minority but without effect". Editors change and so did the policy of Jackson's, but when it ceased to be radical it still reported important events fairly and printed a varied correspondence.

Was Bledington an unhappy village? The strength of the tendency

of simple people to accept circumstances and use every means towards momentary comfort or pleasure must be witnessed to be believed; and contrasts in standard of life were not so sharp as to prevent
communication. But time brought further trouble.

viii How many Villagers?
A retrospective note

Until the early eighteenth century the density of inhabitants in
England had not been great. There had been more fear of loss and
reduction by disease and failure of harvests than any expectation of
gain in numbers or of problems due to such increase. When counts
of village people had been carried out their purpose had not been
"the numbering of the people" but of tenants or militiamen or tax
payers or religious dissidents. But in the course of the century a debate
arose about population; some thought it was declining, others that
there was certainly an overall increase, possibly a large one. It was
seen to be an important question: reduction or increase would bring
problems. Curiously, either change might bring pressure on the food
supply. Reduction might mean loss of produce in time of war, likely
by this time to mean a great call on manpower.

Up to this point we have not compared such figures as are available
so as to assess variations in the number of Bledingtonians. In 1086
there had been 20 adult males and perhaps 90 souls all told. No figure
can be found between that and the Winchcombe Rental of 1355, made
it will be recalled as a memorandum of the Abbey's tenants before
and after the Black Death. It enumerates 39 messuages and cottages,
the steward's house and the priest's house, all of which 41 houses had
been occupied in 1351. Thus the figure we arrive at relates to the time
just before the Plague. If we reckon the average size of a household
as 4½ (a figure assumed by some authorities) we infer a population of
179; there might be some persons outside all these households.

A number of families had lost those of their members who were capable of tilling their land: nine holdings were being managed with the
demesne and eight others were held by tenants in addition to their
home holdings This may well mean that there was the equivalent of
seventeen households the fewer and thus a total reduced to about 100.

We have no other source for nearly 200 years and then two: first,
in 1550 the survey of the "Possessions of the late Monastery of Winchcombe" enumerates eighteen tenants here. The number of holdings

has shrunk: we can add the steward and the vicar and thus reach twenty households. But what of labourers on the holdings of whom a larger number would now be required? We know from wills that two men were employed as shepherds on one of the farms, and that there were men "about the house" in other cases, and we could perhaps generalise—thus reaching however a figure of very little value.

Thirteen years later came the Ecclesiastical Census of 1563 which reports twenty houses and a hundred communicants. Both figures are suspiciously "round" and the meaning of the expression "houses" is doubtful: it cannot include all the dwellings. Twenty may well have been the number of messuages, with two other superior houses, and the homes of workers on the holdings may have been subsumed under these. Taking the other figure, the number of communicants, and assuming these to be two-thirds of the fold, we get the figure of 150—doubtful, but not unlikely. The population may well have varied about this figure for a long time.

Arriving at the seventeenth century, John Smith's Men and Armour of 1608 affords some definite figures for part of the population. Used alone, these give no reliable guidance but one may ask whether they tend to confirm others. Twenty two probable male heads of families under sixty years of age may be inferred. It will not be an over-estimate to add three women and four older men heads: there were also the Vicar and steward. So we reach a total of 31 households, say 140 individuals, a conservative estimate; that there had been some increase is suggested by our next documents.

Two such afford us some indication of the actual number of persons later in the century. The Hearth Tax assessment for 1671, though the list for Bledington is mutilated, shows some 31 names more or less decipherable and apparently there was one other. It gives no account of households that went untaxed, but for some parishes this is done. Sometimes those unassessed equal the others in numbers: we may safely assume in our own case that a number of labouring heads of families did not pay. Taking the number of unassessed at half the others, this gives us a total of at least 46 houses, with probably well over 200 inhabitants.

In 1676 was taken the ecclesiastical census known as the Compton Return which is recognised as having been as a rule carefully done. This gives us the number of conformists (151), papists (none) and non-conformists (5). Persons over 16 years of age were counted and these we may reckon as two-thirds of the total and arrive at a total of 234. From these two sources we may form the hypothesis that by the seventeenth century the population was rising fairly fast. Had we but a good series of parish registers for the century we might now check its truth.

From about 1550 many parish registers afford reliable figures—sometimes even for the period of the Civil War and Commonwealth—of births, deaths and marriages, but here no registers are extant for the years before 1703. From 1605, however, there are some transcripts of registers. These were delivered once a year to the archdeacon when he visited the Stow deanery. The Vicar and the two churchwardens, sometimes the wardens without the Vicar or his substitute, carried them to Stow. Unfortunately, they were not well preserved in the diocesan offices: one set was somehow burned and made partly illegible: others were written on tiny scraps of parchment with fading ink. Sometimes the writing is very poor. There are also many years for which transcripts are entirely lacking. From before the outbreak of the Civil War till after the return of Charles II (i.e. from 1640 to 1661) there are none: for much of this period registration was not a legal duty of the Church. Beside these 21 years there are other, shorter spells of several years for which no transcripts have survived, if they were made.

Thus we have legible records of both baptisms and burials for only 40 years in the century 1605 to 1703. Registers and transcripts afford only the vaguest data on which to estimate the village's population, but a comparison of births and deaths might be expected to show whether circumstances are favouring growth or reduction in numbers. For the forty years mentioned, the number of baptisms is 266 and of burials 160 which obviously suggests a growing population: but it tells nothing of young persons leaving the village. There seem not to have been any steep and sudden declines, due to epidemics or famine. The highest number of burials in any one year is 9 (1703), the average being 4. On five occasions in eight years there are 6 or 8. But when the number of burials is high, the number of healthy births seems to have been high also: a matter of chance, of course, but it does suggest that the deaths are not due to plague. In 1703 the nine burials are balanced by 10 baptisms: one mother and child died soon after the ceremony. In 1612 there had been nine baptisms and eight deaths. In 1685 five of the six deaths are due to the hazards of birth: twins, a mother and child and one other babe are buried. Altogether one child in five died within its first year or fourteen months. (The period between one transcript and another was sometimes longer than a year; the archdeacon's visit might be up to two months' late). Taking all this into account, we should not be justified in associating either the infant mortality or the death of older persons with special circumstances. (We may note in passing that any improvement in medicine and nursing related to child-bed will clearly bring a steady increase in population. It is likely that removal of beds to bedrooms from living rooms, or a sense of the importance of cleanliness on such occasions would also have effect).

Other simple hygienic improvements must have saved some lives. Water-closets in London sent up the death rate but the regular use of a privy in yard or garden was a genuine step forward—but not all houses had space. Some clothes were being made of cotton, easy to wash and iron. Even a little medical knowledge, when it came, could be literally vital. John Lawrence the blacksmith lost an infant son in 1774. He wrote in his book a receipt "To anoint wake children", "2d. oil a . . . , 2d oil ambers, 2d oil worms, 1d oil St. John's wort". "Weakness" was probably tuberculosis.

For what our figures are worth, there had been an increase since the late sixteenth century of about 100 persons. We saw that the excess of births over deaths for less than half the years between 1605–1704 was 106. Disturbance due to the Civil War may have reduced the births for a period so that the excess for the century need not have been more than twice that number. Two hundred more baptisms than burials would suggest a great exodus from the village, but roughly one fifth of the babies were born only to die and hardly affected the total. If we deduct this proportion we get an increase of 160. For the seventeenth century we arrive at the following figures, all partly guess-work: 1671 (Hearth Tax) 200 plus; 1766 (Ecclesiastical Census) 234. Adding to this one fourth of the estimated increase (106, from 1605–1704) for the last quarter of the century we arrive at the figure for 1704 of 274 persons.

Early in the eighteenth century comes the first simple numbering of the people of the village. In 1711 and 1712 Sir Robert Atkyns obtained figures from the incumbents of the parishes of the county and published them in his History. There were here, he says, 53 houses and 260 inhabitants in Bledington—the latter number affording us the figure of five to a house. (This does not mean five to a family; whenever we have details, we find a few houses shared).

If all the villages in the country were increasing in the same proportion, those who believed numbers were increasing, had reason, even though the death rate in large towns was known to be very high.

Where our own emigrants went is a question we cannot answer. We may also ask where our own increase was housed? It is impossible now to find 53 sites of houses standing at that time and difficult to trace more than 35. We learn from the Enclosure Award of 1769 that there were 17 commoners with their messuages and 19 householders in cottages with "titheable" gardens. Presumably these 36 houses are the older and more substantial ones, on the better sites. There is some evidence that there were also small, probably one-storey erections in the yards of the messuages and the increase may have been in these. Later they would fall stone from stone, as may be seen still in the walls of the closes; rough dressing distinguishes them from the normal wall-stones. (There is no sign in Bledington of houses built on waste ground).

Rudge in his Agriculture of Gloucestershire published in 1807 gives a figure for 1770 of 251 and the figure from the first census, in 1801, was 282. Thus the increase was very small. From 1703 we have reliable information on baptisms and burials; registers are regularly kept and the series is complete. From 1703 to 1799 inclusive, 621 baptisms are recorded and 425 burials, an excess of baptisms over burials of 196. Some children still died very early, but there was evidently considerable emigration. What this meant for our social life, we cannot know, but we can ask. Did boys and girls go out with good hope of some success or to a life on the roads? Find work and homes in other rural communities? Contribute to London's high death rate? Join the Army? They had not yet learned to cross the Atlantic.

For the eignteenth century we have a village of between 250 and 280 persons. Since 1800 or thereabouts Bledington has ranked as a small village and till the coming of the railway as somewhat inaccessible. But until then, this was not so. Most of our neighbour villages were smaller (Icomb, the Rissingtons, the Slaughters and Swells) and some now a good deal larger were of similar size (Kingham, Naunton, Oddington). But none was too small to make a contribution to a nation of between $5\frac{1}{2}$ and 7 million.

It may be well to set out a summary of the population changes argued above.

1086	population	90
1351		179 (before plague)
1355		100 (after plague)
1381		100
1550		130
1563		150
1608		? 140
1671		200 plus
1676		234
1704		274
1711		260
1770		251
1801		282

[1] W. H. Hutton *Burford Papers* London 1905 p. 113
[2] Hutton op. cit. pp. 113 & 114
[3] Alan Villiers *The Seamen's Sailor: the Life of James Cook* London 1967
[4] Alan Villiers, op. cit. pp. 31–32
[5] See Chap. VII: The Morris Men
[6] Benjamin Franklin. Autobiography (1818) Everyman Edition pp. 178–198
[7] Maybe this fact accounts for so few spinning wheels surviving in this country
[8] James Boswell. op. cit. Vol. I p. 188
[9] Ibid. Vol. I, pp. 155–6
[10] ed. Nowell C. Smith. *The Letters of Sydney Smith.* Vol. II, Oxford 1953 p. 496
[11] ed. Nowell C. Smith op. cit. Vol. 1, pp. 21 & 22
[12] Jeremy Bentham *An Introduction to the Principles of Morals and Legislation* (1789) Chap. 1
[13] Thos. Spence *The Meridian Sun of Liberty* (1775) reprinted in H. M. Hyndman *The Nationalisation of the Land* (1882)
[14] G.R.O. Ecclesiastical Census 1676
[15] Evelyn Goshawk *Idbury History* privately printed n.d.
[16] E. J. Lainchbury *Kingham, the Beloved Place* Alden Press (Oxford) 1957 pp. 153–155 (Archdeacon Secker's Visitation 1738)
[17] Anthony Trollope, *The Last Chronicle of Barset* passim.
[18] Deed (mortgage) 1734: Papers, Mr Angus Hood
[19] Information re incumbents from various sources, including Hockaday, parish registers, Christ Church records and county histories
[20] a) Stephen Liberty *The Father of Warren Hastings* Privately printed 1932

b) Ibid. *Guide to Investigations re the Hastings Family* MS. Papers, M. K. Ashby

21 Parish Registers 1703–1914. Vicar and Churchwardens, Bledington
22 G.D.R. Hockaday 128. Terriers 1704 and 1829
23 It appears that for part of the period he was also curate at Evenlode
24 Christ Church: Book of Evidences 1778
25 Alan Savidge *The Foundation and Early Years of Queen Anne's Bounty* London 1955
26 See note 3 page 4
27 Churchwardens' Accounts, Bledington. Papers, Churchwardens
28 V. H. H. Green *The Young Mr Wesley* London 1961 pp. 136/7, 214 and others
29 Letter to S. Liberty from E. M. Shilston of Bridgetown, Barbados. Papers, M. K. Ashby
30 M. K. Bennett *British Wheat Yield per Acre for Seven Centuries* in Essays in Agrarian History ed. W. E. Minchinton, Newton Abbot, 1968
31 All inventories are in G.C.L. with Bledington wills
32 Chap. V. p. 162
33 Robert Plot *History of Oxfordshire* Oxford, 1677 p. 74
   Rev. T. Cox *Oxfordshire in the First Part of the 18th Century* 1738 p. 396
34 Two springs of water near the border of the parish were believed to have medicinal value, one at Bould (see Cox p. 394) and one on ground near the present Kingham Station
35 Landboc Vol. I, p. 211
36 Ibid. p. 109
37 Wills of date before 1541 are in the Worcester Record Office
38 Shakespeare's Birthplace Trust, Leigh documents, Bledington Manor Court 1553–1571
39 Chap. V, pp. 126, 127
40 Oxfordshire Record Office. Bundle of Farrant and Sinden documents
41 From this point information re the Lord family is usually drawn from documents in possession of Mr Angus Hood
42 Now the King's Head Inn
43 Document dated July 13, 1767. Papers, Angus Hood Esq.
44 M. Havinden *Agricultural Progress in Open-Field Oxfordshire* in *Essays in Agrarian History* Vol. I ed. Minchinton, Newton Abbot 1968
45 Account Book of John Lawrence 1764 to 1792. Papers, M. K. Ashby
46 Arthur Young. *Agriculture of Oxfordshire.* 1809
47 Ed. Dorothy Hartley. *Thomas Tusser, His Good Points of Husbandry.* Country Life, London. 1931 *February's Husbandry* pp. 131–3
48 Daniel Defoe. *Tour Through England and Wales* 1727
49 Arthur Young *Travels in France,* 1792. Bohn's Popular Library 1924, p. 54
50 (i) H. M. Hyndman. *The Nationalisation of the Land* 1882 contains a reprint of Spence's *Meridian Sun of Liberty*
   (ii) A. W. Waters. *Trial of Thos. Spence in* 1801 contained in *Spence and his Political Works* Leamington Spa 1917 p. 32
51 Arthur Young *Report of the Agriculture of Oxfordshire,* London, ed. 1812: *An Enquiry into the Propriety of Applying Wastes to the Better Maintenance of the Poor*

[52] i.e. the Mill, Tydmarshes', Snows' and Dalbys'

[53] Diggers', Bettertons', Gibbses', and Grayhursts'

[54] G.R.O. Q/RI 25 Bledington Enclosure Act 1769

[55] Enclosed in 1831. See Chap. VII p. 353

[56] Rev. Thos. Rudge *General View of the Agriculture of Gloucestershire* 1811. See under *Bledington*

[57] G.R.O. Particulars of sale of Reddall's properties, 13th November, 1798

[58] Suit in Chancery 1797: Fletcher and other Plainants against Richard Reddall and other Defendants. The story of the suit gathered from documents of 1797, 1799, 1802, 1810. Papers, Mr Angus Hood

[59] Will of Nathaniel Osborne of Tormarton, November 1798. Papers, Mr Angus Hood

[60] Calculation by M. Geo. Broomhall, F.S.S. *The Wheatsheaf*, 1909

[61] Its 18th century decoration has lately been removed

[62] E. J. Lainchbury *Kingham, the Beloved Place* Alden Press (Oxford) 1957, p. 155

[63] Vide memorial stone in wall of Churchill School

[64] *Memoirs of William Smith L.L.D.* by his nephew John Phillips F.R.S., F.G.S., London 1844

[65] i.e. one of the Mattocks cottages. see Chap. V, p. 230

[66] e.g. Margaret Gilkes' deed of gift 1745. Papers, church chest (now G.R.O.)

[67] John Lawrence of Kingham, account book 1764–1792. Papers, M. K. Ashby

[68] i.e. Physic given by the throat, with a horn

[69] A moss that grows on limestone?

[70] Alum used to dress eruption on skin

[71] Oxford Times July 22nd, 1955

[72] Documents in the church chest, recently transferred to G.R.O.

[73] Papers, Mr Cecil Acock

[74] Papers, Mr Angus Hood

[75] e.g. A. W. Ashby *One Hundred Years of Poor Law Administration in a Warwickshire Parish* Oxford Studies in Social and Legal History Vol. III, Oxford 1912

[76] e.g. Document from church chest recording purchase (1756) of a cottage by an overseer, for the sum of £5.5s.10d. (now G.R.O.)

[77] Arthur Young *Eastern Tour* (1771) Chap. IV, p. 361

[78] Edmund Burke *Select Works* ed. E. J. Payne Oxford 1898 Vol. II, pp. 289–290

[79] See e.g. Smollett *Humphrey Clinker*, passim.

[80] For many original statements see E. S. Furniss *The Position of the Labourer in a System of Nationalism*. New York 1920

[81] MS book, Papers, Mrs Myra McLean

[82] Lord Ernle. *English Farming, Past and Present* 4th edition 1932, Appendix 9

[83] Lord Ernle, op. cit. Appendix 3

[84] Sir Frederick Eden *The State of the Poor* Vol II p. 584, London 1797

[85] Rudge op. cit. *Gardens*

[86] M. Sturge Gretton *Three Centuries in North Oxford* Oxford 1902, pp. 130, 131. Vagrants dying of starvation were not uncommon e.g. Tysoe overseers' accounts and parish registers show three cases, M. K. Ashby op. cit. p. 271, A. W. Ashby op. cit. p. 73

[87] This continued to be the case in the early 20th century

88 See Sir Frederick Eden *The State of the Poor* for the speech
89 Reverend David Davies *The Case of Labourers in Husbandry Stated and Considered* (London) 1795
90 Arthur Young *An Inquiry into the Propriety of Applying Wastes* etc. op. cit.
91 E. A. L. Moir *Sir George Onesiphorus Paul* in *Gloucestershire Studies* ed. H. P. R. Finberg, Leicester 1957
92 J. O. J. March 10th 1770

chapter seven

THE NINETEENTH CENTURY (1815-1914)

Introductory; The Clergy in the Early Years; Farmers 1800–1872; Labourers' life to the middle of the century; the Poor and the Poor Law; Country Parson, Victorian; the Wage-earners, the Railway and the Methodist Society; Arch's Movement; Farmers and the Agricultural Depression 1870–1890; Bledington School 1896–1901; and 1901–1914; Religious Life; Church, Chapel, the Temperance Movement and Economic Self-help; On the Farms and in the Villages 1883–1914; The Morris Men.

Introductory

IN THE NINETEENTH century Bledington experienced no internal events so disruptive as "enclosure" but movements from outside had deep effects. Local events were less important than Acts of Parliament.

From Napoleon's final defeat in 1815, after something of a stand-still in political and other movements there was constant change in thought, feeling and event. Our period opens with midland villages in wretched condition. That their population had grown and would continue to do so, unless the number of homes was reduced, could not be doubted. The chief increase was in the number of farm labourers, with their families. Life was still shot through with the inhuman theory of the destiny and status of the working classes which had held the field since the seventeenth century[1] The price of bread had soared and fallen during the wars. It was often at starvation level for men whose wage was nine shillings a week. The incomes of landlords and arable farmers rose and fell with the price of wheat, but was always at a high level with wages rising little if at all. As the need for dwellings became greater old farm buildings were often converted when farm-

248

houses—as happened in almost every village—ceased to be farm centres. As buildings these houses were no worse than earlier ones, but they were crowded together and gardenless, while families were larger. When the poor became destitute, or, as indeed had become usual, their wages would not keep their families in bread, they were dependent upon an ancient Poor Law unsuited to the times; earnings were supplemented by payment from the Poor Rates, thus pauperising a whole class; a condition by which many became degraded, at least in some measure.

Rational protest by the men against this state of affairs, and also joint action for its improvement was repressed by antagonistic and unjust legislation, administered in local courts by magistrates, all members or allies of the landed classes and in the King's Courts often by judges who believed that England's constitution was the best in the world and all Englishmen fortunate.

At large, the power of landlords was still untouched: Parliament, in both Houses, was in their hands. Everyone outside their class was at some risk from their interests. Professional folk—now multiplying fast—were often dependent on them and must be subservient. Even wealthy manufacturers and traders could lack political influence unless they bought land to ensure it.

By 1914, when our period ends, all classes of men, even farm labourers, had the parliamentary franchise. The Poor Law had been amended (in 1834) and though some forms of relief were still hated and dreaded by the poor its application had been limited by the payment of Old Age Pensions (very late—in 1909) and further reform was on the way. Both the body of law and the legal profession had undergone immense change. There was at length (again very late) no property qualification for justices of the peace and they were being recruited in a different way: a working man in court might find himself before a magistrate who had once been subject to conditions not greatly better than his own.

Late in the century subservience, so often called deference, could be avoided, by most men though not often by persons in domestic service The children in Sunday Schools still sang:

> The rich man in his castle,
> The poor man at his gate,
> God made them, high or lowly,
> And ordered their estate.

but the grown-ups did not feel sure of the truth of the statement. As late as 1870 many villages had no school and towns an inadequate number of school places for their children, but by 1914 popular education, supported by the State, had developed from mechanical drill and training not at all designed for the child's own sake, to schools staffed by teachers of fair education trained to give genuinely humane education.

In the last few years of our period, between 1906 and 1914, the workers were guarded from the worst effects of industrial and other hazards—sickness, accident and unemployment (except as regards the last, the farm worker). It is true, however, that country labourers, were still very poor, that their wages would only feed a family if supplemented, as well as being spent by men and women of utter self-control and industry. And yet if respect, including self-respect, freedom to struggle individually and together with one's fellows, for amelioration of one's lot in life are worth something, the changes were beneficent even for them. (Besides, farming was not prosperous: employers could be forgiven).

The position of women was still poor and could be felt (by professional women or by a farmer's widow) to be galling. They did not have parliamentary votes till 1918, and widows might find themselves omitted from their husband's wills and entirely dependent on their sons. But the number of educated women was growing rapidly.

For the poor the climb had been long and painful; endurance was long called for in all aspects of their life. It was not till they at length learned to help themselves that their life could be worth living.

Yet the change was great and could not have been achieved without other accompanying changes. There would seem to have been two sources of these economic tendencies, more certainly one. Industry and commerce had enriched new classes, and the growing wealth caused the continuing expansion of the middle class, the growth and spread of knowledge, and the strengthening of the professions. In towns the number of skilled men and the variety of their trades grew. There were social bridges between classes and communication between them became easier. But also the outlook on society of the new intelligentsia had slowly changed. Since the eighteenth century the summary of Bentham's view of the aim of society, "the greatest happiness of the greatest number" had seemed to more and more folk rational and satisfactory, no matter how weak it seemed to philosophers. Wesley and his evolving church together with the evangelical movement within the established Church with their emphasis on the value of the individual soul in the sight of God had taught despised folk to set a high value on themselves and given them hope for their children.

Further, a great popular literary movement flourished. Poets—Shelley, Burns, Wordsworth—stirred by the ideas of the French Revolution, were it was said "always with the people"; novelists writing somewhat later were awake to the poverty and misery and ill government of the country: they stirred sympathies and warmed hearts in every class. Dickens it is said "drew more English people together than any other influence of the time". The landlord, farmer and labourer laughed at the same caricature and grieved for the same miseries. Trollope held up the mirror at many an angle for the upper classes to view themselves. The spread of enthusiasm for books, with the resulting cheap editions, created a new sort of educated person, not much schooled but informed and also humorous and supple-minded. He might be a lord or a grocer, or horny-handed, and speaking English with an unorthodox accent. Reading became the great winter resource of many country people.

Critics of current values such as Coleridge with his view of the social implications of Christianity[2] and Carlyle's admiring essays on the Middle Ages[2] also reached relatively wide circles among the more highly educated in the first half of the century and vigorous young intellects continued to read them long after that. The press, even when in chains in the early years, was powerful. The Editor of the *Times* was bracketed with Dickens as a reforming power. The farm labourers had good support from him in their struggles; the county papers' reports of their meetings were fair—if not always their editorials.

Upon all this economic, religious and cultural development was based a many-sided generous movement for which any more precise term proves too narrow. Chivalry, let alone fellowship, had long been lacking from the fortunate classes to the unfortunate. But now groups of educated professional men—to speak of country affairs—helped the farm workers' struggling Unions; Bishops and landlords advocated and even provided field-gardens for poor villagers; in our own locality charitable women built schools for children of the poor. The workers' leaders tried to subordinate emotions of resentment and bitterness to claims for justice and hope for the future. In village communities the fissures that had developed tended to close and they might achieve for brief whiles very happy phases. Much of this we shall see affecting and working within our own Bledington.

Two other aspects of the national life, though not always visibly affecting our village life, formed part of its background. First, the place of England in the world at large, the defence and expansion of its interests. From 1792 there had been wars with revolutionary and expanding France. Many thousands of ignorant English villagers met and fought their still more wretched counterparts from France. The war did not benefit the French peasant for a long time, nor did the victory bring benefit to English villagers, but safety from a powerful neighbour and many years of peace allowed our country to return her attention to her internal affairs. All England had been drawn into the struggle. Men of military age drew lots for service. When young farmers and other well-to-do or pre-occupied folk hereabouts had no wish to leave home the overseers of their parish would advertise in Johnson's Oxford Journal for volunteers, offering money to substitutes; it was understood that while soldiers were away their wives and children would be supported on "pensions" from the parish; in 1811 there were three such women-pensioners in Bledington, and this is the only evidence as to men in the forces. It was very common for villages to have crippled men returning but as to loss by death or injury to our men we have no evidence. Nor had there been any Association for Protection such as the Shipton and Ascott farmers had formed, to plan what to do in case Napoleon crossed the Channel. But when in 1815 the government appointed a day for celebration of the final victory at Waterloo we know that our villagers shared the joy that bloodshed was over.

Soon after the middle of the century (1853–6) came the Crimean War, concerning the claims and fears of nations with interests in the Near East. Bledington seems to have had no direct part in it: I never heard even that the women knitted Balaclava helmets to save the ears of British soldiers. But the country was shocked by the general inefficiency of the military planning and commissariat and medical services and by some outstanding blunders of the generals. All this made the aristocratic leadership of the time seem "a system of total incapacity". From that time it received more of the criticism to which, like other systems, it was entitled.

During the century there was much development of the colonies—

in Canada, Australia and New Zealand—and of British imperial rule in India and Africa. What mattered to agricultural villages was the open door to less populated areas, whether British or no. The steamship was bringing them nearer. For decades Bledington men went more readily to the United States than to Canada; men from nearby villages even tried Brazil! But as time went on the colonies took active steps to attract English farm labourers, and letters from successful settlers received in families or published in local newspapers added some degree of familiarity to the hope of better wages, free or very cheap land and freedom from an oppressive social hierarchy.

The expansion of British interests in Africa in the late decades led in 1899 to the Boer War, which proved so difficult and humiliating to Britain. Many Radicals and Liberals opposed the war: villagers who were politically aware had cause for scepticism as to its motives. In the early eighties the troubles of English settlers in South Africa, the Uitlanders, to whom full citizenship was denied were already much discussed—before the English farm worker was enfranchised. There was unusually full implication of village folk in the War. Young aristocrats, squires and sons of "gentlemen" farmers went off with their "Territorial" officers and on their own horses to face the Boer farmers on theirs. Volunteer recruitment was favoured by unemployment. Bledington has no Boer War memorial: no death is recorded or remembered, but there were three volunteers and one of them, a Warren (by now an old name in the village) was taken prisoner at Ladysmith. Our village would, with all England, presently gain by the utterly plain revelation of the physical ill-health of our people through the medical examination of recruits.

Finally, great changes in central and local administration of laws had begun in the late eighteenth century and would continue, at intervals, throughout our period. They would affect not only every community but every citizen. A new pattern for central administration had been evolved: when new legislation extended the functions of government, as happened in the case of education, the Poor Law, and agriculture (all of importance to the countryside) a Committee of the Privy Council was established for it, with a secretary and staff, later a more fully organised Board, with experts serving on it, and eventually a department of Government, with a Minister at its head and a large branch of the Civil Service.

For local control the towns, under the Municipal Corporations Act

1835, were required to have representative councils. At first these had few powers but they could enlarge them through private legislation and thus deal with their own most urgent needs. In the countryside, the Justices of the Peace in Quarter sessions were still the chief authority, as they had been for centuries; civil functions such as the direction of the Vestries in the relief of the poor, the control of the new Police, and a large share in the administration of highways had been added to their judicial functions. Recruited from men of property and from the prosperous clergy, some members, notably clergymen, did careful work and kept some record of it. For their more modern functions they were often handicapped by lack of knowledge and expertise, and for their old, judicial functions both by partial legislation, Game Laws and others, which they were bound to administer and also by their own natural tenderness to the classes upon which they were dependent or from which they were drawn.

That Quarter Sessions of magistrates had too many functions had come to be recognised, and new institutions were created. In 1834 Quarter Sessions ceased to supervise the relief of the poor. A number of magistrates became Guardians of the Poor but to that office they were elected and moreover had advice and criticism from the specialised Central Board.

Another prime need had been the elimination of very insanitary conditions in town and country alike. Sanitary duties were given to the Boards of Guardians—duties for which they, in their turn, lacked qualification. The School Boards set up under the Education Act of 1870 were based on areas too small to ensure suitable members and besides, the regulations of the central education authority discouraged and in time prevented work of good quality. Another function in need of new institutions was housing control. Clearly there was a vacuum of government which must be filled. The new institutions must cover a sufficient area to afford membership of ability and of varied experience. It had to be capable of taking in hand the many-sided work of "local government"—a new term. The background of country life was to be greatly changed.

In 1884 a Royal Commission made recommendations from which followed the Local Government Act of 1888. It provided for elective County Councils. Every three years householders, including women (but not wives of householders) would elect councils. There was a property qualification, though a low one, for councillors. The councils would be large enough to select from their numbers special committees to make recommendations on aspects of the Council's work, though the whole Council was responsible for decisions. Experts were employed but the status of these was at first not attractive to outstanding men.

As matters turned out, County Councils have never been truly representative. Popular control of them such as it has been, has come through Parliamentary elections and legislation regulating the Councils' work. Attendance at day-time meetings in the County town was impossible for all except independent persons, so that County Councils have been manned by the same classes as Quarter Sessions had been. There have been until far into the twentieth century comparatively few elections, sole candidates being common, having been often nominated by their predecessors from among friends of their own kind. A constituency consists usually of several parishes—in Bledington's case, thirteen—and the Councillor was often, till the advent of cars and telephones, a total stranger except in his own village.

It is well known that the counties—notably our own—have been served by some persons and families distinguished for their public service who have held themselves ready to administer new laws with impartial devotion. Where the interests of all classes were common they did work from which everyone profited. For example, on the improved highways elegant carriages, delivery vans, farmers' gigs and traps and young labourers' bicycles all became more numerous and could do longer journeys. But it is also true that the over-representation of property and established classes has meant that there has been emphasis on economy rather than on needs, that the councils lacked variety of view and failed to contribute to the training in government of the classes who most needed it. Rural democracy can never show its paces till in every institution attention is paid to this educational function.

In one matter it was shown that when the councils had not to find money they could respond to popular trends. The windfall of "whisky money" awarded to the councils by Parliament in 1890 was to be spent on technical education but the interpretation of this term followed demand as far as was possible—mathematics, carpentry, science and even physical culture classes were paid for from it.

Another step forward came eventually through the schools for children. The Act of 1902 gave County Councils the general direction under the Board of Education of publicly provided and assisted schools. Their new Education Committees must have, under the Act, a proportion of co-opted members with special knowledge of education and must include women. They must also employ secretaries well qualified for the new work. These provisions rendered the posts of "Secretary" or "Director" of Education attractive to men of high education and generous outlook, as offering opportunities for constructive public service: some admirable appointments were made. The first Secretary for Gloucestershire though not of broad and classic mind was a man of a modern educational outlook. Experienced co-opted members helped to set a somewhat new pattern and a new standard of discussion, to the profit of whole councils.

Meanwhile in the villages the vestries had lost their important civil functions—police, Poor Law, roads. Non-conformists had ceased to attend, labourers had never been able to do so. In 1870 a President of the Poor Law Board had worked out a scheme for rural areas which would have provided new representative bodies for villages as well as counties, and have given considerable responsibilities to both. But Goschen was before his time, or more precisely before his Prime Minister's, and the bill was dropped. But Gladstone's outlook became more democratic and the Liberal Government of twenty-five years later passed the Local Government Act of 1896, popularly known as the "Parish Councils Act" although it also provided for District Councils, Urban and Rural, for sections of Counties. The President of the Local Government Board, H. H. Fowler, was the son of a Methodist Minister. As such he naturally believed—unlike the House of Lords—in the capacity of the lay villager to understand and to manage local affairs. To Parish Councils his Bill allotted good powers.

But in the Upper House the Bill met with the peers' natural preference for the old hierarchical rural situations which gave them—where they owned estates—so much dominance and influence. Their resistance to most Liberal Bills was considerable; to this one it was extreme: 619 amendments were moved! The proposed powers of the Parish Councils were cut down by the very small expenditure in the end permitted. The final Act was thus a greatly diluted measure.

Because of the limitations imposed Parish Councils could not call out enthusiasm or promote spirited or informative discussion of important projects. A village might consciously need (as Tysoe did in 1866) a small sports ground for youths, or maybe a hall for meetings a generation before 1896 and lack it for a hundred years (till 1966): like County Councils they failed to give to villages a modern substitute for their one-time responsibilities. At times in small villages Parish Councils have sunk very low. Farmers have sought office avowedly to "save the rates", excusing this attitude by the depression in agriculture, and others not in their trade have done the same. Even the poor, although they did not pay rates, had so ingrained a habit of sparing and scraping that they could be frightened of the most modest expenditure. Of course, the Councils were not useless. Village needs, e.g. for allotments, could be discussed and some stimulus given to District Councils. In time they would receive some permissive powers, but the limit of their expenditure was not raised till recently nor their prime duties enlarged.

The Rural District Councils slowly became more successful and more appreciated. Each village has had its own representative, and even though, as with County Councils, there has often been no election, the work of the member for the village has been watched and criticised. Their membership has been more varied: wage-earners could not serve but occasionally an ex-worker has done so. The "R.D.C s" had functions related to crying needs, in early days for the much discussed supplies of pure water, involving the condemnation of shallow wells all over our neighbourhood as in many districts, and other provisions, e.g. for privies and for the removal of pigsties to a little distance from cottages and such homely matters.

Local newspapers, school log books, minutes of Parish and District Councils, all bear witness to the frequent epidemics that swept through homes and schools, hindering work and instruction, impairing health and leading at times to tragic early deaths. The present day insistence of villagers on good water supplies and sewage systems is a tribute in part, to the work of the Councils and their Surveyors. Their most popular success has been the provision of houses. Almost every village has its group, large or small, of council houses, all decent in every practical way and sometimes not ill-looking. This work of housing has been done since 1914, outside our period, but together with the great sanitary gains it has proved the value of the local share in administration.

Finally, we should not omit to note the removal in 1911 of a great constant obstruction to change in rural social life. It was during the prolonged debates on the "Parish Councils" Bill that the final struggle between a frustrated representative House of Commons and the hereditary Upper House was foretold by Gladstone.

The great Liberal majority after the election of 1906 framed a number of reforming Bills, relating to education, industrial insurance, licensing of public houses and Irish Home Rule. All these, with others, and at length a budget also were rejected, not entirely by regular attendants at the House of Lords but in part by "backwoodsmen", peers who were persuaded to leave their favoured occupations and come "to the defence of their order". The representative House had to fight it out or become meaningless. After a long and dramatic struggle, the Lords accepted a considerable defeat in 1911, almost at the end of the century as we have defined it. The twentieth century could get going.

An interesting scene had opened Bledington's century. When in 1815 the government had appointed a day for celebration of the final victory at Waterloo, the villagers gathered for a great meal in the yard of Home Farm. Under the immense long roof of thatch-on-rushes of its cartshed[5] and amidst its supporting oak posts (which must have barked many a shin) tables were set and roast beef and plum pudding served to all. The meal had been prepared by the farmers' wives and was certainly blessed by the Vicar. It was a witness to the surviving sense of community, even though a good meal was a sufficient attraction for the poor. In 1953 we all rejoiced in the same manner at the coronation of Queen Elizabeth II. From my seat in the Village Hall I saw a small group of old labourers eating the traditional victuals in a greedy, graceless way as if they were half-starved still, as their predecessors had certainly been in 1815. These men, all born before 1890, had themselves been underfed. They were not representative of their kind, rather our social casualties. But they illustrate the difficulty of maintaining community: only one group had suffered vital insufficiency.

Between 1801 and 1901 the number of our villagers grew quite rapidly and then slowly declined, being still in 1901 20% greater than in 1801. The figure for the first national census (1801) was 282—inaccurate, for two out-village houses were not included—and the figure for 1901 was 341. In the first fifty years it had risen by 27.8%, then was almost stationary for twenty years. Later from its maximum of 391 it fell by fifty. Its composition seems to have changed chiefly by the growth in numbers of labouring folk.

In earlier centuries this had been a husbandmen's village. By 1831 there were 59 labourers and (though the mode of counting varied) the number seems to have been the same in 1851 and to rise later to over 60. Their lives were so difficult for themselves and posed such a problem for government that it might be felt to be then first and foremost a labourers' village.

The whole population was still in 1911 dependent on farming—farmers, craftsmen, shopkeepers, schoolmaster or "dame , and the parson whose income came from the rents of the fields. There were eight, sometimes nine, farms varying in acreage from 290 to 110, employing one man per 20 to 30 acres, beside the two or three small-holders having no regular paid help. Although some handicrafts were dying out means of livelihood were not less varied than earlier: there were some 13 or 14 "manufacturers" and tradesmen. These varied from decade to decade: a representative list would be as follows: miller, cooper, shoemakers (usually 2), tailor, shopkeeper(s), inn-keeper(s), baker, maltster, carrier, smith(s). There might be a drainer or a rat-catcher. Sometimes, not in the early years, there were dress-makers, once a milliner. From 1850 there was for some years a school-master (with ten pupils) as there had also been in the 1820s. When there was no schoolmaster after about 1830 there was always a "dame" teaching a few children to read. From 1876 there was always a school-master with usually a teacher-wife.

Seldom was there any money coming from any source but agriculture unless part of the income of the occupier of Bledington Grounds. It may be doubted whether any family, before 1914, gained a living without anxiety. Grace of life had to be due to grace of spirit. In spite of the Crimean and South African Wars and some other military incidents, England's domestic affairs were her chief pre-occupation in the nineteenth century. Her slow progress out of the slough of the early years was so engrossing, especially in the time of the late struggle of parties, that the growing dangers of the European and world situation could not receive due attention. France and England were extending—with however little deliberation and national intention—their dominion over less powerful communities and over thinly populated regions. Germany with much to be proud of, indulged her pride and ambition and was prepared to sacrifice much to satisfy them. Her system of government lent itself to efforts unified and therefore exhausting to herself and to those who must respond to it. England was very unready for the struggle that began on August 4th, 1914. Into the First World War every village would be fully drawn. Each family with young sons must contribute a member or members to the Forces; on the farms the teams of horses were at once reduced to supply an outdated cavalry, and later their human staffs became so small that farmers' daughters went to plough. Women bore so many and such important burdens indeed that their status lost the tinge of subordination that had so long marked it. The methods and standards of agriculture were presently controlled through the County Council but in truth by the State.

When the men came back from the War in 1918 or 1919 they came as travelled, experienced men who had been shaken from the mould in which they had taken their mental shape. Change in the village was partly brought about by these returning soldiers. But though their mould was broken its impress remained and the changes they made were limited. The First World War did not bring the degree of change which is called revolution, but it serves for a pause, and the end of our period.

The Clergy in the Early Years

In 1815 our Vicar had been, as non-resident and yet taking a great part of the income of the cure, an eighteenth century type,[7] while the curate who took his place from 1805 belonged, by the style of his work, to the nineteenth. William Jones' services, in church and to his parishioners, were much appreciated by the latter, though not of course at all times. Jones was a poor man. His Vicar paid him ten pounds from the stipend he received, and £20 was paid to him by the tenant of the Christ Church lands. He might have been "passing rich on forty pounds", but thirty is different. He was not a University man but he had his qualifications: sometime after his arrival he was licensed as a curate. By that time he was more than fifty years old: probably he had earned a living earlier in some other way. Unlike some of his predecessors he did no farming and had the more time for services not strictly clerical. It seems likely that such a man learned something from Wesley's followers: they had provided examples of simple men being effective channels for religious messages. It would be too much to call him our Mr Crawley[8] but for decades before him our impression is of bare maintenance of church life, while he fills the need.

Some fifteen years after Jones' arrival here, the lessee of the Christ

Church lands, William Brown, wrote a letter to the Dean at the request of the "principal inhabitants".[9] They feel that their curate is underpaid: the Vicar should give him half the value of the living. By that time the income was rising. Christ Church and Queen Anne's Bounty had together endowed the living with two valuable meadows at Westcote, the rent of which would presently be £20: the rent of the Werndidier Farm had gone up from £11 to £18 and Queen Anne's Bounty was paying £3.16s. interest per cent on its allotments of money to the parish. Some small sums were added to these—the rent of the Vicarage and of the close on the Stow Road. Altogether it was now worth close on £80, but not a hundred as Brown and his fellow correspondents thought.

The year after the inhabitants' kind witness to the value of their curate was despatched there are signs that the good man could meet with criticism. A storm blew up in the village. Some travelling comedians (one of whom bore an Irish name) arrived in the village and acted plays there—not to the pleasure or approval of all. The constable, Gilbert, was urged to complain to the magistrate at Upper Slaughter, who issued a warrant for the actors to be brought before him. Alas! they had no legal authority, and were sent to the Bridewell at Northleach for seven days. Not everyone had disapproved of the plays: the offer of such entertainment was very rare. But there was already dissension: some thought that the Rev. William Jones held Calvinistic doctrines, not being aware probably, that the Thirty-Nine Articles did not exclude them. Strong views and disputations of a theoretic nature have been as rare as plays in our history. Were the anti-Calvinists also the enemies of the drama? It seems likely that both objections bear some relation to the spread of Methodism and to the rising movement of evangelicalism in the Church of England.

Among Mr Jones' good works was a Sunday School[10] attended in 1818 by from 70 to 80 children or young people. Doubtless he collected the subscriptions by which it was supported beside conducting it in the church (all among the horsebox pews). He did not flatter himself that this was all the teaching required by the lambs of his flock, as some clergymen did, but bore witness that "the poor would be grateful for weekly instructions gratis". There was at the time a day-school probably taught by Samuel Malins with whom we shall become acquainted, in any case by a teacher who charged fees impossible for the poor of that date.

In 1833 the Rev. John Allen, the Vicar, felt the time coming when he would wish to cease being a schoolmaster. He wrote to the Dean of Christ Church that as he was growing old he would like to reside on his living—if its income could be raised to £150. By that time £10 was being provided from a new source, the Bishop's Augmentation Fund, and the total had reached nearly £90.

There did not seem much prospect however of the desired steep rise, and it was not until 1837 that the Vicar took over his parish and its full income. Allen then wrote to the Dean that he could not possibly live in the wretched Parsonage, and gained permission from the Bishop to live in Stow—though feeling was growing strong that a Vicar should not only serve his parish but live in it.

We do not know how the ex-curate spent the last four years of his life: he was an old man, and his dismissal may have seemed reasonable. He died in 1841, not forgotten by Bledington. Just inside the south door of the church is a memorial tablet "Sacred to the memory of the Revd. William Jones minister of this parish for upwards of thirty-three years". The word "minister" was by now being left by the clergy to non-conformity: its use here suggests that the wording is that of parishioners. Six months before Jones' death the Vicar had died. It was many years before any memorial to him was erected, and then presumably by his family. He had been "for 41 years Vicar of this Parish".

Allen had given some of his energy to an attempt to raise the income of the living, as his successors would also do. He tried to persuade Pyncombe's and other charities together with Christ Church to give new capital in the form of land or monetary investments and had some success.

To succeed Allen the Dean and Chapter appointed the Rev. Charles Raymond Barker, a graduate of Oxford, but not a Christ Church man. There were at this time, or arising in the next four years, two movements in the Church. "Evangelicals" were anxious about the individual soul and its relation to Christ, in which it could find salvation. They stressed the words of Christ in the four Gospels. For that reason and perhaps partly because of the experience and success of the Methodists, they felt for the needs of the poor. Of much more recent origin was the Tractarian Movement. Its early leaders, Keble, Newman and Pusey, were all Oxford men: in its early days it was essentially a movement within the University. It laid stress on the inheritance of the Church as an institution and this involved much learning. Its interests were strictly ecclesiastical and intellectual, hardly at all concerned at first with the social bearings of Christianity. Charles Raymond Barker had close relations with this group. He was a relative of the Puseys and like them belonged to landed folk, sending younger sons "into the Church". It is very unlikely that Barker ever imagined himself ministering directly to this village: the Vicarage was unfit for his use and the people not ready for an interest in ritual and church history. Before two years were over he had resigned. How the church was served in his time we do not know.

A change had come over the relation of Christ Church to the parish. Earlier the Dean and Chapter had left the appointment and payment of the Vicar to the lessees of their property.[11] Now they were not only appointing the Vicar but beginning to do so with some care. They made a general rule about the payment of curates in their parishes; they respond to complaints of their vicars about the vicarage here, and the value of the living. The care of the chancel had been left to their tenants but they took now to instructing their surveyors to report on its condition. Presently they would be willing to consider furthering the Vicar's interest in the education of the poor. They were no longer mere landed proprietors in their relation to the village.

Their choice of a Vicar in 1843 fell upon the Rev. John Oakley Hill, a product of their own college. With him the life of our church seems to leap into Victorian times. As we read the Vestry minutes (from 1854), his correspondence with Christ Church[12] and a short memoir of his life[13] written by his son, we feel ourselves in touch with a well qualified and conscientious minister (it is after all the best word), carefully responding to needs as he saw them. If in early days he seems too much concerned with his house and income, they fall gradually into the background: if he comes with some narrow and ungenerous notions, he sheds them. He came here as a "Broad" churchman, endeavouring to combine some stress on the dignity of the Church's rites with care for the moral condition of his parish. But gradually he drew nearer to the evangelical outlook. Most modern of all, he had a wife as devoted and active as himself.

Before we deal more concretely with the life and work of this husband and wife we must return to the circumstances of their flock.

Farmers and Farming from 1815 *to the Labourers' Revolt,* 1872
The relation of farmers to the village community was losing or had

lost its ancient economic basis. Farmers with their children and their labourers had grown the food consumed in the village but by the nineteenth century their produce was sold in bulk from the farms or taken to market. Sometimes they saw the disadvantages of the change: local farmers meeting in Burford in 1795 thought it their duty to see their neighbours nourished rather than to sell corn to emissaries from other parts.[14] They resolved to sell only to local bakers and mealmen. But that impulse to resist the current tendency was a rare one. Well-fed themselves, farming families would grow inured to their neighbours' insufficiency.

The growing number of enclosures strengthened the strong tendency to a national market, the separated, fenced holdings leading farmers to a more specialised interest in crops and herds and in these as related to personal and family success. Our own farmers, however, were slow to move in those directions. Thirty, forty and even fifty years after enclosure we do not find much progress. In 1801 the total of arable land in the parish was 392¾ acres of which 287 acres were devoted to wheat, barley and oats, eighty to beans, twenty-five to turnips, and only a ½ acre to potatoes, and ¼ to peas. There is no sign of experiment.[15]

The Christ Church estate of 346 acres contained much typical land: it was the custom to lease the whole property to a single tenant who sub-let much of it. As late as 1812 a valuation[16] shows much of the old Home Heath land as worth only 14s. an acre and another 20 acres worth 18s. (This land has long since come to be of very fair quality). The valuer reported that the Heath grounds "have produced little for many years", but "some progress has been made in clearing thorns, though as yet they are not productive". The estate as a whole was "indifferently farmed". Yet in the decade from 1801 to 1810 inclusive the highest average price of wheat ever recorded had been reached—83s.11d. a quarter. From 1811 to 1820 the average reached yet a new high level—87s.6d. and was still "satisfactory" from 1820 to 1826 (inclusive).

The prices of other grains also rose during the Napoleonic Wars and so did those for stock: an area of mixed farming such as ours did not fare quite so well as the grain areas but on the other hand they did not suffer such great risks and anxieties for their harvest. In the last year mentioned (1827) another valuation of the Christ Church land was made[17]—which still did not suggest much progress. It seems that something more than a change of system and prices was needed to bring new knowledge and a spirit of enterprise to the Bledington farms.

There were of course some changes, one of them notable. In 1813 the lessee of Christ Church, an active character—an ex-business man of Chipping Norton—advanced the view[18] that more labour and manure would be applied to the poor lands if a homestead were built near Pebbly Hill and a separate holding established where stock could be reared and fattened. This was done, at a cost of £600. Some years later, about 1820, a smaller holding was formed with a cottage and small yard on the brow of Micklands Hill, a quarter of a mile out of the village. After 30 years more (in 1853) another out-village farmhouse was erected.[19] making with the early Reddall House on Bledington Grounds the fourth and last. In one of the fields of the Micklands smallholding there is a good bed of clay and here a kiln had been established and bricks produced from which garden walls, a few farmbuildings and a cottage or two were built in the village. The last new farmhouse, planned with the assent of Christ Church by Davenport, the then lessee, in the fields more or less opposite his own land was also built of Micklands bricks. These were not of good quality and are still easily distinguished by their poor kneading from the better ones that began soon to come by the new railway. But the house in the new Jay Farm was situated in a modern way, with convenient access to its 100 acres and ample space for rickyards as well as animal yards near to it.

All these new homesteads have been justified: this was the best of the changes consequent on enclosure. The new holdings have been good homes, neat inside and spacious out of doors, and on the whole better formed than some older units. (In 1970 in the hands of enterprising young people they are well-equipped and very productive).

For another change we go back to the years 1829 and 1831, to the completion of the enclosure of the parish—of the 140 acres of the Far Heath and Cow Commons.[20] The latter had still been used as common pasture but some of the strips into which the rest of the ground had been divided seem to have been treated as woodland. The Enclosure Act obtained by the dozen or so of commoners was short; only one Commissioner was appointed. The Cow Commons lay near the river; bridges and culverts had to be provided to make the land adaptable. The little award is full of old names: Spurborough, Barrowshard, Stuthams, Hammerlands etc. This is the last we see or hear of some of them. As Bledington farmers looked around them and saw Ascott and Shipton-under-Wychwood and Kingham unenclosed they might still feel themselves in the van of the locality.

Crops were becoming gradually more varied. Just before the turn of the century some turnips were grown and for the rest, wheat, barley and beans with sometimes a few oats. In 1843 the Rectory Farm—we learn from a list of the indebted farmer's assets[21]—was growing wheat (18 acres), vetches (5), pease (5), turnips and swedes (4), barley (5), potatoes (2) and grass or hay (41). Wherever we find indications of the use of land on the smaller farms there appear to be similar proportions—rather less of arable than of grass.

There is some information as to rents and values at sale. In 1798 a small part of Reddall's estate had been sold for over £70 per acre. In the year of Waterloo, a part of Lord's was sold at £80 an acre. In 1848 the 43 acres of Town Banks Farm went for £75. Still in the prosperous times, 1820, Gilberts' land sold at £62 and when Town Banks was sold again only three years after it had made £75, the price was the same as that of Gilberts'—£62. These five are the highest rates of sale in such records as I have found.

In 1876 when prices were falling and increased supplies of American and Canadian wheat were feared Hangerson Farm was sold at £50. No catastrophic prices appear: the fact that farming here was mixed and that no great capital was required for farms of 60 to 122 acres favoured competition.

Rents were lower than the prices paid might lead one to expect. Hangerson Farm was rented at £2 when it was sold at £50 per acre. In 1798 the average rent of Christ Church land was £1 1s. 8d. When Bledington Grounds was occupied by a sub-tenant in 1870 the rent for its 291 acres was £294. In 1860 Gilberts' was rented at £2 10s. per acre; in 1876 the Home Farm at 30s.

The story of the leases or annual letting of University Farm[23] as it is now called to the Stows shows us the rent fixed in 1808 at 39s. per acre, changing in 1826 to 36s., thus far recognising change in prices after the end of the Wars. In 1862 it rose by 8s. 6d. to 44s. 6d. and remained at that point till 1881. This was a farm of good land, conveniently disposed to its messuage, with the same excellent landlord and the same family of tenants throughout.

Our farmers' conditions of work seem reasonably good, neither rents nor cost of purchase running very high, nor yet going up and down rapidly with seasons and the price of produce, but the deeds now being returned to owners of land as no longer of legal importance show many farmers in debt to investors[22]—often to tradesmen or their widows in Cotswold towns or to a successful Burford brewer or auctioneer of Aston Blank. Mortgages, we have seen, had been taken up throughout the 18th century by the more ambitious farmers, Lords and Reddalls, but throughout the nineteenth we find Gilkes, Stayts, Peglers, Weales all with lands mortgaged. I have never seen a Stow mortgage deed and perhaps there was none, nor one in the name of Hathaway, but the latter family lost their land. Borrowing must have caused great anxiety at times: lenders might call in their money and fresh loans have to be found. In the eighteen eighties Oliver Pegler of Home Farm had eleven times to find new money: it seems always to have been possible. Interest was usually 4% and more than 5% was only paid for brief periods.

Even before the fall of prices, usually thought to have begun about 1866, a few farmers and farmers' sons seem to have found conditions depressing. Only a Pegler youth or two contrived to join a profession, few took to business or trade, but some farmers or their sons went overseas to buy cheap land for clearance in the colonies or to work for wages in the new countries. About 1855 a Phipps went to the United States and settled in Dubuque, Wisconsin. George Gilbert went to Manitoba about 1870, some Stows to a farm on the St. Lawrence and as mentioned above Theophilus Pegler took his family to the Middle West of the U.S.A. There may well have been other emigrants from farming families.

Conditions of the times lent themselves to the formation of agricultural associations. William Stow, perhaps through his connection with the University's estate office, became briefly a member of the Oxford Association and attended the dinners among the gentlemen farmers and squires at which Lords and Bishops spoke, but later he and his son after him joined the Stow and Chipping Norton Association, similar in nature, but frequented by men of more modest standing. Sometimes speeches at the dinners were tactfully liberal, but on the whole their trend was to see a good world threatened.

Often the members were told by their speakers that high rents led to good farming and good profits, but never till late and then rarely that high wages would do the same. Labourers were wretchedly poor and depressed and it is very probable that they were a drag upon the farms. They were also growing in number and the staffs of the farms were increasing, so that the farmer felt the less need, perhaps, to take a profitably strenuous part in the work.

The agricultural societies held annual competitions and exhibitions of livestock—bulls, sheep and fat stock of all kinds. There were also prizes offered to workers showing clearly the kind of service thought ideal at the time—for long service on a single farm, to labourer-fathers of many children brought up without recourse to the parish, and to mothers for the largest number of daughters sent into domestic service. A famous cartoon, ill-drawn but packed with information, shows the well-groomed horses, fat cattle, rams and pigs together with the starved human prize-winners.[24] It was one of the summer pleasures for small farmers, non-members, to attend the shows held by the societies, but they were better suited to the needs of men like Davenport of Bledington Grounds with his many acres and opulent yards than to the descendants of our old commoners. Agriculture on the Grounds farm was sound: the valuer employed by Christ Church reported that this "good stock land" was "in excellent order—such as is seldom met with in leasehold property".[25] But Davenport was aloof from the village, his name hardly appearing in its records nor his neighbours' or sub-tenants' interests in his Christ Church correspondence. His knowledge and his practice supplied no spark to the tinder of his fellow-farmers' minds.

A possible source of stimulus was our next parish of Churchill where Bledington folk had cousins and many neighbourly connections. In 1812 James Haughton Langston had inherited from his father an ex-wine merchant, some 6,000 acres, chiefly in Churchill and Sarsden. Langston was doubly and trebly gifted: he had money, ability, easy access to his fellow men, deep interest in many matters, health and generosity, while his origins kept him free of isolating pride. He was for a while a liberal Member of Parliament for Oxford and Master of Foxhounds of the Heythrop Hunt. But his chosen career was that of estate-manager. He drained his land, pulled down old thatched farm-buildings and built substantial ones. He erected spacious farm-houses (some said the rooms were so large that his tenants could not afford the fires to warm them). When he saw an arable field infested with couch-grass he would send in his steamplough tackle to clean it and woe betide the farmer who let the condition recur.

The stories told of Langston included that of a visit by Bishop

Wilberforce and the great Baptist preacher, C. H. Spurgeon. He more or less coerced them to take rides on his steam-plough. Spurgeon, said to have been a man of humour, must have felt better qualified thereafter to write his once famous "John Ploughman's Talks." Another story relates to Churchill Heath Farm which comes down to the river near Bledington village. Langston's tenants, the Garne family, had developed a fine herd of beef shorthorn cattle: their fame brought a request to visit from some United States enthusiasts. "But", said this more-than-model landlord, "you have no fit space to entertain them. I shall build you a good new sitting room with bedrooms above"· And there, in time for the guests, was the large room, square and ample for talk, with views of the distinguished cattle grazing.[26]

Langston was indeed a creator. He built the new church with a tower like Magdalen's which now gives meaning and literal point to the hill at Churchill; a reading room for the men of the parish; school rooms, (separate ones for boys, girls and infants, praised by Her Majesty's Inspector as the right arrangement for the whole country). He endowed Chipping Norton with its new, classical Town Hall, still daily useful and proudly maintained.

Certainly his message about farming, that open-mindedness and efficiency paid, was heard by some, but his civic spirit was shown in ways hardly open to them. His practical work did not die with him. His heiress continued it later in a project useful to all farmers around and many from far, until today.[27]

The old traditions of village life might suggest that some type of stimulus directed to life as a whole, to heart and mind and vocation, family and community, some type of co-operation in short, might best have served to modernise farms and farmers such as ours but the current patterns of agricultural ambitions and customs were all against such a development. There was in our neighbourhood one co-operative scheme—that of the Chartist small holdings at Minster Lovell, launched in 1842—a scheme of bold idealism whose authors were shortly convicted of illegality and forced to sell the estate.[28] As an escape from foul towns and from the factories of the time the tiny holdings (of from 4 to 2 acres) and box-like houses were good, but unlikely to hold much meaning for farmers.

Too conservative, it seems, in agriculture, our farmers held to good traditions in other ways. They continued to fill the lay offices of the church, which was now again since 1805 bearing some witness to humane values, and to carry the civic responsibilities of the vestry. Harwoods, Peglers, Stows and Tysoes (a new-come family of the old type) were churchwardens decade after decade. Gilberts (father, son, brother) served in turn for forty years. When the church had special needs farmers met them. Humphrey Pegler built new steps to the churchyard; Theophilus, when the church took to modern musical ways, became the first choir-master: Weales, craftsmen and farmers, restored the clock in the tower, presented a new Bible, and made and carved a new pew.

On the other hand the relation even of farmers of small acreage with many fellow-villagers had deteriorated. Labourers had grown in numbers, while falling further in skills and some in self-respect. The legal duties of overseers under the Acts of Settlement and the custom of combining parish relief with wages put more distance between groups. Neighbourliness expressed by legacies had ceased after the middle of the eighteenth century. The cry "Save the rates" would become customary and irrational and long remain so: new police, drainage, piped water would all be resisted as a matter of course. But contacts here were not so broken as elsewhere. Our history is not marred by stories of overseers' striking inhumanity; and after the worst times uniting factors would begin to appear again.

Though even in times of high prices our farmers had not prospered greatly, there had been some increase of comfort and comeliness in their homes. Their wives began to employ indoor servants, daughters of farm-workers. Coming from restricted unkempt homes they must have needed much training in all the kitchen and dairy skills. They were often young enough to learn: one "maid" was a girl of ten years. Sometimes one comes on relics of the decoration then usual—of the wallpaper, preserved on walls of cupboards, growing better in design, substance and colour as one removes layer after layer; or the shards of a jug, such as folk-museums or art schools now treasure, rescued from under stones known to have been laid about 1820. A bill of sale of farmhouse furniture, auctioned a few miles away, was accidentally preserved by a housewife here: one bedroom had been made comfortable and elegant, containing a four-post bed with chintz furniture, a "swing-glass, mahogany frame, and ewer and basin"; there were twelve pictures in the room, and the parlour contained walnut chairs, mahogany bureau, mahogany tea-board and the like.[29]

Such farmers were not hard-pressed or ambitious and did not lose the quiet enjoyment of their fields and homes and neighbours. Varied sensations and reflections could be theirs. Even their wives had some relief from labour and from pressures. No landlords pressed up their rents or like Trollope's Earl of Brentford who "did like the people round" him "to be of the same way of thinking as" himself "about politics" encouraged his agent to know their political outlook.[30]

Labouring life to the Middle of the Century: the Poor and the Poor Law

The annals of the poor of the early nineteenth century are so daunting that it is no wonder that in some histories they are very short and in famous novels otherwise of historical interest they are omitted. Study of them affords no pleasure: the wage-earners' homes are wretched, their arts forgotten, their skills lost.

We left our labourers in 1795 barely able to exist on their wages, or wages-cum-relief. Corn prices continued to rise: official averages have been given.[31] On their effect on the price of bread and on the mind of a villager a homelier record throws some light. In an old note-book found by the writer in a farmhouse at Shenington[32] intermittent entries were made from 1800 to 1828 by a sexton-smallholder. His object is to record whatever strikes him as remarkable, from the immense girth of a cucumber or the depth of a flood to the loud cries in the night of a woman being flogged by her husband. By far the most numerous entries relate to the price of a peckloaf of bread. "In 1763", we read "bread was sold at 1s. 1d. the peck" and in 1780 at 1s. 2d. When the writer started his contemporary record in 1800 it was 6s. 2d Selecting from the entries we find the price in 1812, 6s. 4d. In 1813 and 1814 it varied from 3s. 6d. to 3s. 9d.; in 1815 it was 3s. 4d. and in 1816 2s. 10d. (January), 4s 3d. (May) and 4s. 7d. (November), In June 1817 the peck loaf cost 6s. 8d. and in the September following 5s. 8d. From that time the price steadies at round about 3s. and is only given when it drops or rises markedly—to 2s. 8d. (June 1828) or 4s. (in the following November).

Had the highest of these prices held for long, there must have been an "Irish" famine. As the cost soared and fell no power existed economic or legal that could keep wages related to it. Labourers and their families had to endure in the hope that when the War ended prices would even out at a bearable level. But when the price of corn

271

fell as the Wars neared their end landlords feared that their rents, which had risen with prices, would have to come down and farmers that they would do so too slowly. Both demanded fresh legislation to restrict imports and although there were protests from consumers throughout the country a new Corn Law was passed in 1815 which taxed imported wheat till the price of home-grown produce reached 80s. per quarter. At this figure bread would cost about 3s. 6d. the peck loaf; a family could not have sufficient on an income of less than 15s. 9d. In the early years of the Wars wages generally rose a little. Here they may have risen from the 5s. or 6s. of the seventeen eighties[33] to 6s. 6d. or 7s. At all events in 1834 and 5 the relieving officers of our local "Union" found that no applicants for relief were earning more than 7s. Why did no wages rise more than this? The causes were deep and irrational—customs and assumptions together with economic and psychological interests stood in the way and were supported by the powerlessness of the governed.

"No matter who is careless the crack is in the cup". The labouring classes conformed less and less to a citizenly standard. Stealing of food and fuel grew more common. Wretched homes grew dirtier: they had no wells and carried their water from a village pump; families could not afford soap. There was no fuel but furze and wood picked up from the hedges; bed-clothes were non-existent. The only cooking possible was by boiling. On the other hand others had steadily more of cleanliness, comfort and education. Sale bills of farmhouses mentioned pumps and sinks in kitchens. Farm parlours shone with brightness. Poor curates grew comparatively prosperous and vicars and rectors claimed relations with lesser gentry.

"Crime" even if it could be viewed as more or less harmless conduct for the sake of feeding or warming a family, blasted deeper and wider the gulf between labourers and others. So frequent were thefts in our district that local societies were formed to "encourage the prosecution of offenders", by pooling costs and offering rewards to informers— sums of money large enough to be a great temptation: e.g. one or two guineas for reporting minor offences, five if punishment were transportation and ten for burglary or highway robbery—for which death was the penalty though the rules for informers omitted allusion to that fact. The earliest of these societies known to me was the "Society of Sir Charles Pole's, Bart's. Tenantry in the County of Gloucester" formed at Upper Swell on May 14th 1810.[34] The members undertook to "apprehend" and "prosecute to conviction" and not to "compromise on any account or pretence whatever". Such provisions, in view of the personal knowledge and relationship to be expected on farms is most significant; more so, even, is the provision of a fee of 10s. 6d. for information on the stealing of turnips, presumably from the fields. Other provisions were much as in other, similar, societies, such as those of Campden (1816)[35], Deddington, and Bourton on the Water, the last with members in villages around Bledington including Westcote, on the hill to the south west. By footpath and bridle way it is two miles from church to church. The men of the two villages were intimate: farms on the slopes between employed men from both. In 1812 a Westcote labourer was found guilty of stealing a sack of wheat (when wheat was 17s. a bushel). He had a wife and two children; his wage was 7s. a week. "The man was left every night to lock up the barns. Upon a certain occasion a number of years before he had confessed to having stolen a quarter of wheat". This 1812 indictment sets out that "by this man's own acknowledgment he had deviated from that path of Honesty and Rectitude which is the bounden duty of every man to pursue". Because "the property of Farmers is at various times so much in the power of their servants" . . . "this affair should be treated as a matter of serious nature". We may be sure it was. The Prosecutor was a member of the Bourton-on-the-Water Felons Society and had the help of its solicitor. In another local case before the Oxford Assizes in July 1832 a farmer took action against his shepherd, accusing him of killing and stealing a young lamb. One day the farmer had picked up a lambskin on the way to his fold. Asked whether a lamb had died William Freeman the shepherd had replied, "Yes, a very small one". He had, he said, given the carcase to a dog. But the farmer went to Freeman's house and found his mother about to cook the carcase of a lamb "whole, with the exception of the liver". It was the custom, Freeman said in his defence, for shepherds to have small lambs that had died; and this was not denied. Other "witnesses" were called, as to whether the lamb had been killed or had died. The young man was sentenced to transportation for life.[36]

The inarticulate young shepherd stood alone. His story illustrates at what a moral distance from each other farmers and labourers were now living in many villages. Before the "Felons Societies" all trust vanished. But as to Bledington there is no evidence, and no legend, that any Stow, Pegler or Stayt ever joined one of these and the recovery of a fair degree of community soon after the worst years suggests that suspicion and fear had limits.

As to the homes of our labourers we have both documentary evidence and visible remains, the latter not easy now to interpret. Rudge[37] had written in 1807 of the low condition of labourer's homes and especially of their almost total lack of gardens. The truth of his statement is illustrated by the story we infer from various documents relating to a large group of our cottages. In 1824 William Stayt's farm, with its messuage and orchard in Bennett's Lane[38] was sold by auction. Stayt's forebears had begun to mortgage their farm in 1722, possibly before, and every generation since notwithstanding any advantage from enclosure had added to the debts. William, however, contrived by means of smaller new loans, to "buy in" his messuage for £290 and continued to live in it. He seems to have had a plan for a livelihood: promptly he turned his "brewhouse" (or outdoor kitchen) into a small cottage which he let to a "schoolmaster" (probably the first here since the 15th century) named Malins. Stayt also shared his own house with a tenant, and presently the small farmhouse was divided. But shortly Stayt's neighbours who had helped him to buy his house needed their money and he sold the property to the schoolmaster, who perhaps had better credit, for £350. Assuming values to have remained similar over a few years, two conversions had cost £30. No doubt both Stayt and Malins knew that cottage property was proving a safe investment: when labourers could not pay their rent they applied to the overseers of the poor to pay it for them, which was invariably done. So Malins went on with the conversions: he put a second storey on his own kitchen and lo! there was a cottage. But the fact was that he could not afford the modest expenditure. His scope as a teacher was too small to give him a surplus. In the larger mortgage he now contracted he is named as "Schoolmaster, Milton under Wychwood"—a larger and growing village. As his difficulties grew, Malins' signature on the documents became more and more florid and delicate; but for some time he continued to make cottages, always within the old farm garden. In 1829 his mortgagor, a well-to-do Bledingtonian, Cooper, took over the whole property. By now its four cottage tenants had become ten! But so far as one can tell there were only seven cottages: two more had been made out of stables standing in the old yard, and one from a small outhouse attached to the one-time farmhouse. Thus three must have been shared. The property cost Cooper £395. Again assuming that costs and sale prices were constant the conversions had now cost between £17 and £18 each. Seven tenants at £3 would afford good interest.

In 1847 this property passed to Cooper's niece and her husband Hopgood, a surgeon of Chipping Norton, (the first medical man to be heard of in our documents). Three more cottages had by now been added to it, made from some contiguous buildings, part of another small farmyard. Of these ten homes some were so placed as to have space for the housewife's pails and a tiny garden, others only a few square yards at the back door; two fared a little better, having small vegetable patches. A walk through the narrow lane that bisects the old village allows one to see still a gardenless cottage, the old stables-cottages now garden sheds, and one good-sized cottage with a useful garden, i.e. two cottages now made into one. One or two others still exist, transformed in appearance and usage.

A continuation to the south of this row of cottages on Bennett's Lane is another small group of similar nature and history, though in part older. Here there have been four cottages (they have of course now undergone much change) valued variously through the nineteenth century at from £40 to £50 for the whole group. They had little or (in one case) no garden and were of course tiny. They were in possession of the Gibbs family, which hovered between the status of labourers and craftsmen.

In the case of the third group the evidence lies entirely in an old plan,[39] and in the houses themselves, still existing. There were two old farmsteads on the west side of Church Lane: Hathaways' and Grayhursts' later the Five Tuns beerhouse. From both messuages the land was sold away. By 1841 these two sites accommodated, in all, twelve cottages. Both houses had been divided into cottages and others built on the sites. Not all these buildings are now dwellings and two cottages have become one garage, but they can still be seen.

Twenty six cottages had been crowded on the yards of four small farmhouses. At Tysoe, a South Warwickshire village a similar development took place,[40] as it surely did in others. The common causes were the growth in the practice of privacy in farmhouses, the increase in the number of labourers and the low rent they could pay together with the certainty that it would be forth-coming from the overseers if not from the tenants. What is chiefly of interest here is the domestic quality of the resulting houses—constricting, depressing, unhealthy;

and also the fact that such homes were built or rather contrived in the midst of open country. To account for farmers, clergy, magistrates and legislators, permitting it to happen we must recall the eighteenth century view of the status and function of labourers.

To hope that such conditions did not result in some degradation would be to deny the relation of cause and effect. The wretchedness of the eighteenth century continued and grew—the lack of cleanliness and quiet in the homes, the hunger and cold, the low life in the beer-houses. And yet in Bledington the morris dances were still practised, and a high technique retained, and there were a few remnants of song and play. Many of the labourers attended church services on Sundays sitting invisible behind the high pews (perhaps only a few) of the prosperous, their boys being kept in order by the clerk, wielding a long stick. The Rev. William Jones bore witness in 1819 that the poor of the parish wished their children to learn to read.[41] The overseers would not permit relief allowances to be used for such luxuries as school fees and there was no charitable provision at day schools till 1852 and no public provision till nearly a generation later. But yet some learned to read. From 1806 to 1830 52 % of brides and grooms married in Bledington Church were able to sign the register; since the majority of people in the village were of labourer status, some of these could evidently write and probably read. Later the status of grooms is given and of the bride when she is a domestic servant, but more often only her father's trade is given. Among the literates are seventeen daughters of labourers.

How had they learned to write? No doubt the Sunday School held in church was of use in urging the need to read. From 1825 Samuel Malins was teaching here for a few years. It was normal for school-masters, if not women teachers, to hold evening classes; thus Cobbett and John Clare had learned to read and perhaps some poor men of Bledington. In June 1837 John Benfield who had "no employ" applied to the Guardians for relief: his wife "kept a school" and thus earned two shillings a week. When Malins left the village, female relations of his remained here and continued to teach reading and writing for the next forty years till 1880. A complicating factor is the mobility of labour: change of teacher and school makes against the learning of techniques: from 1813 to 1832, of fifty bridegrooms twenty six come from nearby villages, indicating much parochial interchange.

In sum we may say the Bledington labourers had not given up the hope and struggle for some decency of life. Their wives' burdens were heavier: when there was insufficient food they had to feed the wage-earner before themselves and the children: they had less of sunshine and changing scene, the misery of bearing children on an under-nourished body, and of undernourished children, fractious and ailing.

Conditions in all the southern counties were at least as wretched as in Gloucester and Oxfordshire, and in urban areas even worse. Naturally there was agitation. The growing population in urban agglomerations made possible the assembly of vast crowds, alarming to the government. The channels of debate were stopped in 1819, as perhaps never before, by the "Six Acts",[42] which in effect took away the right of public discussion and the freedom of the Press. To organ-ise a public meeting, under the conditions laid down, was to run the risk of transportation or even of the death penalty; editors of news-papers were held responsible for the matter they printed. They might lose the large deposit they had to make and in addition were liable to imprisonment for "seditious" writings. It was magistrates who defined sedition: they had wide powers. Their license was required before a public meeting could be held. Presently (in the 1830's) "anybody present in a tumultuous assembly might become guilty", as the Chair-man of the Oxford Quarter Sessions said,[43] and in a court of justice "tumult" sometimes meant a rough interjection or two. Cobbett described the few weeks in which the Six Acts were passed as the *Last Hundred Days of English Freedom*. A balanced historian wrote[44] that even before those Days "the bulk of the population not only had no share in government, but they were debarred from demanding a share by laws especially enacted for that purpose and savagely administered. In politics and religion a system like Strafford's "Thorough" ruled the land under the forms of statute and Common Law". Jackson's Journal naturally ceased to comment on the corruption of Parlia-ment or to depict such matters as the Sovereign's ill manners.

As to local justice there had come about great change, tending always to reduce the elements of village responsibility and the sway of custom and to increase the powers and responsibility of magist-rates; Manor Courts in our district were by now very few; the Slaughter Hundred Court had with enclosures lost many of its functions and faded away. The Justices became almost the only agents of local government. They decided "settlement" cases, approved (and sometimes made) appointments to parish offices, audited parish accounts, settled the rate of relief to the starving poor, dealt with breaches of contract, with underweight sales and in short with all sorts of crimes against property. The punishments they could allot in Quarter Sessions included not only imprisonment, but also transportation for life. The personnel of the Bench consisted of landowners and of prosperous clergymen, usually of university education, who could sit beside them as equals.

Justices have been greatly praised for their work of administration but basically they could not give justice: they belonged to a single class and inevitably cared for its interests. The game laws, offences against which provided a great number (said in 1830 to be 25%) of the cases that came before them, had been framed solely in the more trivial interests of landowners and were naturally incapable of just administration. Many other cases were concerned with the faults or delinquencies of the justices' own servants. It is true that they sometimes favoured the poor as against parish officers. Certainly some worked hard—as "hard" went for their kind—and conscientiously, but the times were out of joint.

One of the functions of magistrates was to appoint parish constables. Slaughter remained the locus of justice for Bledington. Thither our constable had to bring all cases, and usually the persons concerned in them. He was a hard-worked, unenvied man. The magistrate was the Rev. F. E. Witts of Upper Slaughter, a man of method. He kept notes, at times of some detail, of his "transactions" from 1815 to 1823.[45] He seems often to have sat alone. When he had a colleague he does not make the fact clear. To him Richard Gilbert, our constable, brought a tradesman who would be fined for "lightweight", a butcher who stripped the "faggots" from a roof, the property of a farmer. One man, by his name a labourer, had assaulted another and they had fought. Gilbert was in trouble himself with the J.P. for the impropriety of his language when he tried to separate them, and later wrote to Witts a "long justificationary letter". He had also to escort a group of unlicensed comedians to whom a part of the village objected; and a vagrant who slipped his handcuffs and ran off while Gilbert was taking him to Northleach Bridewell. Other troubles relate to miseries rather than misdemeanours—for example to "settlements", beggary and the paternity of illegitimate children. In four years we find six cases of removal of pauper individuals and families from Bledington to their place of settlement, mostly to neighbouring parishes and to none more than forty miles away. Two of those conveyed were "single women pregnant". Both of these women had been domestic servants in large houses a few miles away. One of them was carrying her second illegitimate child.

When the Rev. J. E. Witts committed accused persons to Quarter Sessions or allotted them comparatively short prison sentences they were sent to Northleach "Bridewell" or House of Correction. A list survives—beginning in 1791—of thirty persons who were inmates there.[46] All these were labourers or women servants, except four, and those a weaver, a mason and two sailors. The prisoners had stolen hedge-wood, "embezzled" cotton yarn to spin, committed "misdemeanours in service". The list continues for a number of years, it is not clear how many. There are numerous cases such as "disserting" or "leaving" or being idle, in service. A woman was confined for "disobeying the commands of her Master and leaving her place": a main use of the Bridewell and a large use of the magistrates' court was keeping servants, male and female, in order.

During one winter the majority of offences concerned fuel. Wood was taken from hedges, branches were lopped from ash-trees. One man had cut down a tree in a "pleasure-ground". A man suspected of stealing a loaf worth 3d. suffered a month's incarceration before trial and two months after it.

To be a punishment to these folk the Bridewell or Gloucester Prison must have been fearsome. Clearly they had endured "starvation" from cold or hunger (they used the same word for both conditions) as long as they could; then there had been the stealthy deed, the spell in the stocks on the village green, the journey to Slaughter. Apart from the chance of contracting the King's Evil—as Witts noted when he visited the Bristol prison—or other diseases, the discomfort could hardly have shocked these men.

Mr Witt's conscience was genuine, but of his time. The only sign he gives that a "crime' may be due in part to circumstances is in reference to an eleven-year-old child whose parents had died and who had stolen a snuff-box. The magistrate comments that from his seat he "could barely see the child's head". But he sent him to prison for two years. Class government must always be brutal, whether to royal families or to orphan children, because it does not afford the conditions in which human sympathies can work. Nevertheless it is natural to recall another scene, and the saying "Of such is the kingdom of

Heaven [47] and to reflect on the strange condition of our national Christian Church. Perhaps such clergymen as Witts based their culture rather on their Greek and Latin studies than on the New Testament.

After this there is for a time a dearth of documents relating specifically to Bledington but there is plenty of evidence of the world its men and women lived in. It is available to us and had become available to everyone who could buy and read a newspaper. Jackson's Journal was arriving in the village as regularly as Sunday services in the church. All the menfolk of farming families could now read and mostly did. Literate labourers might get an occasional Journal, if only a cast-off. What might have seemed to villagers local misfortunes and tragedies became part of the condition of the whole country.

In 1829 winter came on early. By Christmastime distress was exceptional. It was usual for the poor to have little or no fuel: this year the small stocks of wood they had gathered were used up early. It was not possible for magistrates to act is if thefts of wood merited punishment: they became so numerous. Work was held up by frost and snow and wages ceased. Starvation could not be hidden in village, small town or city. In Oxford meetings were held to find a channel for emotions and a platform for prudent views. What could be, would be done? The newspapers were looked for week by week as in wartime.

In the House of Lords the Duke of Wellington urged—so reported the Journal—that too much should not be made of the distress: it was not everywhere. (It was not rare in the House of Lords to urge such comfort on members). But what was too much?

Many examples of personal catastrophe were due chiefly to general conditions, only in their fatal end to the winter. On December 24th Jackson s carried a tale of the horrors of "settlement".[48] A mother with a daughter of twelve despatched from a distance, travelling towards Worcester, were found in a barn at Oxford, the mother lying naked, dead, with her arms round her child. The mother's clothes had been sold for food. "Miserly relief" had been given them, so said the report.

On January 31st 1830 the overseers of "a Wychwood parish" hired a man to conduct a seller of earthenware and his donkey beyond its boundaries. The poor fellow, said the Oxford Journal, was placed on his donkey, conveyed through the forest into Ascott under Wychwood and left there by himself "not withstanding the weather". (All this of course, lest he should fall ill and be a burden on the rates). There he contrived to clear some ground of snow and lay there from Sunday to Tuesday morning when a passer-by found him there insensible, all but frozen to death. He was put in a cart and conveyed into Ascott where "every attention was paid him", by whom we do not learn. It seemed charity was not extinct.

At last, towards the end of February 1830, the worst of the winter was over. But another such winter and what would happen? The thoughts of many were turned to means of improving conditions. Of course, every suggestion or plan roused prejudice or interest against itself: reform was urgent, but it was beyond the power of man to make it quick.

Charity indeed, though a little like a King Canute before the flood of misery, was the one remedy agreed upon. There was no other means of preventing diaster. Subscription lists were opened everywhere: £70 was gathered in Stow, Witney manufacturers gave one of their blankets to each destitute family and served 4,000 pints of soup each week. In Banbury there was somewhat similar activity.

Oxford seems to have been deeply disturbed. Naturally some members of the Colleges and some townsmen had links with the intellectual and political movements of the time. Bledington readers would note that Christ Church had not been ungenerous. It might presently seem that this dreadful winter had revealed to the Dean and Chapter the condition of the parishes from which they drew funds and had further changed their attitude, already more responsible. The clergy they appointed to Bledington from now would never be absentees and they would be encouraged in good works, both spiritual and economic. Some twenty years later the Chapter would give help to a school for the poor and would experiment in the provision of allotments — influenced perhaps by the Labourers' Friend Society. In 1854 they were prepared to let the 75 acres of Kiln Farm for pasture-allotments but our labourers could not accept so high an offer.

But since the distress had deep and permanent causes there was resentment as well as gratitude: incendiarism began. (The labourers of Shipton under Wychwood promised to defend property; they had a squire who had doubtless earned thanks and even more certainly had great power over their lives).

Before the dread winter there had been many minor crimes, given punishments approaching the fantastic. In April 1829 at the Oxford

Quarter Sessions (young James Haughton Langston was among the magistrates) a man who had stolen a handkerchief and a jacket was sentenced to transportation for fourteen years. Another man who was convicted of stealing nine fowls was to be sent to Australia for seven years,[49] the distinction between seven and fourteen being very abstract for as judges and magistrates would often point out, all transportation might easily be for life, since no arrangements were made to bring the men back. Early in 1830 there were innumerable cases of stealing and poaching, in all the rural areas around.[50] The additional troubles had broken down inhibitions in the labourers. Not a dovecote was safe from raids, ducks and hens were stolen on dozens of occasions, corn and wearing apparel also—all the necessaries of life. Objects of more monetary value, such as silver spoons, were taken far more rarely. Machine-breaking began to appear, and as the year went on became frequent, occurring at Chipping Norton, Filkins and Deddington. In December Banbury was reported "quite free of tumult" but shortly afterwards threshing machines were smashed in half a dozen villages round that town. There was "serious arson" at Deddington—where the Association for the Prosecution of Offenders offered £20 for information as to who had done the deed. But that Association was outdone by His Majesty's Government who made a proclamation offering £500 for information leading to convictions.

Although often at Quarter Sessions the defendants were confused and unready only once in much reading have I found judge or magistrate dismissing a case for lack of sufficient evidence. But at one Petty Sessions sentences were comparatively light: magistrates at Charlbury in May 1829 had before them thirteen cases of theft, mostly of food, as for example, of a shoulder of lamb. One sentence included solitary confinement and hard labour, but the duration of imprisonment was such that the men could see light at the end of the tunnel.

In this year—1830—Jackson's Journal contained regular reports of the Quarter Sessions of a wide area—Berkshire, Warwick and Worcester as well as Oxford, and on occasion, as events developed, those of Stafford, Wiltshire and Essex. (No doubt there was some kind of "Press Agency" available).

By December 1830 reports from some counties had begun to mention group action on the part of labourers: men would join in breaking threshing machines (as in a case at Blockley) or they might go around to farmers and squires to demand a rise in wages. They were at once spoken of as "mobs" and fears of violence were aroused. Sometimes, though the active men were always few, they would be followed by a considerable crowd. There was a question as to how to deal with the "mobs"; the Prime Minister, Earl Grey, sent round to magistrates urging them to severity. They obeyed him: many had long accepted inadequate evidence: now they were content with less. It was not a question of how to do justice but how to produce terror. So many men were accused of "riotous assembly" and like crimes that special commissions were appointed, not consisting entirely of judges, but with great powers. Three hundred men were brought before the Commission in Hampshire, six hundred in Wiltshire. When the Commission came to Reading the Prosecutor offered no evidence against the men accused of certain crimes: there had been "a sufficient number of examples to ensure peace in this part of the country". The Terror had been successful.

It is obvious, and was well known at the time, that many of the accused labourers, even those condemned to death, were men of excellent character. The Oxford Journal reporter on one occasion "observed with much satisfaction that most of the prisoners had previous to the committal of these outrages borne unblemished characters". As late as 1896 an old woman died near Burford,[51] whose husband and brother had been transported in 1831 for 14 and 7 years respectively. She lived with an aching hope for their return. After seven years neither came back: "the one must wait for the other", she said. Fifty years later they had still not come and she died in her chair looking towards the east— as she thought towards Australia. Transportation broke up hundreds of families without hope of reunion.

It is possible that what would most surprise readers of local papers were the speeches of Judges and Chairmen of Quarter Sessions. Some of the latter being local gentlemen, showed sound knowledge of country conditions. A chairman of Berkshire Quarter Sessions told his Grand Jury (1830) that the "general state of crime was accompanied by "universal distress". The poor were beaten down so low in wages and parochial allowances that they could hardly "maintain their very existence". (In any man not a landlord that statement would have been "sedition and incitement"). In October 1830 the Chairman of Oxford Quarter Sessions asserted that "the laws of this country protect equally the poor and the rich and spoke of the "envied and unexampled freedom of Englishmen". In the next June a different

Chairman of the same court declared that "there was no liberty without laws": "the property of poor men" was as "dear to the law as the large possessions of the rich". He even spoke of "this happy country". This same local squire, William Henry Ashurst, did however know some of the facts of life. Everyone, he said, should look to the cause of the troubles. Men should be paid by their employers.[52] Where there were too many labourers distress existed. He was conscious he said of the happiness of many families destroyed. But for stealing a book a man before his court was sentenced to seven years transportation—without, as one should remember, provision for return.

At that session there were 50 magistrates assembled, all landowners or clergy. Eight of them were titled persons; there were two M.P.'s, and nine "Reverends". The men before them were wretched labourers, some accused of setting ricks or buildings on fire, others of theft. Wealth was set over against destitution, fluency against dumbness, mastery of social and legal techniques against bewilderment.

Behind all the inefficiency and injustice lay a century and a half of selfish and tenacious class government, but England had certain other traditions and from these as well as from new classes with their new intellectual tendencies constructive views were emerging. The ideas of Bentham and of his interpreter and populariser James Mill were being refined and broadened by John Stuart Mill; his life-work would show a mind as generous as it was intellectually able. Political economy had become a popular subject of study. The new tendencies were showing themselves in the professions: the generous movement had become larger and more varied: it was emerging in our own locality.

Not all farmers had the outlook of the Felons Societies. A few even sympathised with the machine-breakers and encouraged the men. Occasionally they would refuse to be sworn in as special constables when there were riots. They must have been shocked when two of their number were sentenced to transportation for leading a group to protest for their own kind that rents were too high and tithes oppressive. In Summer 1829 the Oxford Agricultural Society awarded ten guineas to Mr Charles Large of Broadwell, a near neighbour to Bledington, for having "done most for the poor of his parish" during three years past. He had drawn fuel for cottagers and given them material to repair their roofs; and, most constructive, he had "given up land" for them to plant with potatoes.

It was not rare for Jackson's Journal to carry letters and short articles showing knowledge of village conditions. In January 1829 "Oxford Rector" warned of "most deplorable consequences" if "most immediate attention" were not paid to alarming conditions and to the degradation of the labouring population. An article ("Old and New") in February 1830 compared wages and prices in 1732 with those of its own date: the labourer could now procure only *one half* the quantity of bread, *one quarter* the quantity of beer he could in 1732.

It hardly required a prophet or an economist to show that one simple provision would bring amelioration—gardens, whether attached to cottages or detached "allotments". Any village group of farmers could have found a way to provide them, yet how very seldom it was done. Villagers reading Jackson's Journal or the Gloucester Journal in February 1830 would learn of rare local efforts to provide land. In Hook Norton the Trustees of the land set apart at enclosure to grow furze for the poor decided to let it to them for gardens. At Corsham a farmer had let one acre to a labourer of his who had been a great burden to the parish, having ten children. Spade culture had doubled the value of the acre. The family had "every comfort"; the children flourished and had been trained to industrious habits. The Vestry Meeting seeing this success, had resolved that land should be let to the poor, "adjacent to their dwellings, commensurate with the number of their children". Corsham had a vicar "of unwearied zeal" devoted to the "temporal and spiritual welfare" of all his parish, but even he could hardly work that miracle.

It was beyond the bounds of possibility that the poor should as yet help themselves but other classes also demanding freedom from hampering legislation were not without resources. The one fairly safe form of protest was the Petition to Parliament itself. Many were sent. Some were very mild, others plain-spoken enough. One sent round for signature in Gloucestershire spoke of wasteful expenditure of money and its misapplication to "support a corrupt majority in both Houses".

An example of "capricious, partial . . . and unequal representation" was known near home. Banbury with its clergy, its active dissenters, manufacturers, bankers, surgeons, printers, newspaper men, weavers and shoemakers sent a member to Parliament, but he was elected by eighteen townsmen or rather chosen by "Wroxton Abbey" who gave them orders and bribed the town with beer to be quiet about the absurdity. Not all country towns were entirely quiet. Political Unions were being formed too numerous and too popular to be suppressed. There was one at Stow on the Wold, though it did no more so far as I find than send a mildly-worded petition to Parliament.

In spite of the legal difficulties "reform meetings" were being held all over England. The Oxford Journal reported these at Oxford, Abingdon and other towns with great fulness. One held for the "Freeholders and Residents of Berkshire" in January 1831 with the Earl of Radnor, the High Sheriff and two County Members of Parliament present, was addressed with great frankness by its main speaker. As to the poor, "Take the country through, they have no fuel". "The poorer a man is, the greater his need of a vote". He enunciated a still more advanced doctrine—the absence of the ballot in elections had "ruinous consequences".

There were still some to assert that English Parliamentary representation could not be improved upon but they grew fewer. Ridicule of Parliament and its laws became common. When the Lords threw out a Reform Bill in Oct. 1831 the country was not dismayed. Sydney Smith for example talked of Mrs Partington sweeping out the invading ocean with her mop.[53]

On June 4th 1832 the first Reform Act was signed by the Sovereign: it disfranchised some very "rotten" boroughs, distributed the seats to densely populated areas and extended the franchise considerably in the towns. Banbury organised a great procession,[54] Burford was enthusiastic; Stow on the Wold went wild. Over the whole country there was great elation.

While it would be long before the poor could ask good things for themselves let alone secure them by votes it was realised that one of the problems, possibly the most urgent, to which the new Parliament of 1832 must at once turn its attention was the condition of the poor, in particular the Poor Law. The law must be changed: logic and sound sense must inform it and a system of regular and so far as is human incorruptible administration must be provided.

In December 1830 Jackson's Journal had reported a Lecture by the former Professor of Political Economy of the University—Nassau Senior, later to be a member of the Poor Law Commission. All in learned, cold terms he discussed the facts. Villagers reading the speech must have agreed with it. Senior declared that the relief-cum-wages system was ruining the labourer. He compared the dependence of a family on relief with that of the slave: the line between was slight. Emigration would relieve the situation. It cost £12 to send one person across the seas: to send a million would cost less than poor relief, less than three months of the late War. The Corn Laws raised the price of subsistence and ruined the internal corn trade. Laws were becoming more and more mischievous. To increase the "fund of maintenance", the national resources, the men's attitude to machinery must change. Yet it had to be noted that though power looms multiplied goods and reduced costs, thousands of weavers starved. Professor Senior must later have been wearied by the evidence given to the Commission on the Poor Law: the facts had stared him in the face so long.

There must, even without the Reform Act, have been some major enquiry into the Poor Law and the general condition of the poor. The decency of the generality of the labouring classes had stood against much, but it was giving way. The fear of revolution had passed from the higher social classes but it appeared that there might be other threats. The Societies for the Prosecution of Felons and their bribes to informers were being answered by appalling punishments dealt out to tale-bearers. Nobody found out who wreaked the terrible rough justice and thus it was never police court news and rarely reached the newspapers. The symbolic crime of cattle-maiming was common, even in villages where all memory of it has now died out.

And then, what was becoming clear to everyone, the poor rates had long since become intolerably high in many parishes. Where they were less high it was often because landowners and farmers had contrived to banish their poor across their borders for others to maintain—with another result, that their workers had miles to walk to work.

Rates were so high in some parts that they weighed down agriculture, keeping landlords' rents low and depressing the quality of farming. Arthur Young was so distressed by this aspect of the problem that as long ago as 1807 he had made a table of "Rates in the Pound" for every parish in Oxfordshire. In our locality they varied from a shilling at Shipton under Wychwood to seven shillings at Over Norton, eight shillings at Ascott under Wychwood and nine at Leafield.[55] In a Warwickshire parish referred to earlier, the number of poor relieved increased ten times between 1727 and 1827. The expenditure of overseers there had been £59 (to the nearest £) in 1727; in 1800 nearly

£3,000 and in 1827 £1,171.[56] On the other hand, there were a few parisheswhere the problem had been kept within bounds, and others where hopeful experiments had been tried.

Shortly after the new Parliament was elected in 1832, a Royal Commission was set up to study the workings of the Poor Laws and make recommendations for their modification. The enquiries and Report of this Commission and the Poor Law Amendment Act of 1834, which was almost entirely based upon them, deeply affected much of life for the greater number of Bledington inhabitants for three quarters of a century. Until 1908 and Old Age Pensions it was all but inevitable for farm workers, even the strongest and most skilled, to be at times dependent on Poor Law relief. The Report and the Act are as basic documents for the poor as the Enclosure Act for farmers. The first Census (1811) showed 41 Bledington families whose heads were "agricultural labourers" to 20 of all others. Labourers' families accounted for 205 persons out of 325. Similar figures occur in the census details till 1841, from which time they rose till by 1851 there were 54, and by 1861, 77, (if we count the boys described as such but not the "shepherds"). Thus from being a husbandmen's village we had become, it might be said, a village of labourers.

It was to be expected that the Report would be efficient. One of its members was the ex-Professor of Political Economy at Oxford, Nassau Senior, something of whose knowledge and views an intelligent Bledingtonian might have known;[57] another was a politician and experienced administrator, Sturges Bourne, and a third Sir Edwin Chadwick, a great student of basic social needs, interested in sanitation and police, as well as in the Poor Law. Other members impressed themselves less deeply on the future.

Assistant Commissioners—to their honour, unpaid workers—visited and reported on every area. Our own county, with its neighbours Warwickshire and Worcestershire was inquired into by "Mr Villiers". From his report we learn something of the condition of the labourers in our area and of our own villagers. Indeed, the Commissioners' final Report[58]—an entrancingly readable book—is as a whole enlightening to us. We have in these events, and in the Poor Law itself the clearest possible example of the direct and intimate effect of the central government on the village community.

Mr Villiers reported[59] that wages in Gloucestershire averaged ten shillings per week, but this figure had little representative value. In

Bledington in 1834 and 1835 there was clear evidence that they were seven shillings and lower. The same figures ruled over a large area. An old diary for a village over the Worcestershire border gives such figures as seven shillings to labourers and four shillings to their women folk; one worker, presumably resident, was paid £5. 10. a year "and a pair of old breeches".[60]

Villiers reported on Broadway, that the Overseers had tried refusing outdoor relief but their "poor house" was crowded and dirty . . . "a receptacle for vice and disease". The inmates were not controlled. Two able-bodied men had been observed at night conveying to their own home ' huge loads of wood which had been purloined". It seems less shocking to us, but apparently not to Villiers, that a man who possessed two pigs had been given relief. He writes of another whose reason for regretting the deaths of his two children was his being worse off by lack of the relief he had had for them. He found that the "roundsman system" had been "very generally practised", in his area, but that great discredit had come to attach to it. The Slaughter Hundred is specially mentioned to exemplify a method of giving relief to destitute men in lieu of the two other prevalent methods (providing work or supplementing wages),—a third method to be known briefly as "Relief without labour".

From Jackson's Journal we learn that the Overseers at Stow and of of the villages round about including Bledington, had met together to pool and discuss their experience.[61] We infer from Villiers' report their decision to try giving the men money and adjuring them to find work for themselves, instead of sending them "on the round" (most farmers would no longer tolerate this method), or providing parish work, which had also proved impracticable. Mr Villiers had interviewed the churchwardens and overseers of Stow itself and they had explained to him that to give money without providing employment saved much trouble and left the men free to seek work for themselves. Overseers had tried to make it a condition that the paupers should not apply again for relief for some time. But as soon as the money was spent, the men held out their hands again. The method proved to be "a bounty upon idleness and crime" and was "in the end not less expensive than others". It was in association with this mode of relief that men were required to spend some time, and occasionally whole days, in useless occupations, such as "being confined in a gravel pit" or walking up and down between two specified points during working hours, or, as in Bledington, throwing earth uselessly from one spot to another.

It was a matter of course that no Assistant Commissioner in any way represented the poor, nor did Commissioners seek information from those who needed help. The people they interviewed were overseers, magistrates and the like, many of whom were farmers and landowners. Villiers had asked a farm worker at Walford whether some labourers did not prefer the roundsman system as a means of being idle or doing only half a day's work? That might sometimes be the case, was the reply, "but when a man's spirit is broken, what is he good for?"

Another remarkable interview was with a farmer of broad acres at Aston Somerville, in the County. He paid all his workers £36. 8s. a year (14s. per week) and a woman and two children £22. 5s. They could live well and save money on that. They were all industrious good workmen and he could employ many more men at that rate if they applied. He had been an overseer for twenty six years and in his parish there had been only two bastards in five years. But the upshot of this interview, that for many men a decent wage would cut all the knots and that sound farmers could afford to pay it to all the men they could employ was not adverted to by the Commissioners.

It should be mentioned that at points the Commissioners appear to be convinced that the position of the labourers had improved in the recent period. One witness had shown that wages were worth slightly more than in 1798—when the price of corn was extremely high. They had information that 29,000 agricultural labourers had deposits in Savings Banks.[62] But they reveal not even a cursory examination of the meaning in that connection of the word "labourer" or of local factors making for special earnings.

It was clear from the evidence that England was a topsy turvydom. Such facts had emerged as that relief, if it were to provide the barest bread for a family had, over great areas, to be higher than wages. Illegitimate children's relief was supplying their mothers with an income, and children in a pauper family were hardly dependent on their parents and became unruly. A woman might refuse to nurse her mother if the parish would not pay her to do so; or a man threaten to turn his step-children out of doors. Good independent workers had been turned off farms in favour of paupers; the best and steadiest men were the most likely to rebel and even to riot. Other people were paying a great part of farmers' wages but the labourers were no better off and the land was going down in value. And greatest absurdity of all, the whole population most laboriously concerned with the growing of food was, over many counties, half-starved.

Amid all this confusion, it was natural that the Commissioners should decide to be severely practical in their report.[64] There had been some successful experiments: they decided "not to depart from the firm ground of actual experience". They enunciated one principle of reform: the position of paupers must always be "less eligible than that of the lowest independent labourers". No doubt it was deemed to be not within their competence to consider whether this principle should be balanced by freedom to combine to get better wages or by some other means of balancing the cohesion and therefore the power of other classes. The Elizabethan principle that the able-bodied (or the not totally incapable) must work for their relief was taken for granted. The two conditions could be reconciled by providing hard task work and paying for it at a rate below that of wages. This had rarely been possible in the parishes; under other circumstances it could be tried again.

Some parishes had made it a condition of relief that destitute men and their families must enter a "workhouse". In itself the workhouse had been a horrid failure but at any rate, on condition of living in it, few had applied for relief. The men had made desperate efforts to find work and sometimes it had proved to be available. (At what wages or at what distance to be walked, was not revealed). The Commissioners decided to recommend this "residential" condition, but to place workhouses under a different control.

To make use of available knowledge and to avoid local ineptitude, there must be centralisation. There should be a central Board of Commissioners to control the administration of the Poor Laws, with Assistants to frame and enforce regulations for workhouses, to be as far as possible, uniform. The country should be divided into "unions" of parishes, each Union to have its paid officers (the paid assistant overseer had proved his worth in large parishes). Each parish should still raise its own rates and be responsible for the few paupers not required to enter a workhouse—chiefly very old, but not totally enfeebled, persons.

Among other changes the Commissioners recommended was the simplification of the law of settlement, e.g. the Union might be considered as a single parish for purposes of settlement. Thus much of the cruel and meaningless removal of paupers from place to place would come to an end. The Commissioners recommended that relief to children should always be considered relief to parents, so that children could not become in a measure independent. Mothers of illegitimate children should be held responsible for them and no attempt should be made to find fathers. (Some women had taken to naming any man they chose).

As to constructive means of preventing destitution, they considered only two—that of the provision of gardens and other lands for the occupation of the poor, and emigration. They gave a most interesting summary of the evidence on "the occupation of land" by labourers which showed it as almost entirely successful for the worker and his family, and as giving a profit to the owner of the land let to them. But also many farmers and others opposed it, on the grounds that a labourer with land to till in his leisure would arrive tired at his work next day. (It was not noted that on the wages of the day these objectors were asking for an all but fatal limit to a labourer's freedom). After this exposition the Commissioners came to the conclusion that 'since it appears that the land may be let to labourers on profitable terms, the necessity for any public enquiry . . . on these points seems to be at an end". Surely this statement was a thin cloak for disagreement, "minority" reports not being as yet usual? It proved far from true.

As to emigration, the undoubted and considerable increase in the rural population was compatible in the Commissioners' view with the possibility of sufficient employment, but there was no proof on this point. Some immediate relief to the rates would undoubtedly follow the emigration of a considerable number of families. They recommended that it should be legal for vestries to order the payment of the expenses of emigration of those willing to go. None of the suggested provision would meet all cases; take for example in villages, the many accidents on farms, often due to the youth of workers. Anomalies and hard cases could be taken care of by private charity, the Commissioners thought. Fantasies about charitable impulses were a great psychological resource, then and later.

The Poor Law Amendment Act which was passed within a year of the Report followed its recommendations closely. The virtue of the new scheme was that it brought regularity into the Poor Law, with central responsibility and control. The three commissioners appointed had great powers but could be themselves the target of criticism from

Parliament and newspapers. They also in fact continued to gather information about the homes and other conditions of the poor, their reports on which enlightened the nation. They appointed Assistant Commissioners who reported to them on the work being done in all areas and through whom they conveyed praise and rebuke. If discipline was the chief virtue of the new Poor Law it was not one to be despised.

But there was a tinge, a foretaste of another good. For its local elected administrators the Act prescribed the title "Guardians of the Poor". The word, we know, has power: this was the same word that the well-endowed used when they provided for their own orphans (until 1894 there was a property qualification for Guardianship). It conceded to the poor their full humanity and importance. It linked the functions of the persons named with the religion they professed and of which the numerous clergymen among them were official representatives: sickness, age and orphandom would in fact meet with perceptible charity.

Because of uniform practice under the Act its provisions can be sufficiently gathered from its workings here. The whole country was divided into "Unions" of parishes solely for the purpose of relief; thus villages could be grouped as convenience determined. Bledington was included in the Union centred upon Stow on the Wold with twenty-six other villages including our familiar neighbours Oddington, Icomb, the Slaughters and Broadwell. Vestries still elected overseers who assessed their neighbours for poor rates and decided which poor persons—the old and the infirm—might be relieved in their own homes. The new officers, the Guardians, were also to be elected in the Vestries to represent their parishes on the Board of Guardians: magistrates resident within the Union, ex officio, and a few others, nominated by the Commissioners. The principle pervading the new Poor Law, that those capable of work who should be relieved must fare less well than those who earned their own sustenance, was difficult to arrange, with wages still too low to afford food. Hence the provision that the "able-bodied" unemployed must enter the Unions' "workhouse", where they would live and work as long as they must be maintained.

From the minutes of our local Board of Guardians, some details can be inferred as to poor relief in Bledington before the new Poor Law Amendment Act, for example that paupers had been employed to keep the parish roads in order. Since the workhouse of the Union had yet to be built, this custom did not at once come to an end. In 1836 a woman pauper here was still paid four shillings a week and later in the same year William Stayte was being paid 9d a day for this work. At the end of 1836 the roads were "let", i.e. someone contracted to keep the roads in repair. In a nearby village a man was still employed in 1836 "on the round", being paid three shillings a week by his farmer-employer and going to the overseers for the rest of his pay. All such irregularities in the Union came to an end in 1837 (the Commissioners had sent out a questionnaire about them) and a temporary workhouse was opened.

There is a tradition in Bledington that there was once a workhouse here. No other trace of one survives, but we learn from the Guardians' minutes that the overseers still owned some cottages[65] and rented at least one other. The tradition may have arisen from the fact that families could be sent to live in these houses. The property was sold in 1838 for about £33, the money going towards the parish's share of the Unions' overhead expenses.

From 1834, then, Bledington ceased to be a unit for the affairs of the poor. Overseers would still be chosen at the annual vestry meeting to assess and collect rates, and to relieve the aged, but more important than overseers would be Bledington's own representative on the Board of Guardians.[66] The first of these was Edward Stow of University Farm. He found himself at the early meetings one of a group composed of clergy and farmers, the latter men belonging to families like his own, and (still like his own) present today in the neighbourhood—a Comely of Guiting Power, a Hanks of Naunton, a Hambridge, an Edington. At first there were no "Esquires", but one or two of these appeared after the early elections. The clergy did not on the whole represent parishes: some were magistrates attending ex-officio. Sometimes present was the Dean of Gloucester, no doubt a "nominated" member, perhaps of more than one Board in the County. The Chairman we already know: he was the Rev. F. E. Witts of Upper Slaughter whom we saw at work on the Bench. He must have brought great experience to bear and doubtless now a riper mind.

From the first, the Stow Guardians were efficient: they recognised the newness of their task and consulted the Commissioners about every difficulty. They were frequently congratulated by the latter on their plans and the excution of them. No doubt we must trace this success largely to the clergy members, all of whom appear to have been well-educated men. The contribution of the farmers is less certain: they were less articulate. Certainly they knew something of applicants for relief who hailed from their own parishes.

Soon, the paid officers of the Board would be very important. Its first secretary was a well-known solicitor of Bourton on the Water. There were also Relieving and Medical Officers. As these were needed in every Union, they came to form two large new professions. Both— especially the Relieving Officers—became very important to the poor, familiar figures in their lives. At first these can hardly have seemed very beneficent, but later they were on the side of the poor: (the Governor of the workhouse had to see to it that the repressive principle was applied).

The relieving officers had respectively fourteen and thirteen parishes to serve, but were allowed no vehicle or horse: advertisements said "no horse required". Their wages were £52 a year.

It was an officer's duty to visit the houses of applicants. As to the unemployed he had only to report the application, and bid the man appear before the Board at its next meeting. But in the case of the sick, who must be relieved in their homes, he had to know their circumstances intimately. It was often the wife and mother who was ill. The relieving officer must know her condition, the number and ages of her children, and what each one earned, even a nine-year-old's sixpence. Sometimes underfeeding was so evident that he took it upon himself to order the usual relief—a pound of mutton at 6d. So much machinery for a pound of meat! The Guardians never refused sanction to this preliminary provision: often the same relief was continued weekly for a long time. Edward Dickens' wife in Bledington was ill for eight weeks in the summer of 1835: a few of course were ill for longer. Occasionally a home would be found in a state of great distress. In one case the relieving officer threw discretion to the winds and ordered, beside the mutton, half a pound of sugar, half a pound of rushlights and half a hundred weight of coal. When the men were ill, the family's income failed, and it was usual to order loaves and small sums of money—a shilling and two loaves, or half a crown, or even three shillings, but never a sum approaching the normal wage of seven shillings.

All this out-relief was very conditional indeed. One Bledington woman, Richard Beauchamp's wife Hannah, was very bold. Possibly she thought the new Poor Law to be full of helpfulness. Her request was for a midwife or the medical officer to be present at her confinement. The Beauchamps were five in family and their income 10s. 6d. (father's wage 8/- and 2s. 6d. earned by John aged 12). Her application was refused. Weeks later her child was born and she was ill for some seventeen weeks. Then she was allowed her weekly pound of mutton.

On being called to one family, the officer noted that their cottage was "well-furnished" and he "saw fruit on the premises". (An ill-regulated imagination may conjure up a rich bowl of oranges; a moment's thought substitutes apples or plums). Relief was of course refused. One insane pauper (not a Bledingtonian) who was in a private asylum, had a legacy of £10. The relieving officer was required to find the executors and tell them that the Guardians will do nothing for the pauper till the sum has been spent on his maintenance: but the officer was instructed to "take proper steps to see that the pauper was not prejudiced"!

Out-relief for the old, allotted by the parish overseers, but paid out by the relieving officer, was a simple matter: women were given a shilling and a quartern loaf, an old couple, a shilling and two loaves. (Old widowers, it seems, usually went into the workhouse). If the question is asked, how could they live on this income, the answer is that they did not; the butcher "sold" them a pennyworth of meat, a neighbour gave them vegetables, their children gave them small sums. The demand for female domestic servants in towns was growing every year and many country girls were housemaids and cooks. Often they did not marry, and how fortunate their old mothers were then!

It was chiefly on such old folk that Bledington overseers spent at first £1. 17s. per week, a sum that dropped steadily in the first few years, till it was about £1. 4s. by 1840: perhaps 15 or 16 old folk.

Able-bodied applicants for relief had now to enter a workhouse with their dependents but this legal provision could not be applied at once. It was extremely difficult to buy a site for the "institution". Every owner of suitable land in Stow demanded £200 for the necessary acre: no-one rushed to sell. The Guardians had almost fixed on a site when the Vicar of Stow protested that to build on it would spoil his view. At last a good site was found at £120 per acre and "the Institution" was soon erected. It was not a complex building. Something was said of providing rooms for old married couples but nothing came of it. There were two large rooms, one for men and the other for women and children, and besides those a "dayroom" where meals were eaten. The house was ruled over by a Governor and his wife, the latter to be the housekeeper and teacher, (but we do not hear of any teaching being done at this time).

In the workhouse, people of very varying manners and standards of cleanliness must have been forced together. There were always some paupers of weak intellect. and, surely, tiresome, unoccupied children.

In the early days of the Union there was much unemployment. The relieving officer gave information about relief to a great number of men. In Bledington alone, these were numerous. When the Institution was opened late in 1836 he had to explain that applicants must go to Stow, a four mile walk, and be interviewed by the Guardians; if relief was granted they would have to "go inside". He reported all these cases to the Clerk and they figure in the minutes: but in the majority of cases the entry ends "No appearance: case dismissed": the men would rarely appear before the Board—not because they objected to the four-mile walk.

However some, incapable of migrating to find work, as many no doubt did, entered the workhouse. Here, the regulation was, they must be set on work. Bone-breaking was tried, but it was a most objectionable job: a man and a boy ran away because of it, and a revolt was feared. Another idea was to set the paupers to keep the streets and roads clean, but that required more supervision than could be provided. Nothing proved at all suitable till the Governor went to see oakum-picking at the Chipping Norton workhouse. Pulling old hemp ropes to pieces and making bag-strings with the longer threads may well have seemed a comparatively soothing occupation.

The materials of the workhouse food seem to have been sound though cheap and insufficient. When the bread was briefly unpalatable the paupers, with the courage of a group, said so, loudly. The cheapest joints of beef were bought, shin at 2d per lb. and "sticking pieces" at even less. Meat was served only three or four times a week (but at home there had often been none). At other main meals soup was substituted. (One would like to know the recipe: even soup cannot be made for nothing). Men sometimes had cheese; at those times women had butter instead. But at a time when adulteration was rife, contractors had to guarantee that rice and butter and cheese were "of good quality". There seems a gleam of bright light on the page when we learn that the Medical Officer sometimes ordered wine or even spirits for sick persons (1838).

Clothes, too, must have been better than the inmates could ever have bought for themselves. The men's shirts were made of linen shirting, and their shoes were "home-made and of good workmanship", costing 8s. 6d.; women's cost 6s. 6d. Within a year of the opening of the House, greatcoats were ordered for old men who could not work, so that they could take exercise. In their care for the genuine article we perhaps see the rectitude of the clergy Guardians. They could not be associated with shoddy materials.

Cleanliness too, was attained, though the Guardians would not sanction "water-closets on the second floor", thinking that portable closets would serve. Twice a "peculiar illness" pervaded the workhouse, but it was not thought very serious. The "Union", as it came to be called, was quite unlike the Bristol gaol when the Rev. F. E. Witts had visited and found the King's Evil rife there.

Epidemics were watched with care in the workhouse and in the parishes from which the inmates came, both by the Medical Officers and the Guardians. Smallpox occurred in Evenlode and Chastleton in 1836 but patients were sent to a lone house in Broadwell parish, and the medical officer stood ready to vaccinate the poor "for nothing". The other occasional infectious diseases were "diarrhoea and cholera", but the numbers were never great in early years.

There was usually one at least "imbecile" or "deranged" person in the workhouse. When their condition was severe they were referred to as "lunatics" and "idiots", and in that case were sent, after a time, to the county Lunatic Asylum or to a "licensed house for the reception of lunatics" at Hook Norton. (This house with relics of its one-time barricaded appearance still exists).

The features of workhouse life that paupers most disliked were the discipline and the indiscriminate mixing. No list of rules is given but an example is seen in the conditions of churchgoing. Inmates might attend one service a week if, when it was over, the parson or minister would sign a declaration that the pauper had arrived punctually and stayed to the end. The regulated life was utterly intolerable to some. One night a blind man and a woman, Jane "Wearing" of Bledington got out through the windows of the "day room" and crossed the boys' yard which as yet had no walls. The Warings were at this time a very poor family, lost to respectability (Jane "left her two bastard children behind her") but there was always something dashing and generous about their personalities.

The Governor and Matron, and the Guardians were distraught about the escape. They offered a reward for the apprehension of Jane and her blind companion but could not hear of them. Then they distributed a leaflet describing them and offering the reward. The two were fairly hunted. At last they had to show themselves, to beg food. They were found at Woodstock and brought back. From that moment Jane was unmanageable, "in a state of mental derangement", and was presently sent off to the County Asylum. Her companion, bereft of his friend and guide, wanted to give up life. He was "in a state of melancholy and determined to starve himself", secreting all the food delivered to him. They watched him lest he should attempt to kill himself more speedily, but presently he was reduced to weeping and obedience. Jane, it seems, was not very deranged. The Asylum returned her to the workhouse and after a time she escaped again. Although she was in workhouse clothes she was not found for six days,—and then at Evesham.

The minutes of the Guardians afford a little information of a kind we have lacked—upon the "morals" of our Bledington poor. One man whose family apply for relief is in prison for poaching· and in 1838 the family of another man is destitute because he is in prison. The next week his wife is a widow. Had he suffered capital punishment? It seems more likely that he had committed suicide.

The number of Bledington folk living in the workhouse seems to have averaged 9 (1847) or 8 (1848). There were constant applications to the Guardians for relief, beside that regulated by the overseer. Sometimes there would be 8 or 9 in a week, at other times three or four, in addition to invalids being visited by the relieving officer. Workhouse relief was very inexpensive to rate-payers: 699 days' residence in 1847 cost only £15 while out relief was £48.

From 1836 "Died at Stow Union" becomes a familiar phrase in our parish registers. Till the "Institution" was abolished some still spent their last years there for lack of any other possibility. Many a proud old woman unable at last to keep clean was taken off to it by a mixture of ruse and force. No newspaper reported such occurrences; they are known still by a few with long memories and referred to on rare occasions in talk.

The workhouse never became a tolerable home of rest. Up to 1914, if you met an agricultural labourer out in the fields, here or elsewhere and he talked of his life, he would ask—not being a Methodist or

299

devoted churchman—"what is there for us to live for? Nothing to look forward to but the workhouse".

It should be said that in the course of the century it was ruled that old couples who so chose must be allowed a room for sleeping: during the day they joined separate groups. The time would come when the children were better provided: a school was opened, apart from the main building. But it was never possible to give assurance that there was a modicum of privacy or of comfort.

One function of the workhouse has gone unmentioned,—the reception of vagrants, who were seen on the roads everywhere. If you walked to Stow from Bledington in the afternoon you would be sure to see one or two between the Oddington turn and Stow, on their way to the "Union". Usually they stayed only one night, doing a stint of labour before they left the next day. Hospitality to them was one of the two great functions of the workhouse till well into the twentieth century. A wash, a meal, a dry bed, and then away: that was tolerable. These facilities, also, must have been used by ex-Bledingtonians.

The regime of the new Poor Law was certainly healthier than the previous state of affairs. Confusion had been eliminated, if not inhumanity. After only nine months, our Guardians were convinced that labourers were "more industrious, orderly, and anxious to obtain employment" than before they began their work. (Also in the new circumstances wages began to creep up). The sick, too, benefitted, the Guardians thought, by the "greater regularity of attendance". Because the poor were so reluctant to submit to some of the new conditions of relief, the rates came down. In February 1837, the Guardians computed that there had been a saving of 40% of the cost of relief as compared with the last years before the Union was formed. Wives were working oftener in the fields and so were children.

Again, earlier Unions being made single "parishes" for purposes of settlement had reduced the number of removals, though they could still occur. One sick woman (1836) refused to be separated from her mother, by removal to her "settlement", and was refused relief. But now that more people could write letters without difficulty it became usual, gradually, for parishes to subscribe to the maintenance of those who had a legal claim on them, without their presence.

The effect of hunger, unemployment, pauperism, the legal terror and the subordination of their class to all others meant that labourers and their families were socially almost completely detached from other kinds and ranks. It was impossible for a boy or girl, unless by a chance in thousands, to rise to sufficiency and to improve his status. Going from school to school in villages from 1915 to 1924 I saw the labourers' children apart, dulled, without impulse, sitting near to happier children, but invisibly barred from them.[67]

And yet even in Bledington, though here workers were poorer than the average, channels to a tolerable and even to fairly good life would presently open. But before we consider steps forward we ought to realise where the labourer stood in 1834. Everyone who reads village history must come to ask: how did the English labourers' position in the late seventeen and eighteen hundreds compare with that of slaves? Many a man given the opportunity of selling himself with a prospect of sound food and shelter must have done so for his family's sake.

Till the middle of the century and long afterwards poverty continued, with insufficient or unsuitable food, though no longer slow starvation. After that time some channels to a better life opened. They were in brief, the railways, the colonies, and the new police. How many would be free to take them and have the energy to do so? The last-mentioned had best be dealt with here. The old constables, unpaid officers of Hundred Court or Vestry Meeting, had not been useless. They had known everyone and at least by elimination knew where to look for miscreants. But two developments had changed the situation. First the voluntary associations for prosecution had taken a great deal upon themselves. Some of them began to keep dogs to track sheep-stealers (one set up a pack of blood-hounds) which made flesh creep and not only that of offenders! Also, a spreading modernity was canals, to be followed in the eighteen forties by railways. These two cheap new means of transport offered both new forms of plunder and new means of eluding even the new "Peelers" and "Bobbies"—members of the paid and trained police forces some towns had formed from 1829. Ten years later it was legal for Justices in Quarter Sessions to set up police forces for Hundreds. There began to be areas with and others without police forces: naturally, persistent offenders removed their habitations from one to the other.

Many thought the time had come for change, but not Bledington. In January 1842 a printed form was carried around the village, householders and others being invited to object to a proposal that our county as a whole should be policed. In all, thirty four men signed. But a majority in the Hundred favoured the project and a Gloucestershire force was inaugurated. Our parish was called upon to pay £30. At the Easter Vestry Meeting rate-payers expressed their unanimous conviction that a police-force was "wholly unnecessary and useless and that the charge should be immediately reduced and as soon as possible abolished".[68] This strong expression may mean that the village suffered from little misbehaviour within its own borders but the lack of dissension suggests a poor, narrow debate. Nine years later the Battle of Mickleton Tunnel on the railway that was being built near us would afford vestrymen a profitable lesson in the need of a police force not based on parishes.

The nearest station for a County Constable was Stow on the Wold. (The vestry continued to nominate village constables—in 1864, not two but five, including wage-earners). It was probably not till 1890 and after that the County "Bobby" became a familiar sight—when a bicycle increased his speed on tours of duty.

The new force had an effect on justice. Policemen were wage-earners and this odd form of representation had some tendency to even-handedness as between classes even though policemen did not tend to identify themselves with evil-doers. After the mid-century magistrates' justice improved, though it had far to go.

A few rural labourers joined the local police; it was a more favoured ambition to join the Metropolitan Force.

Country Parson. Victorian

We have forecast that the Rev. John Oakley Hill would exemplify here a Victorian outlook and conscience: he arrived six years after the Queen's accession, from a background which naturally had much of the eighteenth century about it. He was born in 1803 at Knighton in Radnorshire, but of an English family, not quite without property and of clerical traditions. (His brother had a career similar to his own and a great uncle of his was patron of a small living). The family traditions were cherished. John attended Lucton and Ludlow Grammar Schools, of which the former had been founded in Queen Anne's reign by a maternal ancestor of his. He matriculated in the University of Oxford at sixteen and became an undergraduate of Christ Church, living as many famous men had done, in Peckwater Quad.[69] He graduated in 1825,—some thirteen years before the Pluralities Act (1838). He was nominated by his great uncle to be vicar of the parish of Ullingsworth cum Little Cowarne in Herefordshire, and was in

1826 ordained Deacon by the Bishop of Hereford. Whether he served his first parish at all, we do not know; probably he merely shared the stipend with a curate (in the modern sense) who cared for more than one parish. In the next year (1827) he was appointed Chaplain of Christ Church and was ordained priest by Charles Lloyd, Bishop of Oxford, "his Chaplaincy being his title". Shortly before his ordination he had taken his M.A. degree. One of his duties as chaplain was to say Latin prayers in the Cathedral, from the Latin version of the Prayer Book made at the Reformation for the use of Collegiate churches.

In his early career Mr Hill moved fast: in 1828 he became—like his predecessor here, John Allen—a schoolmaster. He was Headmaster of Monmouth Grammar School, with one assistant, and forty pupils, all boys. The work was undoubtedly well done: he instituted a sound reform dividing the schoolroom in two, and the boys into classes, one to learn classics and the other English, Arithmetic, and the rudiments of Latin.[70] He and his brother, his assistant, were good teachers: the school's official visitors thought the Head's salary insufficient; and when he left Monmouth the townsfolk presented him with two beautiful papier maché trays, still cherished in the family in 1933. (Even this detail of his story is typical of the comfortable and cultivated middle class of the time).

Hill liked his school-work well, but his ideal for himself was that of country clergyman and when the Dean and Chapter offered him one of the parishes in 1832 he accepted. A few years after his appointment to Ashenden cum Worton the Duke of Buckingham made him his Chaplain at his Woolton seat. We see the new attitude of Christ Church to plural responsibilities in their refusal to approve of Mr Hill's adding this work to that of his incumbency. He gave way. For this sacrifice he was rewarded in 1843 by the offer of the cure of Bledington. The stipend of the post was poor, but higher than some others, and though there was no vicarage house worthy of the name, that was still true of many parishes. Thus, one of the young clergyman's first efforts was to prepare for a family by increasing the income and building a house.

A vicarage near, if possible next to, the church was part of his ideal vision, but no-one would sell land nearby and the patrons pointed to the ample garden or close of the ancient parsonage house five minutes from the church. The vicar's objection to building on the old site was that there were poor cottages very near to it, which he thought unsuitable, but the Dean and Chapter would not regard them as an objection. So Mr Hill pulled down the old small house and built his new one on its close, not near the brook or the cottages but high and dry, at the other end. It was a modest enough house (built by the Milton under Wychwood firm of Groves who would later build the village school) but it contained a study for the Vicar. Its style, with slate roof, brick walls and "sash" windows, did not accord with that of the good Cotswold farmhouses, rather with the contemporary English taste in vicarages: but part of the plan at that time was a decent veil or barrier of trees around the vicar's home, so the breach with tradition has never painfully struck the eye.

The new Vicar's "living" was £88 and the village poor: it seems strange that a man well qualified and of relatively prosperous background should have deliberately settled here "for good" as the villagers said, but he seems to have done so. He lived in his new home as a bachelor for four or five years but in 1848 he brought his bride to it. She also fitted well into the contemporary ideal picture. She was, we are told, a "charming bride", well-descended—from the Bagnalls, not the modest family who farmed and kept school here awhile but "The Bagnalls of Staffordshire", and from the Coxwells of Ablington Manor. In the course of the next year a child was born, the first son of a vicar to be born here for a hundred years. We hear of no more children, but even a small vicarage family had social claims and educational needs beyond those that could be met from the living's income.

This had increased steadily and prospects for the clergy had been improved by the appointment of the Ecclesiastical Commissioners. Like Allen before him, John Oakley Hill made a continuing effort to raise the income. The farm called Werndidier or Werndydyr in Radnorshire, the first gift to the living from Queen Anne's Bounty, was a constant subject of debate. It was not far from a town with which Hill had connection—so he wrote to the Dean. He knows it for "a miserable place"; and it was very distant from Bledington: a predecessor of his once spent half a year's rent on a visit to it. Hill offered to exchange for it two good meadows he had bought in Bledington, which at the moment would bring in more rent; if Werndydyr were his own, he would build a house on it, which would lead to better farming and more rent. The Dean and Chapter were inclined to agree with this proposal, but the Bishop was shocked at the thought of exchanging fifty-two acres for six.

Persistent proposals to acquire land, and application to Christ-Church, Queen Anne's Bounty and the Diocesan Fund for money for the purpose were in time rewarded. The living was still worth under £100 in 1857, but the Ecclesiastical Commissioners having come to the rescue, by 1862 the value had risen to £136. Further efforts in the next nine years raised it to £150; at which figure there were then many poorer livings.

Hill's latest efforts to improve his own and his successors' home was its extension: it had "no washhouse, or cellar or larder". The Warneford Charity (there appear to have been many charitable funds to apply to) promised £50 and Christ Church found the rest. At this time Christ Church seems always to have helped those who helped themselves and as they were patrons of a number of livings, it was not so small a work. The country over, many poor vicars must have been carrying on a similar long campaign. There is pathos in a request from Hill to the patrons to warn applicants for parishes like Bledington that they will find neighbouring clergy well-to-do and, one gathers, social difficulties arising from the fact. (The statement was true in relation to the Kingham rectors but not of others nearby).

But Mr and Mrs Hill were not pre-occupied by their own circumstances to the exclusion of other matters. When they first considered their parish, it must have had an eighteenth century look. The stocks still stood on the green, though they were unlikely to be used again. In the church there was a number of "horse-box" pews for respectable families (hiding the fine old bench ends) and mere "formes" or benches for the poor; the pulpit and clerk's desk were of the "three-decker" type. A verger walked up and down past the seats occupied by young men and lads and if there was unseemly conduct the "thwack" of his stick on the miscreant's back would be heard all over the church. But the attendance of the young men in spite of this attention gives a glimpse of the place of Sunday services in villagers' lives.

The clergy of the nineteenth century liked to find their villages old-fashioned and quaint. The brief memoir of Mr Hill by his son tells of the remnants of old songs, of the children's maypoles, and the rhymes with which they begged on St. Thomas's and St. Valentine's Days and of the Mumming Play acted in the Vicarage kitchen at Christmas time. Percy, the small son, saw it but could not later recollect the play, only the unwonted appearance of the men, with their false beards and strange garments and the quaintness of their antics. Once the Morris dancers with their Tom Fool came to the Vicarage lawn. Many country vicarages made their own cider or shared the village supply. The Temperance Movement had not reached the villages yet, but it would do so soon and would make vicarage families very conscious of the inebriating contents of their cellars, and presently humorous about them. Hence the stories as, for example, of the Shenington's vicar's wife who insisted on her gardener whistling while he decanted her best brew and of young Percival Oakley Hill being found at the cider cask with a beaker in his hand when his speech was the merest lisping. Presently he atoned for this with thirty years of temperance advocacy. The church bells were another item in the old traditions. They had ancient customs, as for example, being rung at six in the morning on St. Thomas's Day. The ringers had their festivities and their high skills. Admiration for the latter could at moments unify the village: everyone loved the Christmas chimes and the "firing"[71] of the bells on very special occasions.

New traditions were also to be started off, notably a more intimate and pervasive patriotism, expressing itself chiefly in sympathy with, and adoration of the royal family. When the Prince of Wales married the "Lovely Sea King's Daughter" the Vicar and his wife "made it a children's feast day", erecting a triumphal arch, and providing tea on the lawn: they had arranged too, for the bells to be chimed and "fired". In 1871 when the Prince was very ill with typhoid and a rumour went round that he had died, young Percy was sent to toll the bell, happily much too soon.

More modern aspects of the life of his working folk came home to the Vicar in his early days. When he first arrived he may have heard that a cottage at Bould had been licensed for Methodist meetings some ten years before. There were Benfields at Bould and also in Bledington and in 1847, four years after Mr Hill's arrival a group of labourers began to hold Methodist services in the Benfield house in this parish. Five years later the group built a chapel[72] in the lane, not far from the old Steward's House. Many years later it would be called a "hen-house", but it was not too small for activity. As soon as it was built a Sunday School was started there. The Vicar had realised that the "poor" children of the village were unschooled and ignorant and he started in his own house, not only a Sunday School but a "day school" also. He himself said in a letter to the Dean in 1854 that he does so "to counteract the efforts of the Dissenters",[73] but such a motive would never have sustained alone the hard work of teaching, He had "acted as village schoolmaster for two years" and had had for scholars "twenty five to thirty poor children and twelve children of farmers and tradesmen". His two kitchens had been used as school-rooms.

The work was not a temporary enthusiasm but went on throughout his charge of the parish: Mrs Hill did much of the teaching for some years and then Miss Naomi Malins was employed. Later she was described as "imperfectly educated": probably that was why the day-school came to cater for infants only.

There was no chance here—the Vicar said in reply to questions sent out by the Senior Common Room of Christ Church in 1854 to all the incumbents of its parishes—of building a National School; the neces-sary local contribution towards land and building could not be raised in so poor a parish. He had at first, he wrote, supported the school himself, but now he was receiving some subscriptions. He could have added that the Churchwardens sometimes helped by supplying coals from the church rate.[74]

From the answers to another enquiry twelve years later we learn that the day school served infants only: grown children were attending school in a neighbouring village (i.e. Kingham) where they are charged 3d. per week. (We gather that the "children's pence" in Bledington were much less). But to the Sunday School big and little children alike belonged—sixty or more. We learn nothing as to what was taught in either school beside reading and writing and "the basis of morals"— as the Vicar wrote—"the Scriptures". We learn now (1866) the annual rewards of the school mistress—a cottage, £4 and the children's pence. The school property, i.e. cottage and schoolroom had been acquired and built by the vicar in the first place but Christ Church had obligingly bought it from him: its use was their contribution to education.

In 1866 Mr Hill described the folk of his parish as "industrial[75] agricultural, respectful to the church"; farmers were all churchmen, but "twenty labouring poor attend the Wesleyan chapel". Nowhere do we find any allusions to home conditions or the state of minds as distinct from souls. Yet he must have been acquainted with them, since he baptised and buried and had taught his folk; and moreover, was Chaplain to the Stow workhouse, driving there twice a week in his pony carriage. Simply, they were no part of his charge. Religion and morality were his business. It is not too much to assume that great poverty was taken for granted and even decreed by Providence.

But in the field of religion he and his wife worked hard especially at the Sunday services. They had found them old-fashioned on their arrival. A few singers had sat together in the gallery across the west end of the church: there had been a small band of "serpents" and other instruments but they presently failed and Mrs Hill accompanied the hymns on her flutina. The psalms were said, the clerk reciting, with some mispronunciation, ("I was a lion (alien) unto my mother's children"), alternate verses. This was the time when clergy ladies began elaborately to decorate churches for festivals; there were little books about how to do it, forerunners of modern "Flower Arrangement".[76] Here, at Christmas time, the sole decoration had been small twigs of holly stuck in holes in the pews on either side of the nave, but in the sixties Mrs Hill organised a little band of farmers' wives and daughters who brought armfuls of evergreen branches to enwreathe the pillars and laid scripture texts on the window-sills. These were cut out in snow white cotton wool laid on crimson cloth, the whole bordered with holly and yew. There were flowery designs for Easter and the magnificence of corn and fruit at harvest.

The greatest improvement of the services was musical. It seems that when the Hills arrived hymns from a collection of about thirty, Allen's Primary Hymn-book, were sung. Soon Tate and Brady's Metrical Psalms (till now the psalms had been said) were attempted, but what gave the people a large part in the services was the introduction, about 1868, of Hymns Ancient and Modern—a choice of hundreds of hymns, many with fine, rhythmic, sometimes rousing, tunes, suitable for children, for boys, for simple souls and cultivated minds, gathered from the ages and from churches, far and wide.

The history of the effect of hymns is one of those that can never be written, but to stand in Bledington church next to an old labourer singing beautifully and confidently, and to know the dignity of his life and the quality of his work is to make a very firm connection between the music and words of hymns and the old man's character. The hymns must have had some immediate effects: when lads found themselves singing "Awake my soul and with the sun", and turned the pages of their hymn-books and knew that later would come

"Soldiers of Christ arise
And put your armour on."

"Tread all the powers of darkness down
And win the well-fought day".

the need for thwacks would be much reduced. And when Mr Hill saw how many of the hymns were the work of the Wesley brothers he must have seen reason to drop contumelious references to "dissenters'. Like the English Prayer Book in its early days and since, but with added potency of song, the hymns gave glorious meaning to common experiences. And from them family occasions—christening, marriage, burials would gain in meaning and worth.

Enthusiasm for the hymns brought a demand for a different instrument. A harmonium was bought and young Mr Theophilus Pegler of Banks Farm became choirmaster and taught simple part-singing The choir and Sunday School came down from the gallery so that the congregation was more compact and the singing had more volume. Hymn-singing is a folk art. It probably did something to reduce the appeal of the lay Morris dances and to confine them to a smaller group.

John and Maria Hill did twenty eight years of good, if limited work and were "faithful" as their parishioners recorded in brass on an eight-day clock when they left in 1871. The Vicar had long ceased to be so keenly interested in "real property" and become by conscientious exercise of his office a keen low church worker, nearer and nearer to evangelicalism. Maria had broken new ground for later clergy wives and in a measure for other women by her activity in the parish. Mr Hill, in virtual retirement, became vicar of Little Rollright, a parish containing one large farmhouse (where once famous shorthorns had been bred) and a few cottages. But his and his wife's real work in those late years was to conduct a mission in their own house, on the outskirts of Chipping Norton—caring to the end for the souls of the poor.

Their priorities, as we say today, were right: but the health and comfort and status of the majority of their parishioners did not figure on their list. They followed every good movement if it were widespread, being naturally members of the majority of their clerical kind.

The Wage-earners, the Railway and the Chapel, 1842 to 1872

We left the labouring folk adjusting themselves to the new Poor

309

Law. Very few of them, possibly none, would pass their whole lives independent of relief but some would have long spells of wage-earning and, so far, of independence.

Certainly the position of the workers was now clearer. It was healthier for farmers to pay their own labourers and for labourers to be limited to a single employer whom their work must satisfy, and who might lose his best men. But in one way for many labourers and their families life was for a long time even harder than before 1834. Poor Law relief had taken note of the number of children in a family, but wages did not: the father of three, four or five children had a lower income than before. He had one resource—to encourage his employer to give work to his children and, where possible, to his wife. Thus a vicious circle was set up: low wages meant child and house-wife labour, and the employment of families prevented any upward movement of the men's pay. A man's best time as to income was while his children were young. Boys of ten or fewer years from this time earned regular wages, a few pence weekly, on farms. Fewer boys went to school than earlier, and they attended less regularly. The number of illiterate young people rose again. Small boys collected stones from the arable fields where that was thought beneficial, led horses at plough and even at harvest with loads of corn behind them, and they helped the women to weed the root crops. Long before boys were ten years of age they were left in the fields to scare birds. When schools were opened farmers would often say they could not "manage" without child labour: but the farmers within our own parish many years later accepted compulsory schooling with a good grace.

The men's wages steadied gradually when they were no longer supplemented by the overseers, settling at 6s. 6d. and 7s. The poor harvests of 1843 and 44 brought back the general misery and there was a renewal of rick-burning and other breaches of the peace, but these died away. Indeed, from the end of the fourth decade some streaks of light stray into labourers' lives from other classes. The franchise had come to some quite poor tenant-farmer neighbours. Many groups and clubs for discussion were being formed by working men in the towns and the Trade Union movement was too widespread to be successfully repressed. True, the Tolpuddle affair had shown how Trade Unions would be resisted in the villages, but in the long run what had to be permitted to the towns could not be denied to the country.

The wage-earners had in every way to recover from the worst times —not only in their economic status but in their physique and in all that aspect of life covered by the short term "morals"—in reasonable confidence in themselves and in others, in honesty, in the courage to speak their minds, in responsibility for their children and their homes. It would take a long time as well as different conditions to achieve all this: and perhaps in parts it would be for some a new achievement. Not till after 1914 would their physique do their country credit: there was some lack of sobriety in otherwise decent men till 1900 and beyond. Yet some did more than recover, achieving a high degree of responsibility in their daily work and a rare integrity of character beside the literacy and wider knowledge required by modern changes.

It must be remembered that the wage-earning group was joined sometimes by the sons of smiths and carpenters and coopers and other craftsmen when these had several children: these had not to recover from injured physique or personality. But the old shepherd and bell-ringer I knew in Shenington—gentle, sensitive and expressive—did not have these advantages; nor did the elderly man of Bledington whom I knew much later, who was still living in one of the gardenless cottages where cooking was difficult and cleanliness impossible. He had spent his childhood in another cottage, set in a garden but shared by two large families, having one bedroom each. He took me round his former home instructing me in "the way we managed". This neighbour had a true feeling for history, always trying to infer the past from stones, and implements and furrows in the fields, and— more remarkable in his circumstances which had been worse than merely poor—he was capable of understanding and sympathy for persons in many social ranks. There is literature celebrating the qualities of nineteenth century rural workers, e.g. George Sturt's account of "Bettesworth"[77] and his wife—the most realistic and detailed of all such studies. Another such book is A. G. Street's *Gentleman of the Party*.[78] An ex-farmer writing on a labourer cannot be suspected of fantasy or flattery, yet in the "Gentleman" we have a man of fastidious scruple and honour, spending a life-time on farms. But Street's great stroke of apparently unconscious realism is that though his hero and his wife maintain so high a quality their daughter becomes a prostitute and their son a criminal. Themselves they could save but their children would not accept so harsh a life.

Readers of Wordsworth will think of his countrymen—of *The*

Waggoner, with his great skill and horsemanship, of *Michael's* heroism and tragedy, of the old man living in a charitable institution among people with whom he could not talk, bereft of everything and yet finding something exquisite in life by which he could live. G. M. Young with his love of Oxford and faith in orthodox culture wrote of "Wordsworthian illusions about peasants".[80] If the qualities the poet and others saw were not illusions on what were they based? Perhaps always on severe labours directed to essential ends and on the exercise of skill, with its basic effect on minds, together with the leisure to ponder given by frequent solitude in the fields. You could as soon make a mob of shepherds and carters as of scholars from the Bodleian Library. Also, something resulted from the fact that the farm workers' horizons were so closed, so absolute, giving no possible room for ambitions, for mere dreams, only to make the best of the present, the best of a man's self as well as of his circumstances. Ambition whether on his own account or for his children must lead to risk and strain if not to despair. If a labourer's children struggled for themselves except by means of emigration it must be for many years with the same result: the *Gentleman of the Party* accepting his position was in his way successful and his children came to ruin.

Many skills among our workers were very deep in the tradition. Pre-enclosure skills were by implication belittled, but they had been in some directions highly developed, sustained by the visibility of the work done in the open field and by public comment. There had been competition, says an old writer,[81] "as who keeps their team in best order and best geared, who sows best, so that the corn comes up evenest . . . who mows best by leaving the stubble even cut . . . or has the fewest sheaves blown down after a high wind". Hereabouts there was a special skill—the building of field fires, for ashes to benefit the subtle clay. The heaps of weeds roughage and wood burned, smokeless for days, leaving small mounds of powdery ash. Marshall[82] described them in 1796 and I saw them built in 1949, to clear ancient orchards and neglected gardens. After all, the worst times had lasted not more than two generations and not all the damage was irretrievable. Most remarkable, the art of folk dance had here survived and would continue to sustain a considerable group for the best part of a century yet. The church when clerical absenteeism quite ceased could teach again the christianity of the Sermon on the Mount, and thus it may be helped the men "to keep no score of wrongs".

The long hours of the labourers' work must always be remembered. Lasting for a great part of the year through all the hours of light, they were a severe limit to improvement of life, as was also the weight of the work. The latter began to be assuaged through the improvement of tools and by machinery which was welcome in so far as it lightened work; it was in speeding up that it brought or seemed likely to bring unemployment and "the workhouse". The horse-rake was introduced, alongside the large heel-rakes, for hay-making. Grain had been tossed with shovels for the wind to blow away chaff, but gradually the winnowing-drum won its way: a man turned a wheel with a fan attached inside the drum: so much dust and pricking chaff was prevented that it was never unpopular. Flails continued to be used for threshing on small farms long after 1830, although the "threshing machine", which both threshed and winnowed the corn, had spread rapidly. There was no need for farmers to invest in it: "small" men bought them and took them from farm to farm. On more progressive farms the dibbers for sowing the grain, which had superseded the broadcaster's bag, very slowly gave way to seed-drills. John Purser of Ilmington (whose unpublished autobiography, in the absence of writings by Bledingtonians, is useful) saw corn "dibbed in" as late as 1890. Two men walked backward, with a dibber (a rod with a cone-shaped steel end) in each hand, making holes for the grain, and two women followed them dropping it in, both parties walking bent. This was one of the back-breaking tasks that were not uncommon.

Soon after 1862 Samuelson's (of Banbury) "self-delivering" reapers which "laid the sheaves off very neatly" began to be seen with their sails flying on the large farms at Churchill, and second-hand ones came later on to the Bledington farms. But always there was the combination of laboriousness with variety of work. To a modern farmer the staffs employed on the farms from the mid-century until 1914 and even after the First World War would all seem large, having declined by one-fifth from 1851 to 1914. The numbers varied: Humphrey Pegler on 187 acres had 14 labourers, while Edward Tysoe on 290 had only 9. Pegler's staff of one "man" (how many were boys?) to 13½ acres, and Tysoe's one to 32½ were the two extremes. On the six largest farms (290 to 110 acres) the average was one "man" to 21.[83] All the men worked long hours, but even so in haytime and harvest more workers were needed. Women and girls worked and, notably, young boys were given stiff and even dangerous tasks. It was common for the

313

last (they were still too small to wield the men's tools) to lead the horses from the hay and harvest fields with great loads behind. John Purser[84] gives an account of one day's work. "As a boy of thirteen" he was going to market from Ilmington to Stratford on Avon (eight miles) with three horses and a large load of grain on a heavy four wheeled waggon. On a lonely road, with no house near, a cotterpin broke and let a wheel off. Down came the load. He had to unload the sacks and then go off to get a new cotter-pin and find a man—"and still only half way to the mill". Not all accidents ended so well, with a mere "late home that night". Skill was essential from moment to moment, for the safety of man and boy. Rough and firm discipline in farming groups did not always prevent disabling accidents. And disablement meant reduced wages or, at worst, years of workhouse life.

Endurance was the quality the men must have beside skill. Good men stayed on Stows' or Jonah Hunt's Farm for twenty or thirty years: life could be tolerable there, especially when presently a hard time for farmers brought some fellow-feeling. Typical of one of these established men was John Hall, born in 1838, who worked on Stow's farm for sixty-one years as "carter and day-labourer". (He must have started at about ten years). He and his wife brought up a family of daughters one of whom became a teacher in the village school, another lived a hundred years to die known and acclaimed as a citizen of Reading: a third is our greatly respected neighbour still. When "Old Age" Pensions came in 1908 John was entitled to draw one and was urged to do so. He refused and when his friends pressed him he wept bitterly: money you hadn't worked for was charity. He would earn "as long as there was earning in him". (It may be worth remembering that John Hall's father was a blacksmith). The refusal of pensions was not for a while very uncommon. John Purser tells of a neighbour, who as a child had had to wear other families' clothes and to fetch soup for his mother from other women's kitchens who would never he declared "have a damned pension". In his own words he "couldn't bear to 'old me 'and out for it'", so sour had been the taste of charity. This feeling may well have characterised those who were sons of craftsmen or small-holders. It is connected also with a quality in Bledington men and women which was not found in all agricultural villages—a complete absence of servility, an attitude to which the asking or expectation of favours were foreign. It found active expression in frankness and indeed bluntness of speech, not always welcomed by newcomers to the village. Here there had never been a demand for low curtseys or lock-pulling or charity other than the unconditional and never-advertised gifts of friends.

There is no doubt that some labourers showed great power to rise above circumstances. Did their wives share it? After 1865 or so, there were no full-time women labourers on the farms, though women still shared some of the most laborious of the farm-work—e.g. the meticulous hoeing of turnips, and the corn "dibbling". Where cottages were small and viewless and children young, the women's life was maybe harder day by day than the men's work afield. Many of them had their skills, careful of every ha'penny and of every wild edible that did not require sugar. Very rarely, one might have such a special skill as did John Hall's wife, who made print bonnets, caned, frilled and gophered—the folk-wear of the day—for women in Bledington and Stow.

When the family enjoyed a fair cottage and had some slight economic good fortune, such as after 1850 a son's or husband's spell of railway work, they could make a home with some small comforts, with pictures on the walls and a book or two, as in Fred Hall's—a Bible, *Pilgrim's Progress* and *The Altar and the Household*, a book of readings and prayers for family use. No doubt the wives missed for the most part, the effect on the men's spirits of the wide views from the high land, of the quiet and the natural variety of the fields, and had little compensation in that kind at least from their small children, poorly fed and frustrated.

Life for families was often difficult. The reason why one can discover so little as to when and how many labouring boys and young men emigrated to the towns and to other countries is that often boys never came back and some communicated only once or not at all with their parents. It was different with girls, who went less far. The unmarried daughter or the one who married a railwayman was the hope of parents for an old age spent outside the workhouse, in dependence made tolerable by family feeling.

The women shared with the men the comfort of religion and of the companionship of church and chapel. For twenty five years Mrs John Hall gave the church a thorough weekly clean for sixpence and "would ha' done it for nothing if the church-wardens 'adn't 'ad the money". It would not have been possible for a Methodist family to have prayers before the men went out at half-past six in the morning[85]

315

unless the wife and mother had greatly wished it.

We have gone ahead somewhat and must return to trace two other changes which affected the workers' condition. The view that field gardens or "allotments" could make a great contribution to their lives (expounded and resisted in the first third of the century) has been mentioned. In 1831 the Labourers' Friend Society had been founded, chiefly to advocate the provision of allotments. Its members were mainly landowners, some of them noblemen and clergy, among whom were a few bishops, including our own, of Gloucester. "His Most Gracious Majesty" King William IV headed the list for a few years. One of the Society's activities was to hold small meetings "under distinguished patronage" in county after county. It also published a little periodical and report *The Labourer's Friend*, outstanding contributions to which were made by the Bishop of Bath and Wells who had no fewer than five hundred tenants of allotments on his episcopal estates. His Grace had seen in his youth the ill effects of enclosures in Westmorland "from Penrith to Solway Firth" and in one of his first cures in 1806 he had started a small allotments scheme and seen men become "more regular, more industrious, more content": those who had been in receipt of relief needed it no longer. The success of the field-gardens on his episcopal estate had, he said, "satisfied every wish", of his generous heart. But the true base of the Bishop's views lay in his religion. "God", he said, "has made of one blood all the nations and all the classes of people upon the face of the earth". Thus no man and no class existed merely to support another. For many this was still a revolutionary view.

Around this seemingly innocent plan to allow a man to dig for his family after an eleven or twelve hour day on the fields, battles in an old war of theory still raged. Some held that a man would be made weary for his employer's work and would feel an independence which would not accord with his divinely appointed place. Nor did exponents of this view add the corollary that he must receive a share of the produce of the fields he tilled sufficient adequately to shelter and feed him. However, the Bishop of Bath threw down a bridge to these opponents. "Protection and encouragement are required from the higher orders; the labour of their hands from the lower; thus are we all brethren one of another". Brotherhood on such terms was acceptable to many. It was often possible for the clergy to encourage the use of "charitable" land for gardens and a usual view among them was

316

that labourers might without harm to their employers have one-sixteenth of an acre (ten poles) on which to grow vegetables, on the strict understanding that no produce was sold. In Bledington the only land in public control was the six acres of furze-land allotted to the poor at enclosure which were the responsibility of the churchwardens. Furze had little value as fuel and by 1840 coal was reaching the villages. The Vicar, Oakley Hill, encouraged the wardens—so says his son—to offer the land to cottagers and this was done: in what year is not known One may ask the relation of six acres to the need. From 1811 to 1841 there were not fewer than 40 farm labourers: in 1851 the Census Report gives the figure of 50. Ten years later the number is 68, but there had been an increase: the total population numbered only 5 more than in 1841; the new figure in fact included a number of young boys and one woman. By 1850 homes had neither multiplied nor improved. The crowded cottages were still and would long remain in full use. At least one cottage, sometimes 2 or 3, were being shared wherever we have figures. In 1841 two men and in 1851 two men and a woman lived "in barns, sheds or the like". Wages permitted of little expenditure on food other than bread.

How much of all this was known to the Chapter and Senior Common Room of Christ Church we cannot know, but in their earnest effort to serve their parishes they had responded very generously to the teaching of the Labourer's Friends. The theory that there should be a limit of ten poles was not for them. They were willing and anxious to provide holdings large enough for a cow or pigs, as very generous landlords occasionally did. When at last in 1854 a suitable farm—Kiln Farm or Micklands fell vacant, the whole 75 acres was set aside. But to make a success of a field-garden, let alone a small meadow, capital and equipment are required. It had been clearly shown in many villages that a pig was the necessary complement of even a quarter-acre allotment. Without the animal spare potatoes and other vegetables could not be used, and without the by-product, manure, the soil ceased to be fertile. And when that happened the rent for the plot could not be paid. Among the crowded cottages of Bledington pigsties were an impossibility, and in fact only one of the seven fields of Kiln Farm appears to have been used. Maps of the parish show till 1922 this field and the "Poor's Plot", as still used in that way. There were about a dozen allotments.

The tale of the allotments may be briefly told till the end. About

1880 an enterprising man chose Bledington as the centre in which to build up a business as corn chandler and bacon curer and to these added other small matters such as the offer of a small and convenient meadow for gardens. But this land was sold after ten years. It was not till 1914 that the working men put forward their own demands for allotments. By that time their Parish Council had powers to rent land for the purpose. The men declared they would no longer cross the muddy fields in winter, nor yet go the long mile round to the Poor's Plot. But no land was available.[87] A year or two later private enterprise afforded eight acres within easy access of homes and these continued in use as allotments till 1965, after all the publicly and charitably provided ones had ceased to be used.

There are no stories of labourers evolving into successful farmers from allotments but certainly wives and children profited. Even by 1914 farm wages had not risen so as to permit a family a sound diet, nor to pay the rent for a sound cottage with a good garden: allotments were still essential.

In 1872 there arose in our own wider district and from the mind and spirit of the workers themselves a strong movement to remedy their own condition. But as to the economic gain of Bledington families—important though not great—the main cause was of urban and commercial origin. During the fifth decade railways were "ironing all England". In 1845 an Act of Parliament was obtained for the establishment of the Oxford Worcester and Wolverhampton Railway which would not only convey passengers from Oxford, but also much local freight to various towns in the Black Country, on small subsidiary lines. The railway would run beside the Evenlode river from Oxford to Kingham, passing between that village and Bledington. Unfortunately the Railway Company was badly administered throughout its career. Since it was often on the brink of bankruptcy and chose to quarrel often and violently with its great precursor, neighbour and source of capital, the Great Western Railway, its works were from time to time seriously interrupted.

When news of the projected line reached Bledington, everyone expected change. Railways, with their special tracks and steam engines, were far more revolutionary than turnpike roads or coaches had been, and they would clearly cut through the country at more frequent intervals than could canals. The last had been almost entirely concerned with goods. On railways everyone would be free to travel: the special provision for the poor, open trucks with seats, would be far cheaper and less laborious than any other means of travel they had had. The farmers considered what new markets would be open to them and how much less it would cost them to send their corn and meat and small products to comparatively distant towns. Active young workers confidently expected a chance of jobs. Though the great contractors employed Irishmen and North Country men, there were sub-contractors for smaller works and presently there would be permanent jobs on the finished lines. Building the track and laying the first lines was heavy work and involved absence from home, but the wages were better than those offered on the farms. The work was at first not constant.

Some of the technical and labour problems interested everyone. There was notably the long war of the gauges, of which an acute phase occurred on the O.W. & W.R. The Company had undertaken to lay broadgauge rails, so that G.W. trains could run over them, but in spite of the terms of its Act, it only laid them in combination with narrow gauge and even so disputed every short length. This problem was of the mechanical type which would soon affect so much of life. Others had more human aspects. There was the battle of Mickleton tunnel[88] thirteen miles down the line from Kingham, which excited all the neighbouring districts. It was more like a struggle in the American mid-west than in the sober English Midlands, more dramatic than the local skirmishes in the Civil War. The tunnel had been started in 1846, but there had been troubles with contractors. Work had been stopped in 1849, and not resumed till two years later, when a new Contractor undertook it. But he too found the Company's management unsatisfactory. When he and his men threw down their tools, but remained in their places, the Company decided to take possession. Marchant the contractor and his navvies took up stations to hold the tunnel. The time neared the week-end, best even then for getting a sight of events. On Friday the Company's men tried to turn off the defenders by force and there were blows. Meanwhile the chief engineer of the line, the famous Brunel, arrived with a large body of reinforcements. Someone sent for local magistrates, and Brunel postponed action. The next (Saturday) morning two J.P.'s, Gloucestershire worthies, arrived with a body of the newly established police, armed (so the story goes) with cutlasses. Perhaps no-one greatly feared or relied on the new Police. At all events the magistrates read the Riot Act twice, but the two sides still threatened each other. Meanwhile the Company had offered the work to the firm of Peto and Betts who employed large bodies of men which they switched from one job, and one line, to another. Peto and his force marched across from Warwick, turning up late on Saturday intending to take up the tunnelling on Monday. The navvies could hardly be prevented from joining the engineer's force: they were accustomed to getting quickly down to work, to earn good money. During the Sunday night Peto gathered more men from other works, who arrived at three o'clock in the morning of Monday. The attacking force was large enough to dispose itself partly at the Evesham end of the tunnel and partly at the hither end, towards Kingham and Bledington, and even divided, hoped to over-awe Marchant and his men by numbers and settle the matter before the magistrates could return. There was a battle at both ends, hopeless for the defenders. Police arrived but quailed before the sight. Heads and limbs were broken and one man produced a pistol, but before he could use it (supposing he meant to do so) someone knocked him down with a spade. That was the sign for the end: Marchant's handful could not resist two thousand. Sanity reigned and a parley took place, interrupted briefly by excitement as a detachment of troops from Coventry marched up—only to march back again.

By the time, early in 1853, that the tunnel was completed the rest of the line was more or less in readiness for use and its opening to traffic was fixed for a day in April. But the Inspector from the Board of Trade, summoned just before the great day to give his approval, refused to give it because signals and points were lacking. The directors ate their festive dinner, but there was stillness on the railway. A second time the Inspector found objections but the line was at last opened in June 1853.

The O.W. & W. Railway had endeared itself to the neighbourhood: it is charming and relieving to find even greater incompetence than one's own. The name given to it, "The Old Worse and Worse" was always used with a smile: it continued for a long time to be fitting. The second-hand defective engines bought led to frequent break-downs. But yet there were some trains and the possibility of coming and going. Its influence on the village became steady and pervasive. Individual lives were often greatly changed.

Stow on the Wold and Chipping Norton, especially Stow, lay too high for the main line to approach them, but the Norton folk wanted a connection, and perhaps looked forward to an ultimate line from the O.W. & W.R. through to Banbury, already on the main Great Western line to Birmingham. Local money was enthusiastically raised[89] and £10,000 offered towards a single branch line to run from what is now Kingham Station to Norton: the contractor Peto offered the rest, and built the line, opened in 1855. The halt in Kingham parish became in due time Kingham Junction. Presently the line from Chipping Norton to Banbury was built.

In 1861 Theophilus Haddock Pegler was asked to sell land for a new line from Kingham Junction westwards to Bourton on the Water. The line was built and presently extended to Cheltenham. Thus it was in due time possible within a mile of Bledington to board trains going south to London, north to Birmingham or Crewe, west to Cheltenham and east to Banbury and beyond. This did not have the effect of causing Kingham or Bledington to grow to any marked extent, though in the future it would cause their population to become more varied.

In 1862 the O.W. & W.R. ceased to exist: it had been taken over by the Great Western Railway, a line of very different traditions, less risky and much less amusing, but a place on its staff was well worth having.

For the present the most traceable effects of railways on our village relate to employment. Many plate-layers were required for the successive extensions on the line: most of the Bledington railwaymen were for a long time in this rank. How many of them there were is not clear till 1861. In the census figures of 1851 we found three men called plainly "labourers": it is possible that these were working on the line. In 1861 eight railway workers were named, seven as "labourers": what the eighth did does not appear. These figures are not of course, a full measure of the effect: a number of young men may well have left home more or less permanently joining Peto and other contractors, or going to stations along the line for other employment.

We shall see presently that for the girls of Bledington also the railway was important. There was now for them only one way of earning a living—by going into domestic service. There were a few "situations" (the word used) in the village itself. In 1851 there were eleven women servants, children's and other nurses not included. (The age of one "servant" was 10 years). Employers' names were given and it is clear that the "places" were mostly in daughterless farmhouses. One farming family kept two servants and the Bledington Grounds family two, beside a children's nurse.

In the marriage register we find that of the 52 women married in the sixteen years from 1855 to 1870 (inclusive) 42 were domestic servants. Of the others, one was a housekeeper and two dressmakers. For the remainder no occupation is given: they were doubtless "girls at home", farmers' daughters.

The servant-brides were for the most part employed away from home in large outlying farmhouses or in towns. Their holidays were few and short, but unlike many of their brothers, they kept in touch with home, an important fact for their families. They could and did bring their "foreign" bridegrooms home for the wedding. From 1870 the occupations of brides cease to be given for many years but we learn the status of their fathers and their grooms, and see thereby the importance to young women of the railway. From 1875 to 1911 eight bridegrooms of a total of 89 are railwaymen—three plate-layers, two engine-drivers, a signalman, a porter, and a "railway servant". Most of these are second-generation railwaymen, their fathers' rank very various, from gangers to stationmasters. They are not Bledingtonians, but come chiefly from villages on the main and branch lines. The brides too had their own railway connections. Altogther ten of them in these years are daughters of railwaymen, their fathers' work varying very much as does the railwaymen-grooms'. A number of the fathers must have taken to railway work when the lines were first constructed. Some of the posts, those of signalmen, guards, engine-drivers and stationmasters were more responsible, and better paid than others; railways gave a hope the farms hardly offered at all, for young men profitably to change their jobs.

There was another worth while gain in the form of good new clothes and these a uniform they could take pride in. The Great Western Railway was worth good work: the men developed high standards of skill, service and responsibility, and moreover genial and kindly manners. Kingham Station became worth a visit for its strict order and the beauty of its gardens. (What explains the difference between those gardens a generation since and their ugly unkemptness in 1970?)

Events of a different nature ran parallel to the coming and development of the railway. In 1847 John Benfield whom we knew earlier as unemployed and three other men applied for his cottage to be licensed as a meeting-place for dissenters. Already in 1835 a near relative of John's had licensed his cottage at Bould for Methodist meetings. The Benfields were, or rather are, a fairly old family here. They had talents for music and dance, and were sound workmen. His cottage was one of those formed out of the Stayts' farm out-houses. Here in the single ground-floor room services were held, the tiny group sang, heard sermons, and knelt beside their chairs to pray. Any action other than vocal must soon have become impossible for their numbers grew.

The names of the group other than Benfield were recent in the village: probably one or more of the men had come from a Methodist group elsewhere. Soon the Wesleyan authorities recognised the group as a Methodist Society. It became essential to have a chapel, not only for adults' worship but to house a Sunday School. Five years after their first license in 1852 the building, in what soon came to be known as "Chapel Lane", (the old name for the walk past the church being no longer in use) was completed. It was 26 feet by 20, built of brick and cost £150. How this immense sum was raised no-one knows. Forty years later their successors would raise over £250, from their own wages, by special works of various kinds and by begging from all and sundry.

The little group proved themselves fully capable of conducting their Society. Their worship was as orderly as it was enthusiastic and the Sunday School prospered. Reading must have been taught to the children there, at home or by Mrs Benfield. It was almost impossible to be illiterate among them: Wesley's Hymn Book and the Bible were the basis of their religious life. Thus, they not only had letters but also literature and language and ideas. Cheap Bibles were obtainable: no home, no packed box of young man or woman going away was complete without one.

As for interpretation of what they read, they were not left entirely alone. The Minister of the Stow "circuit" visited them and preached to them occasionally and their "local" preachers had to pass tests. Nevertheless, they had little of dogma. The year they built their chapel, the Vicar opened his day and Sunday Schools. He himself said he feared the Methodist influence, but they do not appear to have feared his: their children attended his day school for a year or two before they went on to the farms.

Country labourers had long been taught by their superiors in rank to look for rest and compensation for all troubles to a life beyond the grave and Wesley himself led his followers to put their spiritual salvation and religious practice so far first that they had few political thoughts and no plans. And yet Methodist ways certainly threatened the view of the ideal village that had come to be cherished in so many minds—of a squire and vicar administering the community, or—lacking a squire—a gentleman-vicar doing so alone, with farmers and tradesmen kindly patronised and genially though humbly responsive; and under all an obedient, lowly class of labourers and female servants. But Methodists were nurtured on the history of another people than their own, not taught to them but read for themselves, a people whose prophets were sometimes peasants and whose kings had tended asses or sheep. They were all brothers and sisters together even if the sisters might only occupy the lesser offices. Even the Minister came among them as a brother. Their chapel was the only public place where they were not subordinate and could enjoy social warmth as well as responsibility and many-sided activity. But it should be said that the chapel drew to itself only about half of the labouring families. Reporting to Christ Church on the state of the parish in 1857 the Vicar wrote of twenty farm workers as frequenting it, but this may well have been an understatement and at times of festival the little chapel was crowded.

Vivified religion together with the generosity of parallel lay movements was permeating society by many channels. One may think of George Eliot's Adam Bede, published in 1859, treating of "simple" village folk as of equal interest with their middle-class neighbours, of the country clergy such as the Rev. Lord Sydney Godolphin Osborne,[90] Charles Kingsley, Canon Girdlestone,[91] and the Rev. C. W. Stubbs,[92] all of whom saw village conditions and believed their own eyes. But before they could influence events the attention of the public had to be attracted—dragged—to rural workers' needs.

Arch's Movement

Bledington men still tell how when they were boys their elders told them how they had been stone-breaking on the road when Joseph Arch walked past or how they had gone to huge meetings in Ascott, Milton or Chipping Norton. In our neighbouring villages of Warwickshire and Oxfordshire there occurred early and outstanding events in the last and most widespread "revolt" of rural labourers, that of 1872-3. The word suggests an unorganised, ill-regulated struggle, doing some injustice. The causes were poverty, long hours of work (in winter all the daylight hours), miserable cottages and tyrannical restrictions, e.g. employers' objection to the men having allotments or keeping a pig or fowls. This time the aims of the leaders were more considered and the national climate much less adverse than in 1830: there were men who were literate and vocal though others remained unlettered and ignorant. Work and journeys on the railways, the penny post, the cheapening of newspapers, the increased proficiency of reporters all modified the situation. But the country workers' position was still very weak, for lack of good feeling and information, and their only political influence lay in the charitable interest of educated, humane men. The same conditions ruled all over the country except where there were many smallholdings and in the neighbourhood of urban industry in need of labour. There had been earlier trouble in Norfolk and Herefordshire.

The main objects of the "revolt" were simple—to get less miserable weekly wages and reasonable hours of work, better cottages, and gardens or "allotments" the men could till for themselves. A secondary object was to assist men to move away to industry or overseas: that would be profitable for them and raise the value of those left at home. The leaders had before them a clear pattern of the means by which all this might be done—a Trade Union such as those which were improving the lot of townsmen.

The very first event in the movement was a letter to a local paper. A few labourers of a Warwickshire village whose wages left them starving when the weather was bad had appealed to a neighbour, a joiner and a member of a Trade Union. Henry Taylor wrote for them a letter to the Leamington Chronicle showing that the men and their families almost as soon as rain set in must starve or go into the workhouse. The letter brought in gifts of money (about nine shillings for each family) and they were tided over the bad patch. A small group of men of two other villages, Barford and Wellesbourne, who read the letter went similarly to another workman not dependent on a single farmer-employer. Joseph Arch[93] had been a farmworker since he left school at ten years but by his middle-age he was a champion hedge-cutter and also skilled and strong at field drainage work. He worked independently by contract, seldom in his own village but travelling from farm to farm over considerable distances.

These two men, Arch and Taylor, became leaders in a local movement, both going on later to spread the fire over wider districts. Arch became a national figure. He had many qualifications to represent the farm workers and to give them acceptable and companionable leadership. He had experienced every aspect of their troubles—early labour, boyish humiliation by the segregation of "smock frocks" in the church, resentment at some of the customs of the "parson's school", the long hours and the low wages, and the harshness of the Poor Law.

Without advantages he could not have served his less fortunate neighbours, but they were not such as to divide him from them. His good cottage was his own by inheritance. As a child he had been well fed largely on produce from the half-acre garden behind the home cottage. His school had not altogether failed him: the master had taught him some arithmetic and elementary mensuration. His greatest good fortune lay in his family, especially it seems, in its women. Both his mother and his grandmother were strong women, standing over six feet. His mother had encouraged him to read and learn after his schooldays and spoke to him of many matters with good sense. The Bible was read in his home and a little Shakespeare. As a youth Arch joined the Methodist Church and became a local preacher. His journeys took him into Wales, where he attended chapels and was welcomed as a preacher. The Welsh, more fortunate than English country folk, had lost neither freedom not fluency of speech and Arch seems to have learned from them: at all events he had had much practice in formulating his thoughts and in making his voice heard. In his later life Arch was not able to take full advantage of all his opportunities, e.g. as a Member of Parliament: they took him too far from his base. Yet he could learn from his travels, there is evidence that he had great native discernment and balance. His phrases could be as terse as the Latin quotations of the classically educated: best evidence perhaps of both intelligence and of good basic education (if education is preparation for life) was his permanent consciousness that the enemy and he shared a common humanity: he spoke harsh truths harshly but was never a hater.

In the movement to which he gave the first powerful impetus the Bledington men would take no prominent part, but they knew at once its importance and took a deep and excited interest in it, attending meetings, reading and discussing reports and comments in the Oxford, Cheltenham and Gloucester papers. But they threw up no leader:

once again our village was to be on the outskirts of events. There were fifty or more labourers—a large enough group. Their circumstances were usual enough yet there must have been some difference between our village and those where events were more stirring. Perhaps it lay in the smaller acreage of farms. Certainly these were on the whole larger in the villages "under Wychwood". Some of our farmers owned their land, none were subject to large landowners. At any rate, there was little acerbity here between masters and men: there was no very deep social gulf. It was the time when education was becoming universal and compulsory in the country, to the disgust and anxiety of some farmers: but ours were themselves pressing for a Board school, to which they would send their own children, and which they would support with conscience and at times with friendly encouragement. There had been a change at the Vicarage. The Reverend John Ashford Hartshorne M.A. was a "Broad" churchman and much concerned with the social relevance of Christianity. He had been struck by the way social conditions outside were reflected within the church, labourers and their families being confined to benches at the back and in the aisle, while others sat in pews. He was himself a poor man, relatively, with no private income and a stipend of about £160: perhaps he tried to imagine life on an income at its best a sixth of his own, and so insecure as to be far less in rainy weather.

When Arch was approached by his neighbours the chief question he discussed with them was whether the men were ready—ready to combine, to organise, to pay subscriptions, to hold on. Farm by farm, village by village, they were helpless. The explosive moment, it seemed had come: at his first meeting he spoke to over a thousand men, summoned without a placard or a written notice. At, say, fifty labourers per village attending they had gathered from a large area. In the weeks immediately following Arch, Taylor and other speakers held meetings on village greens all over South Warwickshire and then went on to North Oxon. Often the meetings were immense (It is not possible to understand the movement without realising that the men were habituated to trudging many miles over wet fields: the first meeting had been held in February).

Arch had no need to convince his hearers of their own case: he could devote his speeches to extending their view of the difficulties of their situation. Tenant farmers were not free: liable to twelve months' notice to leave their holdings, they dare not have a view of their own, political or religious, nor could they safely invest money or begin an enterprise. It was true that losses of the farmers were pressed down on labourers, but gains were called up to landlords as rent. The farm labourers' Union had landlords as well as farmers to fight. So went Arch's argument.

What made this the right moment for the effort? There was no single great cause: discernible reasons can only be arranged at random. The second Franchise Act had been passed some five years earlier; schools had been opened in a majority of villages; there was a fair sprinkling of Methodists, i.e. men who had received sound "adult education"; in some parishes garden allotments had been provided, which meant better feeding, more stamina. (In 1870 New Zealand mutton was first sold in Milton under Wychwood and doubtless in other large villages).

The pace of organisation was admirable. In Arch's own neighbourhood a Union had been formed within a fortnight of the first meeting, and in six weeks, a number of village unions joined to form in a single one for the county. In May at a great meeting in Leamington the National Farm Labourers' Union was formed. Here other hopeful factors in the situation became evident. The delegates from the villages wore smocks and hob-nailed boots; the "platform" was differently dressed. Among the speakers were an aristocrat (Auberon Herbert); another M.P. (George Dixon of Birmingham); a Congregational minister; a local doctor and a business man, philanthropist and social student (Jesse Collings). Further, this and other meetings were fully reported by the Leamington Chronicle whose editor gave enthusiastic support to the movement, becoming its Teasurer. Journalists as a profession tended to be stirred by the human situation they saw and even when aiming at impartiality between the sides gave the publicity that was bound to help. All this showed the stirred sympathies, the tenderer conscience and the greater variety of outlook of the nineteenth century.

News of the meetings reached the London *Daily News* early: famous war correspondent Archibald Forbes was sent to report them and his articles brought money to the new Union, and publicity to the reactions of farmers and landlords. The latter varied: in a single village the largest owner gave notice to all his workmen-tenants who joined the Union that they must leave their cottages, but another (a woman) called in an arbitrator between herself and her men and raised their wages as he recommended. Lord Leigh, nearby, lived up to and improved upon the mild reputation of his ancestors, once Lords of the Manor of Bledington: he raised the wages of his workers to fifteen shillings.

The attitude of the farmers was more important; on the whole it was they who paid the wages. Late in 1872 the Oxford Journal had reluctantly followed the London press so far as to recognise that the new movement had some importance. It had long since ceased to be a critic of the "establishment" and speakers at the Union meetings were never reported at all fully. What it did thoroughly was to show the attitude of the farmers. It was springtime and there was urgent work to do. Their choice in South Warwickshire looked uncomfortable— put up wages or have the men absent "on strike". At meetings in Corn Exchanges, at Chambers of Agriculture, wherever a number of farmers met, they passed resolutions deprecating "combination which would foster discord between men and employers", and urged individual farmers to dissuade men from joining the Union. At one large meeting, reported on March 23rd 1873,[94] and later on many other occasions farmers threatened to "throw out the whole body of labourers". An editorial noted that "with few exceptions farmers were bent on resisting the demands of the Union". Often farmers talked of the men's "excessive demands tending to set class against class". Education in village schools was discussed. It was a "misnomer to call that education which ignored . . . the duty to the Creator" and of the labourers to other classes: education in village schools was too elaborate—the Revised Code "set the standard too high".[95] At one meeting a practical man recommended the formation of companies to buy and let out steam-power machines to defeat the labourers, but it was easier and might be quicker to threaten to discharge all their workers who had joined the Union, on the ground that it was supporting men on strike: such threats were frequent and sometimes carried out. Some farmers were willing to give an advance of one or two shillings in the weekly wage to non-Union men. Our farmers raised wages by two shillings without this condition. The story is told of a Bledington worker who one Saturday evening threw eleven shillings into his wife's lap, crying out "Missus! We shall never be short of money again!" As a rule the most unsympathetic farmers were those of broad acres who had large elegant homes, were sending their daughters to boarding schools and in general were tending away from village life and their labourers.

Sometimes resistant farmers were urged to take longer and more humane views. At the Oxfordshire Agricultural Society's dinner in May 1873 the Senior County Member of Parliament, an old man and a favourite, urged the farmers to "meet the men in a fair and liberal spirit". He remembered the troubles of 1830. In the Swing Riots the County had avoided the disgrace of a Special Commission. Then wages had risen from eight shillings to ten. He bade his audience remember that a man like an animal worked the better for being fed: and further, it had been proved that where better wages were paid, labour costs were lower. Supply and demand would settle much: the supply of labour was declining.

The President of the Society went so far in a short speech as to admit that "in some parts wages were unquestionably low" and that the price of provisions had risen. Things "could not have gone on much longer". The labourer was not an ambitious man, he said: give him a good cottage and increase the number of allotment holdings at a fair rent. (At that point there were cries of "No! No! That won't do"). But the President had no good words for the Union: it fostered and lengthened strikes and created "disaffection". When their Member spoke of a reduced supply of labour some of the diners must have called to mind a report from the Wellesbourne area shortly before. The Executive of the Union were finding work for discharged men. Contractors for the new railways in New Zealand would take any number, who need not possess a penny. Waterworks, factories and dockyards in the north offered work. Groups of agricultural workers with their families were preparing to leave Fenny Compton and other villages for Brazil[96]—a new destination; seven Methodist families left Fifield for New Zealand;[97] two Shipton families went down on the *Cospatrick* in 1874. There were well-known rumours that pay and conditions in America and Canada were attractive: a letter in the Journal from a Nebraskan farmer set out the facts for his area very convincingly:[98] day workers could earn as much in a day there as in a week at home. Both men and girls could earn excellent wages and be boarded too.

Conference and reason between employers and employed were lacking. In August there was strife nearby. At Wootton, ten miles from Oxford, there was first a strike and then a more extensive lockout. Three hundred men from the area came in procession to the Martyrs' Memorial,[99] headed by a band, and there held a meeting.

Farmers had refused to meet the 180 Union Members of Wootton and had determined to discharge every one of them: 120 were already out of work, as well as others at Tackley and the Bartons. Speakers ranged further afield, speaking of conditions in general. In Dorset workers were bound "hand and foot" in tied cottages. Nearby the Duke of Marlborough was "transferring cottages and allotments to the farmers to strengthen them against the workers".

The next news of Wootton was that soldiers had been sent from Aldershot to help get in the harvest—a bitter pill for the men. The secretary of the Union declared that but for the soldiers the workers would have persuaded the farmers to go to arbitration. However there had been "the devil of a row" in Parliament about the soldiers. At the local protest meeting Henry Taylor urged the men to look to Parliament for permanent redress: they must be determined to get the franchise.

Sympathy for the labourers tended to be remote. Sometimes shopkeepers (who knew their circumstances only too well; many were deeply in debt to them) were friendly, but farmers rarely; and the church, they felt, was against them: the parish clergy taught them, they said, to be content with misery and dependence. And not only the parish clergy; locally the new Bishop of Oxford, Bishop John Fielder Mackarness, devoted his first address to his clergy to an unkind attack on nonconformists.[100] He denied to their ministers and preachers "the validity of their call", and that was a large theological matter, but he went on to accuse them of filching "promising sons of the church" and to taunt the ministers with desiring a social equality with the parish clergy which nothing, not even a revolution, would give them! (A discouraging speech to any of his clergy who tended to look for harmony in the villages). On the other side of us Bishop Ellicott of Gloucester had ensured his fame among the labourers by an unlucky speech in the early days of the agitation in which he quoted an old mischievous saying "Don't nail their ears to the pump and don't duck them in the horse-pond". But Arch, who naturally took this as having reference to himself, dealt with that. Speaking in Gloucester he referred to the Bishop's "unorthodox belief in adult baptism"[101] one poor joke deserved another. The Bishop had the great grace to change: speaking the next year at Stow on the Wold to the clergy of the rural deanery which included Bledington, he said the clergy should stay out of disputes, but encourage the payment of equitable wages and the improvement of cottages. The Church was, he said, the Church of the poor as well as of the rich: the country clergy "had been ever the true friends of the rural poor".[102] Good resolutions for the future are often couched in historical terms. Religion at this time had an importance in the "climate" of village life which it is not easy, now, to grasp. To be cut off from a church was to be largely an outsider: hence in part the social importance of village clergy.

It is sometimes said that the labourers' movement mixed religion and economics overmuch. Since the Bible was for many their only source of fine phrase and literary rhythm it was natural they should use its terms. They undoubtedly spoke sometimes as if Australia or New Zealand were heaven: but then a man who had only misery here, and no higher hope than a shilling or two more as a railway porter could go to New Zealand, build his own house, become a farmer and have for example (as John Purser did) a prosperous milk business. Mr Dunbabin[103] tells of a speaker who said that God would send angels to see how old folk lived on three shillings a week. But that was truly prophetic: in the course of time, He did; the pensions promised in 1908 were worth more. Certainly Arch and Taylor were not at all confused: they had quite clear the two directions; down to earth and up to heaven. Livelihood was the topic of the Union meetings held in the marquee the Milton men would shortly acquire to accommodate their large meetings. The life of the soul was the business of the religious meetings some of them held in it on Sundays.

Winter was naturally a quiet time for the Union. With the spring weather of 1873 the leaders had extended their operations into our immediate neighbourhood. Meetings were held in Chipping Norton, in Woodstock and in the villages "under Wychwood". In Ascott and Milton there were already some Union members. The meetings in both these villages were immense. Arch is said to have spoken to 2,000 people: men must have come from very far. In his local speeches so near to the Gloucestershire borders Arch talked of our county. Bledington men heard of the wages paid in their own and other Gloucestershire villages. Their lives were described: halfway through their thirteen hour summer day men were "no better than a wrung-out dishcloth": not a married man but was in debt to the village shop.

In May our area presented a short drama to the nation—its action all in low-life but vivid and to many, somewhat shocking. After a Union meeting in April, the day labourers at Ascott under Wychwood demanded that wages should be raised by two shillings a week. The account we have of the events in the first act of the play is that given by the farmers in a letter to the Times.[104] The chief of these was Robert Hambidge (sic) an active, keen farmer of 400 acres, an important character, though mostly off-stage. It would appear that wages were usually ten shillings. Hambidge consented to give an extra two shillings to some men, but not to the older or "infirm" ones. This proposal he made "in a most friendly manner". Readers of the farmers' letter and of many other documents are struck by the high interest expected upon the investment of a little courtesy (one may often note this expectation). But men learning to co-operate could hardly so instantaneously abandon their weaker brethren, and on the next Monday morning the men did not appear.

Hambidge was content with the offer he had made and his neighbours followed him in it. The men had left him "in the middle of a backward barley-sowing", with his twelve draught horses and four working bullocks, his superior flock of 500 sheep at turnips, "and milking cows, bullocks and young stock". But he was not without resource: his shepherd and a young yearly servant were still at work and a day or two after the strike began he "borrowed" two men from a relative five miles away. And then, with, it seems, all his fellow-farmers, he rode off early in the morning to Stow Horse Fair. They felt they had good reason to suppose the strike would soon be over. There were about seventy labourers in Ascott and its 1700 acres were divided into seven or eight farms, relatively large for this area. There were no residents more well-to-do than Robert Hambidge, nor had there ever been a resident lord or landowner. The Vicar had recently deplored this lack to his Bishop, as the cause of an unruly quality his parishioners sometimes showed. It is said that the poor of other villages that had been within the Forest also kept a certain rough independence and herein were superior to villages further out. It is certain that Ascott retained its ancient dances and games in exceptional vigour.

The farmers of Ascott were a comradely body. They rode to fairs together; they agreed on a common policy towards the strikers. (They would pay able-bodied men the same wage as had been agreed on by a group of nearby large-scale landowners—twelve shillings a week—and also piecework should be available for those who chose it). It is to be noted that they signed their letter to the Times in a curious way. With each name, they gave the public office each occupied—

Churchwarden, Waywarden, Guardian of the Poor, Overseer, Feoffee of the Ascott charity. When they called a "parish meeting" to consider the men's demands it was like a vestry meeting The pattern is that of Bledington at the time: with the land, they had inherited or assumed from the old commoners the community responsibilities which had been borne by them and their like for centuries. Hambidges were worthy folk (I was well acquainted with a member— of the next generation), genial within the circle of families sharing their interests. But they were not imaginative and had not noticed that farmers were no longer the major part of the community.

On the eventful day Hambidge's two borrowed men set out from his house but at the gateway into the field where their work lay they encountered a large group of women, wives (nearly all of them) of labourers, two or three of them carrying sticks. The women urged them not to work, not to be blacklegs, and waved their sticks, but finally invited them to a drink at the inn. The men, or rather the eighteen year old workers, gave up trying to enter the field and returned to the farmhouse to get instructions, accompanied by the women who "jostled" them somewhat. The master had ridden off to Stow Fair and the poor young men dared not face the women again, nor yet the master without having done their day's work. When at last they ventured out, accompanied by a police constable, they saw nothing of the foe. Such was the central act of the odd play.

Hambidge decided to prosecute the women. The nearest magistrate, the Vicar of Shipton, tried to dissuade him, but failed. On Wednesday May 17th the women were summoned before the magistrates—only two of them—at Chipping Norton. Both were vicars—one of Shipton and one from Swerford on the other side of Chipping Norton. Sixteen women, two of them with young babies, were convicted of "assault and intimidation" and of "unlawfully molesting and obstructing" the two labourers. Some were sentenced to ten days in prison with hard labour and the others similarly, but for seven days only.

Word had gone around the countryside that the women were to be tried and a great crowd had gathered round the police station. Many of the "rioters" wore badges of blue ribbon—the sign of Union membership. The crowd expected to see the women brought out to go to Oxford by rail, but the Police feared they would be "rescued" and kept them hidden. It grew late, and the train had gone; then the crowd stoned the police station and a constable's house; windows

334

were broken. (Jackson's Journal bore witness that the ringleaders in this action were not wearing the Union badge). The Mayor came and threatened to read the Riot Act but did not need to. It was Wednesday and after midnight the crowd ceased to exist: it had become weary, hungry individuals, thinking of the long trudge home and the next day's early start. At two in the morning Oxford police drove up in a "brake" and took the women, babies and all, to Oxford prison.

Again the Times and the Daily News had sent reporters; the matter was raised in the House of Commons—"by certain officious members" Jackson's Journal said. The Journal was firmly behind the clerical magistrates who had acted, it said "strictly in accordance with the law". They were supported also by the Lord Lieutenant, the Duke of Marlborough, who had shown himself to farmers a liberal land-owner; and he forwarded also a testimonial to the magistrates signed by "298 occupiers of land and others" from 29 Oxfordshire parishes expressing "entire approval of the course adopted and the hope that the sentences passed will check any further attempts to interfere with the freedom of labour".[105] Arch summed up the matter presently at Ascott: Christian ministers ought to live in the affections of their parishioners and not to administer unjust laws". He and other Union leaders began to demand stipendiary magistrates for the countryside.

But there were protests also at the centre: the Home Secretary pointed out that the law offered other possibilities to the Bench: the women could have been warned or bound over.[106] The same Minister had asked for the comments of the Lord Lieutenant of the County on the events, but found that the Duke was among those looking for ways to defeat the Labourers' Union in his own village. Labourers seem to have been excluded from the sympathies of most larger farmers and many landowners, but in the larger political world the situation was summed up as showing "class influence in the administration of the laws".

The play was naturally watched to the end by villagers round about. At the end of a week the "seven days" women were awaited by a large crowd outside the prison and taken home to their village where an immense meeting was proceeding. Between two and three thousand people were addressed by Arch and Taylor and others in less canny and moderate terms than usual. There must be stipendiary magistrates and manhood suffrage. They all knew the vote was not worth having without the ballot, but the Ballot Act would soon be in the Statute

Book. The "tyranny of the countryside" was known now through the length and breadth of the land, the speakers said.

Three days later, on Saturday, the other women, sentenced to ten days, were received by a still larger crowd, and all sixteen received a cheque at the hands of Arch.

On the whole the Union's struggle had been conducted with more restraint on the workers' side than on the other, yet the prudent leaders had had their difficulties. There was a little machine-breaking: young Urban Rose of Broadwell slept a night or two beside his new mowing machine: a group of "taskers" (men who went round threshing with flails) burnt a threshing machine on Icomb green. But their most basic trouble was the mental condition of many potential members of the Union—they were so unpractised in thinking beyond the next few meals, the next contact with their employers. How seldom shepherds and carters saw that their interests were identical with those of the day labourers; their wages, though a shilling a week higher, were actually lower per hour. Thus men of a little more stamina, a little more ability did no more than look benevolently on. Labourers had forgotten entirely ancestors who had rights and status: in our own village, for example, some whose forebears are known to have been commoners for a hundred years had lost almost all contact with other classes except that of service.

Many a rural anecdote reveals the mind of the poor who had no advantage of stimulus in chapel or school. Two such from Milton and Leafield have substance enough to have been recorded:—[107] An old woman had died suddenly at Milton and her widowed husband was the sole witness at the coroner's inquest. Question after question was put to him, in answer to all of which he shook his head, or sat as still as a statue. Finally a neighbour said, "You tell 'em, Ned, what you sin and done". Ned woke up and told his story, the end of which ran

"So I mäade 'er a drop of browth out o' a bit o' bäacon as we'd got
    and I took en up. 'Er was laid out very quiet and I sez 'Näance',
    and 'er never moved and I sez 'Näance, thee bistn't dyud, you,
    bist?' And dalled if 'er wasn't as dyed as a nit.',

Another has further significance. The Vicar of Leafield visiting cottages in Holy Week spoke to one woman of the Crucifixion of which, it seemed, she had never heard. "You say, sir, as all this 'appened long since?" "Oh, yes, nearly two thousand years ago". "Well, then, Sir, let's 'ope as tent true". This latter tale may seem to

336

have less point today: in the latter half of the nineteenth century for all those who took refuge in the hope that the labourer was receiving what he needed for salvation on any level it should have been electrifying.

There had been, as we said, a little change and hope in the air, for labourers, in 1872 and 1873. But cheap meat and corn for them brought loss—at least in the short run—for farmers, and that threat was intensified by some very wet seasons and poor harvests. There was therefore, no chance of a further rise in wages. It remained true that starvation wages were not good for farming but not all difficulties in the situation could be resolved between farmers and labourers: political and social change was required. Membership of the Union fell off and in many villages branches ceased to exist. Nevertheless wages did not fall back to the old level. Bledington labourers continued to be paid eleven shillings; nor did they work quite as long hours as before 1872.

. The village community was at last free of the old lingering view, held before this time for round about two hundred years, that one class of persons could and must be a permanent sacrifice to all others. This view had incidentally been a partial cause of intolerance and discourtesy between churches, but now came a change. Our Bishop, a fair representative of his kind, bade his clergy in 1883 recognise that Nonconformists "served the same Lord" though they must uphold to the full "the theology and claims of the Church of England". There could now be mutual respect between the two most influential groups, "Church" and "Chapel", in many villages including our own. They even occasionally held friendly meetings on the green together, to pursue some charitable work, for example to support the newly established hospital at Moreton in Marsh.

Farmers and the agricultural depression
(circa 1870–1890)

Farmers are the fundamental category of villagers—as essential as the land on which the community dwells. The Bledington group was still very stable. They were slow to change their agricultural methods and continued to fill ancient communal offices so far as these remained in the third quarter of the nineteenth century. Here, as hereabouts, it was still chiefly they who attended the vestry meetings and took office as churchwardens, overseers, waywardens and constables. It

337

was they, usually in the vestry, who protested against some of the changes urged or forced on the community by external authority; and on the other hand, as new institutions took form—the School Board, the Parish Council, the church choir—they would take an active share in those much out of proportion to their numbers.

One may get an impression that the families composing the group changed little also: the names Stayt, Stow, Pegler and Baker occur generation after generation till late. But even these changed: Bakers disappear at last; Stayts and Bricknells cease to be farmers; Peglers vanish and return. The families who replaced these do not stay so long—Harwoods, Gilberts, and Phippses leave after two, sometimes, three generations. (On the big Bledington Grounds only Davenports stayed two generations: no family has ever settled for long since 1850). Other families, making up the number to eight or nine, may sometimes be here only one generation, but as it happens that is not so very important. Until the twentieth century newcomers on the smaller farms closely resemble the group they join, coming from similar, often nearby, villages, and from holdings of similar size: they fall easily into the old patterns. Work, family, neighbourliness, with life and service in and to the community are the main features of their lives. As the later years of the nineteenth century yield two examples of men breaking the bounds of custom, it may well be that earlier individuality has gone unrecorded: even so, custom largely ruled; divergence was made easier by modern developments.

The farming group by 1840 was ceasing to be separate and becoming less dominant. With the increase in population and the complexity of industry, due to machinery, and to the growing transport and retail trades, farmers and their families could easily choose friends on their own economic level but with other means of livelihood. Wells the Wheelwright and the first Harwood, a craftsman of many gifts, were friends brought into the group. Daughters of these families received their education, such as it was, together with farmers' daughters; and their sons became farmers, sometimes within the village.

Farmers' holdings were less constant than the group of families. The old farms retained their identity, but they were differently grouped among the farmers. The tenant of Rectory Farm might also hold the Hill Barn Fields and Pebbly Hill; the Stows usually held the Coombs' or Ledsoms' fields as well as the University's land; at one time Harwoods farmed Gilberts' fifty three acres as well as their own eighty six. But these arrangements proved temporary: when a tenant departed or an owner died and it was convenient to reduce a farm's acreage, an old holding was detached, and let afresh.

By 1870 some considerable changes in methods of work had taken place elsewhere. Even here machinery had become the commonplace which it had been elsewhere by 1850. Underground drainage was an ancient enough idea. On our farms the water was led off a few short brookside slopes by elm pipes—logs with holes driven along their length—and by covered ditches with thorn boughs laid along them, but larger scale works had become possible about 1840 through the use of coarse clay pipes laid end to end, and through plentiful and cheap labour. Strong skilful workers took to the trade of drainer; one of these lived in Bledington in 1851. Some difficult arable land was dealt with, though the grassland still took its chance with only ridge and furrow drainage as at least a little still does. There was one large-scale operation. In 1846 and 1850 the Government had set aside altogether four million pounds to lend to landlords, so as to hasten drainage and in 1865 the owner of Bledington Grounds (by this time Sir John Chandos Reade of Shipton under Wychwood) had borrowed £1500 for this purpose. On these 271 acres there was a charge of £91 for 17 years. But none of the smaller owners followed this example.

A number of these were in no position to borrow more money. Two Stayt Farms (Banks Farm and Fletchers'), two Pegler farms (Home Farm and Banks, bought from Stayt), Gilberts' (the one-time Rose's) and the Weales' smallholding had all been mortgaged for many years before 1870. (We have seen that some farms were mortgaged or bought by means of mortgages from the early seventeenth century and that continued to be the case till 1914). But though interest could be the equivalent of a landlord's rent even that conditional ownership was often well worthwhile. Here however, little if any land was held under conditions irrelevant to agriculture such as political or religious complaisance, and seldom at high rents.

During the period of disturbance owing to the labourers' revolt a fair price was being paid for corn and other products. There was no reason why farmers should not be fairly prosperous though it is doubtful whether those of Bledington could be so described. The labourers' protest shamed them into paying somewhat better wages but these were no great tax: a little extra machinery made possible a reduction of staff: and this was made easy by opportunities on the railway and in towns tempting young men to leave.

But after 1873 comes the period sometimes referred to as the "great depression" in agriculture. First came the wet, cold seasons from 1875 to 1880. Then imports from the new lands of the United States and Canada grew rapidly. A quarter of wheat worth some 56s. in the late sixties was to be worth about 40s. in 1880, just over 31s. in 1886, and still less (24s.) in 1894. Prices for stock and for dairy products fell much less far, being perishable, while their market was growing. Presently the effect of imports was in a measure helpful to mixed farming: cheap cereals made excellent feed for cattle.[108]

Land at Bledington had long been described as "pasture, meadow and arable", the proportions of these varying from farm to farm: and there was little land that could only be profitably used for corn. Yet even here there must have been alarm. The drainage of the Grounds had doubtless been carried out with a view to improved arable and the farmer who purchased it in 1870 must later have had great anxiety; much of Stows' Farm, held on lease, was good arable that any farmer would hesitate to put down to grass. On the whole Bledington seems to have escaped a great deal of trouble. Just across the Oxon. border on the lighter land was a large corn-growing area, stretching as far as Banbury and then beyond into Northampton county. The area in Oxfordshire alone totalled over 60,000 acres. Farmers near Oxford city gradually found alternative products—the town was growing fast and with it the demand for milk, butter and eggs; but further to the northwest and north there was no such attraction. Old fashioned farmers on large hereditary holdings and with a certain balance at the bank were accustomed to think that they could live through several bad seasons to recoup their losses in good. They blamed the terrible weather of 1879 and hung glumly on. But in 1881 and 1882 a number of them became bankrupt. When they were "sold up" they and their creditors received a few pounds for good heifers and whole teams of horses went for what should have been the price of one. These almost complete wrecks spread depression over the whole area: a farmer could not sell out and begin again on a smaller farm or in a new line.[109]

The effect of all this was more and more public trouble in whole communities. In Banbury and Chipping Norton and Stow the solicitors and banks, dealers and auctioneers all experienced reduction of profits or business. Samuelsons at the Britannia Works, unable to sell their mowers and reapers, first reduced their men's wages and then

340

were forced to dismiss many of them; the unemployed and their families were fed at soup-kitchens. Failures on large farms could disturb whole villages and from many of them groups of labourers, often eight or ten at a time, left for the United States or Canada.

It was everywhere seen that smaller farms held on where the four hundred to thousand-acre holdings did not, but landlords having been forced to reduce rents, had not the capital, nor yet the inclination, to split up the holdings; the new ones would have needed new farm buildings. Hence the necessary changes were very slow to come, even after the situation was to some extent understood. By 1884 farmers were being urged at their Agricultural Society dinners and by their bankers to cease to hope for better corn prices and to concentrate on milk and butter, beef and mutton. The policy "down corn, up horn" was economically compulsory.

One of the developments following on the change was the decay of old markets and the opening of new ones. The Langston Arms Hotel had been built about 1880 next to the railway station at Kingham Junction and shortly afterwards a cattle market was opened there. It seems a remote spot, but perhaps the fame of the Garne herd half a mile away helped early sales. The market had ups and downs, but was never abandoned and today it flourishes. Within a twenty minute walk from Bledington Church, it did something to make up to our farmers the lack of a good retail market for milk and eggs.

They seem to have gone haltingly on; there were no bankruptcies here, save one forty years on, and that not due to farming hardships. For younger and bolder spirits there was a way to avoid that final failure at the end of the steep decline—emigration. We know of several members of farming families who crossed the seas. An example had been set as early as 1846 when a member of the Phipps family, who were small holders and tradesmen, had taken his young family to Wisconsin, where in time they modestly flourished. In 1876 Humphrey Theophilus Pegler had inherited Banks Farm; he sold it in 1882 for the amount of the mortgages on it and departed for Harwich, Massachusetts. About the same time the heir of the Gilberts went to Canada, settling in Manitoba, whither John Gilkes had gone a few years before. And later, a family of Stows settled on the St. Lawrence in Western Ontario.

In spite of these signs of discouragement it seems that rents and the sale price of land did not drop so severely here as in other parts. The evidence comes from a few various sources.[110] but perhaps is sufficient for the generalisation. The rent of Stows' farm, £2. 4. 6. per acre in 1875, fell in 1892 to 30s. Since this land was leased the rent sometimes fell late in depressions and correspondingly rose late after the upward turn.

In 1860 Gilberts' 140 acres were let without the farmhouse at £2.10.0 In 1870 the rent of Bledington Grounds—before the great depression —was only £1 an acre, but it was kept rather low because the tenant was paying off a loan for drainage which raised his payments by another 6/8 an acre.

Hangerson, with good land, but almost all of it between a quarter and half a mile from the farmhouse, was sold at £51 per acre in 1876, when its rent was quoted as £1.17.1. Banks Farm was let in 1885 after the "break in land values"[111] at £1.13.4., having been sold shortly before at £56.5. only £3 lower than the £59.4.0. of 1862. A good proportion of this was old heathland but it was continuous with its good house and outbuilding, standing apart yet near church, shop and the children's playground, the green. It had points of attraction for the farmer and his wife, if the latter had any choice.

On the whole then, Bledington farmers fared better in these hard times than many. A good living may not have been possible, but if they had to sell it was perhaps rather because they took farming too much as a way of life, accustomed and mentally comfortable. They had little or no impulse to learn and exert a new style of management, much less did they develop an attitude of exploitation.

Within the farmhouses there was now little tendency, as there had been in the early eighteenth century, for farming folk to strive for a new culture, a new social level. The reason for this was no doubt in part economic: the farmhouses remained as they had been modified a century or even two centuries before; as the century progressed, life ebbed out of the newer rooms and was lived in the warm, busy kitchens; the resident maids became a thing of the past. Music of a limited kind, together with tea parties and occasional "concerts" given by themselves and other villagers to support charities, came to be (apart from religion) the cultural heights of the farmers' and craftsmen's families.

The status of farm wives had fallen low. They had long since ceased to figure in deeds relating to sale or lease of land: sometimes now it happened that one was entirely omitted from her husband's will, left dependent on the heir to the farm. They had to bear with the view that women's minds were trivial, unsuited to take part in decisions. Many a farmer's wife watched her husband's prosperity diminish and pass and then was required to move to another, smaller farm without so much as seeing the house. Yet one woman in Bledington was for a short time an Overseer: it seems certain that this was because while her husband had been ill she had carried out his duties and when he died she finished his period of office.

Women's subjection, like the labourers', had been due to divine arrangement. Changes for wives were on the way, but more slowly than for their fellow sufferers.

Bledington School 1876–1914

A community can develop far without the power to write down its words. It develops skills in growing its food and customs in apportioning its land. It names its utensils and every tree and mound and brook. Indeed, it finds words for all aspects of life. It has almost always its arts: song, dance, sculpture, embroidery, drawing—some or all of these.

Writing is for long necessary only for selected purposes—trade, governmental messages, the recording in portable form of stories, poems, songs, that hitherto have been "written" only in human memory. But writing and consequently reading was necessary for modern life—for contact between distant peoples, to avoid catastrophic plague, to keep powerful foes at bay.

All this Bledington had seen in the course of its history. The power to write and to read came to be a widely desired addition to life and began to spread through the impulse and effort of the young, just as songs and plays, working skills and sports had done. But the time came when literacy had to be acquired under compulsion by all the very young, with for decades no reference to their own childish wishes and needs or the methods natural to them, or even to parental choice. The school resembled for a time rather the workhouse for the adults than a nursery, playground and workshop for the young. This was a strange development, illustrating the complexity and the unfortunate quality of what had befallen this and other villages. The past miseries of plague the intolerance of religion, disastrous harvests had a less arbitrary quality.

As far back as the thirteenth century there had been two literate

343

families, both originating with minor officials of Winchcombe Abbey. They arrived here able to read and write for certain practical purposes while connecting that ability with religion. We saw that between 1282 and 1322 fifteen Bledington boys had been taught some Latin. They had entered into their studies voluntarily and were themselves to profit by them as churchmen or stewards of land. At the same time and for long afterwards education was given to many through words in the form of stories, sermons, and hymns all of which had been already written down. The Bible seemed to be the source and inspiration of all these and there was a great popular movement to read and possess at least sections of the great Book. But the powers and authorities of our larger society could not approve popular freedom to read a work in which the polity described and the outlook inculcated were so different from those desired.

Later this resistance gave way to some extent and in the sixteenth century knowledge of reading spread and copies of the Bible were multiplied on printing presses. Instructions were in fact given for access to a chained Bible in every church. In our village progress was slow. In 1551 our own Vicar knew little of the Bible's contents. Great changes in society caused demands for changes in religious teaching. Dissenting movements, since they were concerned with interpretation of the sacred Word meant a spread not only of literacy, but of literature; the demand for reading was linked with imaginative and doctrinal content, not with utility.

On the other hand the making and reading of records was coming to be used for many purposes—to "remember" every occurrence and decision, to convey every kind of message. For example, manor courts which had relied much on custom and on local tradition and memory, began to use written records and gradually ceased to be held as did that of Bledington in the late sixteenth and very early seventeenth century.

In the walls of our farmhouses built from about 1580 there were small oak-lined recesses designed to hold one or two large books— the Bible and a Prayerbook. By then the touching and elegant English of the church service had begun to endear words other than those of folklore, folk-song and play to hearers who were sensitive to their rhythms. Lay song books also began to be common at that time. We know of no formal provision for popular teaching in Bledington up to this time except the brief existence of a chantry, very slightly endowed. But deep wishes and a special impulse make importunate learners.

In the seventeenth century farmers, especially freeholders, of whom Bledington had a good number, felt that their sons if not they themselves, ought to be able to read the documents relating to their property, drawn up by professional lawyers and scribes. In 1647 occurred the meeting of commoners which left a full summary of their rules, signed by 21 of them. Coopers, weavers, smiths, tailors (never here all at one time) began to make a very brief record of work done for their neighbours and sums owed to them for it.

Beside the reasons for literacy given by religion and work and art there were in due course those of prestige. Literacy became essential to "gentle" status. The tenants of one of our larger holdings, three families in succession, from about the year of Elizabeth's accession (1558) had this status or the ambition to attain it. The last of these lived for three generations in the village, having few connections with their neighbours; their literacy did not spread to others.

Yet, gradually, in the yeoman class, illiteracy tended to be shameful. It was in 1682 that a Hathaway so valued his Bible as to leave it ceremoniously in his Will.

By the eighteenth century and possibly before there must have been some cottager, at least at times, teaching reading here. But it was our close neighbour, Churchill, that carried the torch for villages around. There was a school there from 1722 for girls, where the teaching copied something from apprenticeship—the girls learned to sew for households and to read. Its private schools kept there by men for a full living, were exceptionally good, prepared to give more than the elements of the three Rs. There is reason to believe that both Kingham and Bledington boys walked or rode the mile or two thither. At Kingham itself there was "no free school. No charity school".[112] in 1738, (and similarly in 1796) and beyond a "dame" school, no school at all. It seems that the good rectors, the Lockwoods, charitable and active, did not think them necessary. The founding of Jackson's Oxford Journal in 1750 and its distribution about the villages argued widespread literacy and did much to promote it.

In the early nineteenth century there was here, as we saw, a well-attended Sunday School and a small day-school for those who could pay fees. By then had come the time of isolation and poverty, and often degradation, for the poor. Yet the curate bore witness to the desire of labouring people that their children should have schooling. And at this time a school-master here was ready to teach those of any age and appears to have made a living, for a time. But there was still no general and reliable provision.

In the new or vastly extended towns of the time there was social breakdown—lack not only of community but of inherited decency. To meet these conditions and to further its own special aims in 1811 the *National Society for the Education of the Poor in the Principles of the Established Church* had been founded. Its work grew and spread until a majority even of villages had a "National" School. The church's principles included the duty to be content with one's station, but such teaching may or may not distinguish between the will of God in the matter and the current arrangements of society; the outlook of the clergy came to vary very much. But the view of the fixed place of the poor as the burden-bearers of society was still very prevalent and many were prepared to teach it rigorously to the very young. At the worst though, the teaching of these schools included that of the value of the individual soul and some glimpse of the many-sided attraction for children of the Bible's contents.

In 1846 the National Society conducted an Enquiry into the provision of schools in villages. In Bledington there was still a Sunday School and a Day School attended by 12 girls and 18 boys, being taught by a man and his wife in a single cottage room.[113] Support for the teachers came from fees, and from the church rates out of which coal was bought, while their cottage was supplied by the incumbent himself. From the census report of 1851 we learn that there were still two teachers, man and wife, but only ten scholars. A year later, our new Vicar opened a school in the Vicarage. This was the most effective attempt yet made to give our children letters: it had growing needs to meet. By this time a Bledington boy could not hope to get work on the railway or a girl in any but a rough farmhouse kitchen, without the power to read. Yet still not all the children attended school: Kelly's Directory gives the figure of 30 pupils for 1856 (the same as in 1846) and that figure presently dropped to 20.

By this time however there was a "National" school at Kingham. We know that by about 1870 our older boys were attending it, and they may have done so from its foundation in 1850: the children in the little Bledington School were nearly all "infants".

In Stow a National School had been opened in 1844. The Vicar there

346

refused to modify a rule that pupils must attend Church services on Sunday. As Baptists were still numerous there the school did not solve Stow's problem and illustrates one reason for the Board Schools soon to come. (In Bledington, be it said, there was no such difference. The Methodists were content to use the school and to allow the Church-wardens to buy coal from the rates, while the Vicar seems never to have required any doctrine to be taught that raised objection). Chur-chill had a "National" school provided by its model squire, in model buildings, with good teachers.

Why was the Bledington school between 1850 and 1876 so small? We had two successive good parsons, ready to help with education: Christ Church had already provided a specially built room, and might, had the need been proved, have helped to enlarge it. By far the greater part of our population were farm labourers, whose families could hardly exist without wages earned by every member who could so much as run errands. Small boys and mothers both worked. There were only a few examples of women labourers, but most mothers worked at times and then needed their girls at home. At what age boys began to work is not quite certain: the census reports show them working by ten years of age. In 1857 and doubtless for a number of years about that time, the Stow on the Wold and Chipping Norton Agricultural Society was offering prizes for young men who had worked long on particular farms and were still working there. £1 was awarded to a boy of thirteen who had started work at 5 years, and so had worked on the same farm for eight years and £1 to each of five others of whom two had started at 6, two at 7 and one at 8. The names of their masters are local—Mace, Hopp, Tysoe and Smith—respectable names, and the offer of such prizes was obviously thought respectable: no doubt it was better even at five or six years to suffer exposure than to be half-starved. Such a state of affairs was incompatible with education, and literacy under these conditions would be a miracle.

Meanwhile it was not only Bledington children who could not hope for a decent wage without letters: the nation was in the same position. Its industrial revolution had favoured its monetary wealth but its social consequences had been disastrous. A sturdy and intelligent people had become ignorant, unhealthy and unskilled. Sooner or later this state of affairs must be the worse for national industry. Many things had to be done and one of these was the provision of some degree of modern education for all children. The nation was

347

nearing a decision in this matter. The Government had begun to support voluntary effort as long ago as 1833 when it had offered grants towards the erection of school buildings. It had also set up (1839) a Committee of the Privy Council to administer these grants, and later the Education Department (1856) under the more direct control of the government and with more varied functions, and had presently appointed a Royal Commission reporting in 1861 on "measures required for the extension of *sound and cheap* instruction to all classes of people."[114]

This task in a country with terrible mistakes in its social past, largely devoted to trade and consequently to private monetary wealth, and ridden with controversy about religion, was indeed complex. But a more generous outlook was slowly spreading. In 1870 the statesman W. E. Forster, introducing a Bill to ensure that there should be a school within the reach of almost every child, omitted the word "cheap", stating his problem thus: "How can we cover the country with *good* schools"? We hope now to trace the evolution of Bledington's "good school": it took time, for all the conditions and events that have been mentioned were a part of its background and past.

The Education Act of 1870, "Forster's Act", provided machinery and finance for schools in all areas where they were lacking. In each such parish a School Board was to be elected, which would have the duty to impose a rate for the purpose of building and supporting a school.

Bledington was ready for this Act. A petition in favour of having a Board at the earliest moment was signed by 23 of our 35 rate payers. The school-to-be was envisaged as providing for the whole village, not "for the poor". Farmers and their wives wanted a school within easy reach for their own young children but that was not all: it suits with our village's background that no social distinctions were ever made in the school, but it was not, it seems, a common state of affairs in the country. Her Majesty's Inspector J. P. Palmer[115] reported in 1877 that in many schools "the farmer will not let his daughter (nor his son except in earliest years) sit beside the children of his labourers". He was often told by country clergymen that over-education led to social discontent, to their wives having no servants or useless ones. He doubted whether the English were ready for common schools. (Later we find our farmers persistently keeping children from school to work on the land, but some of the children were their own).

Every year literacy had grown more pervasively necessary for all children. Railway connections were being extended, the shop contained more varied products, some of them in packets with printed labels. In 1867 urban labourers had become parliamentary electors: in 1866 working folk in Chipping Norton had founded the Co-operative Society. There was a Friendly Society in Bledington before 1871. In 1872 and 1873 Arch and his colleagues had roused the farm labourers, making them feel that they must be prepared to join their own Union, to make claims for themselves, to travel, to vote.

In 1874 the first Bledington School Board was elected. A year before that a great difficulty had been removed. The Agricultural Children's Act had been passed under which no child under eight might be employed on the land, unless on his father's own holding. From eight years a child could be employed part-time if in the previous year he had attended a school a given number of times. Three years later it became parents' legal duty to see that their children "received efficient intruction in reading, writing and arithmetic".

In the matter of the school building the specifications of the government's Education Department left little choice to the Board. Messrs. Groves of Milton under Wychwood, who have left many a good impress on Cotswold villages, perforce erected in Bledington the building of worst proportions, also of poor materials, in short the ugliest in the village to date. It consisted of two communicating rooms, one 39 by 18 feet; the other 18 by 16. These with the closets outside, with open pits under the seats, quite near the only door, were the sole provision. In the larger room, to be used by older children, about a third of the floor took the form of a series of broad steps, with a long bench on each, a "gallery". On this the children could sit close together for oral lessons or singing, every movement visible to the teacher.

Heads of grant-aided schools were required to keep a daily log. Instructions for record-keeping were vague and 500 blank pages were provided—an invitation in effect to fulness and to a touch of the personal quality of letters or diaries. From it and from the school registers, we learn in some detail of the life lived within the school walls.[116]

Members of our Board were chiefly farmers, but trades were represented, and the Vicar was usually a member and often, but not always, Chairman. The first Secretary was a Pegler, a member of a family with a turn for culture, especially in his case for music. We find

349

members of the Board frequently visiting the school (which was their prescribed duty, always discharged). In early days the Board showed a natural understanding of their teachers' and childrens' need for encouragement and help. One member would go to school to play accompaniments to the children's singing, another brought his magic lantern to entertain and inform the children. Farmers' wives came and helped with the needlework when the Master's wife was ill. On May Day, for some years, after the children had sung their songs at every house in the village, "friends and lovers of children" provided them with "a plentiful tea" served by the Board's ladies.

As to the essential nature of education for young children there had been much ferment in Europe since Rousseau. It had reached England from Pestalozzi's school for orphans of Napoleon's war where he had worked out his fatherly and yet systematic methods and from Froebel's insights into the infant mind. Robert Owen had used Pestalozzi's basic ideas in his factory school and Dickens had read Froebel "avidly". While Dickens was writing of Dotheboys Hall a parson in Hampshire was planning to open a village school. Before becoming Vicar of King's Somborne the Rev. Richard Dawes had taught science to undergraduates in Cambridge; he had read Rousseau's Emile and Cobbett's account of how he had taught his sons; for several years he observed and considered the life of his village. From all his experience and reading, together with the view that he should do as he would be done by there issued Dawes' own "common sense", as rare and fine as genius.

King's Somborne School, opened in 1842, offered education to all the village children.[117] It based its work on the interests of little children, on the affections of parents, on the developing impulses of adolescents. Babies learned to write the names of their mother's pots and pans, of their brothers and sisters, of flowers and fruits; older children told in writing of their own experiences. In higher classes science and mathematics were taught, always starting from processes and problems that already interested the boys and girls. The pupils read very difficult books on subjects of their choice; the school library was shared with the grown-ups, parents often reading the same books as their children. Perhaps the greatest achievement was the teaching of the principles of cleanliness and health and gaining the co-operation of the homes in carrying them out: the children had toothbrushes and washed their feet twice a week! "School" was not given for nothing: the Vicar wanted proof that parents approved. Even labourers found the weekly twopence or so required of them. Farmers' sons and others came from miles around. The pupils were so enlivened, worked so much together, that all differences of station were lost sight of. It was a distinction, said Matthew Arnold, to have been educated at King's Somborne.

King's Somborne was not unique. In his evidence to the Commission of 1861, the Rev. James Fraser wrote of the thirst for education in many villages, giving touching examples of sacrifices made by boys to attend night schools. "The people seemed to feel that they were perishing for lack of knowledge". There are signs that Bledington School Board could have given understanding and some help to a fine school and that His Majesty's Inspectors were ready at that time to give leadership towards such work, but the government's Education Department placed a comprehensive bushel over all these humane lights. The Newcastle Commission of 1861 referred to earlier had had to consider the immense task of teaching the three Rs to the large, deprived, ignorant population of our towns. To ensure attention in the schools to every child and his progress they had advocated (in 1861) an annual examination for each class of children from seven years to eleven. The aim was worthy, but there were those who knew that this short cut if taken would make against the reliance on natural purposes and interests that make a school live. Perhaps no one thought however, that it need be fatal: the Commission made some other recommendations of a a more liberal kind.

Unfortunately the Minister in charge of the Education Department, an able classical scholar and lawyer, was a man of odd and harsh personality, who hated and feared the lower classes.[119] He was the last powerful holder of the view that they should be trained simply as servants and burden-bearers (I wish these words could be printed in red): no thought that children should be taught for their own sake and in accordance with their own nature had touched him. But he believed that literacy was necessary for modern workers. Lowe based his "Revised Code" for grant-earning schools on the recommendation of the Commission but went further than they providing that children's progress should be regularly tested by *individual* examination. This Code was never fully discussed in Parliament but it shortly had the force of law. Except for a small allowance for attendance, grants would only be paid in respect of children who passed the annual examinations in the three subjects. The new Code made teachers' salaries dependent on the number of children's passes, put an end to all government encouragement for pensions to teachers and to the scheme of "pupil-teachers" which had begun to provide assistant teachers of modest qualifications. (This last scheme was of great importance to villages, at this time singularly lacking in economic and educational "ladders" for the young).

By 1876 the Code had been modified slightly but remained a terrible skeleton. It applied to all schools: its influence went beyond teachers and scholars. The Board of Education's Inspectors, once men with a liberal and hopeful mission, welcome in the schools, became dreaded visitors. School Boards given no ideas, no encouragement of their own good impulses, grew incredibly stingy. (The two teachers of Bledington School of a hundred children shared for a long time a single blackboard and a single chair in spite of urgent requests for a second).

Reading, writing and arithmetic were taught for four years very formally with the least possible reference to real life. One small reading book lasted a class for a whole year and was handed on to their successors torn and dirty. In our school one year when the classes received new reading books there was uncontrollable excitement. Everything possible was learned by heart. To pass, to earn grants and presently to leave school a child need not know a single geographical fact, a story or a line of verse, write a sentence, much less a letter of his own, or if a boy, have the slightest practical skill.

Boys and girls who passed all the annual tests from seven years to ten, could go to full-time work; it was more usual to have to attend another year. Farmers' children and others stayed on, and two years after the qualifying "Standard IV", were at last required to "read a short ordinary paragraph in a newspaper or other modern narrative" and in arithmetic might be asked to deal with something concrete, "a bill of parcels", the alternative being "a sum in practice".

For girls there was one mitigation of the scheme: it was a condition of grants that they should learn to sew though needlework earned no grants. Even this subject suffered from a most formal mechanical approach. Further, "the scriptures" must be "read daily". But they also earned no grants. They had to be on the timetable—but the Bledington log-book nowhere mentions them till 1902.

School had no attraction: children stayed away for the slightest reason until the day of examination drew near. Some of our own children, paralysed by the school methods, went back to Miss Malins who had kept the dame-school to be coached for the "labour examination" at ten or eleven years.

The School had opened in March 1876. There had been no difficulty in getting the children to try the new school, whose walls they had watched rising from the field in the Lower Oar. No fewer than 113 presented themselves in the first few days though some 72 had been expected. The new school master found that of the children over six years of age 15 had attended the Kingham "National" school, 30 a dame school in the village, 14 (chiefly newcomers to Bledington) at various neighbouring village schools. 23 had been at no school at all. Of all these entrants only two, the master thought, could have passed "Standard I".

By 1876 the Code had been a little supplemented. Small grants could be earned for singing and this was taught in our school from its first week. At first it was heavy and not "cheerful" but later was sometimes "light, cheerful and enjoyed". Two decades later it had begun to be realised by "cultured" persons that English villages had inherited treasures of lovely song, but songs for schools were specially written: the children sang about the pitter-patter of rain on the pane, the "tap-tap" of the cobbler. They were required to rejoice in their privileges: "My English Fatherland", "Oh, I'm a British Boy, Sir", (the vigorous rhythm and emotional expression of these songs must have been welcome). Outside school and out of sight there were simple country dances and exacting Morris; inside it was at least a mitigation of immobility to have jerky "Swedish exercises". Probably whatever the life in school might have had to offer there would have been difficulties about a high attendance. Old customs could not be dropped at once. There was not only work in the fields and on the family "allotments", but lighter matters—Saints' Days on which the children had always knocked on doors with old formulas—"Remember St. Thomas"—for gifts. There were Club Days in surrounding villages and fair days at Stow, meets and annual point-to-point races of the hunts.

The poverty of the parents affected school in many ways. In 1891 school fees ceased to be charged, but for labourers' children they had been only 1d. or 2d. The economic compulsions to absence were stronger than legal threats against it. The master continually recorded

353

absences for work. "Parents have a custom of taking all the family into the fields with them at harvest". In April boys were away helping to plant potatoes in the family allotment, and in October they were collecting the crop as father dug them. The master was more indignant about farmers (he named eight of them) who tempted the boys by pay for crow-scaring and other jobs. All the big girls would be away in some weeks of June taking care of babies and home while mothers turned swathes of hay or tedded them. Often they were away on washing days, or taking mother's place while she was ill. Even small children would be taking meals to workers in the fields, gleaning corn, carrying buckets of water. In early days they willingly sprang to do any work that would keep them away from the school. Often the six weeks of the summer holiday did not cover the whole harvest-time and then there would be a half-empty school, the children present feeling jealous and rebellious.

Two causes of absence strike another note, though with these also poverty had much to do. First, weather: the slow-flowing brook still floods briefly once or twice each winter, sometimes even in the summer, in spite of the works of the Thames Conservancy Board. Earlier, floods might come any time from October to May; once a flood cut off the homes of 40 children, invading a number of them. The school building "heated" by an open fire itself deterred the children. On more than one occasion ink "froze in the ink wells during the writing lesson". It could be too cold for much writing for a whole week. On some days in January 1881 and at other times "chilled feet, bad boots and severe weather" caused poor attendance. In the previous year "the weather, scarcity of work and constant limited supply of proper food tell on the children". One headmaster, an exceptionally successful teacher, mentions the effect of weather very frequently: he will not have children in school in wet shoes or clothes. Often the children spent half-hours marching or singing to get warm, without much effect. From 1880 it had been the School Board's duty to make by-laws about attendance and to prosecute parents who did not obey. The chiding of H.M.I. on the subject was almost useless; it was possible to prosecute two or three parents but not twenty.

Worst of all causes of absence were the epidemics of physical trouble and illness, that hindered the work very frequently and at times emptied the school altogether. Here, also, the school building itself increased the difficulties. In the very first year, 1876, we read of many

354

cases of fever. At the same time children were suffering from scabs and towards the end of the year there were references to "scarlatina". There were no rules for closing the school and no quick reference to medical authority. In 1882 half the children in the school (58 of 110) were ill with measles and the children were "very weak and feeble". Sometimes—and it was natural enough—the children had barely recovered from a fever when they succumbed to another epidemic: in 1896 whooping cough was followed by measles; three years later there was scarlet fever succeeded by influenza. In 1892 many children were absent with "eruptions on face and hands". To the end of our period children in school were often "verminous and scabby", suffering from ringworm and diarrhoea. In December 1887 one child had "all the symptoms of a decline"; she died in February. The master does not often survey the number of cases: they would vary from week to week and he has in mind not so much hygiene and medicine as individual children and his depleted classes. For many years attendance did not rise above 66%.

The staff of the school was usually of two persons, at times the master and his wife, the latter teaching the infants, who began to attend at three years of age, and the girls' needlework. When the wife did not teach, the assistant was an unqualified girl, known as an "Article 68" teacher: she must have passed her "standards" and have been vaccinated. Everything depended upon the master. There were about a hundred pupils to be taught, of which thirty might be in the infants' room and of which some were always absent—which was more troublesome than if they were present. The assistant, unless she were the master's wife, always needed his support in keeping the children in order: at first there were no pictures for the infants, no toys, no "activities".

The master's pleasures took the form of relief: he would be "glad" that attendance was no worse, that the Board had at long last acceded to some trifling, yet to the school essential, request, that the children had returned after an epidemic, that the results of the examination had not had the effects of reducing his salary. And yet it was to good masters that the school owed mitigation of the iron role of the Code and almost all its good quality. They were poor and hard-driven men; no doubt that accounted for their sympathy—under the necessarily severe discipline—with their pupils' lives.

Mr Greenfield (1881–1891) showed understanding of children.

He kept the school calm through the ordeal of examination-day by the prospect of walking to Sarsden House, to tour the garden, the head-gardener showing master and flock his greenhouses and borders, or he took them to Icomb Round Tower—a poor "folly" not of much interest but commanding a view of Stow on the Wold crowning the opposite broad hill to the West and on the other side a long and beautiful valley which if the children were fortunate would be for a time a great lake of golden light. It was he who organised the May Day singing and feast and the New Year's "Post Office" from which the children had each a present. He taught singing, in a simple natural fashion, not by "solfa" and exercises in using the high notes, as Inspectors sometimes recommended, so that the songs were enjoyed. In the eighth year of his rule H.M.I. commented in his Report that the headmaster was "wearing himself out", and in the tenth year he died.

From 1880 small grants could be earned for the school by older children in two subjects chosen from a list (grammar, geography, elementary science, history). By 1885 Mr Greenfield was teaching grammar and geography to the few children who remained at school after the Labour Examination. But H.M.I. pronounced that "two class subjects were too much for the children". The fact was, of course, that they were too much for the master. The grammar of his entries in the log is not without fault, yet it was geography that was dropped. Strange, it seems, to omit rivers and mountains and ships and foreign children and exotic plants in favour of parsing sentences, but in fact school geography at the time was hardly less abstract than such analysis: mere lists of towns and capes and bays were learnt together with definitions of islands, promontories and the rest.

The generous movement in thoughts on education continued. Matthew Arnold, one of His Majesty's Inspectors from 1851 was an opponent of payment by examination results from its inception. His fame as poet and critic helped him to win some of his educational battles, e.g. to get the learning of poetry into schools. Scientists were complaining that schools of all types ought to be giving their pupils some knowledge of nature and of some manual skills. Sir John Lubbock's highly readable and humane books were read by thousands. His ideas were not original but for most of his readers they seemed both revolutionary and attractive. For him the task of primary schools was not to bestow knowledge but to foster interests: teachers could only teach well what interested themselves. Reading should not be abstracted from life: lessons in practical subjects would help children's reading.

In 1888 another Royal Commission on Education (the "Cross" Commission to enquire into the working of the Elementary Education Acts) issued its Report. A minority of its members shared these humane views. They advocated suitable and roomy school premises, and staff sufficient to give children individual attention and sympathy. The system of cramming, they wrote, was more and more prevalent, "threatening to destroy the love of knowledge".

The majority went less far, and it was their recommendations which were acted upon in the new Code of 1890. Individual examination in the three R's was no longer the major test for grants: rewards could be given for the quality and success of the whole school, including discipline and achievements in other subjects. Seven years later lingering traces of the Revised Code were swept out of the schools: children were free to advance as fast as the knowledge and judgment of teachers and inspectors permitted. But it would be a long time before teaching in the schools as a career attracted any but young people for whom it was almost the only opening: the monitors[120] and "Article 68" teachers in our own school do not include any farmers' daughters or other relatively prosperous folk till after 1914.

In 1892 Irving Senior was appointed headmaster here. He was an orderly, efficient teacher, capable of taking some advantage of the improved opportunities. The pages of his log are tidy to a miracle, his hand-writing is consistent, neat and without any other sign of individuality. Senior's teaching matches his hand. It lacks poetry—literally and perhaps in spirit. The verse extracts for repetition are commonplace rhymes, except one,—a passage from Henry V. In his time there were no outings to the tops of hills. But arithmetic is taught with some practical reference, logically and with success. In music he teaches the children the solfa notation and persuades the School Board to hire the Church harmonium, which had to be conveyed along Church Lane for a weekly lesson. In his time the "gallery" which imposed a dreadful formality on some of the work was taken out and all the floor was available for movement. It was no longer a sin to speak quietly to a fellow pupil.

This capable fellow could speak with confidence to his Board and they responded, making small improvements in the school's equipment—another blackboard, a chair each for teachers, a cupboard.

357

But the Board would not pay for paper, preferring the all-but-per-manent though unhygienic slates.

Irving Senior had his success with the children: not once does he mention disciplinary trouble. When in school they work hard and well and on a few occasions in summer-time the master records an attendance of 90% for a week. Not till 1900 did Senior include geography or history in the curriculum: in history there seem to be no lessons, but only a "reading-book" of historical stories. But along his own line he could innovate. He gave the elder boys and girls a lesson on the value of the figures that the 1901 census would gather and on the way to fill in the forms, so as to help their parents.

But Senior too had his troubles. Still all the old out-of-school attractions affect the children. Each autumn the children go "apple-scragging" with their parents: the owners of orchards had agreed that they should be free to gather the remaining apples from the trees and to collect the windfalls. Later in his record (July 1900) he says that 23 pupils are absent "for most trifling reasons", only three in the hay-field. Shortly after, H.M.I. threatens to report the Board for neglect of their duty to see that children attend school: compulsion is still essential. In one way the Head himself is responsible for absences. It is he who refuses to have children in school wearing damp shoes and clothes: if they arrive so he sends them home.

When Irving Senior left in 1901 the school was orderly and much was effectively taught. It had earned respect though only limited liking. H.M.I. bore annual witness that "the children pass an excellent examination". It was as good as it could be under the old administration, with the master helped by unqualified girls, and his wife to teach sewing. Only the family has greater powers than the school to dull and even shorten lives if it fails. The last remnants of "payment by results" were—in 1901—about to be eliminated.

Even so, the school had far to go before it could make a great contribution to the childrens' development and to village life. Indeed, to listen even now to discussion in village meetings upon matters very important to the gathering and within everyone's comprehension is to feel that the generations of native villagers present had little help in gaining powers of expression and reasonable confidence.

Reasons for change in the schools were multiplying. Humane common sense was being reinforced by an urgent anxiety in the minds of business men and manufacturers. Britain's early inventions in machinery, and her early civil engineering had given her a great advantage. But Germany with her more paternal government had a better understanding of some aspects of education. She was training more skilled men than was England: her schools, though not giving a liberal education at least related their work to their pupils' own future livelihood. Indeed, experts declared that England was lagging behind almost all European countries. Within the schools the infants' classes had made progress: pictures were on the walls and "activities" on the little desks. "Conversation lessons" though artificial were an improvement on the demand for silence. In "junior" classes foundations must be laid for later work. How to do this without a deadening formality was little understood. There had to be far more provision for "secondary" education. The last was a vague term: no one knew what kind or kinds of schools should provide it.

Essential to the basic life of a great number of children was change of another kind. Ill-housed, ill-fed, being taught in a building which itself contributed to ill-health, they needed economic and physical change before they could be educated—a fact that was to be dramatically brought home to minds open to such matters, as we shall shortly see.

School Boards were not affected by the Local Government Acts of 1888 and 1896. Education had never been among the spheres of local courts, vestries or magistrates: to require their successors to serve and control it would be a great departure. In the towns the Boards had sometimes administered extremely successful schools in spite of central misguidance and mistaken regulations, but in country parishes they had often failed. Experience in other spheres had shown that it was undesirable to have single-purpose institutions, requiring separate elections. The idea gained ground that education should be one of the functions of the new, more comprehensive, councils created under the local Government Acts.

Reasons for change and improvement in the schools were multiplying.[121] An urgent anxiety had grown in the minds of business men and manufacturers. Britain's early inventions in machinery, her civil engineering and chemistry, had given her a great advantage. Germany with her more paternal government had a better understanding of education. She was training more skilled men than was England: her grammar and "middle" schools and technical colleges had been reorganised and multiplied. Indeed, experts declared that England was lagging behind almost all European countries in all her educational provision. Statesmen and still more Members of Parliament not in office began to take a continuing interest in schooling. England, it was clear must have more educated persons, more skilled workmen, more scientists. This economic anxiety could be useful to reformers already asking for change on other grounds.

A second alarm was later to affect all schools. This did not reach its full intensity till after the passage of the very important Education Act of 1902, an Act planned during the late stages of the Boer War, which did not end till May 1902. The Boers had given way at last, but England—who had thought of herself as a foremost nation—had much humiliation to digest. Through various inquests the cause of the slowness and failures of campaigns had been studied. Military authorities had been shocked by the remarkable number of recruits who had proved physically unfit for service—from 40% to 60%. The nation's physique, it seemed, had sunk to a very low standard. The decline was far from having been generally noted: the medical profession had at first no wish to be represented on the Interdepartmental Committee on Physical Deterioration. Doctors had not our schoolmaster Senior's intimate knowledge: the poor could not pay for medical help until Friendly Societies were both efficient and widespread, and even then women and children were not provided for. The discussion and the Committee's Report of 1904[122] opened many eyes. London crowds were seen to be composed of undersized and ill-featured folk. For thirty or forty years after this date observant persons—especially if they had travelled in other countries—were shocked when they rode on country omnibuses by the pallor, bad breath, lameness and toothlessness of passengers. It would take time for connections between poor physical conditions and the problems of schools to be realised by politicians and the public. Yet educational progress had to wait upon improvements in feeding, exercise, and clothing. Bledington's head teachers had found their children often too hungry, too ill, too wet to learn: H.M.Is had found the school's temperature at freezing point and the air unbearably "stuffy".

The Revised Code in 1862 had slipped almost unnoticed through the House of Commons, but in 1902 members gave to the Education Bill "59 nights of vigorous debate". The Conservative majority in Parliament was with the Church in its claim to receive rate aid, while still appointing teachers and controlling religious education in the schools founded by the National Society. In many villages there was only one school and that a "church" one and rural nonconformists felt that rates should not be used to support religious tenets and social interests and outlooks contrary to their own. In these villages there was much dissension, which "School Board" villages were happily spared.

The new Act would not stimulate keen popular support and interest in village schools but much attention was given by opposition and government alike to two other matters—the proposed new education authorities and plans for more advanced education for older children. The resulting Act was something of a mule—not life-giving but capable of carrying heavy loads of superstructure.

County Councils had already discharged some small educational functions in a promising way. They were now put in local charge under the central Board of Education, of publicly provided and aided education in their area. They were given the duty of ascertaining its needs and planning to meet them. The need everywhere for more "secondary" education was recognised (that meant, for longer and more advanced teaching for abler children). Many "Board" Schools, had, like our own, done little about religious training: now nonconformists and "churchmen" alike were anxious for more serious work. In the schools handed over to or built by the new authorities (to be known as "publicly provided schools") forty-five minutes of each day must be devoted to Bible teaching not distinctive of any church or sect—a provision which left the subject largely in the hands of teachers. In small schools with the head-teacher in close touch with all the teaching, this was a highly successful arrangement. The text of the Bible was the base of lessons. The children in almost all schools gained access to one subject which necessarily afforded them stories, ideas, language and vital human characters, some of them in various ways inspiring. It was always popular when at all well taught.

To provide a channel between County authority and village there was to be a body of school managers, two chosen by the Parish Council and four by the County Council. They would, under much regulation and guidance, appoint teachers and keep watch over the building. It was not provided that parents should be represented, or otherwise brought into touch with the school, and chance would more often than not fail to provide a single parent-manager. Four places of the six would as a rule be in effect filled by the Local County Councillor who would choose persons of superior social standing.

361

Village schools had now two distinct governors—the Board of Education working through His Majesty's Inspectors and the County Education Committee. The latter had their work to learn, but they were helped by growing public attention to life within the school walls.

In 1908 the Board issued a pamphlet making suggestions as to suitable subjects and methods for rural schools:[123] the country environment, if not the village community, now seemed important. The sentiment for the countryside, for agriculture and gardening, and later for local building, which was growing strong in many minds first touched the formal life of many schools through this missive. Nature-study and gardening would make their way gradually till they appeared in most school time-tables. Three years earlier the Board had published its first *Suggestions for Teachers*.[124] The title struck a modern note. Teachers were left to decide the best methods for themselves, while considering the results of other teachers' experience as expounded in the pamphlets. There followed other *Suggestions* each better than its predecessor.

Thus the background of the work of Mr and Mrs Hill who were appointed to Bledington School in 1903 was different from Senior's, in 1902. Our School Board was still in charge: it was in 1904 that the school came under County supervision. The Hills were both teachers, he certificated and trained, she having in addition to his help, motherly and teacherly commonsense. Their reign was a halcyon period and —it almost follows—brief: such competent teachers were wanted in larger schools.

Formal examination of pupils had now gone; interest was fostered and encouragement given.[125] The infant class had already made much progress since H.M.I. had first suggested "a few bright pictures" and commented on the teacher's gloomy face. Mrs Hill went to visit a successful infants' school at a distance to get ideas—an example of the simplicity and directness they brought to bear, a sign at once of confidence and humility.

Geography was now a permanent part of the curriculum: Canada and New Zealand—the homes of ex-villagers—were studied; imagination was stirred by the thought of tropic and arctic climates. The children read stories of explorers. "Nature study" linked the school with field and garden and gave some impulse to exploration on foot and with the eyes. The enumerated topics remind one of the old artificial "object lessons", but there was also "field work in Spring". One February day in 1904 the children brought in snow-drops, wallflowers, "nut-blossoms", and "hawthorn buds". One may suppose that the "hawthorn" was blackthorn, but children and master learned fast and had "very great liking" for the work.

A change had come over the Bible teaching. Hitherto no-one outside the school had taken any interest in it: now once a year it was inspected. For three years a local clergyman was the inspector; he was followed for three years by a nonconformist minister. By now Bledington's vicar was "the Radical Parson", Stephen Liberty. He welcomed this arrangement but tactfully refused to serve, except in emergency, in his own parish.

Every year the ministers report that the children reply with spirit and pleasure to their questions. Always they know the stories well; they have learned much by heart; they "have a good grasp of the morals they have correctly deduced", and they sing and pray with reverence. Bibles were too expensive to be obtained from school funds. Master and children prepared a "concert" of songs and "recitations" for the village and with the proceeds bought Bibles, to be used in school first and to be given one by one to scholars as they left.

But the Hills departed after three years to Stow on the Wold. The next headmaster was an enthusiast but physically delicate and not in every way efficient, indeed he left under a cloud. However, he did one beneficent work in school and village. In May of the year he came he asked the children to bring flowers to send to his sister's poor London school. The wealth they tumbled on to the school floor overwhelmed him. Always from that time forward successive heads have encouraged the children to send money to orphanages, flowers and messages to sick neighbours and the like. Thus, the children learned techniques of generosity. For the last half century at school and in grown-up life, villagers have made laborious collections and arranged "sales of work" often in the past of excellent needlework, and given entertainment to raise money for every sort of good work. No village has put in more hard work for hospitals, "Navy" homes, spastic children, cancer research.

But how much there was still to learn about conducting school life! In 1905 the master caned a boy for sulks, and another for wilfully tearing a reading-book. Nearly every book the latter had handled had been returned with leaves torn. The inference that a boy who tears books hates them, and that punishment will intensify boredom and dislike could not be made yet. Punishment was still the only treatment for masturbation, for stealing, for falsehood and for all the little aggressions that relieve frustrated children.

The staffing of the school of 90 children was still very inadequate except when the headmaster's wife was also a teacher. In 1906 the head was paid £90 with the use of the schoolhouse. The highest salary paid to an assistant for some years yet was £30. Sometimes the assistant was an "Article 68". There were at times in addition two monitresses, paid in 1907 one shilling per week, this sum rising later to 1/6d., then 2/6d. Only one pupil-teacher[126] appears in the log—old John Hall's daughter, who successfully went through her course—the first Bledington youth of either sex to enter a career in education since the seventeenth century.

Meanwhile the County Education Committee composed partly of County Councillors and partly of persons co-opted for special knowledge was at work. The new administrative and larger rating areas were proving useful. After four years of agitation a new stove had been provided at Bledington instead of the draughty open fire, and it was now "a pleasure to work in a cheerful clean room". The day of one blackboard for three classes was soon left far behind. In 1904 School Managers—at first, members of the old School Board—had been appointed.

The Secretary to the new County Committee first visited our school in 1907. He was enthusiastic for reform in the methods of his rural schools. Teaching in gardening was being given in Bledington school in 1908. But the Secretary's chief interest was to urge on teachers a special approach to all subjects: the "Charlotte Mason method", evolved by a woman who had been a governess in a private household. She started all her teaching from literature, from the best books. There was much to be said for this, in country schools. Literature was at that time the art most available for country folk, for appreciation and practice too. But it was not best for all minds. For some it was absurd: there were also the impulses to construct or collect from which to work. The pressing necessities of agriculture surrounded the school; and the multiplicity and variety of plant and animal life; the needs of man's physical nature, of cooking and gardening. It seemed a mistake for the Secretary to identify himself with one method, a "fad", the teachers called it, and here, so far from the Secretary's base, they need not give way.

Bledington School Managers, the deposed School Board, seem to have been determined to use such powers as they had—somewhat obstructively it seems. In particular they resisted the idea that schooling and the children's physical condition had to be considered together—in spite of the fact that epidemics, including in 1913 diptheria, still came thick and fast, first emptying the school and then sending the children back feeble and lethargic. In 1907 an Act[127] had been passed providing for the medical inspection of school children, but not for the carrying out of the medical officer's recommendations. The County Education Committee adopted a plan for each parish to have a Care Committee to help parents in finding ways to carry out the doctor's advice. But our Managers refused in 1911 and in 1912 to take any steps to form a Committee. In 1914, Sir Francis Hyett, Chairman of the Education Committee wrote to them himself to urge the following up of cases of ill-health, but they still continued to declare that it was both impossible and unnecessary to form a Committee. We have seen elsewhere that the village as a whole found questions of hygiene and ill-health difficult and unwelcome. The whole school had been at work for a generation, but it had not unlocked minds, nor bred up ex-pupils to understand and care for itself and its work. The final tragedy that converted the village to a different view of hygiene was not to occur till twenty years later, in the schoolhouse.

As to hygiene within the four walls of the school, little was done till after the First World War. The first urge towards personal cleanliness combined with facilities for it came from the Lever firm of soap-makers. The Master accepted their suggestions and the materials for a "clean-hands" campaign. The children responded with gusto and learned the pleasures of cleanliness. Seven months later the Master writes that the results of the campaign are still to be seen. Nevertheless the little heads were still itchy from vermin, and ringworm continued to be a constant trouble. Only towards the end of the Second World War one misses from the log any mention of impetigo, pediculosis, scabies and "infectious eczema". Could there be a firmer proof of the school's lack of success?

In 1906 the first group of Labour members in the House of Commons, with a natural realism about the needs of the poor introduced a Bill, shortly to be an Act,[128] permitting the provision, where

365

necessary, of meals in and by the schools. But our County Education Committee considered that in their villages the need did not exist: in one or two villages, they reported, volunteers were providing hot cocoa! In 1924 a lecturer for the National Milk Campaign talked to the assembled school, using a highly theoretical approach. In 1928 the Master received a questionnaire about the children bringing meals to school, but it came at a time when only two children stayed at school and asked no questions about what was eaten in the homes. In 1931 the Horlicks Malted Milk Company sent along packets of their product and the Master's wife heated water and made the drink: how good it must have seemed.

It is not surprising that authorities did not see it as the school's or or the education authority's duty to provide meals, but it is useful to note the slow recognition of underfeeding. Walks through the villages in the school lunch hour would have shown some children making a mid-day meal of bread and margarine and jam.

The ill-success of the school had, it seems, worn away the feeling of the village for education. In 1909 the County Council was eager to improve the practical education. It proposed to erect craft and cookery rooms, attached to our school, to serve as a centre for classes in those subjects for several villages. A Parish meeting was called to discuss the proposal and arrived at the unanimous decision that "such a school in this district is not needed and could be a burden".

The School was a long way yet from the ideal it would some day, at least for brief periods, attain—in which children would gain sound knowledge of their surroundings, easy use of their hands and tongues, some music and a little poetry, beside the three R's.

Religious life: Church and Methodist Chapel: Temperance and Brass Bands.

It is time to record changes in the religious life of the village. Vicar J. O. Hill had departed to his new charge in 1871 and had been succeeded by the Reverend John Ashford Hartshorne M.A. During his forty three years of service here the latter saw and took part in many changes. His outlook was that of a "broad" churchman and of a practical man. He had a continuing adapatability and efficiency which made him a "profitable servant" not only to the church but to the village.

366

About the time of his arrival, church rates ceased to be legal, the last being levied here in 1872. Thus the financial responsibility of churchwardens and vestry became heavier. All church members needed to feel more keenly the call upon themselves. In church services there had been changes before Hill left: the church was being warmed to some extent and evening services were being held after dark. These had a certain popular quality to which the congregational singing and the emergence from the winter dark into the light and warmth of the large oil lamps contributed. The collection of money during services came soon, though not at once. At first it was very occasional, but presently frequent. There was a general approach in style of church life to that of the Methodist chapel, but naturally considerable differences remained.

The vestry was still until 1896 the only parish meeting for civil local government; churchwardens still managed the "Poors' plot" and levied the poor rate, but it was no longer possible for them to help support the Vicar's school by paying rent for a room and buying a small quantity of coal for it each winter, as they had done for some years. The new Vicar soon ceased to keep the school going and shared the wish for a School Board. As the vestry became more concerned with the detail of provision for the church, Methodists and some others ceased to attend, but gradually as its church business became more detailed attendance of church members improved and women began to be present.

When Vicar Hartshorne arrived he was shocked to find the chancel in poor condition, as it had been since 1840 and often in earlier times, and the gallery at the West end ugly and in need of repairs. His outlook is further indicated (it was somewhat in advance of many rural clergy) by the fact that he was equally shocked to find labourers still by custom confined to the back of the church and sitting on backless benches. One of his first-formed purposes was to make their places and their seats "as advantageous as the rest". In his second and third years he must have witnessed the effects of Arch's movement, not quite without sympathy. He shared quietly the view that Christianity had social implications and the Church a concern with communities as well as individuals. He was not markedly evangelistic but "broad" in a modern sense, mildly affected by such influences as those of Charles Kingsley and perhaps Sidney Godolphin Osborne with his knowledge of social facts or Canon Girdlestone who supported the rural labourers' claim for better wages and conditions.

From the beginning of his cure the new Vicar encouraged his laity. In the first vestry meeting chaired by him we find him insisting on the ordinary forms of proposition and seconding: in one held shortly afterwards the "thanks of the meeting" are offered—another complete novelty in the minutes—to a churchwarden for building new steps to the churchyard. Before long, a choir was formed, which met regularly to practice hymns and psalms. In due course the laity raised money in new ways, by "concerts" and sales. Soon women took a greater share in the work. From 1883 Mrs Taylor taught in the Sunday School and played the harmonium at most of the services till 1895. The laity had a new status in the Church.[129]

But the new Vicar's most striking work was the restoration of the church. Since about 1850 there had been throughout the country a strong movement, with which Vicar Hartshorne was well acquainted, for the preservation and restoration of ancient churches. But shocked as he had been by its condition, he did not rush into the work of restoring his own. He first interested archaeologists and architects not only in its dilapidation but in its beauty. First came an unsigned but learned article in *The Church Builder* for October 1876, on its "rare relics of mediaeval art" and "specimens of each successive age of architecture". Later, in 1882, a well-known architect, J. E. K. Cutts, wrote of the church in the Journal of the Bristol and Gloucestershire Archaeological Society. His knowledge had been gained in the course of the survey he made of the church as preparation for a scheme of restoration.

Our church was fortunate in not having been treated earlier. Ruskin, in a study of the old church at Calais, had urged respect for the effects of time upon ancient buildings, and encouraged those in charge to modify them as little as might be. William Morris, it is said, seeing two tiny Gloucestershire churches, both mediaeval, one of which, profiting by "neglect" had remained singularly unchanged in its original quality, and the other recently spoiled by "restoration" had been deeply moved and was at this very time (1876) founding the Society for the Preservation of Ancient Buildings, to prevent the "excessive energy" by which some architects had smudged out the effects of time and with them much delicate beauty. It was good that the Vicar, so modest a man, was in close touch with this up-to-date movement.

The scheme prepared by Cutts was to have cost £1450, but in 1879 it was greatly reduced and an estimate obtained for £555. Christ Church then consented to basically repair the chancel; the ugly and unnecessary gallery at the west end was removed, revealing the high fine arch into the tower; the walls of the whole church inside and out were cleaned and pointed. The fifteenth century pews, freed by the removal in Vicar Hill's time of the "horseboxes", were largely renewed. Their carved ends blurred by time, but not much damaged, were given new oaken frames. Sorely needed work on the bells[130] had to be postponed.

But much work was done on the windows. Possibly had the earlier, so much larger, estimate been accepted the glass might have fared better, for little was saved of an ancient window of green, patterned panes, and the conservative principle was a little lost sight of in some re-arrangement of figures. But the restoration certainly preserved for us jewels of translucent colour and lovely form as they have already been described: the "kneeling effigies" in the clerestory; "Our Lord and Mary Magdalene" and St. George and the Dragon, and the "crowned female saint" in blue mantle and sleeveless fur-trimmed robe, with her "rosary and sceptre". St. Christopher still carried the Christ-child, and in the chantry window, which seems to have suffered somewhat, there are still six apostles with their signs and symbols. The tracery lights in the north windows still show the boy with the chrism box, a chalice and host, an eagle and nestlings, and royal roses.[131] The old soft leading was replaced by less pliable metal and the work has lasted securely for nearly a century.

What part the parish played in raising money and how much was given by the Church Building Society and other central funds is not clear. It is certain that we may regard the work as largely that of the Vicar.

To finish here the story of restoration: the simpler defects in the bells were remedied a few years later: some were given new head-stocks, wheels or frameworks, but presently it was no longer possible to peal them: they needed recasting. In 1931 the parish, led by the Rev. Stephen Liberty, put the work in hand. Three of the old bells were recast in Burford and three new ones from the same foundry were hung. One of the twin bells cast in 1639 and inscribed "And Charles he is our King" recast later at the expense of two parishioners, stands now in the church.[132] The story of the building, modification and preservation of our church could stand as an emblem of a religious outlook always struggling for its life and always saving it.

For some reason, thunderstorms seldom burst with great force over the village but in 1876 a thunder bolt brought down a couple of wretched cottages standing behind the chapel. No-one would attempt to rebuild them and the trustees of the chapel, foreseeing the need for its extension, bought the garden in which they had stood. They had no money, but a friend in Chipping Norton lent them £50 free of interest. In 1880, or thereabouts, a young minister arrived to take up the cure of the thirteen village chapels which together made up the Stow "circuit". Paying his first visit to his Bledington flock he was shocked—somewhat as Hartshorne had been on seeing his church—by the building in which they met. It was "like a hen-house". It was not till eight years later that the small community decided that it was essential to enlarge their crowded chapel. The average number in the congregation was eighty, and there were eighty-one "sittings".

A plan to lengthen the chapel and to build a wing for the Sunday School, of 19 by 18 feet, was made. For this, the builders' estimate was £150. If earlier the society could not raise £50 for its extended site, how could it find three times as much? But the need was urgent and there were so many officers in the little society—trustees, "organist", class leaders, local preachers, Sunday School teachers, circuit steward—that many of the men had the habit of activity. A list of about half the members shows them to have been mostly farm workers and railwaymen with two skilled tradesmen—"most of them poor" wrote their minister, "but responsible men". The Chapel's work was prospering.[133]

Enthusiasm mounted, and a special meeting was called, of which unusual details have been by chance recalled. A speaker exhorted members and friends to promise all the help they could. John Hall (two villagers bore this name) presently rose to his feet. He had left farm-work to become a railway linesman: his wage was over ten shillings a week, but he had a large young family. "I'll give five pounds!" he called. But his wife tugged at his trousers, and he sat down. Chastened, he rose again. "I can't give that five pounds", he said, "but I'll collect ten". (And so he did, and more, telling everybody up and down the railway line about his beloved chapel). A number of other collectors were enrolled, the musical folk promised a sacred cantata, the women would make garments to sell. Relations in the

Colonies were written to: better off Methodists and other friends within a range of ten miles (quite a number of them members of the Church of England) were to be approached for help. The Minister, with his small salary and so many chapels to think of, promised seven guineas. On a sober estimate the trustees saw their way to £135. Then the Minister and Trustees applied to the Connection's central Chapel Committee, to which the Bledington society had contributed their annual mite, and fifteen pounds was obtained.

Meanwhile as the work was proceeding and as the end of the chapel was taken down much decay was found. The sum needed rose to £220. On the other hand, the membership grew and the Sunday School with it. John Hall's daughter who remembers the chapel from this time described—her old face glowing—how the members and their families spent Sunday. There were class meetings at nine, morning service at 10.30., Sunday School after the mid-day meal, and finally the evening service.

After the re-building in 1888, the chapel with its 34 new seats, was still crowded but it was warm and bright and cleaner, more orderly and airier (with its new Archimedes ventilator), than most of the cottage homes could ever be.

With both church and chapel restored and fitted for half a century's further work we can turn to consider their effects on individuals, on each other and on the community. These, especially their significance for the individual mind, are not easy to know: there is no written evidence but one has known persons. At church, did the beauty of stone and glass, the recitals of Cranmer's prayers and collects touch minds and fill them with wise thoughts and charity? Some, no doubt. On the other hand the formalised services lent themselves in some members to a conventional, diluted attention in which the imprecatory psalms were read or sung with little sense of their contrast with later teaching. In both churches there was music, the singing of fine hymns, not infrequently the same words and melodies. Both congregations had musical families, the Church its Peglers and the chapel "the Stayts, all members, all singers".

On the whole we know more of the effect of the chapel on individuals. All members were literate; the best of them were great readers of the Bible. In a few homes it was read book by book and large sections of the New Tesament were known by heart. S. T. Coleridge fervently recommended the Old Testament as the best school for statesmen but

371

he had little hope that the poor could share its lessons. Yet village life was as much illuminated by stories of Naboth's vineyard and scores of others, and by the teaching of Amos, as was the life of nations. Nor is there any likelier explanation of the patience, charity and good cheer shown by old labourers and their wives, whether "church" or "chapel", than the ethical teaching of the gospels and the hopes and sense of privilege they drew from the same source.

There was in fact at this time great similarity of teaching in the two churches. There were no great theological differences except concerning the appointment of clergy and ministers, the necessity or dispensability of the "laying on of hands", but that was seldom thought of here. Similarity of services had grown. A broad and evangelical outlook on the part of Vicars narrowed even the difference in selection of hymns and readings and of emphasis on teaching. But there were social and economic differences. While there was no wealthy member of either congregation, and Church parson and Methodist minister were both poor men,[134] yet the one church was linked with government and high status in the world, the other was an enclave of the poor, still excluded from social opportunity and civic office. The result of these circumstances was that many Methodists had few ideas outside their work and their religion, and they were more strongly marked by the latter. Churchmen were more open to ideas and suggestions from the business and commercial world. In the matter of education, there was no very striking difference. In both the laity were called on for service: the Vicar was more and more dependent on lay help, though his laymen would not carry so much of the burden as Methodists must.

But in spite of all that similarity the churches remained apart. In 1882 our Bishop, addressing his clergy, advised them concerning their relations with dissenters. They should recognise them as Christians and regard them with charity but they must not abate one jot or tittle of the Church's doctrines or the Church's claims—hardly a clarion call to positive friendship. In the seventies you might still read in the County papers of clergymen who refused to sit on committees with dissenting ministers in promoting a charity both were concerned with, and of others who boycotted—sometimes under dreadful circumstances—the burial of dissenters in their churchyards. Bledington has nothing ugly on these lines to record, but it was not till about 1935 that a Vicar stepped across the chapel's threshold, asking to be shown round. He was the Rev. Stephen Liberty, a gracious, friendly personality and something of a scholar.

Both churches affected the village's secular life: the good Hartshorne was sometimes chairman of the School Board, sometimes after 1896 of the new Parish Council. Farmers—churchmen—who had manned the Vestry offices became Parish Councillors, playing a conscientious part, though "saving the rates" was a cloak for something of meanness. Methodists would not for decades occupy these offices but they contributed some new and largely lay institutions:— a brass band, the Temperance Club, a branch of the Oddfellows Society. Their work in these had a genial and fraternal quality that became less prominent (at least temporarily) when the little society dwindled.

It is certain that the chapel had a strong communal feeling and effect and that in this way it had something to teach institutions less comradely in their ways—should they ever wish for the lesson.

We turn now to an account of the lay institutions mentioned, each of which did something to illuminate and lighten hard, homely lives.

There was always a "drink evil" in poor villages—men spending too much, and going home to wives and children maudlin and worse. In Bledington even after tea and cocoa had become common, and later still when hops and lemons made housewives' summer brews good drink, there were always two and often three licensed premises till the twentieth century. It is possible today to see the conditions under which the men drank. The Kings Head Inn has still two small low-ceiled rooms with fixed benches round the walls and a table on which mugs can be set, with little space for anything but drink and and talk, and darts when there are few drinkers. There were similar rooms at the Five Tuns, one of them almost a cellar. Though drink was not the basic evil there was a widespread movement to attack it directly, favoured by dissenting churches and many clergy of the Church of England. Total abstention from alcohol was advocated: no doubt it required a less constant strength of mind to sign a pledge and stay away than to drink less than others in the "pub". By 1862 the temperance movement in the form of total abstinence societies had reached our area. In that year the Temperance Society in Bourton on the Water could attract 200 people to a lecture in the Methodist Chapel and at about the same time Chipping Norton had a strong branch of the United Kingdom Alliance, formed to press for strong legislation about licensing.

Something was needed to fill the blank left by mere abstinence. Hanging about home was impossible and perpetual work on allotments was not for all natures. The brass band arrived to provide for some a genuine and most superior hobby and diversion. It had become possible through the publication of cheap musical scores and the invention of valves that made wind instruments easier to play—not that they were put within easy reach of farmworkers, but passion solves difficulties. By 1872 the Chipping Norton Temperance Club had a brass band and the Wyck Rissington Band that played at the Bledington festivities at Lammas time had a similar origin.

The music of the bands and the processions they led never met with the approval of artists and cultivated folk as would, in time, folk songs and dances but clearly they suited the folk of the time, so starved of sound and colour as they were. Sadness and dullness were briefly quelled by the loud and stirring sounds; they gave attraction to village fêtes of Friendly Societies and Bands of Hope (the children's temperance clubs) to which the bands called their hearers. In rural areas, they were usually associated in some measure with chapels and often with outdoor religious services resembling those of the Salvation Army—as here on Sunday evenings in front of Rosepool Barn, now the Village Hall.

Bledington's Temperance Band came very late.[135] No-one knows the precise date of its beginning. but it was before the end of the century. Having come, it was a great and lasting success: it is spoken of with more affection than any other minor institution. In some families three generations played: till 1949 trumpets and drummers could be heard practising in the cottages.

Musical talent was available: the Stayt family had already a small string band meeting at their cottage. A more than sufficient number of men and boys enrolled: an old photograph shows a large crowd of musicians with their supporters. Practices were held in the small Sunday School wing of the chapel. Boys were taught in special sessions to read staff notation and to play their instruments and their parts: the band-master led them up and down Heath lane, puffing and blowing with the difficulty of marching and playing at the same time. (No schoolmaster born could have taught them the staff notation in the abstract and artificial condition of the school at the time).

The band played for all Bledington fetes and for festivities in other villages also. They charged modest fees or collected money to pay for the costly instruments and keep them in repair. (A euphonium cost ten guineas and a cornet as much). A special activity was playing at Methodist Camp Meetings in a number of nearby villages—Chadlington, Milton, Lyneham, Chilson and Churchill.

The success of the band shows the gifts that survived among the working people and the enthusiasm and persistence of which they were capable. Certainly though its connection with "temperance" was tenuous it held youngsters from the "pub" and reduced the dependence of many on drink. Its value is shown not least by the fact that a rival band, based on the King's Head, sprang up and kept going for some years.

Economic Self-help

The chapel had restored to a large group of responsible labourers, on the level of the spirit, the status they had lost in the eighteenth century: that is, they felt they were living a life worth while. The church, too, was by the eighteen-eighties accepting them with less emphasis on their condition in the social world. (But the school which might have done so much to raise the spirits of their children and to give them the means to improve their individual or united prospects was ill-inspired to that end). The temperance movement and the brass bands had been useful props for some temperance and fields for work and self expression. Farmers were not prospering and the raising of wages was not, it seemed, an available way to a better economic foundation for life. A hopeful outlook made the men ready to seize every chance to help themselves.

In 1870 young Percival Oakley Hill saw the annual fête of the Bledington Sick and Provident Society as an ancient institution. It was not that, but it was old enough to have achieved more than economic importance. Its fête took place at Lammas-tide, making use of one of the ancient holidays. The last Monday in July was "Club Day". On the previous Saturday sons and daughters returned to their village homes, amusing themselves in the evening at stalls and shows on the green. Sunday was a family and church (or chapel) affair. A full account of the activities of the great day itself might still be heard a few years since.[136] In the morning, quite early, the Wyck Rissington

375

Brass Band (before our own was formed) played its way into the village followed by men from nearby hamlets and villages, members of Bledington's well-managed Club. Bread, cheese and beer were provided for them in the long room over stables at the King's Head Inn. And then a procession of Club members formed behind the band and followed it into church, where the Vicar preached. Meanwhile a dinner of beef and ham with Yorkshire pudding and Christmas puddings were being prepared for 130 persons. Mrs John Hall and her daughter Mary had begun preparations on Saturday, kept holy the Sabbath and resumed in the early hours of Monday. Twenty five shillings was paid to Mrs Hall for all this work, to be shared with numerous helpers.

The dinner eaten, there were speeches by one or two clergymen and doctors and after that a parade of the village—first the Club's banner, with the device of clasped hands and the legend "Bear ye one another's burdens", then the Band, followed by members and all who would. The long hours of evening were filled with games on the green—throwing the disc, the ancient Aunt Sally game, coconut shies, shooting galleries, dancing, and general good-fellowship. At 9.30 the band played its final tunes as it marched out of the village, and the major feast and fête of the year were over.

The festivity filled a great need and left vivid memories, but as to the business of the Club, no notes remain. It was too popular, too much respected to have been a primitive "sick and dividend" society, dividing annually the residue of the pool of subscriptions not drawn upon in illness, thus adding a small gamble to insurance. Sometimes village clerics had helped to transform such clubs (which had had to refuse or turn off elderly or weakly members) into permanent societies on a far better and kinder basis, and this may well have happened here. Even so, the Club had not the necessary investments and organisation to be accepted for work under the National Insurance Act of 1911, and after long service it came to an end.

Since 1898 the Club had had a rival in the village, to which most of its members now transferred. This was a branch of the Cirencester Benefit Society. Founded in 1890, it had at first been registered as the "Working Men's Conservative Association", but had soon shed the political limitations. It had spread rapidly in the West Midlands and has held its own in a hundred towns and villages against the greater Friendly Societies, such as the Ancient Order of Foresters and the

Oddfellows. Beside the charm of local origin, it had an adavantage in having followed some societies in making sound provision not only for payments in time of sickness but also for savings for old age. It seems always to have provided for subscriptions and benefits on a very varying scale: members could pay small or large monthly subscriptions and could add to or reduce their "cover" as need arose. It was thus qualified for service in the more prosperous times when they at last arrived.[137]

In 1898 a branch of 21 members was formed here, with a young man of 19 as secretary. It continued to grow and still exists with 103 members, rather more than half of whom are scattered throughout England. As time has gone on benefits have been varied, children's and women's societies formed and mortgages made available.[138] In later years a branch of the Foresters has been established here and there have been groups of Oddfellows but these have been too small to last.

It must not be forgotten that for very poor families with unintelligent or sickly or injured heads the need to set aside several pence each week could never be met: they lacked all insurance. Till 1914 wages of 12s. a week were still common on farms and 14s. the maximum.

The Friendly Societies are a proof of the hopefulness and extraordinary prudence many labourers and their wives could show: to screw out the weekly pence for "the Club" was difficult, but the reward was great. Sickness pay did not disqualify for Poor Law relief: indeed, the Guardians were inclined to help more generously those who helped themselves. But after 1884 it was even more important to be insured so as to avoid "relief", for if a man accepted it he forfeited his franchise.

The second of the thrift organisations managed by working men for themselves was the cooperative movement. In 1866 a small group of working men in Chipping Norton determined to buy coal by the ton instead of a stone or two at a time. So great a saving was made that they formed a small Co-operative Society on the model of those started twenty years before by urban working men to buy various commodities in quantity and sell to themselves. At their first public meeting in 1867 (four years before Arch's revolt) the Vicar of the town spoke approvingly and an encouraging letter was read from the Earl of Ducie, the worthy son-in-law and successor of J. H. Langston of Churchill.[139] (Although local shopkeepers might have feared losses

377

from this development, there was never any overt resistance to it, as to the claim for a better wage when Arch's movement touched the district: the landed classes had no concern with the profits of shops).

An early enterprise of the new Society was the making and sale of bread—a very portable commodity. It began to send delivery carts to the villages and to invite householders to membership. Then it ventured to send grocery also. Normal prices were charged for goods and the surplus, the private trader's profit, was returned to members or accredited to them in proportion to purchases. The village housewives valued their "dividend" which. if they could keep their hands off it, grew in a pleasing way, and would pay for a good domestic pot or children's boots. Presently they could buy meat and shoes and furniture from the "Co-op" and provide for funerals and even insure lives. Only a little good sense and much self-control was necessary for this co-operative thrift but there were still a few who must buy where they could get into debt. The Society never found the way to more than pure economic usefulness to villagers, though it could give stimulus and experience to Norton men who could attend meetings.

Earlier means to thrift had included "allotments" provided by others, though most exacting of the men's own exertions. The Poor's Plot had about 1860 ceased to be used to produce rather useless furze, and Christ Church had provided allotments at about the same time.

But all this was little enough. The cottages were still wretched. Some families were dependent on poor relief on the slightest misfortune. None of the labourers could make provision for old age. The younger men, less hopeful than their fathers had been, were liable to ask "What is there to live for? We all end up in the Workhouse". Old ladies with next to no income and unable to tend themselves, but determined to stay in their own homes were tricked and dragged to Stow. (What else could be done?)

Even voting after 1884 for Liberal candidates at Parliamentary elections was a very indirect means of self-help.

On the Farms and in the Village
1883–1914

From the passing of the Poor Law Amendment Act in 1834, and throughout Queen Victoria's reign (1837–1901), the gulf between farmers and labourers was being very slowly narrowed though there would never be an easy bridge between. The interests of farmers and workers would never coincide: in course of time farmers' clubs and the workers' trade union and political interests would express and confirm the difference. Yet the underlying sense of community in the village was able to grow. From 1876 all the village boys sat on the same school benches and after 1884 farmers and labourers both voted in parliamentary elections—quite frequently for the same candidate—and from 1896 they would hear each other's views in the annual parish meeting. It is true that in discussions there was disparity: farmers had more confidence and self-possession and therefore better if limited powers of expression. Only once before the young men returned from the First World War, conscious of service done and wide views gained, would wage-earners make demands of the Parish Council. By the end of the century some of the more prosperous railwaymen owned their own cottages, and were gaining some experience and some confidence in their Trade Union, but there were few of them compared with the farm workers.

Change was more constant and at times very visible and dramatic. In school the start of the new century was emphasized: the children felt they were living at a magic moment—a feeling that would be justified by the most thorough re-making of village lives after the mid-century. In 1900 there might be seen on the greater roads of the Cotswolds a new kind of vehicle, to be for long less important than railways, but gradually to become more pervasive. A Burford lady wrote in 1902[140] that "steam horses confined to iron rails had proved beneficial enough but there was nothing to be said for letting them loose to the terror of man and beast in the country roads". The combustion engine was a still better steed than was steam: no very heavy fuel to carry, no feeding, watering, grooming or stable to clean. In 1903 there were three motor-cars in nearby villages, all driven by clergymen. Two years later there was one in Kingham village—a "5 horse-power, single cylinder Humberette", owned by the blacksmith-engineer, Caleb Lainchbury. His son describes it and adds "what wobbles developed at speeds of about twenty miles an hour!"[141] Doctors slowly abandoned their horses to follow these examples, to the relief of their own lives and their patients'. The "motor" became a common sight. Villagers had long been able to use the telegraph, and since 1904 it was possible in some post offices, though not in Bledington, to use the telephone.

The railway continued to improve its services. In 1905 the Kingham-

Banbury line was joined to the Kingham-Cheltenham by "the loop". Every day groups of people from Kingham and Bledington gathered on the bridge over the new rails to see and feel the express train thundering through "from Newcastle-on-Tyne to South Wales". Once or twice later, the Royal train from Scotland was run on to a siding in our parish for the night. "We saw nothing of the Queen but her bath-water" villagers said, but "with one thing and another" the loop had quickened life.

The common basis of village life was still the farms. After the first adjustments to enclosure, these had undergone no revolution. Their number was still usually the same. In every decade from 1831 till after the Second World War there were from 10 to 8 farmers, beside smaller men with under 40 acres. Slight changes in the number of larger farms were due to individuals sometimes taking on additional holdings. Later the holdings would fall apart again. We have detailed information for the year 1901.[142] Bledington Grounds comprises 288 acres; two composite holdings (Rectory Farm with Pebbly Hill and Home Farm with 3 small units) are of 272 and 119 acres; 4 farms have between 109 and 86 acres, and the eighth 42. Besides these there were eight small-holders, with from 37 acres to 12, the last made up of two orchards. Other holdings were of less than 4 acres—tradesmen's closes for horse, or orchards attached to houses. Ownership also was a good deal distributed: Christ Church retained its land and in 1913 acquired also Home Farm of 86 acres: the University retained Lower Farm: Bledington Grounds was being as usual farmed by its owner. The Earl of Ducie was a small owner, since he had bought the mill and its few acres, across the river from his Churchill estate. Only one farmer, except at the Grounds, the widow Harwood, was now an owner. Stayts, one family of Peglers and Gilberts had all mortgaged their property for its full value and finally sold it. Peglers and a Gilbert heir had both emigrated—one to U.S.A. and the other to Canada, but still half the farming families bore old names: Stow, Gilks, Harwood, and another Pegler. Hawker, Jefferies, and Hunt were new here but were those of farming or small-holder families in nearby villages. Two of our small-holders also bear old names—Cook and Benfield; a third, Malins, approached its century here. There was a fairly new name—Drinkwater—at Bledington Grounds.

All but one of the larger holdings were engaged in "mixed farming" (one, Gilberts', lay too low for ploughing) but there was comparatively little arable. Only some 40 of the 270 acres of the Grounds were ploughed. On Harwoods', Stows' and Lords' or "Manor" Farm the proportion was rather higher. Jonah Hunt on Rectory Farm liked arable farming and raised his proportion, growing barley with some success. The rotation on arable—but the order of cropping is doubtful—included wheat, "broad red clover", beans and barley (the two latter fed to horses and cattle) and fallow. Mustard was sometimes grown on the fallow and ploughed in as green manure. But more important, our farmers were rearing stock, producing milk and butter, and selling off calves. Every farm had a few geese; turkeys were tried on Home Farm; maize from America being cheap, farmers' wives were keeping large flocks of hens. Oats from the River Plate were very cheap.

As the population in towns increased transport of products by rail grew more frequent. Bledington with other villages around began to despatch milk to Oxford and London, chiefly the latter. Almost all the larger farms did so, leaving the local milk and butter market to the hard-working wives of smaller farmers.

The monthly cattle market at the Langston Arms by Kingham Junction Station was doing well, especially in sales of Shorthorns. There is no report of outstandingly good breeding here but the market set standards and provided opportunities to acquire sound animals. The number of cows varied on the farms between 9 and 16; smallholders might have from 7 or 8 to 2: they also kept pigs and poultry and grew apples, perhaps half of them for cider. The old pear orchards still contained beautiful old trees, but of little value, and only one or two apple orchards were well kept.

As to methods practised in the fields, it is significant that the number of labourers declined very slowly. In 1851 there had been 51; after the First World War there were 44 (and even in 1931 the number was 40). The reduction the country over was one third, here less than a fifth—a proof of conservatism in farming ways. There was still a sufficient number of labourers both to form a class with a common basis and yet to contain groups. In late August and September 1914 there was still the ancient sight of old and young, men, women and children thronging the harvest field. A photograph taken in 1910 shows a hundred persons on John Hunt's wheat-field; the same number gathered on Hawkers' Home Farm fields. The latter still supplemented its regular staff with casual workers from many miles away: two families lived for weeks in its barn. Their legend was assured by a fight one night, between the heads of two families, attacking each other with sickles; men leaving the inn at closing time saw the sparks flying in the dark from these weapons.

But though sickles were still used to reap corn on a fair-sized farm, methods were changing. Only Bledington Grounds acquired the early "manually operated" reaping-machine which had to be accompanied by a man who turned the corn against the knife. Other farms did not buy reapers till the "rack machine" had become common. On this, revolving "sails" both brought the corn to the blade and cast it free from the machine. Soon followed the binder, with its mechanism for tying the sheaves. No doubt the slow rate at which harvest machinery was bought was due to the small proportion of arable land, but also to conservatism: though there was some borrowing there was no concerted scheme for exchange.

The first mowing machine for grass seems to have been acquired about 1884[143]—a tragic occasion. The worker in charge of it lost a hand on the first day: at night some of his fellow labourers drove in stakes among the standing grass. It was a late date for machine-breaking but there were old reasons for it and a newer one: farm labour, always a dangerous trade, had become more so.

For transport on the farms two-wheeled carts were used for most purposes, though the old wagons came out in hay-time and harvest—occasionally, even in the nineteen-fifties; tractors, rare everywhere, had not appeared here by 1914. Every farm had its team of horses and its carter.

Low wages and plentiful labour no doubt prevented a rush for machinery. There was little reason why it should be popular till the versatile tractor came. Wages here could still be as low as twelve shillings "before the War", though thirteen and fourteen were paid. It was, by 1900, some years since employers had become legally due to pay compensation for accidents where negligence could be proved, but the provision was for the most part a dead letter: farmers did not insure and labourers had no funds for court cases. We glimpse the economic gap between the farmer and worker. Since the failure of the Agricultural Labourers' Union in this area there could be no rectification of the labourers' risks except through Parliamentary action.

By 1914 every fair-sized farm had drills, a mowing machine or harvester, and most also a cultivator (drawn by three horses), a set of drags, and some a hay-tedder (but little girls were still kept from school while mothers helped to make hay). The all-metal zig-zag harrows had superseded the old harrows with short wooden bars studded with steel tines, which had been so long preferred. The threshing drum, powered with a steam engine, owned and let out by one farmer, was horse-drawn from farm to farm. On all farms the small machinery such as turnip or chaff-cutters had improved. Machinery would take a spurt forward when oil-engines, being light and easily moved, became cheap, but they do not appear to have been introduced by 1914. The farmyards were museums of old tools, most of them in occasional use: breast-ploughs still used for removing turf, fagging hooks, scythes, sickles, "dumpicks" or dung-forks, curious implements for pulling together tightly the lips of wool-sacks—all these hung or stood around the sheds and barns.

Farming experiment was far to seek but individuals turned aside to make money by buying and selling. A small farm, Hangerson, became the base of a horse-trading business. As many as thirty horses might be seen along the road to Gloucester market; one large farmer traded in hay and corn and one family supplied some London shops with meat and presently they themselves moved into the London retail business.

On the whole, then, our farmers from the late eighteen seventies until 1914 led a poor and rather harrassed life, shared—although there was some improvement from the nineties—throughout the country. The import of cheap grain[144] from the new countries impoverished large arable farmers. In 1883 traditional explanations of poor results such as small crops and wet harvests still received too much weight: the general trend was not yet fully acknowledged. Prices had fallen from an average for wheat of 51/10d. in the seventies, to 35/9d in the eighties, but the fall was concentrated in the last five years. Two disastrous years when the average fell to 29/9d. were painfully felt: there were many bankruptcies of farmers in the Banbury area, and landlords lost money also. On our own comparatively small farms there were no bankruptcies: the loss from bread-corn prices was partly compensated by cheap American corn for stock-feeding. They had besides, no very important social interests or status to maintain as had farmers who had hunted and sent their daughters to expensive schools. The rents they paid seem to have been gradually lowered. From 1855 Banks Farm was let at 33/4d. per acre; for some years after 1892 Stows paid 30/-, a decline from 39/- paid from 1881 to that year. Land was sometimes sold for as little as £30 per acre.

Farmers' wives retreated into their kitchens, dispensed with the servants they had had in earlier decades and added to their egg-production butter-making and even calf-rearing. They were as essential to the farms as their Elizabethan counterparts but did not gain the same consideration. They kept their homes real: the quirks and oddities of art that were seen in the homes of tradespeople in towns, as well as in finer houses (wax models of bouquets of flowers, stuffed birds, the huge third rate pictures of sailing boats in harbour or waterfalls) never appeared in their rooms. Occasionally farmers and their wives would patronise the travelling artist who made a drawing of the head of the family or of its home. They read Dickens and the younger folk *Queechy* and other romantic books: the girls were taught music, not to sing drawing-room songs but to be ready to play for hymns sung at home or at Sunday School. Their life was more strenuous in labour than in thought or enterprise.

In 1892 Bledington men read in the Oxford Journal reports of speeches agitating for reduction in rates on farming land. By now the County Councils were busy on their road-making and other works, and their rates were rising. By 1896 the pressure had been successful and rates on agricultural land were by law reduced to half, and a few years later to a quarter. This naturally spared landlords from reduction of rents as well as helping farmers.

But farmers began also to express their need for better conditions from landlords and to look to Parliament for help. Richard Stow was an active member of the Stow and Moreton Agricultural Society, which had an unusual number of members farming medium acreages. These urged each other to use their Parliamentary votes in their own interests and to refuse leases which did not provide compensation for improvements, and for unfair disturbance, and give reasonable freedom of cultivation.

All this led up by 1900 to the formation of clubs exclusively for farmers. The Banbury Farmers' Club made exceptional progress, recruiting members from as far west as Chipping Norton. Such Clubs multiplied fast and in 1908 the National Farmers' Union was founded. As it developed the Union would do more than any movement had done to change farmers' habits of mind. It emphasized their common concerns which were economic only, while it also provided a certain scope for ambition and sociability. It is in part responsible for the scorn sometimes expressed for farming "as a way of life". Monetary profit was coming more to the front, though still on small farms home consumption of products was important. Here, bacon, milk, butter, eggs and fowl were all used at home and sold to neighbours till the First World War, the mill still ground local grain and a good deal of bread was made at home. Certainly farmers went about their work in a more leisured way than now. No work was done on Sundays except the tending of animals, not even in the wettest summers and harvest-times. There were gay occasions, notably making cider together with the village press—an autumn frolic that would not cease till the nineteen forties.

Our farmers still served church and village: one would chair the vestry meeting, or the Parish Council, another train a choir, others act as members of the School Board and visit the school in its working hours and their own: not, of course that these offices were always discharged with talent or with liberality but office could call out both and the framework and custom of service remained. One may speculate that Bledington farmers might have taken readily to an economic-social ideal and brought to modern agricultural change much of value from their own lives, but private capitalistic enterprise with a minimum of occasional co-operation was then the prevailing inevitable model in the influential Farmers' Union. Most of our farmers did not become Union Members for a good many years, in fact till the nineteen forties. Once they acted together in protest: those who sent milk to London withheld it for a higher price. Two local farmers' churn-carts were held up in the road to the station and the milk emptied into the ditch. Some sort of organisation was needed.

The relations of farmers with their workers had never been so distant as in parishes of larger farms. There was little or no "conspicuous expenditure"; servility was never given, never much cared for. And now the worst days had passed: for labourers life was still hard enough "in all conscience" as the country phrase went, but starvation diet was something of a legend, though still the children did not have suitable food. Cheap corn meant more and better bread. There were more opportunities for young men: by 1909 the number of railwaymen had grown to 20. Many village families had relatives in London and visits were exchanged. Now that literacy was the rule and postage inexpensive families remained united and in contact, in spite of migration.

A group remained for whom improvement was very slow to come. They earned the lowest wage of twelve shillings a week and lived in the gardenless cottages. One cottage at least was still shared: later I was shown through it in 1954, by a man who had spent his childhood there when it was shared by two families—large, as under such circumstances they are apt to be. He explained to me how some of the children had slept in an upturned table: its framework kept off the draughts. This group sometimes suffered from unemployment and then their children's malnutrition and ill-health distressed our schoolmasters.

These were hardly the circumstances in which neighbourly and easy relations could exist between farmers and their men but in slightly better instances they could be good. By 1914 John Hall had served the Stow family as carter for fifty-five years and had not yet left his post. His record was applauded by the local Agricultural Society on his employer's motion. John's wife had before her marriage been a servant in the Stow farmhouse. There was and is between Halls and Stows a mutual regard, warm and respectful. Jonah Hunt on Rectory Farm (with other holdings) had a complicated relationship with his workers: from the farm they had not only milk and butter, mutton and bacon, but coal also. (It is said he bought six trucks of twenty tons each year). None of these things were "presents" in lieu of wages, but prices were low and long credit was given. It is said that, excepting youngsters, none of his workers ever left him. Farmers and workers had some shared ideas: one or two of the former had struggled from small beginnings and knew hardship.

Yet a certain meanness in farmers' attitudes to workers could be seen, due no doubt to the tendency to defend their economic position by saving money rather than by more active processes. It is said that after the passage of the National Insurance Act in 1911 two labourers sought compensation for injury, one of them being awarded £50 and the other £18. After that no farmer would permanently employ the man who had received the larger sum. The same attitude was seen in the long absence of any effort to supply convenient field-gardens. Both employers and employed had found that they must look to Parliament for improvements in their lot. A report in the Oxford Journal asserted that almost every qualified Bledingtonian was known to have voted in the 1906 election, when the Liberal Party were returned and took office, though there were rain and high winds all day and a man and horse were in danger of drowning in the floods. Some of both groups had great hopes of the new Government—farmers wanting security against hazards such as being "rented on their own improvements" and all labourers hoping for old age pensions.

Certainly wage-earners and their families were better off after the Liberal innings between 1906 and 1914. They were fortunate that the House of Lords could not throw out the Old Age Pensions Bill as they had done so many others. The Act had at once a most direct effect on village lives. It provided, quite outside the Poor Law, five shillings a week for men and women of seventy years whose income from other sources was less than £50 a year. That provision included some farmers' and tradesmen's widows as well as poorer folk. (Sadly, persons already relieved by Guardians were not eligible). The Act brought the most unalloyed material blessing ever to befall the village poor. The very workhouse, the number of inmates reduced, became more tolerable. In 1909 there were sixteen pensioners in our village.

There was unusual attention in the Government's programme to what concerned country life as such. It included the provision of small holdings, which might provide an escape from low wages and low status. The more truly conservative were politicians the more they should surely have approved such provisions. Since 1800 there had been other Acts to encourage garden allotments but they had been half-hearted. In 1887 an Allotments Act had recognised that without the possibility of compulsory purchase of land very little could be done. It was almost a dead letter in the countryside though a few townsmen gained. Late in the century Denmark had proved that agricultural small holdings could be a success with many aspects—economic, social and educational. This vital success provided our reformers with a new impulse. In the new Small Holdings Act of 1907 the right administrative setting was at last adopted. The Board of Agriculture became the critical supervisory authority and the County Council was given the duty to ascertain the demand in its area and the power to obtain the necessary land on reasonable terms. In Bledington there were old holdings of from five to fifty acres but they were held by small farming families and tradespeople. No labourer, but for some remarkable chance, had access to the small capital required and often labourers' literacy was inadequate for necessary purchase and sales, But garden allotments were within their scope, as they had shown on the Poor's Plot and Christ Church allotments.

The new Small Holders Act had a great welcome and some County

387

Councils became great landowners. By the beginning of 1908 the Gloucestershire County Council had received 166 applications[145] and they were still arriving at the rate of six a day. Applicants desired an average of 26 acres. For garden allotments, more local provision was no doubt fitting. Nothing happened in Bledington till early in 1914 when thirty men sent a petition to the Parish Council "for small holdings" by which they seem to have meant allotments of an acre or so. At the Parish Meeting that year it was agreed that the Council should obtain land. Two farmers, both holding land within easy reach of most homes were approached. One simply declined: the other offered part of Skeythorns (the ancient Skey's Thorns) on the road to Icomb but the distance was far too great; and that was the end of the matter till after the War. Within a year of November 1918 (the end of the War) our Parish Council received permission from the Board of Agriculture to purchase land. Meanwhile the Oar Ground, part of the ancient Lower Oar came into the market. But the Parish Council had no desire for the responsibility of purchase and suggested to the County Council that they should acquire the land—which they were "disposed to do". But at the sale the County's Agent stopped bidding while the price was still reasonable—as the village thought, and with reason, for it was bought to become a small holding for fruit growing. So haltingly went poor men's hopes in the country. That was the end of the hope of public provision. At last in a few years' time a farmer offered some large plots for garden allotments behind the school— a very eligible spot for evening cultivation. On these an incalculable deal of hard, dutiful, out-of-doors labour has been carried on in the last half century. But they were not agricultural small holdings.

These two Acts—Old Age pensions and Small Holdings—were the only important measures proposed by the elected House and not rejected by the Lords. There had been also among the rejected ones an Education Bill and one concerned with the licensing of public houses, the latter approved by sections of every church and class and party, but opposed by vested interests shared by a number of members of the Upper House. Another project important to our labourers was compulsory insurance by employers for accidents at work.

The struggle between the elected and hereditary Houses (in great measure so out of date) absorbed the minds and energies of politicians and statesmen: the international developments which were to lead to the First World War were fully reckoned with by very few even of

388

the best informed and remained only distantly threatening to the most intelligent villagers. Three years after the Parliament Act of 1911, with its partial victory for the Commons, came the outbreak of War, with England's people not united and her military machine inefficient. Every village would be forced to make its full contribution as may be seen by the War Memorial which alas! is nowhere lacking.

The War is the great watershed at which, with a few anticipations, we pause. How was life in our village just before we approached it?

It is usual to find that after literacy has become common a village has its poet—or at least its versifier. Ours occurred in the earlier years of this century. He was so active that if you met him in the streets he would button-hole you and pour out his rhymes. But also he had a sense of history and for the importance of contemporary event. From his verses and collection of cuttings of his articles from the Oxford and Cheltenham newspapers (pasted into an illustrated catalogue of ironmongery)[146] we can gain a picture of the village in 1909.

But first a word on our numbers. We infer from the census taken two years later that there were nearly 400 villagers; the number had been increasing since 1901 at the rate of about six a year. There were, much as usual, ten farmers, some small holders, and four shopkeepers. One shop was quite large, supplying many outlying houses and some small villages: others were tiny, selling small matters like reels of sewing cotton. There were twenty railwaymen and no fewer than sixteen Old Age Pensioners with a varied and rather new range of craftsmen and tradesmen: a slater, a market-gardener, baker, carrier, photographer, an undertaker and three butchers, besides carpenters, miller and smith.

In 1909 the weather was exceptionally severe and produced economic shadow if not gloom. Hay and corn were "in whole or part spoiled", beekeepers gained no honey, floods invaded homes. But spirits could rise. There were innumerable pleasures, mostly of a communal nature, including meetings and "concerts" and other entertainments, a Band of Hope for children, but with adult members also; the Temperance Band was large and active, and another Band, based on the inn, had a brief lively career. There were Sunday Schools at both church and chapel whose friends provided "treats", several within a year, sometimes taking the children to a high field with a glorious view, for sports and tea. In 1908 "Pleasant Sunday Afternoon" meetings had begun. They took place in the chapel but were not distinctively Methodist: folk of any Church or none attended at will if they could enjoy what passed. For politics there was a Bledington branch of a Conservative Club and one public meeting to give support to the licensing Bill at that time before Parliament—not a party meeting: the Temperance movement crossed boundaries

Most of the occasions had two characteristics in common: they had some connection with religion and were the setting of much individual activity; men, women and children all contributed. Speeches and addresses were given notably at the "Pleasant Sunday" meetings: usually but not always the speakers were men, their subjects such as Character Building or the lives of missionaries; women sang solos, adolescents gave "recitations" of narrative or humorous verses or "dialogues"—playlets with two or three performers. Only the short recitals by musical families probably reached a standard cultivated persons could care for, or that could escape the smiles of superior persons who were also a feature of the time, though not numerous here.

Our reporter, if not a Methodist must have been well disposed towards the chapel; but certainly the latter favoured popular activity, by its dependence upon its members. Most of these occasions transcended sect. A churchwarden and his family played a leading part in "P.S.As." The annual Methodist ' Camp Meeting" on the green was attended by 500 people, certainly not all Methodists, who were almost crowded out of their own chapel at their Anniversary Services.

This kindly and fruitful peace owed much to the elderly vicar, the Rev. John Hartshorne. He had long shown his accord with the village community and in the time of ill health appreciation of his long and reasonable service was shown in the consolatory messages sent him from many a meeting.

Newspaper notes on "religious" activity, stressing its social amenity and simple pleasures may seem to leave out Hamlet from the play. But its core is evident enough from memories of the old Vicar, and of the gentle devoted Methodist school manager, musician and delicately conscientious worker, George Stayt: of the stern upright old John Hall, who when pressed to apply for an Old Age Pension wept with misery. For these and others the reading of the New Testament, the contemplation of the life of Christ and acceptance of his teaching on human nature and the duties of human relations, was the centre of life.

But there was a very large margin around this centre. The contrast between two of our farmers shows the range of impulse and feeling in villages. Both were men of force: both had risen from smaller farms to the largest of all our holdings—William Jefferies to Bledington Grounds and Jonah Hunt to the Christ Church property. Both were remarkable presences—Hunt bearded, broad and sturdy, about the work on his farm more tattered than his men, but on other occasions full of dignity in well made clothes of finest Chipping Norton tweed. Jefferies[147] was tall, immense: he weighed, it is said, 24 stone and could duck under one of the old wagons (seven hundred weight tare) and lift its four wheels well off the ground.

Hunt was of communal mould, a special constable, school manager, a parish councillor. He was also a Methodist, and officer of the Society, a great supporter of the Temperance Band. Outside his offices, his activities were less usual. He loved children and festivity, together or apart. To every Sunday School or other "treat" he went with his portable boiler to help provide tea, and with the dolls his wife made for the girls' prizes for the three-legged and other races. He would go too with the Temperance Band to village "Clubs" to dispense non-alcoholic drinks, and would visit the old folks' section of Chipping Norton workhouse carrying gifts. He loved old ways but new ones too, and that was no doubt one reason why he prospered so as to set up two of his sons on good farms and to enjoy a modest but comfortable retirement.

Of Jefferies' farming one hears little, but much of the races over his ground. There the Heythrop Hunt ran their annual "point-to-point" and for a few years a regiment of Hussars raced there in brilliant uniforms. He became a familiar of aristocratic huntsmen; the year the Prince of Wales competed at the Hunt Races it was Jefferies who seized his hand in congratulation.

In everything he did Jefferies showed his exceptional vitality; he lived in his chosen way irrespective of his resources. Presently he was bankrupt. Bailiff's men took up residence in his house but became his friends and helped to barricade it against the police. Summoned to the County Court he was repeatedly and roughly rude to the Judge. The local courts knew him too: forced for lack of money for fees to send his children to the village school the Board prosecuted him at last for their unpunctuality and absence. He was determined to be and was outside society.

The paths of these two villagers naturally crossed, once with violent effect. Jefferies bought a stag, of all things, and kept it some winter weeks confined and fed, to be hunted by himself and the under-graduate clubs who kept horses at Home Farm. (He was following the mode, it is said, of Blenheim's more stately cruelty). The day came, but the stag would not take to the more or less open country: it leapt gates into the inn yard, broke into the pound and gardens and then ran in an aimless roundabout course[148] with Jefferies and his young followers confusedly in chase. Presently it doubled back over Rectory Farm where Hunt was walking with his gun to get a hare or rabbit for his wife. This was no hunt! This was shameful! What about his crops! He shot the stag.

A few nights later after midnight a crowd of undergraduates mobbed his house and with long poles smashed every window in it, their noise shocking the village.

Both of these men were long recalled in talk, but Jefferies more often, as if young farming folk liked to think of this powerful erratic tempera-ment among so much that was middling and moderate. Life led out too little into greater spaces—a complaint that would not so very long continue to be made.

A small vignette may bring to an end this account of farm folk. Stock and dairy and farmyard animals and poultry were more im-portant than corn, but work with them was so diurnal. There was birth and slaughter—dramatic enough, but sad and messy. Harvest comes but once a year, with heat, sunshine and long daylight. It was a social event and in every fortunate year still brought its sense of achievement and success. The last load from the last farm to finish was escorted home by a cheering crowd. One year, recalled by one young at the time, the wagon came home over the little town bridge, into the gateway of Home Farm. It was late and the men leading the horses carried modern "hurricane" lanterns, with oil lamps inside: others in the crowd had in their hands little old horn lanterns, with candles. Safely through the gate-posts, the horses stopped. Farmer Hawker and his wife stood beside a barrel of their own cider, handing horn tumblers to everyone who came. Our farming was somewhat backward, but it was life, not a mere specialism.

During the latter eighteen hundreds Christianity as our villagers professed it and political democracy which both rest on a supra-rational faith in human value were creating a better community. But would it one day rise again to such united achievement as in its ancient arts and in the re-building of its church in the fifteenth century? At any rate the nineteen hundreds would show that it still had hold on art as well as on religion.

The Morris Men

One activity in the village at this time has so far gone unmentioned. It was age-old but still a vivid streak of life, equal in its intensity, for some, with the high moments of some old Methodist's meditation or an heroic schoolmaster's devotion. It was a treasure and hidden in the most effective of all ways: by the blindness of those who might have seen. Over and above its own value, it raises interesting questions.

Once it had been part of the inheritance of the whole village[149]: in the early twentieth century it belonged almost exclusively to a small group of farm-workers—those whose minds and whose leisure were not absorbed by religion or the sociabilities of the inn and who had the necessary gift. The share of women and children in the old arts had come to an end as property and social division had dominated life (though the school revived some May Day celebrations). Even among the men they were rapidly vanishing: yet, strangely, it had retained its fine quality to the last.

Living in Bould, the hamlet on Idbury Hill, as late as 1913 was an old man, Charles Benfield, who had been fiddler to the "morris side", the dancers of the ancient morris dance. He no longer played: some years earlier his fiddle had been broken and he had never been able to buy another. There was also Edwin Gibbs in 1913 seventy five years old who went about whistling the old dance tunes and when talk touched on the dances in the King's Head would rise and demonstrate the steps. John Hitchman had been "fool" to the last side, George Hathaway (the ancient name again) had carried the "bag"—a box in the shape of a heart—when the side had gone touring. There was plenty to talk of when these men (with Jonathan Harris and Thomas Wright) chanced to meet: the old dance names alone would decorate a talk—Princess Royal, Lumps of Plum Pudding, Trunkles, Ladies Pleasure, Bledington Hey Away, Young Collins, Balance the Straw and the rest.

Until the late eighteen eighties and into the nineties the side had danced on May Day and in July at the "Club" festivity on the green at home and had also gone to other village "Clubs". In 1887 they had paid a visit to another Morris group, celebrating Queen Victoria's Jubilee with the Longborough "side", and in 1900 there had been a last visit to Fifield. Earlier our side had danced often with Idbury and Lyneham groups and sometimes at Shipton and Ascott under Wychwood. Their connection with Longborough was the most intimate, it seems. To a great extent the two villages shared the same repertory of dances, but the style of their dancing differed and an element of controversy as well as competition spiced the pleasures of meeting.

Naming of dances after villages as for example *Bledington Hey Away* or *Longborough Swaggering Boney* is misleading, meaning chiefly the place of record, though also it may indicate difference of style. Hathaway dancers, for example, who began their lives in Bledington, would later be dancing with Stow. Hathaways had started families in the Slaughters and other villages, and many were morris men. Even when dances bore such names as *Idbury Hill* there were very similar dances under other names in other villages.

But style varied from village to village: the forest men leapt high, while the Bledington side prided itself on keeping their feet close to the ground, but executing many small foot movements: Longborough did the "jump" every two bars and Bledington every four. The refinement, the detail, of the dancing is one of its great features—the variety of figure and step and movement. The social pleasures were dependent on the intrinsic beauty of the dance, on the music, as well as the movements, and on the demand for the use of all the men's faculties and their physical endurance. These were the cause, too, of the long devotion to the cult.

The nature of the dances called for onlookers. Six men formed a "side", dancing mostly in pairs. They were accompanied by a fool or squire who with his bladder on a stick kept the space for the dance whilst amusing the crowd with quips and cranks and antics.[150] There was also the man with the box: the men needed money for dress and instruments and indeed for shoe-leather, not to mention drinks.

By 1890 it had not always been possible to form a complete side in Bledington. Benfield and Hathaway had bestirred themselves to recruit and instruct a "young side" who should maintain the tradition of visits and competitions. But this plan, successful for a time, broke down. The swiftness of step and the elaborate figures are best learned by small boys, with their wonderful absorptive and imitative power, and by this time men, including members of the side, left the village too often for the old traditions to be steadily carried forward.

A few signs and remnants of other kinds of tradition remained; for example, the ancient oaken may pole on the green, round which social dances had taken place, men, women and children or young men and maidens dancing together. As late as 1924 there lingered a trace of the ancient folk-song, Arthur o' Bradley's, and verses of a May Day Song; and as has been told there were crude remnants of a Christmas Mumming play.

The traditions of the dances were of vital interest only to the dancers, even here. They took place in the evening with the Aunt Sally game and the quoits. Visits to other villages also took place late, after the evening meal and the working hours, except on a few rare holidays. In middle-class minds when the morris was known at all, it was a "rough frolic", associated with uncouth relaxations, such as beer-drinking. Certainly there had been a famous local fracas. The rough forest men of Field Town loved a fight and had a bout with the Lyneham side, but such exuberance was rare: the essence of the dances was delicate skill and imagination—art, in short. Quite other causes than coarseness had to be sought for their being so nearly lost.

In our new school in the eighteen-eighties the boys and girls sang poor specially-written songs and did "Swedish" exercises: no-one knew that they could have already from their fathers that "grandest" most exacting of dances, the *Gallant Hussar*. Some atmosphere, some repression had confined the dances and much else to lowly classes, not here alone but everywhere. As we have seen the labouring folk were reclaiming something for themselves, but chapel and brass band and friendly society had not broken down the social fences.

But now to the older labourers came the astonishing experience not only of respect but equal friendship with men who had enjoyed, if not wealth and rank, much that is best in our, or any, civilisation. As early as 1907 a "gentleman" (Cecil Sharp) had admired and conversed with an old dancer at Stow where at least one Bledington family had relatives skilled in the old group dancing. The Slaughters and Long-borough had been visited also. It is possible that Bledington folk had also heard of the learned young man from Oxford who had made his home in a cottage in Ascott under Wychwood where he had fired the villagers, especially a group of young men, with interest in old dances and songs. R. J. E. Tiddy's chief interest was in the old mumming plays of which he had collected versions in Icomb and other villages.[151]

In Bledington, he found only crude fragments but heard of men who had only a few years ago ceased to form a "morris side". It was in 1913, some eighteen months before the beginning of the War, that Tiddy brought Cecil Sharp to Bledlington. Together they sought out the men with the treasure.

Sharp, like Tiddy, was a University man of distinction, a member of Clare College, Cambridge.[152] Like Tiddy, Sharp had learned his approach to ancient dance through another study—in his case, the collection of folk-songs. Of these, England had once had as rich a store as any country but it was long believed that none existed in this country. Other nations' modern music was based on popular, indigenous melody, and scholars had concluded that this was the natural and necessary basis: lacking this, England was evidently a basically unmusical nation building on borrowed foundations such music as she had.

But as long ago as 1844 songs had been collected in Sussex, and in 1889 a West Country village clergyman, the Rev. Sabine Baring-Gould, had gathered a few fine tunes and songs from old neighbours of his and published them. His books, especially *Old Country Life*[153] were widely read and soon others were collecting songs. One of these was another village parson, the Rev. Charles L. Marson who, together with Sharp, found, not a few, but hundreds of songs, often with what they deemed lovely tunes. Words, because they had had a commercial value for broadsheets in times gone by, had been modified and spoiled, but the melodies had still their beauty.

It was found that many rural areas had such songs, and Sharp looked for them everywhere. It was in contacts with country singers that he learned how to approach the slow and reticent minds of rural folk. It was not easy. He would seek out an old man or woman who was reputed to know an old song. It was usually difficult to persuade them that he was not greatly interested in recent songs but wished to hear the old traditional ones, which no-one had valued but the singer himself and an old crony or two. Then, too he would often find—so deep were the treasures buried—that the song could only be recalled under special circumstnces. A man must be in the company of particular friends at the inn, or must be in the act of ploughing: a woman could only recollect her words while she ironed her linen, or worked at hoeing or weeding. Once a woman singer who had interrupted her task of picking up potatoes in the field to sing had seized the lapels of

Sharp's coat in her enthusiasm, exclaiming "Isn't it lovely?" Such experiences revealed to Sharp and Tiddy and others that the men and women who had retained elements of the ancient culture were like themselves, artists—lovers of form and sound. On their side, the rustic singers found Sharp as one said, "common but nice". Common: he did not fear to lose his dignity, had no condescension, no complex "superior" accent (mannerisms then so common) but directness and patience together with great competence. He had, notably, techniques for recording songs and dances: the notation for dances he had rescued from old records and modified for himself. A musician and enthusiast for ancient music and dance living a few miles from here gave, later, a sketch of Sharp at work.[154] "Another dancer whom Cecil Sharp discovered pulling mangels was asked for particulars of a certain dance. The veteran took Sharp behind a haystack and the pair capered together, the old man singing the tune at the pitch of his voice until the data necessary for the perpetuation of the dancing were in the collector's note book". By chance the dancer's employer came on the scene unnoticed and was "thunderstruck" to see his labourer's accomplishment. At Eynsham "men straight in from the fields in their working clothes, sodden with rain, danced in boots heavily weighed with mud, . . . and gave me as fine an exhibition of Morris dancing as it has ever been my good fortunate to see".[156]

Sharp's experience here was similar. He visited Charles Benfield, the fiddler at Bould, but the old man could not play the tunes: his fiddle had been broken some years before and he had never been able to replace it: so on another visit Sharp brought him a new one. At once Benfield tried to play the tunes "but the result did not please him". Thoughtfully he examined and fingered his new bow and said "It looks alright and it seems a nice bow but somehow it won't keep time with the other hand"—a reflection of the inability of these old musicians and dancers to dissociate dance movements from the tune and vice versa".[155]

On another visit Sharp met Edwin Gibbs, then in his seventy-fifth year, who demonstrated the steps of the Bledington dances, whistling the tunes the while. Gibbs had seen dancers of the modern revival and criticised their style. It was "not danciful enough", but "all caperin', and runnin' and reevin' about". But then the Bledington style was exceptionally precise, and the new dancers had not learned it.

397

Benfield's new fiddle soon learned to dance, and Sharp recorded from him the "magnificent tune" of the "grandest most strenuous of all Morris dances, *Gallant Hussar*", together with the tunes (and from others the dances) of *Trunkles, William and Nancy*, and *Leap Frog* or *Glorisher* "all superb dances" with also three jigs:—*Princess Royal, Lumps of Plum Pudding, Ladies Pleasure.*[157]

The work of collection was continued, not always by Sharp. Collectors of dances were astonished at the number of villages in this area that retained or had only recently lost their morris and other dances, and often at the number of dances. There were Sherborne ("a terrible place for dances"), Lower Slaughter, Swell, Spelsbury (where the morris was danced once a year on the church tower) Oddington, Leafield (or, its older name, Field Town), Field Assarts, Ramsden, Little Barrington, Wheatley, Brailes, Ilmington, Finstock, Bloxham, Bampton, Eynsham, Asthall, Brize Norton. Not all the villages in this folk-dance area were in Gloucestershire and Oxfordshire. Chipping Warden was in Northamptonshire, Bidford in Warwickshire, Oakley in Buckinghamshire. The area had been defined, no doubt, before the county organisations had been established. Scholars in the subject, notably Joseph Needham, the Cambridge biologist, have mapped the areas where morris dances have been found and have concluded that they "are restricted to those territories which between the 5th and 11th centuries were Saxon".[158] Some have speculated on a still longer past. It is certain that their continuity has been very remarkable.

The dances first recorded in Bledington were naturally those most completely recalled. After the First World War Cecil Sharp resumed his work, but he died in 1924. The work of collection was then continued by the Travelling Morris, a group of Cambridge men who toured the Cotswolds in 1923 and on other occasions, keeping in touch with the new dancers and noting new dances or fragments, with also an occasional song. In the course of time it was established that the Bledington repertory,—very largely shared by Idbury and Fifield—included 28 dances.[159] Of these some seventeen were so fully recorded that they are now commonly danced by Folk Dance Clubs. Their names have great interest, not explored in this book, for example—Hey Away (or Hey Diddle Dis), Idbury Hill (or London Pride), Maid of the Mill, Morning Star, Old Woman Tossed Up, Over the Water to Charlie, Bonnets so Blue (or Boys of the Bundle) Cuckoo's Nest, William and Nancy, General Monk's March,

398

Glorisher (or Glorishears) also known as Sunflower, Constant Billy, Young Collins, Balance the Straw, Ladies Pleasure, Lumps of Plum Pudding, Princess Royal (the last three are jigs), Jockey to the Fair, Shepherd's Hey, Lord Sherborne's Jig, Greensleeves, Trunkles.

Notable visits were those of the Travelling Morris in 1924 and 25. They camped on a midsummer evening at the top of Idbury Hill and "gave a show" in the garden of the manor house, having fetched the local men to join them. At the end Richard Bond "was so overcome with emotion that he insisted on making a speech. The dancing was 'proper pretty', he said, and he had never seen Trunkles so well done, and 'it takes a bit o' doin'", He had hardly dared to hope to see any more dancing before he died. That night he had the "first good sleep he had had for the better part of a year". It was then that Bond sang Arthur o' Bradleys.[160]

The movement to value and record folk song and dance was paralleled by other rural interests. A large literature of the country side was being produced based partly on sentiment, but also at times on intimate experience. The most realistic of these writers was George Sturt of Surrey whose study of an old labourer reported precisely the outlook, the language, the hour-by-hour life of such men as the Bledington dancers.[161] Bledington's own most distinguished near neighbour was one of these writers, a journalist of rural affairs. J. W. Robertson Scott had bought the large dilapidated farmhouse, Idbury Manor, and there wrote books describing, among other matters, the country workers' housing[162] and the hardships of small farmers. Presently he founded there his famous quarterly *The Countryman* which dealt with every aspect of English country life and was read and also written by every sort of countryman and woman. By the nineteen twenties history was also being written and rural economics studied by men who were the descendants of long lines of small farmers and wage-earners, not necessarily more liberal than their colleagues from more well-to-do or professional classes, but with a stronger impulse to study the groundwork of country life.

Mr Robertson Scott had entertained the Travelling Morris in 1925 with hospitality of field and hall and table while remaining himself a little taciturn, doubting—their spokesman suggests[163] the value of a movement so far from concern with material problems.

All these rural movements were in part specialised off-shoots of what we have called the "generous movement" in nineteenth century

England (strengthened of course by new institutions, new economic interests). Others might have more material value, more effect in future years; none, not even in the churches, led to so complete a negation of social fences as the Morris dances: the least stress on status between dancers would have been a crudity. Till a few years ago one could be present at meetings of old dance-friends; one may still be admitted to see the friends' letters.

Nothing had brought more solace to some poor men than their dances. They had supplied them with a little of the more-than-bread man lives by. To the village as a whole they are a glory parallel to its beautiful church. The name of Bledington may be heard wherever dancing is regarded as an art—in foreign lands, at international meetings and festivals, in schools and colleges and clubs.

Odd, that this treasure should have been pushed into holes and corners. What had caused such repression? Puritanism was perhaps responsible for a while, but it is too favoured a whipping-horse in this as in other connections. Other countries had Puritan movements yet retained their ancient song and dance. Wherever in Germany a company gathered on pleasurable occasions till 1914 and beyond singing would start up and innumerable songs follow—not only ancient songs but recent ones, the repertory having been increased all along the years. In Austria dancing still remained in many villages. I myself saw it in 1922 and 1924 at village gatherings in the Salzkammergut— slow, processional dances of great dignity, clearly religious in origin, some others resembling formalisation of rough fighting; still others were courtship dances. They were not confined to men. In Austrian homes, small instruments hung on the walls and when the spirit moved, as it frequently did, the family took them down and made music.

In England then, some local, some English circumstances had led to the all-but-complete break. Ralph Vaughan Williams, a musician sensitive to social affairs,[164] held that it was due to aristocratic power and wealth in the eighteenth century, with the enthusiasm that grew up for things foreign and the "corollary that the type of music which the foreigner brought with him was the only type worth having". The isolation of the aristocracy was a factor and one which may be traced further back, and in part to the court, but there was more— the whole long process of commercial, industrial and agricultural change, the division of society into landed and landless, rich and poor, citizen and pauper, served and serving.

But what on the other hand had caused the survival of fine remnants of popular culture in small groups of the least fortunate of men who valued an art as a most precious part of life? Their very poverty and remoteness isolated them from some inferior and adverse movements, but also the misery of their homes, from which their wives could not escape, drove them out to enjoy something of their own.

At any rate, art survived and the men were brought before the war into a new experience, a new brotherhood. The dances had begun in an ancient, pre-Christian religion and, with that religion, had suffered a partial eclipse. Then had come a reconciliation or toleration and only in modern times neglect and contempt.

It has seemed to me that when Bledington has reached a high point in its life, as in the re-building of the church in the fifteenth century, in the religious and social life of our evangelical period and in the constant charitable work of the twentieth century much has been owed to the insights of Christianity into human life. Now the brotherhood of the arts had brought back at least briefly another value, another expression of community.

[1] See 18th Century Introduction, pp. 249–250
[2] See e.g. Religious Musings (1794) Lines 126–300
[3] Thos. Carlyle *Past and Present*
[4] e.g. in Banbury a hospital, at Idbury a school
[5] Pulled down in 1953
[6] In the next ten years the number grew again—to 403 in 1911
[7] See page 188
[8] Anthony Trollope. *The Last Chronicle of Barset*
[9] Christ Church Calendar of Estate Papers, Dec. 10, 1817 (No. 89)
[10] Report of the Parliamentary Select Committee on the Education of the Poor, 1818
[11] The number of Christ Church and in general of Oxford graduates among the vicars suggests that Christ Church was often asked to name a candidate
[12] Christ Church. Calendar of Estate Papers 1843 (several Nos.)
[13] MS. Papers, M. K. Ashby
[14] M. Sturge Gretton. *Burford Past and Present* new ed. London, 1946. p. 90 quoting from J.O.J. July 1795
[15] P.R.O. 67/11 See W. E. Minchinhampton *Agriculture in Gloucestershire during the Napoleonic Wars* B.G.A. 1949 & 1950

[16] Christ Church Calendar of Estate Papers No. 72 6th July, 1812
[17] Christ Church Calendar of Estate Papers 27th Feb., 1827. No. 105
[18] Christ Church as above, 9th January, 1813. No. 78
[19] Christ Church as above 1854. No. 174
[20] G.R.O. Bledington. Act for Enclosing the Far Heath and Cow Common 1829, Award 1831
[21] MS. Papers, M. K. Ashby
[22] Various deeds etc. Papers, Messrs. R. Bolter, N. Pearson, and M. K. Ashby. Also Christ Church, The Treasury: Bundle labelled *Home Farm, Bledington* (for Peglers)
[23] Oxford University. *Gloucestershire Estates*, University Farm, Bledington, *Historical Details* as sent to Mr Frank Stow
[24] Frederick Clifford. *The Agricultural Lock-out of* 1874. Edinburgh & London 1875, facing p. 356
[25] Christ Church. Calendar of Estate Papers 6 & 7 Oct. 1864 (No. 174)
[26] Ex. information, Mrs Lilian Rose, of Heath Farm, Churchill.
[27] The market at the Langston Arms. See p. 452
[28] A. W. Ashby *Allotments and Small Holdings in Oxfordshire* Oxford 1917, Part II
[29] Sale Catalogue, Little Compton Farmhouse 1799. Papers, late Mrs Alexandər
[30] Anthony Trollope *Phineas Finn* Penguin ed. Vol. I p. 271
[31] Chapter VI p. 297
[32] Transcription of a diary intermittently kept, 1814–31. Papers, M. K. Ashby
[33] Chapter VI, p. 81
[34] "W.B." *Nineteenth Century Stow* p. 17. Stow on the Wold 1911
[35] Evesham Journal March 17th 1967. M. Sturge Gretton *A Corner of the Cotswolds* London 1914 pp. 29, 30
[36] J.O.J. July 21st 1832
[37] Rev. Thomas Rudge, op. cit.
[38] Deeds in the possession of Mr Cecil Acock and Mr Roland Bolter
[39] Papers, Mr Roland Bolter
[40] M. K. Ashby *Joseph Ashby of Tysoe* Cambridge 1961 p. 105 et al.
[41] The Select Committee appointed to inquire into the Education of the Lower Orders, 1818. Evidence, *Bledington*, the Rev. Wm. Jones
[42] See e.g. E. Halévy *A History of the English People* (Vol. II) 1815–1830 London 1926 pp. 67–70
[43] J. O. J. January 8th 1831
[44] G. M. Trevelyan, *Recreations of an Historian*. London p. 108
[45] G.R.O. D. 1283 Rev. F. E. Witts, Journal 1815–1825
[46] G.R.O. Ms. Register of Prisoners, Northleach Bridewell Oct. 1791–August 1816
[47] New Testament, Mark Ch. X v. 13–15
[48] J.O.J. December 24th 1829
[49] J.O.J. April 1829
[50] J.O.J. January 1830
[51] M. Sturge Gretton, *Some English Rural Problems*, p. 69 Student Christian Movement 1922

[52] i.e. not in part from the rates
[53] Sydney Smith. *The Letters of Peter Plymley* London 1929, p. 227
[54] George Herbert. *Shoemakers Holiday*, ed. Christiana Cheney Plate VII Oxford 1949
[55] Arthur Young *Agriculture of Oxfordshire*, 1809
[56] A. W. Ashby. *One Hundred Years of Poor Law Administration in a Warwickshire Village*. Oxford 1912. Appendix I
[57] See p. 285
[58] Poor Law Commissioners' Report of 1834, H.M.S.O. Cd 2728, 1905
[59] Op. cit. Supplement. Report of Mr Villiers: Gloucestershire
[60] Evesham Journal. Feb. 3, 1836
[61] J.O.J. April 3, 1830
[62] Poor Law Commissioners' Report. Supplement. Report of Mr Villiers: Gloucestershire
[63] Poor Law Commissioners op. cit. p. 229
[64] Op. cit. Passim.
[65] One had been bought by Overseer Pegler in 1756 for £5.5s.10d. see page 313, note 2
[66] For all references to Stow Union see G.R.O. G/STO Stow Board of Guardians
[67] M. K. Ashby. *The Country School, its Practice and Problems*. Chapter V. *The Country Child*. Oxford 1929
[68] Vestry Minutes, Bledington 1842, Papers, Parish Council
[69] Details from letter to Rev. Stephen Liberty by Percival Oakley Hill, 1933. Papers M, K. Ashby
[70] P. Oakley Hill refers to William M. Waterlow. *A History of the Charities of William Jones at Monmouth and Newland*, 1899
[71] Ringing the whole peal of bells together
[72] Documents of Methodist Chapel. Papers, M. K. Ashby
[73] Christ Church, Calendar of Estate Papers. Letters from J. O. Hill 1854, 55, 57
[74] Churchwardens' Accounts 1858–59, 1859–60. Papers, Churchwardens
[75] He must have meant craftsmen
[76] e.g. W. A. Barrett. Flowers and Festivals. London 1868
[77] George Sturt. *The Bettesworth Book*. London 1901 *Memoirs of a Surrey Labourer, Lucy Bettesworth* 1913
[78] A. G. Street. *The Gentleman of the Party* London 1936
[79] Wordsworth *To a Redbreast* written 1846, published 1850
[80] G. M. Young "Macaulay had no Wordsworthian illusions about peasants". *Macaulay* in *Victorian Essays*. Oxford 1962 p. 43
[81] Charles Varley A New System of Husbandry. Vol I quoted by E. B. R. Creen in *On Open Town Fields*, Agricultural History Review Vol. IX, 1961
[82] William Marshall *Rural Economy of Gloucester* Vol. II *The Wolds* 1796
[83] Census Report of 1851
[84] Autobiography. MS. lent by the author to M. K. Ashby. Extracts from this work, not including this story, have been reproduced in *Our Ilmington by John Purser*. Wellington N.Z. 1964 (see E. M. H. Ibbotson. *Ilmington in the 19th Century*: the local Historian August 1971
[85] John Purser gave an example of this

[86] Bishop of Bath and Wells. Remarks on the Present Distresses of the Poor, Reprinted in Labourers' Friend Magazine, May 1836 and June 1836. Also various speeches to the Labourers' Friend Society.

[87] For details, see section *On the Farms and in the Village* p. 512

[88] Terry Coleman. *The Railway Navvies*, London 1965, pp. 110–114 E. T. Macdermot. *History of the Great Western Railway* Vol. I, 1927, pp. 494–6. Lainchbury op. cit. p. 130

[89] E. J. Lainchbury, op. cit. p. 131

[90] Wrote letters to The Times, selection published London 1888

[91] Vicar of Hulberton, Devon and of two Gloucestershire villages; known as "The Agricultural Labourers' Friend"

[92] Vicar of Cranborough, wrote *The Land and the Labourers* advocating smallholdings and cooperation. London 1884

[93] Joseph Arch. *Joseph Arch, the Story of his life.* London 1898

[94] J.O.J. March 23rd

[95] For Revised Code see Section *Bledington School*

[96] J.O.J. June 1st 1872

[97] Groves op. cit. The History of Shipton under Wynchwood p. 47

[98] J.O.J. May 3, 1873

[99] J.O.J. Aug. 10, 1872

[100] Report in J.O.J. April, 1872

[101] Joseph Arch, loc. cit. Ch. VI

[102] G.D.R. Gloucester Collection 530. Addresses by Ellicott, Lord Bishop of Gloucester

[103] J. P. D. Dunbabin *The "Revolt of the Field": the agricultural labourers' movement in the 1870s.* Past and Present XXVI 1963

[104] Reprinted on June 7th 1873 in J.O.J.

[105] Cf. D. McClutchey. *Oxfordshire Clergy 1777–1869.* Oxford 1960

[106] Hansard. House of Commons. May 26, June 9th and July 4th 1873

[107] Groves op. cit. p. 53

[108] See e.g. C. S. Orwin and E. H. Whetham. *History of British Agriculture 1846 to 1914.* London 1964 Chs. 9 and 10

[109] Cf. Audrey W. Taylor, *Gilletts, Bankers at Banbury and Oxford.* Oxford 1964

[110] Family papers, chiefly annotated sale catalogues

[111] F. M. L. Thompson, *The Land Market in the 19th Century in Essays in Agrarian History* ed. W. E. Minchinton. Newton Abbot p. 45

[112] Lainchbury op. cit. pp. 154–155

[113] Church Schools Enquiry Report 1846–7. Published for National Society 1849. (Library of Department of Education and Science)

[114] Commission to enquire into State of Popular Education (1861). Report. ("Newcastle Commission")

[115] Committee of Council on Education, Report 1876–77, p. 420

[116] Log-books and registers of Bledington School used from this point

[117] (i) Matthew Arnold. *Reports on Elementary Schools 1851–1882.* H.M.S.O. 1908 p. 21—a very brief reference.
(ii) Rev. Richard Davies. a. *Hints on an Improved and Self-paying System of National Education from the workings of a village school.* London 1850

b. *Suggestive Hints towards improved secular instruction . . . to bear on practical life*

[118] Commission to Enquire into the State of Popular Education 1861. Vol. XXI pt. I. p. 53

[119] J. F. Hogan. *Robert Lowe, Viscount Sherbrooke*. London 1893. Early Chapters

[120] Ex-pupils of the school, otherwise unqualified

[121] General references: M. K. Ashby. *The Country School, its practice and problems*. O.U.P. 1929 Curtis & Boltwood. op. cit.

[122] Interdepartmental Committee on Physical Deterioration. Report, H.M.S.O. 1904

[123] T. S. Dymond. H.M.I. Adviser on Rural Education, *Suggestions on Rural Education* H.M.S.O. 1908

[124] Suggestions for Teachers, H.M.S.O. 1905

[125] Bledington School. The Log Books

[126] Pupil teachers received some tuition from the head-teacher, usually before school hours

[127] H.M.S.O. Education (Administrative Provisions) Act 1907

[128] H.M.S.O. Education (Provision of Meals) Act 1906

[129] Vestry Minutes, Papers, Bledington Churchwardens

[130] H. B. Walters *Gloucestershire Bells* B.G.A.S. Vol. XLII

[131] Cf. Ch. III, p. 112

[132] *The Ringing World*. Sept. 11, 1931: Evesham Journal May 25th 1935: Vestry Minutes and Churchwardens' Accounts. Papers, Bledington Churchwardens

[133] Letters, accounts etc. relating to the Methodist Chapel. Papers, M. K. Ashby (gift of Mrs Viner)

[134] The Vicar's income varied between £130 and £150

[135] Minutes and accounts of Bledington Temperance Band. Papers, Mr Will Stayt

[136] Conversations with Miss Mary Hall, Mrs Viner, Mr W. Stayt, Mr George Beacham

[137] Information from Mr E. A. Smith, Secretary, the Cirencester Benefit Society

[138] Conversations with Mr George Beacham, and papers, Mr Beacham

[139] Papers, Chipping Norton Co-operative Society, Secretary, Mr Walker

[140] Mary Sturge Henderson. *Three Centuries in North Oxon*. O.U.P. 1902 p. 168

[141] Lainchbury. op. cit. p. 184

[142] The Overseers Special Expenses Rate Book. Papers, Bledington Parish Council

[143] From this point much is owed to conversations with Mr N. Pearson, Mr C. Holdam, Mr and Mrs Roy Hunt and Mr and Mrs Harry Slatter

[144] e.g. Oats from the River Plate are said to have been sold at 16s. and 17s. per cwt.

[145] Cheltenham Free Press, June 11th, 1908

[146] Papers, Mr W. Hunt of Oddington

[147] Another account of this odd character may be found in Charles Fenby *The Other Oxford* London 1970, pp. 112–4

[148] Cheltenham Chronicle, March 27, 1909, and papers, Mrs W. Hunt

[149] Cf. Ch. V. The Seventeenth Century pp. 9–14

[150] Mr Rolf Gardener writes of the last Bledington fool: "John Hitchman was squire and tomfool of the Bledington side (died Nov. 1929). In 1924 he told us "When I weren't a-playing squire I used to dance nearside-hindermost" (a nice

description) As fool with the pig's bladder and cow's tail he styled himself "Billy Lapem'."

[151] R. J. E. Tiddy *The Mummers' Play* Oxford 1923
[152] Maud Karpeles *Cecil Sharp, His life and work*, 1967
[153] S. Baring-Gould. *Old Country Life*. London 1889
[154] *The World's Work*. August 1912, quoted by Mr R. L. Dommett in a letter to M.K.A.
[155] Cecil Sharp. *The Morris Book* Pt. III London 1907–13
[156] Fox-Strangways *Life of Cecil Sharp*. Oxford 1933. p. 96
[157] Letter from Mr Rolf Gardiner to M.K.A. Oct. 10th 1962
[158] JosephNeedham's Map, *Essays and Studies* by members of the English Association Vol. VII Oxford 1921
[159] See typed list, unsigned, in library of English Folk Dance Society
[160] Letter from Mr Rolf Gardiner to M.K.A. Boxing Day 1962. Bell, *Ancient Poems*, etc. *of the Peasantry of England*. Arthur o' Bradley's Wedding pp. 138–143 London 1857
[161] George Sturt *The Bettesworth Book*. London 1901
[162] J. W. Robertson Scott *England's Green and Pleasant Land*
[163] Mr Rolf Gardiner, Letter to M.K.A. already cited
[164] (i) R. Vaughan Williams *National Music* Appendix 1 p. 9
(ii) E. Barker (ed.) *The Character of England*, containing J. A. Westrup *Music* pp. 403–7

postscript

SINCE THE SECOND World War Bledington has undergone something of a revolution by the settlement of a large number of families from other traditions, but so far its pattern has held: those newcomers who have not cared to take a place within it have been negative or limited factors. Can its unity survive a further influx? It can only do so through reconciling and fruitful impulses and purposes.

When our history began, the felt dependence of all its folk upon shared methods and means of livelihood—common methods of tilling the soil, customs modified by meetings of commoners, work administered by fieldsmen elected by them—ensured a true community. Man, woman and child had common purposes and inescapable responsibilities. There were also shared conceptions of the powers beyond man himself, seasonal ceremonies and social arts to express emotion, the last so adequate that they would serve some villagers for a thousand years.

Yet in such a society life was hard, short and sometimes catastrophic or ugly. Differentiation of function, the coming of priest, soldier, landlord, and later craftsmen, clerks, teachers, made possible growing ease and wealth. But they did not ensure it: they also brought fissures. Were fissures essential? Family culture can break or serve and enrich a community as we daily see. Even the hedged and private farm can as a barrier be overleapt.

The conquest of 1066 brought to our country lasting divisions of race, language, power and wealth. After a long period of absorption and recovery our records seem to show two periods of happy, realised sense of community. Late in the fifteenth century the parish largely rebuilt and glorified the church. The people were at one, not in gaining but in lavish spending of their meagre excess of gains. And then again, four centuries later, after the barest recovery from deep social division, and from very great privation for the largest group, the village had brief and joyous experience of community. At this time the Church

407

and the Methodist Society both prospered and included in their membership or their influence almost the whole village. In the first of these two periods there was still much of common agriculture, but by 1876 this had been left behind for more than a century, though there was still fairly complete, if less direct, dependence on farming.

The two periods of unity shared two characteristics: religious inspiration and popular enjoyment of art. In the first, the art may be called classical: it is based on long and consistent development and on the work of professional artist-craftsmen, in the service of a communal end, supported by the devotion of the community. Meanwhile the ancient lay dances, songs and ceremonies continued to express the basic common life. By the latter period, these old arts had declined; the new art was religious but had also to provide for homely popular expression. The place of folk song had been taken by hymns, the official books of these containing beautiful tunes and good words: "mission" hymns were hearty and crude. There were other popular forms of music, verse and plays. All these expressed generous and consoling sentiments.

On an official level there was still division between orthodoxy and dissent but this mattered little in the village, where the laity shared festive and other services and enjoyed the sharing. They helped each other's projects and charities.

In both periods there was emphasis on early Christian teaching, in the first through oral and visual teaching of stories and legends, in the second through much reading of the gospels, with the teaching of the founder concerning the unity of the human family despite all appearances to the contrary—in Christian terms on the Fatherhood of God and the consequent brotherhood of man.

In 1876 and thereabouts the Bledington community had had a recent searing experience of inhuman denudation, contrasting not with wealth but with situations of comfort. Even at that date much misery was set beside the situations of all-round sufficiency which farming almost always affords, and the crafts usually.

What conditions are the necessary basis of community, here and elsewhere? We are able to care for the people with whom we can and do from time to time identify ourselves. We need a policy within which no social barriers greatly impede sympathy and knowledge. As time goes on we see some barriers worn down and others—always with great loss—flung down. But these are succeeded by others. We may see the gulfs between capital and labour, skilled and unskilled, Catholic and Protestant, being bridged, only to see them widening between, for example, the races and to see a tendency to dig them between classes based upon degrees of intelligence as measured by artificial tests—both of these bringing exceptional dangers.

But fear inhibits: only hope and faith inspire. Can we persevere, equipped with democratic and Christian faith in the immeasurable value of persons and with a human political ideal to match it, but also with patience and humour, not asking for the moon—so beautiful in the distance, on approach so arid, rocky, horrid.

index

413

417

419

425